Publisher 2000:
Get Professional Results

About the Author

Roger C. Parker (Dover, New Hampshire) is the author of 26 books, including *Looking Good in Print: A Guide to Basic Design for Desktop Publishing* (often called one of the ten most influential computer books of all time). There are more than 1,500,000 copies of Roger C. Parker's books in print in more than 37 languages. Roger's books emphasize the marketing aspects of personal computing, including desktop publishing, presentations, and Web site creation and design.

In his roles as contributing editor and columnist, Roger has published more than 150 articles for *Home Office Computing*, *New Selling Times*, *Newsletter Design*, *Technique*, and *Corel Magazine*. His monthly "Alternatives to Price Competition" column ran for more than ten years in *Audio Times*. Roger teaches advertising and marketing at New Hampshire College and has developed curriculum and conducted more than 175 desktop design seminars throughout the United States and Australia. He's been a guest speaker for the Magazine Publishing Association's Folio Conference in New York, a keynote speaker at PageMaker Conferences throughout the United States, and a speaker at Ragan Communication's Corporate Communicators Conference.

Publisher 2000:
Get Professional Results

Roger C. Parker

Osborne/McGraw-Hill

Berkeley New York St. Louis San Francisco Auckland Bogotá
Hamburg London Madrid Mexico City Milan Montreal New Delhi
Panama City Paris São Paulo Singapore Sydney Tokyo Toronto

Osborne/**McGraw-Hill**
2600 Tenth Street
Berkeley, California 94710
U.S.A.

For information on translations or book distributors outside the U.S.A., or to arrange bulk purchase discounts for sales promotions, premiums, or fund-raisers, please contact Osborne/**McGraw-Hill** at the above address.

Publisher 2000: Get Professional Results

1234567890 DOC DOC 019876543210

ISBN 0-07-212298-6

Publisher
Brandon A. Nordin
Associate Publisher and Editor-in-Chief
Scott Rogers
Acquisitions Editor
Megg Bonar
Project Editor
Jody McKenzie
Acquisitions Coordinator
Stephane Thomas
Technical Editor
Terrie Solomon
Copy Editor
Lunaea Weatherstone
Proofreader
Stefany Otis
Indexer
Karin Arrigoni
Computer Designers
Elizabeth Jang, Liz Pauw, Dick Schwartz, Roberta Steele
Series Designer
Jill Weil
Illustrators
Bob Hansen, Michael Mueller, Beth Young
Cover Designer
Dodie Shoemaker

This book was composed with Corel VENTURA™ Publisher.

Contents at a Glance

Contents

Part II
Get to Work with Publisher's Wizards

Part IV

Using Publisher to Project a Professional Image

Preface

I admit that I resisted learning Publisher because it just seemed so overwhelming. Too many choices made it hard to make any choice at all. However, Roger C. Parker makes me want to delve right in and start churning out professional publications.

I already knew that desktop publishing makes creating publications easy. This book makes using Publisher to create effective marketing materials even easier. Disguised as a software tutorial, this is really a blueprint for business marketing success. They say the Web can make a small business look big. Publisher and Roger C. Parker help that small business look good.

A software tutorial may not be able to guarantee business success, but I can assure you that anyone who invests the time in learning Publisher "the Parker way" is assured of good-looking projects that will help, not hurt, your business image.

Jacci Howard Bear, About.com Desktop Publishing Guide
http://desktoppub.about.com

Acknowledgments

An author may write a book, but it would never make it to publication without the help and support of many others.

I would like to thank Megg Bonar and her staff at Osborne/McGraw-Hill, Terrie Solomon for all her editorial assistance, Winston Stewart for his contributions, and last, but not least, my family for allowing me to take the time away from them to write this book.

Roger C. Parker

Introduction

I **can't think of any software program on the market that can make as immediate an impact on your firm's bottom-line profits, or the success of your nonprofit organization, as Microsoft Publisher 2000 can.**

Consider: it may take months—even years—for the effects of a new or improved word processor, spreadsheet, or accounting program to have a major impact on your firm's bottom line.

But Publisher 2000 can make an immediate difference by making it easier and less costly to keep in contact with your customers and supporters and by allowing you to quickly produce a professional advertisement, brochure, newsletter, or Web site—one that generates immediate results. Within hours of installing Microsoft Publisher 2000, you can be doing a more effective and efficient job of communicating with your firm's prospects and customers, your association's members and supporters, or your far-flung family and friends, even if you've never had any previous graphic design experience.

If you're a new business or association, Microsoft Publisher 2000 can help you create the marketing materials you need from day one: business cards, letterheads, envelopes, and address labels, as well as brochures and flyers that explain what you do and why you're good at it. Microsoft Publisher 2000's Wizards will help you create an appropriate image that will be consistently applied throughout all your print communications. Right from the start, you can project a professional image.

If you're an existing business or association, Microsoft Publisher 2000 can help you jump-start your profitability. With Publisher, you can produce promotional materials such as postcards and informative newsletters, resulting in new business from new customers or repeat business from previous customers.

Microsoft Publisher 2000 is extremely flexible. It can grow with you, as your resources expand. In the beginning, you can use Publisher 2000 to produce projects that will be created on your desktop ink-jet or laser printer. Down the road, as you graduate to four-color printing, Publisher 2000 can prepare the files necessary for professional-quality printing by service bureaus and commercial printers. So, whatever your printing requirements, Publisher 2000 is there to help you.

Wizards are an intrinsic part of Publisher 2000's power. Publisher's Layout Wizard's help you lay out your projects so they project an attractive, consistent appearance. The Color Wizards help you choose colors that complement, rather than compete with, each other. Other Publisher 2000 Wizards guide you through the process of organizing your files to be taken to a service bureau for printing.

Study after study show that attracting new business is the number one priority of most business owners. The following pages describe, in detail, the marvelous power of a software program that can help you produce the materials your business or association needs to attract new business or new supporters.

Inside this Book

In Part I, you'll learn all about Publisher's capabilities, how to use Publisher's frames and objects, and the basics of using Publisher's Wizards.

In Part II, you'll jump in and create a newsletter, brochure, catalog, and Web site with Publisher's various Wizards, and see how easy it is to create professional-looking documents that effectively convey your message.

In Part III, you'll see how Publisher handles long document creation, how to create documents without using Wizards, and how you can create an online presence from your print publications.

In Part IV, you'll learn how to create a logo and add it to your documents, how to use photographs in print and online publications, how to get the most out of Publisher's addressing options, and what to keep in mind if you decide to have your project printed at a commercial printer.

Conventions Used

This book uses several conventions designed to make the book easier for you to follow:

- *Italic type* is used to call attention to important terms or to words and phrases that deserve special emphasis.
- Small capital letters are used for keys on the keyboard, such as ENTER and SHIFT. Key combinations are connected by a hyphen, such as press CTRL-F2.
- Menu commands are separated with vertical lines, such as File | Print.

Tip: Tips are shortcuts or advice to help make it easier to get things done.

L▶ Note: Notes point out unusual features, functions, and capabilities, or things to watch out for.

New in 2000: New in 2000 highlights features that are new in this version of Publisher.

Cross-Reference: Cross-References tell you where in the book you can find more information about a particular topic.

Professional Pointer

In Professional Pointers, the author gives you insight and guidance on a particular topic or feature learned from years of experience.

Conclusion

After reading this book, I'm sure you'll share my enthusiasm for Microsoft Publisher 2000. You'll find yourself looking forward to preparing your next brochure, flyer, or newsletter rather than feeling that you don't have the design experience to produce a good job. Because, with Publisher 2000 and its Wizards, it's virtually impossible not to produce a professional publication.

Let me know how your project comes out!

Sincerely,
Roger C. Parker
Write Word
P.O. Box 697
Dover, NH 03821
http://www.NewEntrepreneur.com

Part I

Meet Your New Marketing and Publishing Department

chapter 1

What You Can Do with Microsoft Publisher 2000

In this chapter, you will:

- Learn how to affordably and easily make professional-quality publications and Web pages

- Enjoy instant professional results using Publisher's Design Wizards and predesigned layouts

- Project a professional, easily maintained image with minimal effort and learning time

Microsoft Publisher 2000 is a powerful yet easy-to-use software program that helps you communicate more effectively in print and on the Web. With Publisher 2000, you can effectively promote your association, business, church, or school by efficiently keeping in touch with clients, prospects, members, and supporters. Microsoft Publisher is for you—whether you work for yourself, prepare marketing materials for a large corporation (or a department of a large corporation), or donate time to help schools, non-profit associations, or religious organizations.

In conjunction with your desktop printer and/or professional commercial printers, Microsoft Publisher helps you prepare marketing materials that project a professional image, getting marketing and promotional messages out as quickly and inexpensively as possible.

Microsoft Publisher 2000 is equally effective on a personal level, helping families, friends, and neighborhoods communicate with each other by creating invitations to yard sales, family newsletters, and personalized holiday gifts such as family calendars.

Making Quality Affordable

Few businesses and organizations can afford the high costs of professional design and production. Graphic design and production typically cost between $50 and $100 an hour or more. At these prices, design fees can quickly eat up your marketing budget before you even begin to print and mail your message.

L▶ Tip: Publisher's Design Wizards are very user-friendly, interactive guides that walk you completely through the document-creation process by asking you a series of questions. Once Publisher has sufficient information from you, and you come to the Finish button of the Design Wizard, Publisher automatically creates the document for you.

By eliminating outside design and production costs and by providing a framework to get you started, Publisher 2000 permits you to concentrate on your message, not waste time choosing typefaces, type sizes, layouts, and colors (unless you want to—you can always design your publications from scratch). Working with Publisher 2000's Design Wizards leaves you more time to fine-tune your message and permits you to get more done in less time. By doing as much work yourself as possible, you can devote more of your marketing resources to printing and mailing your publications. This helps your marketing dollars go further. Fifty dollars worth of postage permits you to communicate with a lot more people than fifty dollars worth of freelance graphic design or production talent.

Professional Results from the Start

With Microsoft Publisher 2000, previous design or desktop publishing experience is not necessary in order to achieve quality results. Even if you have not had any graphic design or desktop publishing experience, Microsoft Publisher 2000 helps you achieve good-looking, professional results.

Publisher 2000's enhancements include the addition of what Microsoft calls its Design Wizards. These versatile Design Wizards will get you quickly started by providing the framework necessary for creating a wide variety of business communications. Publisher 2000's Design Wizards range from the basic printed needs of every business or organization—such as letterheads, envelopes, and business cards—to specialized communications such as brochures, catalogs, greeting cards, newsletters, and postcards.

New in 2000: Publisher now features 29 Design Wizards.

Cross-Reference: For more information on Publisher's Design Wizards, see Chapters 4, 5, 6, 7, and 8. A glance at the Microsoft Publisher Catalog, shown in Figure 1-1, reveals the wide range of publication types you can quickly and easily create with Publisher 2000, as well as the design options available for each type of publication. Each time you select a publication type, you can choose the look and desired format of the publication by reviewing the Design Master Sets options displayed in Publisher's right-hand window.

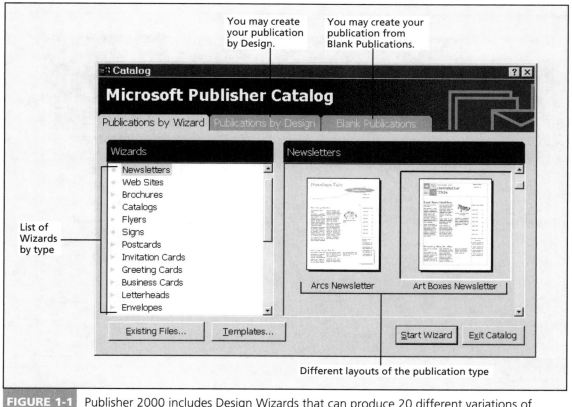

FIGURE 1-1 Publisher 2000 includes Design Wizards that can produce 20 different variations of 29 different types of documents

It's important to note that Publisher 2000 does more than provide you with just generic publication types. Publisher's Design Wizards offer detailed guidance for various types of specialized communications. Instead of just "brochures," for example, you can select from Informational, Price List, Event, or Fund-raiser options. Each option offers different suggestions for headlines, captions, and visuals. For example, you can choose from among 15 different types of postcards, as shown in Figure 1-2.

Publisher's Design Wizards not only help you design your publication, they guide you through the process of completing your publication by offering detailed, context-sensitive suggestions. After selecting a publication type and design from the Microsoft Publisher Catalog and clicking the OK button, Publisher presents you with an onscreen *template*, or framework, for completing your publication. Publisher's Design Wizards also save you time by automatically inserting your firm or organization's previously saved name, address, phone, fax, and e-mail information in your publication. (See Figure 1-3.)

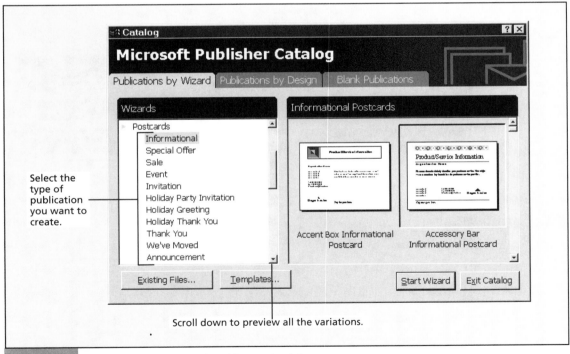

FIGURE 1-2   Choose the Design Wizard best suited for your message

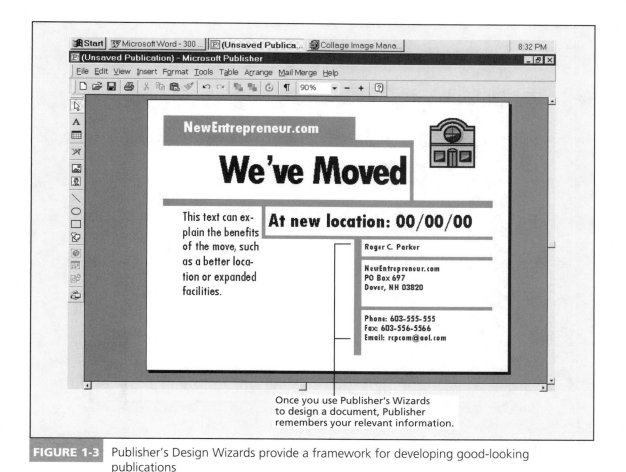

Once you use Publisher's Wizards to design a document, Publisher remembers your relevant information.

FIGURE 1-3   Publisher's Design Wizards provide a framework for developing good-looking publications

Cross-Reference: For more information on entering varying sets of personal information, see Chapter 2.

In just minutes, you can easily complete your publication, creating a customized publication that effectively communicates your message. In the background, while you're working, Publisher automatically will make any type size or other change necessary to create a good-looking publication, as shown in Figure 1-4. Note that Publisher automatically reduced the type size of the headline to accommodate more words.

Tip: You can also save variations of your important information for your primary business, home/family, secondary business, or other organizations.

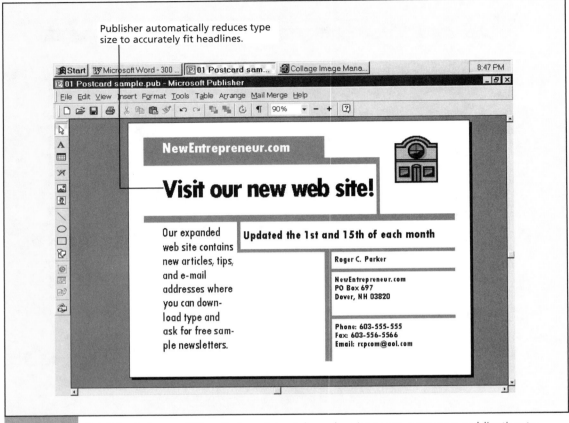

Publisher automatically reduces type size to accurately fit headlines.

After producing your publication, Publisher can address your postcards, newsletters, or brochures as it prints them. (You can even assemble a database of customer names and addresses with Publisher, if you don't already have one.)

Cross-Reference: For more information on using Publisher with mailing lists, see Chapter 14.

Of course, Publisher 2000 does not force you to use its Design Wizards. You can also create your own custom publications, choosing margins, colors, column layouts, typeface, and type size choices from scratch.

Cross-Reference: For more information on creating custom publications from scratch, see Chapter 10.

Taking Advantage of the Web

In addition to preparing the print communications your firm, association, or church needs to succeed, Publisher 2000 makes it easy to take full advantage of the Internet. Creating a Web site follows the same process as creating a print publication. Publisher 2000 offers you several ways to create a Web site. If you want to get on the Web as quickly as possible, you can convert an existing brochure or newsletter into a Web site. Or you can use Publisher's Web Site Design Wizards to create quickly and easily a professional-looking Web site for your business or personal use. Start by selecting a desired Web site design from the Microsoft Publisher Catalog. Then insert as many pages as necessary, choosing the page layout most appropriate for the content you want to include on each page of your Web site, as shown in Figure 1-5. Publisher 2000 offers different page layouts for stories, calendars, events, special offers, price lists, and links—or, if you prefer, you can create a Web site from scratch.

Cross-Reference: For more information on creating Web pages with Publisher, see Chapter 11.

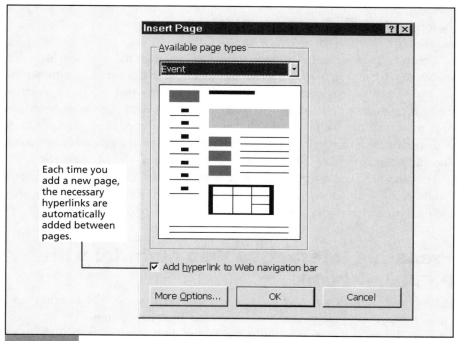

Each time you add a new page, the necessary hyperlinks are automatically added between pages.

FIGURE 1-5 You can use the Web Site Wizard to create an eye-catching Web site. You can also create a Web site from an existing brochure, catalog, or newsletter

Publisher 2000 Grows with Your Needs

Publisher 2000 is capable of growing with you as your firm or association's marketing needs become more sophisticated and your design abilities and printing budgets grow.

You may start by outputting your work on your home or office desktop printer. If you don't need many copies, you can produce the final copies yourself on your black and white or color desktop printer. Or you can prepare black and white master pages on glossy paper that you can take to a copy center for quantity duplication.

Later, you may need to produce more copies as your association or business grows and you want to improve the quality of your publications by taking them to a duplication center or commercial printer. You can use Publisher to prepare electronic files for four-color professional printing, which is of a much better quality than any four-color printing you can currently get from a desktop printer. When you use a professional printer, there are several additional factors that impact how you must create your desktop-published document for commercial printing. It's best to get all the facts about how to prepare your files for any professional publisher before doing too much work on the project that the printer may require you to redo.

Commercial professional printers specialize in high-speed, high-quality color work on a variety of special papers. By taking your project to a commercial printer, you can choose from a near-limitless choice of paper colors, paper coatings (from glossy to textured), and differing paper weights or thickness. More important, you can include four-color photographs, use edge-to-edge printing, and specify the exact colors used in your publication using worldwide color matching standards like CYMK colors and the Pantone Color Matching System.

You may start out by printing documents on your desktop computer, but Publisher 2000 can grow with you as you advance to the point of preparing professional publications that rival those produced by fancy design firms.

Preparing Interactive Web Material with Publisher 2000

Publisher 2000 makes it easy to tap the growing power of the Internet, and equally important, makes it easy to harness the interactive potential of the Web. You can add order forms, registration forms, and reply forms to your Web site so you can capture the names and addresses of Web site visitors, as well as, when appropriate, sell directly to them.

Publisher 2000 may even provide you with a springboard to a new career. As you become comfortable translating ideas into finished print and online communications for your own firm or association, you may find there's a market in your area for preparing print and online communications for others on a volunteer or freelance basis (making new friends and developing new business contacts). As your design and production skills develop, Publisher 2000 could be the tool you need for major career advancement.

Projecting a Professional Image Using a Brand Identity

Publisher 2000 makes branding—creating a unique and easily recognized image—very easy. There are five aspects to a successful branding program: uniqueness, appropriateness, consistency, quality, and frequency.

Uniqueness

Your print and online communications must appear distinctly different from those of your competitors. Just as the arrangement and size of your eyes, nose, and mouth give your face a unique and easily recognized look, your marketing communications should appear different from others your customers, prospects, and supporters encounter. Type, layout, white space, colors, and graphic accents are some of the tools that, working together, create a unique marketing brand image.

Microsoft Publisher 2000 helps you project a unique image by offering you a choice of 20 different Design Master Sets. Each Design Master Set, identified by descriptive and easily remembered names such as Accent Box, Bars, or Straight Edge, consists of a unique combination of layout, type, and graphic accents.

Professional Pointer

When you design any type of publication, you need to develop an eye for when enough is enough in terms of adding additional elements such as Attention Getters, Boxes, Dots, or other decorative elements. Sometimes, if you add an element to your design, it will be the perfect thing to complete the project. However, if you are not selective about items you add, you can make the design too busy or too full. Knowing when to stop and when to add elements is a skill you can practice and master, but it takes effort and restraint to accomplish.

You can preview the appearance of the various documents associated with each Design Master Set by clicking the Documents by Design tab in the Microsoft Publisher Catalog and using the vertical scroll bar to scroll through the various options, as shown in Figure 1-6.

Once you have chosen a Design Set and publication type, you can modify it by applying one of more than 60 different color schemes. Each color scheme is based on five colors, carefully chosen because they work well with each other and project a unique image. Choosing a color scheme is as easy as trying out each alternative by clicking on it, as shown in Figure 1-7, and observing whether or not it projects the image you feel is most appropriate for your firm, association, or family.

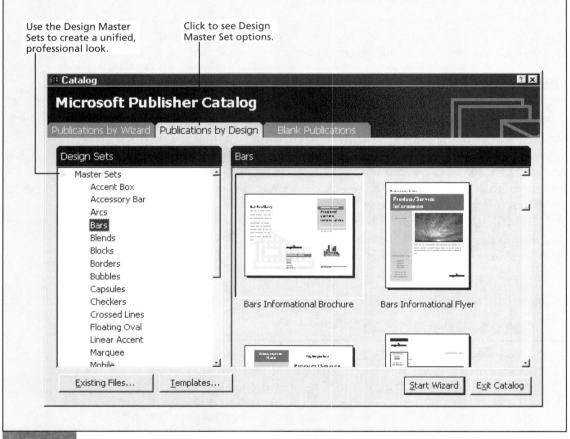

FIGURE 1-6   Click the Publications by Design tab in the Publisher Catalog to review the layout and typography of each publication within the Design Master Set

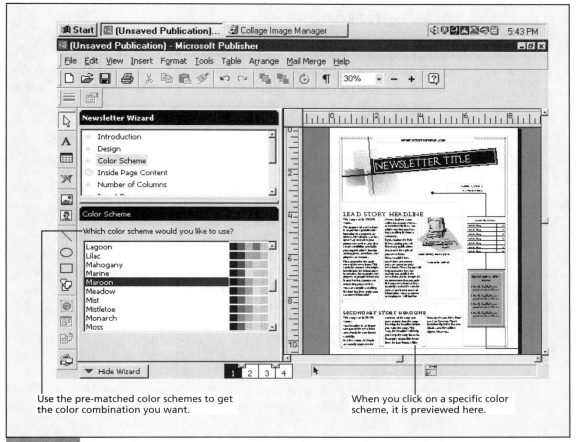

Use the pre-matched color schemes to get the color combination you want.

When you click on a specific color scheme, it is previewed here.

FIGURE 1-7 Apply one of the more than 60 different color schemes to each of the 20 different Design Master Sets by clicking on the scheme to see it displayed onscreen

Once you have chosen a color scheme, there are many ways you can further customize your publications. In many cases, you can choose different column arrangements—that is, one-column, two-column, or three-column layouts. You can also add Publisher's Design Objects, such as Calendars, Coupons, and Reply Forms, as well as graphic accents such as Attention Getters, Boxes, and Dots.

By the time you're through modifying Publisher's basic Design Master Sets and adding your firm's logo plus the text and graphics associated with your message, your publication will project a unique, customized image.

Appropriateness

To succeed, the documents used in your daily business and your marketing communications have to project an appropriate image. They must "feel right." The colors, layout, typefaces, and graphic accents should project a safe or conservative image for accountants and lawyers, for example, or a contemporary look for firms and organizations serving a youthful market.

By offering you a choice of more than 20 different Design Master Sets, plus additional Special Event, Fund-raiser, Holiday, and Restaurant sets, 29 different document types, and more than 60 different color schemes, Publisher 2000 makes it easy to choose an image that is both unique and appropriate for your business.

Appropriateness is achieved by choosing the Design Master with the typeface, layout, and colors that accurately project the image you want for your firm, association, or religious organization. In general, bright colors, like those used in the Bluebird, Monarch, Parrot, and Sunrise Color Schemes, are associated with contemporary or informal images. Darker, richer, more subdued colors, like those used in the Alpine, Burgundy, Cranberry, and Sapphire color schemes, communicate a conservative, quiet, and more expensive image.

Likewise, "quiet" layouts, like those associated with Publisher's Accent Box, Bars, or Punctuation Design Master Sets, project a more dignified, or upscale, image than layouts with more attention-getting graphic accents, like those associated with Publisher's Blocks, Borders, or Tilt Design Master Sets.

The typefaces associated with each Design Set also project different images. The Bookman Old Style typeface used for the title and headlines in the Art Boxes Design Master Set, shown in Figure 1-8, projects a strong, serious, "no frills" image. Sans serif typefaces, like the Gill Sans used for titles and headlines in publications created with the Accent Box Design Master Set, project a more contemporary image, as shown in Figure 1-9.

Professional Pointer

The terms "serif" and "sans serif" originated in the "ancient" days of manual typesetting. A *serif* is any sort of a short line or a slight ornamental flourish found on the ends of the strokes that comprise the letter, so typefaces with these additions are called "serif typefaces." *Sans serif* describes characters that have no short line or slight ending flourish at the end of the keystrokes that comprise the letter. These typefaces are called "sans serif typefaces." Oftentimes, individuals with limited typographical knowledge easily confuse the two terms, but I have a "trick" for you to remember, so you won't get the two terms confused: the word *sans* means "without" in French, so sans serif means "without serif." If you are new to dealing with typefaces, being able to use these terms will help you keep in step with the experts.

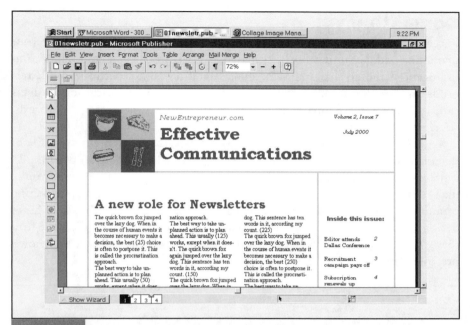

FIGURE 1-8 Thick serif typefaces, like Bookman Old, project an image of strength

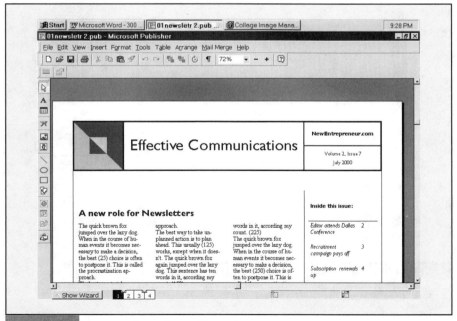

FIGURE 1-9 Sans serif typefaces, like Gill Sans, project a clean, contemporary, no-nonsense look

Consistency

Success is also based on projecting a single, consistent image throughout your marketing and day-to-day business materials. All of your print and online communications should share the same look. Branding cannot occur if your letterheads and envelopes look noticeably different from your brochures, business cards, catalogs, "compliments-of" cards, flyers, invoices, newsletters, postcards, statements, Web site, and weekly reports.

Each of Publisher 2000's Design Master Sets can create an entire family of documents, each projecting the same image. Each Design Set can produce 29 different types of publications. These cover all of the publication types you're likely to need for your day-to-day business needs as well as a variety of marketing promotions. A thank-you card produced using the Accent Box Design Master Set, as shown in Figure 1-10, is reminiscent of the design used by the same firm that sent the newsletter produced with the Accent Box Design Master Set (shown previously in Figure 1-9).

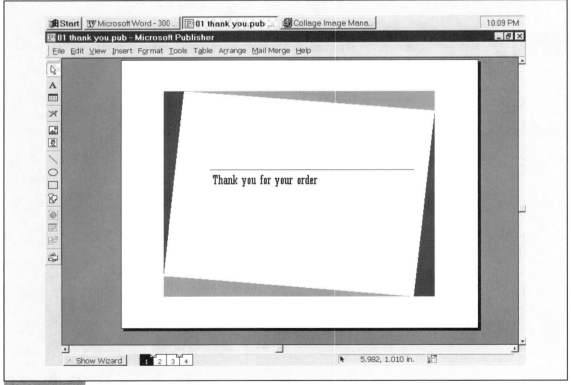

FIGURE 1-10　Using the same typeface and border for a thank-you card matches the newsletter previously shown in Figure 1-9

Professional Quality

You only get one chance to make a first impression. Your firm or organization is judged by the image your marketing materials project. Poor choice of colors, layout, typefaces, or graphic accents can do irreparable harm. Since you never know which of your marketing communications are going to be seen first, it's important that each and every publication or document projects as professional an image as possible.

Publisher 2000 ensures professional results because the design work has already been done. Professional designers with backgrounds in small business and organizational marketing created Publisher 2000's Design Master Sets. You don't have to worry about choosing the right typefaces and type sizes, creating balanced layouts, or choosing compatible combinations of colors, because the work has already been done for you.

All you have to do is develop your message, and Publisher 2000's Design Wizards will help you choose the right format for it, regardless of whether you're creating a business card, envelope, letterhead, newsletter, postcard, or Web site. Professional-quality results are guaranteed.

Publisher 2000 also helps you project a professional image by checking your spelling and grammar as you create your publication and by checking for potential problems while preparing your files for commercial printing or posting to your Web page on the Internet. Design Checkers identify potential problems and suggest remedies.

Frequency

Successful marketing is a *process* rather than an *event*. Long-term success does not come from a single newsletter, a single brochure, or a Web site that remains unchanged from month to month. Rather, success comes from an ongoing series of marketing communications. The more frequently you communicate with your market, the more success your firm or organization is likely to enjoy.

Maintaining visibility creates marketing success stories. The more often you communicate with your customers, prospects, and supporters, the more likely you'll be remembered when it comes time to buy (or contribute).

Publisher's ease of use makes such frequency possible. Frequency is ultimately based on efficiency. By working efficiently and by eliminating design and production costs, you can produce more marketing materials—more newsletters, more brochures, more postcards, and more thank-you cards—and you'll be able to afford to mail them to more people. In addition, by doing the work yourself with Publisher, you can keep your Web site frequently updated with fresh content.

What You Still Have to Do for Yourself

Although Publisher's Wizards take the work out of preparing full families of customized documents that project an appropriate image, the ultimate responsibility for the success of your marketing communications still depends on you.

It is still your responsibility to develop your marketing message. Although Publisher's Design Wizards can help you format that message, it's still up to you to create the message—in other words, to write the text, choose the illustrations, and take whatever photographs are required. You choose the Design Set and color scheme most appropriate for your publication.

Here are some of the marketing functions you're responsible for:

- Determining the purpose of your document.
- Deciding on the action you want your customers, employees, stockholders, contributors, or volunteers to take.
- Choosing the arguments to which your audience is most likely to respond, and write the text, prepare the illustrations, or take the pictures that best develop your arguments.
- Choosing the best level of duplication or printing for your document, including—when appropriate—choosing the right paper to print your document on and the best way of distributing it to your audience (for example, as a self-mailer or inserted in envelopes).
- Choosing the right commercial printer for each of your publications. This typically involves preparing and submitting quotation sheets, comparing printing bids, submitting your files to the printer, and picking up and approving the finished publication.

Most important, while preparing your publication, you still have the responsibility of ensuring that your document is adequately proofed to keep you from making embarrassing mistakes. Although Publisher's AutoCorrect will flag and, if instructed, correct most spelling errors as they occur, double-check it to make sure the right words have been inserted. You still have final responsibility for the spelling of proper nouns, and for correct phone numbers and zip codes.

In addition to proofreading, you remain responsible for numerous details such as making sure headlines are not hyphenated (do not contain words split between two lines) and subheads do not appear by themselves at the bottom of a column. You still have to eliminate widows and orphans—individual words or lines of text isolated at the tops of columns. But by taking the hard work out of document design and formatting, Publisher's greatest contribution may be to create time for you to do these other important tasks.

What's Different in Publisher 2000?

If you have used previous versions of Microsoft Publisher, you are likely to be pleasantly surprised by Publisher 2000's greatly enhanced capabilities. Publisher 2000 enhancements can be categorized into three main areas: ease of use, better color handling, and improved commercial printing options.

Added Ease of Use

Publisher 2000's ease of use is the result of added design options as well as an improved interface. Not only are more Design Master Sets available, but the variety of types of pages you can create for each type of publication has been increased, offering you far more design flexibility.

For example, the Publisher's Catalog Wizard, shown in Figure 1-11, is new to Publisher 2000. With this Wizard, even one-person businesses can quickly and easily create catalogs to show and describe a variety of their offerings to customers, prospects, and supporters. When creating catalogs from a single dialog box, you can choose from among several available page layout options for each page,

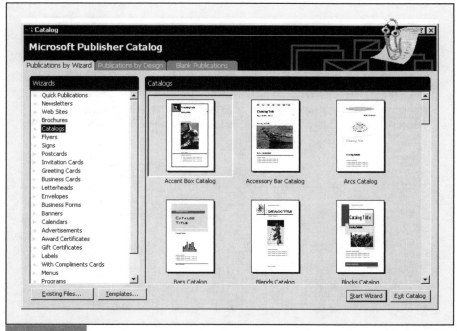

FIGURE 1-11   The Catalog Wizard makes it easy to select and preview the most appropriate layout for each page of your catalog

including a choice of one, two, three, four, or eight featured items and additional formatting options such as a calendar, table of contents, or text.

New in 2000: Publisher's most noticeable improvement is the addition of the Catalog Wizard, explained in Chapter 7.

More Design Gallery Objects

Publisher 2000 features more Design Gallery Objects—those pre-formatted building blocks for calendars, coupons, reply forms, and graphic elements that can be added to more than one type of publication. More important, the Design Gallery also helps you inadvertently avoid losing text or graphics you add to pages of your publication that you later delete. If you delete a page of a newsletter or catalog containing text or graphics, Publisher automatically saves the text or graphics in the Design Gallery's Extra Content area, shown in Figure 1-12, making it easy for you to rescue them and place them on another page. The first words of the text in each rescued text frame appears as a caption below the text frame, making it easy to locate a desired article, headline, or pull-quote.

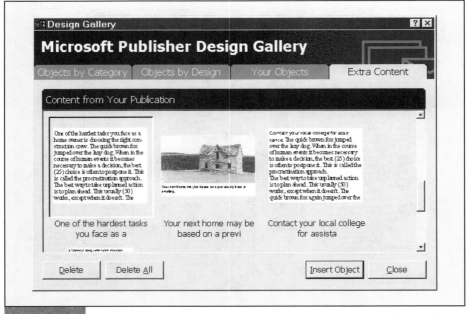

FIGURE 1-12 Clicking on Publisher's Design Gallery's Extra Content tab reveals text and graphics previously placed on deleted pages

Many subtle improvements have been added to the Publisher screen. A Show Wizard/Hide Wizard button located in the Status Bar along the bottom of the page is easier to access than opening the View menu and selecting the commands. Increase Font Size and Decrease Font Size buttons in the Formatting Toolbar make it easy to select a different type size.

New Clip Art Gallery

Another important ease-of-use feature found in Publisher 2000 is a new Clip Art Gallery, which makes it easier to search for decorative illustrations and insert them into your publications. As shown in Figure 1-13, you can search for clip art by entering keywords in the Search for Clips window. When you locate a desired image, you can simply drag and drop it into your publication.

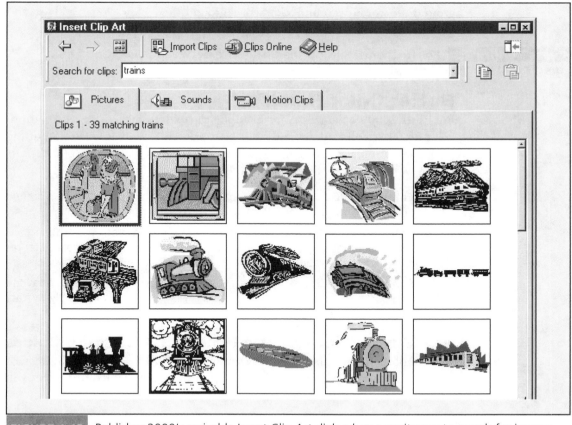

FIGURE 1-13   Publisher 2000's resizable Insert Clip Art dialog box permits you to search for images using keywords

Cross-Reference: For further details on the new Clip Art Gallery, see Chapter 12.

Contributing to Publisher 2000's ease of use is its consistency with other Office 2000 software programs. Publisher 2000's menus and toolbars are similar to those used in other Office 2000 programs, as is its use of the Office Assistant to provide help as needed. In addition, many Publisher designs are now shared with other Office 2000 applications, such as Word, Front Page (for Web site creation and management), and PowerPoint (for presentations).

Easier Page Navigation

Publisher 2000 includes easier page navigation, including a new Status Line that makes it easier to go directly to desired pages. The new page number interface also makes it easier to see at a glance whether you are looking at Publisher's Background View or Foreground View. (Background View allows you to add text and graphics that will appear on every page.)

Cross-Reference: For further details on the difference between Background and Foreground Views, see Chapter 3.

Better Color Handling

Publisher 2000's enhanced color-handling capabilities make it easier to output color on office color ink-jet and color laser printers as well as when outputting your publication at a copy shop or commercial printer. Publisher 2000 permits you to work with three different color models:

- **Composite RGB**   Choose this option when printing publications in limited quantities on your office color ink-jet or color laser printer.
- **Process colors (CYMK)**   Choose this option when your publication contains four-color photographs and your copy center or commercial printer requires color separations for printing on a four-color output device.
- **Spot color(s)**   Choose this when your publication contains black and white photographs and is going to be printed in black plus one or possibly two accent colors, as Figure 1-14 shows.

New Support for Pantone Matching System for Colors

Most important, Publisher 2000 now supports the Pantone Matching System, or PMS. The Pantone Matching System ensures that your printed document will

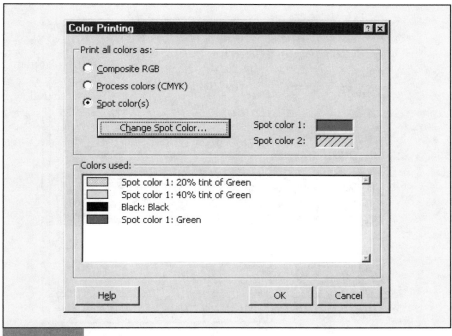

FIGURE 1-14   Use Publisher 2000's Color Printing dialog box to choose the type of color processing output you need for your final product

look just the way you want it by permitting you to assign colors by number, using references to standardized books of accurately printed color samples. Separate sample books, or specimen books, are available for coated (glossy) as well as un-coated papers. Selecting colors using the Pantone system, shown in Figure 1-15, avoids the problems inherent in trying to relate what you see on the screen of your monitor to the color that emerges from a printing press.

Publisher 2000's enhanced color output capabilities are accompanied by en-hanced color management features (see Figure 1-16). For example, you can now recolor pictures with Publisher 2000, if you have chosen two-, three-, or four-color printing at a copy center or commercial printer. Select the new Leave Black Parts Black option if you want to add extra depth to your picture.

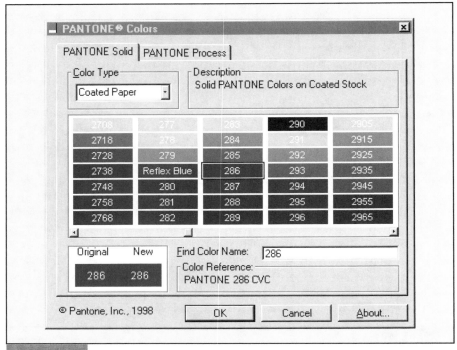

FIGURE 1-15 With Publisher 2000, you can assign colors based on the industry-wide Pantone Matching System

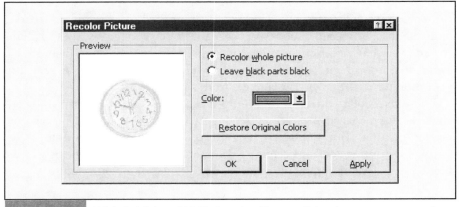

FIGURE 1-16 With Publisher 2000's Recolor Picture dialog box, you can recolor all or part of a picture

Working with Copy Shops and Commercial Printers

Perhaps the biggest news with Publisher 2000 involves its smooth integration with service bureaus, copy shops, and commercial printers. Service bureaus are independent firms that convert computer files into high-resolution films that are used by commercial printers, although many commercial printers do this work themselves.

You can preview Publisher 2000's new commercial printing and output options by selecting the new Pack and Go Wizard, located in the File menu. The Pack and Go Wizard prepares your files for commercial printing by splitting large publications across multiple disks, embedding TrueType fonts, including linked graphics, creating links for embedded graphics, and printing composite and separation proofs. The Pack and Go Wizard ensures that all necessary linked graphics and fonts used in your publication will be brought to the printer (or brought home, if you want to work on a business publication on your home computer). If your publication includes linked graphics, such as links to charts created with Microsoft Excel, the Pack and Go Wizard makes sure that a copy of the appropriate Excel file accompanies your Publisher file and that the two files are correctly linked.

Cross-Reference: For additional information regarding the Pack and Go Wizard, see Chapter 15.

Publisher 2000's Commercial Printing Tools, located in the Tools menu, permit you and your commercial printer to choose the right file format for four-color process printing, or two- or three-color spot-color printing. You (or your printer) can also adjust the color trapping (overlap). Trapping eliminates white spaces that might show up between adjacent colors when your project is printed at a commercial printer.

If you select Tools | Commercial Printing Tools | Fonts, the Fonts dialog box (see Figure 1-17) displays a list of the fonts included in your document. Check boxes permit you to embed either the full character set of the TrueType fonts used in your Publisher file or just include a subset of the fonts actually used in your publication. If you only used 12 different characters of a particular font in a headline, for example, you can embed just those 12 characters in the Publisher file instead of the full alphabet, numbers, and punctuation included with the typeface. This, obviously, creates smaller files.

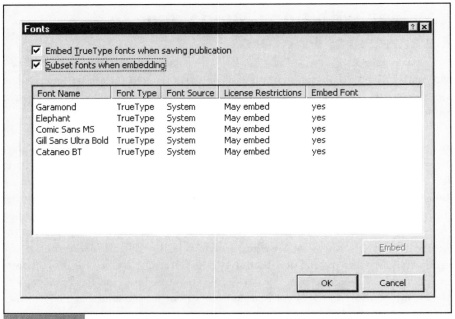

FIGURE 1-17   Use the Fonts dialog box to include all the characters of a TrueType font in your Publisher file, or just those characters used in your publication

Tip: If these advanced features seem intimidating, don't despair. They are there mainly to help you get the best possible results from your commercial printer or service bureau. If you are going to be printing your documents on your office desktop printer, you do not need to concern yourself with these features.

New Graphics Manager

The Graphics Manager is another important new addition to the Publisher 2000 Commercial Printing Tools. The Graphics Manager, shown in Figure 1-18, lets you replace embedded graphics with links to the original files of scanned photographs (or other graphics) used in your publication. Linking copies of the original files and sending them along to the commercial printer, rather than simply embedding them, makes the original files available to your commercial printer in case last minute fine-tuning is needed.

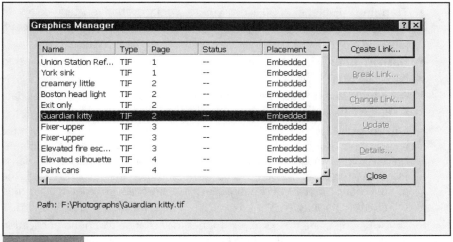

FIGURE 1-18   Using graphics linked to the actual files in the Graphics dialog box lets your commercial printer fine-tune the original files if necessary

Is Publisher 2000 Compatible with Previous Publisher Versions?

Publisher 2000 is very comfortable opening publications created with Publisher 98 and Publisher 95. However, Publisher 2000's Wizards may not be able to completely revise publications created with Publisher 98's Wizards.

Publisher 2000 can also save files in Publisher 98 format. Because Publisher 2000 incorporates so many new features, however, Publisher 98 may not be able to support many features that you take for granted working with Publisher 2000. Significant differences between Publisher 2000 and Publisher 98 include:

- **Type**   Publisher 2000 can embed fonts in document files. Publisher 98 cannot, so the document will not display and print properly unless the fonts are installed and available.

- **Color**   Publisher 2000 can assign CYMK and Pantone colors. Publisher 98 will convert these to RGB (or screen) colors. You also lose the ability to create four-color separations.

- **Trapping**   Publisher 2000 allows you to slightly overlap touching colors, to ensure complete color coverage on a commercial printing press. Publisher 98 does not support this feature.

- **Dashed lines**   Publisher 98 converts dashed lines around coupons to non-dashed lines the same width.

- **Date and time formatting**   If your publication automatically updates date and time information, formatting may be lost.

- **Linked graphics**   With Publisher 98, you cannot link graphics; you must embed them in your Publisher document file. This loss creates two problems. First, files with embedded graphics are often very large—sometimes too large to fit on a diskette. Second, because the graphics are not embedded, the printer cannot quickly and easily see those graphics in order to fine-tune them before printing.

- **Layout**   Some line breaks in text frames may change when the publication is opened in Publisher 98. Publisher 98 Wizards will be unable to revise publications created with Publisher 2000's new Wizards.

Professional Skills Summary

In this chapter, you learned to recognize how you can use Publisher 2000 to create professional-looking, affordable publications and documents, as well as Web sites. You learned about Publisher 2000's new features that simplify creating documents and publications you want printed by a copy center or professional printer. You also learned how to use Publisher's capabilities to project the type of professional image you want to project, including tips and advice on how to create or fine-tune unique, appropriate, and effective materials. With Publisher, you'll be able to save money *and* maintain control over that print project—no matter how large or small.

chapter 2

Getting Started with Publisher 2000

In this chapter, you will:

- Complete an introductory overview of Publisher 2000's main menus

- Learn about Publisher's shortcut menus

- Customize and work with Publisher 2000's standard and special-function toolbars

Publisher 2000's menus are organized much the same as other Office 2000 programs. Because of these applications' similarities, you'll find it easy to transfer habits and knowledge gained working with Microsoft Word or Excel to Publisher 2000.

Publisher 2000 features 10 main menus arranged along the application's screen top. Click on any one of the 10 main menu options, and Publisher will present a drop-down list of specific commands listed under that menu's category. You can also open any of Publisher 2000's main menus by holding down the ALT key and pressing the specified underlined letter for that menu option.

Surveying Publisher 2000's Main Menus

In this section, we'll take an introductory overview of Publisher 2000's main menus, but keep in mind that this introduction is not intended to be a comprehensive look at every menu option. Instead, we'll hit the menu highlights, emphasizing what's new and pointing out some of the more important commands we'll discuss in detail later in this book. This overview approach will help you whether you're a newcomer to Microsoft Publisher or you've upgraded from an earlier version.

As you begin this overview, remember that the exact configuration of each menu will vary slightly, depending on whether you have previously selected a text or graphic object by clicking on it. You may also experience slight differences, depending on the document type you currently have open.

Like other Office 2000 programs, Publisher 2000 offers personally customized menus that automatically move your most frequently used commands to the top of each main menu, but—depending on how often you use each command—you may not want Publisher to change your menus' contents. To keep your menus static, select Tools | Options. Publisher will display the Options dialog box. From this dialog box, click first on the General tab. Then click Menus Show Recently Used Commands First, to make the menu options static. Doing so, however, will affect the way menus are displayed in all Office 2000 programs.

Hiding and Revealing Infrequently Used Commands

Like other Office 2000 programs, long and short versions of each menu are available. This saves valuable space by hiding infrequently used commands until they are needed.

When you first select a menu, the short form appears containing two downward-pointing arrows at the bottom of the menu, as shown in Figure 2-1. Click the two downward-pointing arrows to reveal the full menu. If you don't immediately make a selection from the initial command options, Publisher 2000—after a few seconds—will automatically open to reveal the full menu with all available commands, as shown in Figure 2-2. Notice that infrequently used commands appear against a light gray background.

Note that Publisher 2000's menus are context-specific. If you previously selected a text frame, for example, the long and short Format menus will contain commands dealing with type, as shown in Figure 2-3. If, however, you have previously selected a graphic, such as a photograph, the Format menu contains commands dealing with graphic images, as shown in Figure 2-4.

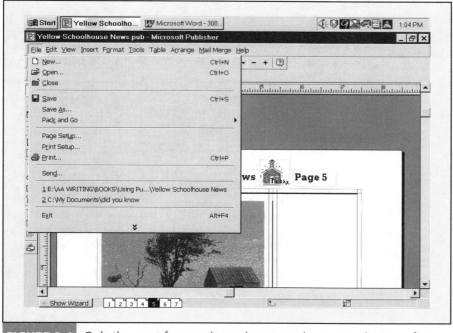

FIGURE 2-1   Only the most frequently used commands appear when you first open a menu

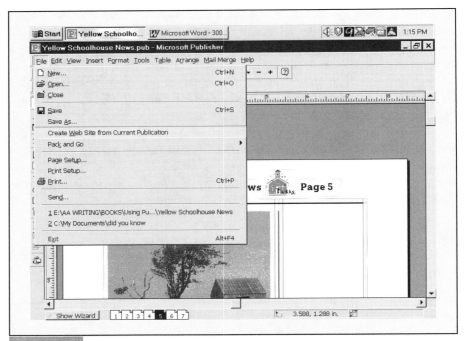

Click the two downward-pointing arrows at the bottom of the short menus, or wait a few seconds, to reveal all the commands

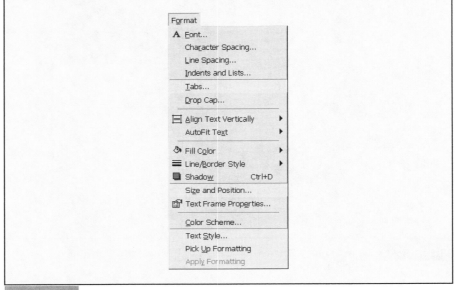

Open the Format menu while a text object is selected and the menu reveals commands dealing with formatting words

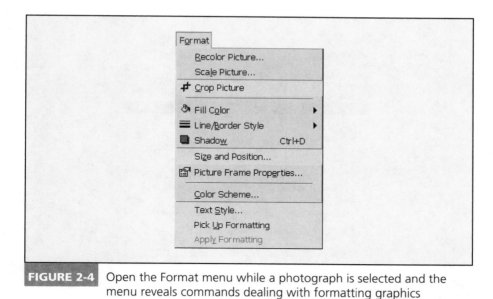

FIGURE 2-4   Open the Format menu while a photograph is selected and the menu reveals commands dealing with formatting graphics

Understanding the File Menu

As with all Office 2000 applications, you'll use the File menu to open, close, save, and print documents. Also common with other Office 2000 applications, the Open, Save, and Save As commands make it easy to locate documents and save them in multiple formats. You can easily access up to 50 of your most recently saved documents. The Send command, which is new, also makes it easy to electronically send files over the Internet.

New in 2000:   Publisher's new Send command makes sending files over the Internet a simple process.

The Pack and Go command is one of Publisher 2000's most important additions on the File menu. With this feature, you can easily take your Publisher 2000 projects, complete with fonts and graphics, to another computer or to a commercial printer. (See Figure 2-5.) The Pack and Go Wizard splits large publications across multiple disks, embeds fonts, and makes sure that linked graphics are included when you transfer your files. The capability to embed TrueType fonts in your document file is an extremely important enhancement, because it eliminates numerous problems when you are working on more than one computer or using a commercial printer.

New in 2000:   Publisher's new Pack and Go Wizard automates taking large project files with you—whether to another computer or to a commercial printer.

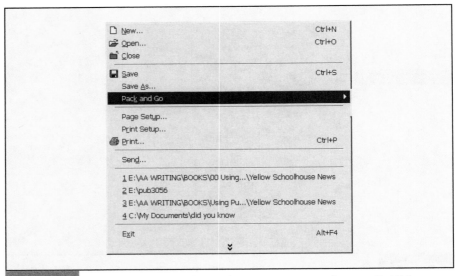

FIGURE 2-5   Select File, Pack and Go when you want to take your Publisher projects to other computers or a commercial printer

Exploring the Edit Menu

Publisher 2000's Edit menu contains several important commands that perform tasks beyond the usual Cut, Copy, Paste, Find, and Replace commands that you would normally find in other Office 2000 Edit menus. Some of the Publisher-specific Edit menu commands are:

- **Undo (shortcut command: CTRL-Z)**   Previous versions of Publisher limited you to the last command or change you made in your document. Undo will be accompanied by the name of a specific element you want undone, such as Undo Formatting, Undo Cut, or Undo Create Object. With Publisher 2000, you can undo up to 20 changes in your document, until you have saved the file. Once you have saved the file, the Undo command will no longer perform multiple Undo operations.

- **Redo (shortcut command: CTRL-Y)**   This menu option restores the action undone by your use of the Undo command. Redo returns the document to the state it was before you used Undo. For example, if you delete a graphic and decide you want to put it back, use Redo to restore the graphic. Be cautious, however, because the Redo option shows on the Edit drop-down menu only when you have the entire set of Edit menu options displayed. If you do not see the Redo option on the Edit menu, but you see two small down arrows at the bottom of the Edit drop-down menu, you must click the small arrows to expand the Edit menu to display all its options.

New in 2000: Publisher now features multiple levels of the Undo menu option. If you have not yet saved your file, you may undo as many as 20 of your last actions on that specific document.

- **Can't Undo and Can't Redo**   These commands appear as shadowed menu options when you cannot select them.

- **Delete Text, Delete Object, Delete Page**   Before you can use any of the three Delete options, you must first select the item you want to delete: either text, an object, or a page. Once you highlight the item, the Edit menu will then display the commands you need to perform the deletion. As with Undo, you must be sure the Edit menu is displaying all its options. If you do not see the Delete option you need and two small arrows appear at the bottom of the Edit menu, click the small arrows to expand the menu to display all its options. For example, if you have selected a text frame, you can either delete the text within the text frame using Delete Text, or delete the text frame itself using Delete Object.

- **Highlight Entire Story (shortcut command: CTRL-A)**   Use this command when you are replacing boilerplate or "for position only" headlines and text, when you work with Design Wizards, or when you want to copy an entire text file's contents to another file, for example.

- **Edit Story in Microsoft Word**   This feature works only if you have Word V6.0 or later also installed on your computer. Use this command when you are working on long documents. Right-click on the text frame, and Publisher displays a free-floating menu. Select the Change Text option. Then select Edit Story in Microsoft Word. You can now use all of Word's more powerful editing features, such as outline numbering or changing text from numbered to bulleted lists, with only a few mouse clicks.

- **Personal Information**   Use this command to enter *only once* your entire set of primary or secondary business, organization, or home/family information, such as address, phone number, or e-mail address. (See Figure 2-6.)

New in 2000: Publisher's new Personal Information feature eliminates the need to constantly re-enter your firm's—or your clients'—addresses, phone numbers, and e-mail addresses. With the Personal Information feature, you can store specific information that can be instantly updated for your primary business, secondary business, other organization, or home/family.

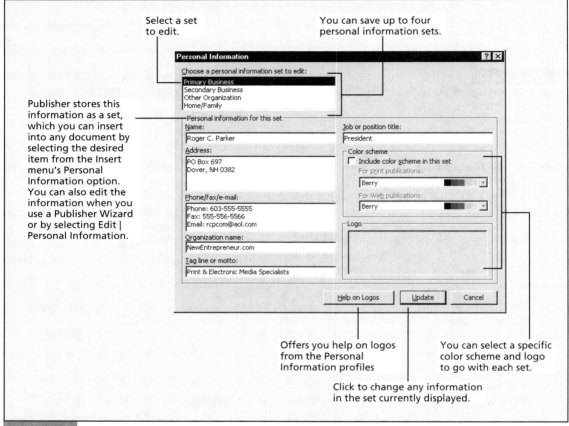

Select a set to edit.

You can save up to four personal information sets.

Publisher stores this information as a set, which you can insert into any document by selecting the desired item from the Insert menu's Personal Information option. You can also edit the information when you use a Publisher Wizard or by selecting Edit | Personal Information.

Offers you help on logos from the Personal Information profiles

You can select a specific color scheme and logo to go with each set.

Click to change any information in the set currently displayed.

FIGURE 2-6 Select Edit, and select Personal Information to enter your logo, name, address, phone number, and e-mail information into your personal profile

Using the View Menu Commands

Publisher 2000's View menu options change the way your document appears on your computer's screen. Five important View menu options are:

- **Picture Display** With this menu option, you can work faster with documents that contain several large graphic images, such as scanned photographs. Instead of showing the actual, detailed image, Publisher's new Picture Display command displays a lower graphics resolution (a lesser detailed image). To use this feature, click the View drop-down menu and select Picture Display. Publisher then displays the Picture Display dialog box. (See Figure 2-7.) Remember that with Picture Display, when you print your documents, all graphics images will still print with full detail.

- **Hide Boundaries and Guides, and Show Boundaries and Guides (shortcut command: CTRL-SHIFT-O)** This menu option hides nonprinting elements you've added to your publication, such as margins, columns, and horizontal or vertical guidelines. This feature makes it easier to preview how your document will look when printed. Note that this command affects *only* the image on your monitor. You can reverse this option to see boundaries and margins again by

Tip: If you choose either the Fast Resize and Zoom or the Hide Pictures options from Publisher 2000's Picture Display option, remember that the only aspect affected is how the picture appears on your computer screen—not how the picture prints. With both options, the picture prints at maximum resolution.

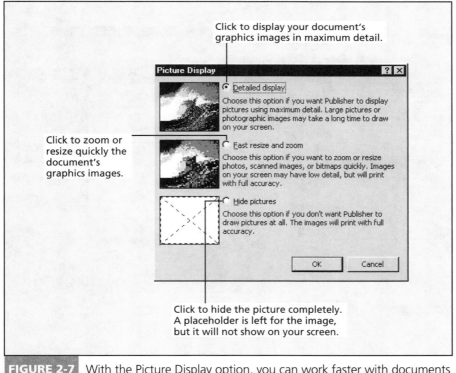

Click to display your document's graphics images in maximum detail.

Click to zoom or resize quickly the document's graphics images.

Click to hide the picture completely. A placeholder is left for the image, but it will not show on your screen.

FIGURE 2-7 With the Picture Display option, you can work faster with documents that contain several graphics images or large graphics images

L▶ Tip: How completely you can use the Show Wizard command is determined by whether you created the document using a Publisher 2000 Design Wizard. If you created a document from scratch, your options with this menu command are limited.

clicking the View drop-down menu, and selecting Show Boundaries and Guides.

- **Show Wizard and Hide Wizard** If you created a document with Design Wizards, you can easily change a document's appearance with the Show Wizard command. Depending on the document type, you can change the design, color scheme, layout, paper size, customer address, or forms. (See Figure 2-8.) To work without the Design Wizard, select Hide Wizard from the View drop-down menu.

This window outlines the type of Design Wizard you are using, its layout, and content details.

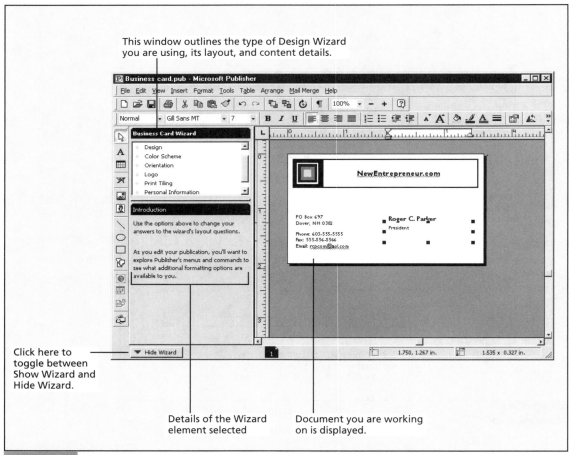

Click here to toggle between Show Wizard and Hide Wizard.

Details of the Wizard element selected

Document you are working on is displayed.

FIGURE 2-8 When the Show Wizard option is active, your screen's left side will display context-sensitive directions to alter the document's appearance

The Insert Menu

With Publisher's Insert menu, you can quickly add text and graphic elements to your documents. You can add text files, Design Gallery Objects, previously saved graphic images (including clip art), or scanned images. For example, you can select between multiple image sources, such as a flatbed scanner and a digital camera, as well as acquire the image, as shown in Figure 2-9.

Before you can add any element to your document, you must first place a text frame, graphics frame, picture frame, Word Art frame, or clip art frame within your document by using Publisher's toolbar. To add an element to a frame, you must select the frame by clicking on it.

You can use the Insert menu's Design Gallery option to add a Design Art Gallery object to your document, or add additional selections to the Design Art Gallery with the Add Selection to Design Gallery option.

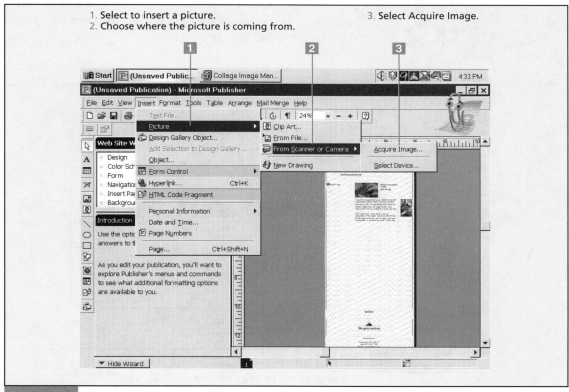

FIGURE 2-9 From Publisher's Insert menu, you can add a variety of digital images and objects to dress up your documents

With the Insert menu's Picture option, you can add a picture directly from your digital camera or image scanner by selecting the From Scanner or Camera option, and then selecting Acquire Image. In addition, you can use the Insert menu to add clip art, art from a file, or a new drawing.

Cross-Reference: See Chapter 3 to learn more about Publisher's frames and how to use them.

From the Insert menu, you can also access the Form Control menu, which is great for adding interactive elements to any Web site you create with Publisher. (Note that if you do not have a Web site file open on your desktop, the Form Control option remains shadowed as inactive.) When you select Form Control from the Insert menu, Publisher displays a nested menu that features interactive Web page enhancements such as single-line text boxes, multiline text boxes, check boxes, option buttons, list boxes, and command buttons. Adding features like these to your Web site makes it easy for your Web site visitors to introduce themselves to you, and explain their needs and preferences. (See Figure 2-10.)

Tip: Remember, to access the Insert menu's Form Control option, you must have a Web site open on Publisher's desktop; otherwise, Form Control will remain shadowed and inaccessible.

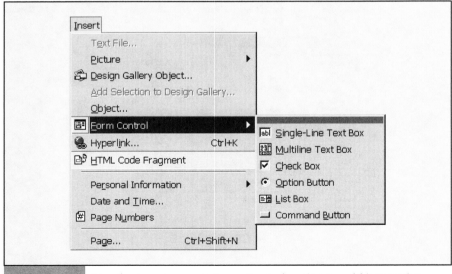

FIGURE 2-10 Use the Insert menu's Form Control option to add interactive elements to your Publisher-created Web sites

The Format Menu

The Format menu contains the commands you need to control your document's or Web page's appearance. Publisher's Format menu's content changes depending on whether you have a text frame, graphics frame, or table selected. The majority of Publisher's Format menu commands are the same as those in Microsoft Word, but the following list discusses the exceptions that pertain only to Publisher:

- **Align Text Vertically**   If you select the Align Text Vertically option from the Format menu, you will have three choices: Top, Center, and Bottom. This feature places the text you select at one of the three available options, and if used correctly, can give you more enhanced text placement capabilities. Remember, however, that you must first select a text box to make the option available and unshadowed on the Format menu. Note also that whichever option you select affects the entire text frame. (See Figure 2-11.)

- **AutoFit Text**   When you create headlines, use the Format menu's Best Fit option so the headline will automatically expand to the appropriate type size to fill the available space. You'll find this option to be especially useful when you are adding headlines to Design Wizard-created documents. You can also choose Shrink Text on Overflow if you have a bit too much text to fit the available space. (See Figure 2-12.)

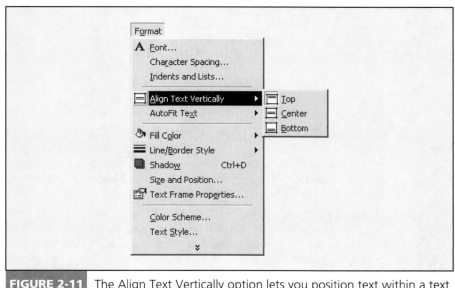

FIGURE 2-11   The Align Text Vertically option lets you position text within a text frame at the Top, Center, or Bottom

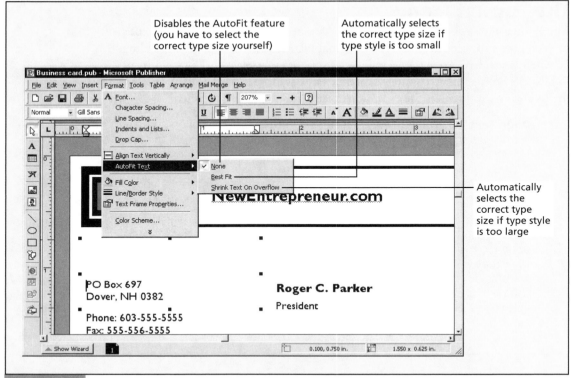

FIGURE 2-12   Use the Format menu's AutoFit Text when you want Publisher to choose the right type size to fill available space

Tip: Use Publisher's AutoFit Text, Best Fit, and Shrink Text on Overflow options with restraint. Your best-looking documents will be based on your consistent use of a few type sizes. In addition, if you use text too small to read, no one benefits from this decision.

- **Fill Color**   Fill Color gives you the opportunity to add color backgrounds to your frames, by selecting harmonious colors from your previously selected Master Design Set. You can also change color schemes or add a special effect by selecting either the More Color Schemes, More Colors, or Fill Effects option. (See Figure 2-13.)

- **Size and Position**   When you select the Format menu's Size and Position option, Publisher displays the Size and Position dialog box, which you use to precisely adjust the size and placement of any text or graphic object. (See Figure 2-14.) If you click the Size and Position

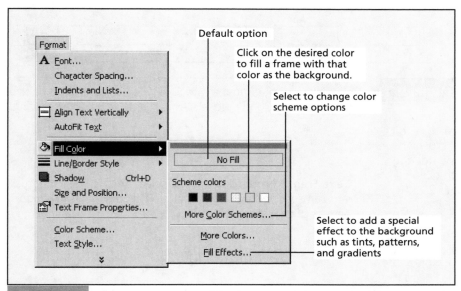

FIGURE 2-13 The Format menu's Fill Color option lets you add color backgrounds to your frames

dialog box's Show Toolbar option, Publisher 2000 displays a new feature, the Measurements toolbar, which you can use to fine-tune letter and line spacing. For convenience, you can move this toolbar anywhere on the screen. (See Figure 2-15.)

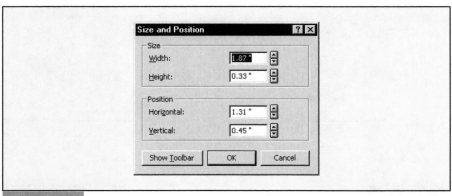

FIGURE 2-14 Select Format, Size and Position when you want precise control over the placement of text and graphics

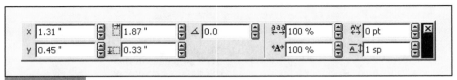

FIGURE 2-15   With Publisher's Measurement toolbar, you can control frame size and position easily and precisely, as well as letter and line spacing

Tip: If you are coming to Publisher from Microsoft Word, you may be wondering where the Paragraph dialog box is. Well, Publisher 2000 does not have one! Select Format, Line Spacing to adjust text line spacing within paragraphs or add extra space before or after paragraphs.

- **Text Frame Properties**   If you select Text Frame Properties, you can specify the margins, columns, and column spacing for any specific text frame. (See Figure 2-16.)

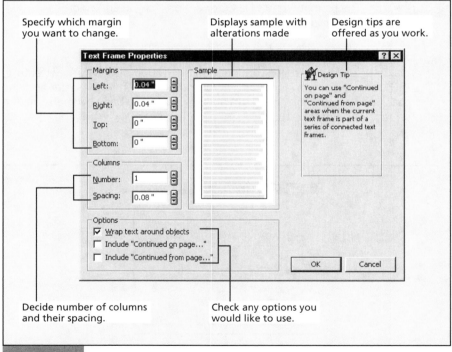

FIGURE 2-16   With the Text Frame Properties dialog box, you can control specific spacing within a text frame

Option	Description
Color Printing	With this option, you can print colors as they appear on your computer monitor, or use process or spot colors. When you select this option, Publisher displays the Color Printing dialog box. (See Figure 2-17.) If you select Spot Color(s), Publisher activates the Change Spot Color button option. When you click this button, Publisher displays the Choose Spot Color dialog box for fine-tuning your spot-color options. (See Figure 2-18.)
Trapping	Trapping determines how much adjacent colors will overlap each other on the printing press (thus avoiding gaps between adjacent colors). From this menu option, you can select Preferences, which will display the Preferences dialog box (see Figure 2-19), or Per Object Trapping, which displays the Per Object Trapping dialog box (see Figure 2-20).
Graphics Manager	This option shows at a glance which graphics files are embedded in the document and which are linked.
Fonts	Select this option, and Publisher 2000 displays the Fonts dialog box, with which you can determine which TrueType fonts you will embed or insert into your documents.

TABLE 2-1 Tools Menu Options Specific to Publisher 2000

The Tools Menu

Publisher's Tools menu offers access to utilities, such as spell check and Design Checker, but the most important addition to this menu is the Commercial Printing Tools. When you select the Tools menu's Commercial Printing Tools option, Publisher presents a drop-down menu offering the advanced commercial printing options listed in Table 2-1.

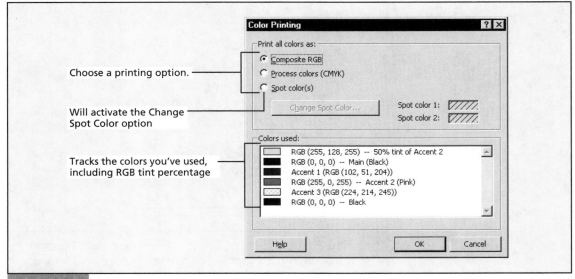

FIGURE 2-17 Publisher's Color Printing dialog box provides commercial printers with all the color-printing details about your Publisher 2000 files

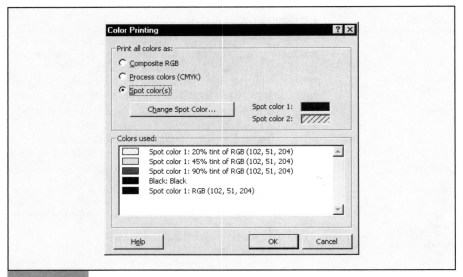

FIGURE 2-18 Use the Choose Spot Color dialog box for fine-tuning your spot-color options

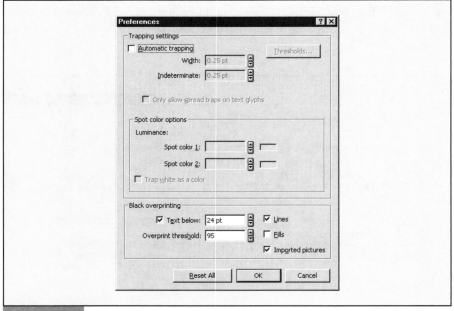

FIGURE 2-19 Use the Preferences dialog box to activate Automatic Trapping, vary the luminance of spot-color options, or set details for black overprinting

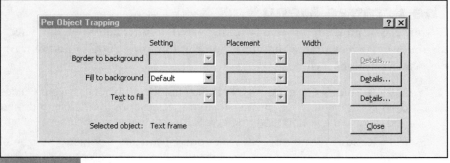

FIGURE 2-20   Use the Per Object Trapping dialog box to specify the Setting, Placement, and Width of the selected object's Border to Background, Fill to Background, and Text to Fill settings

New in 2000: These commercial color-printing options make Publisher a full-featured professional desktop publishing application. When you understand and effectively use these options, any commercial printer you use will be pleased when they receive your Publisher 2000 files.

The Table Menu

Not significantly changed from previous versions, Publisher 2000's Table menu contains the entire repertoire of commands to create and edit tables that any Windows-based software application user should readily recognize. Use the Table menu, shown here, to insert or delete rows and columns, and to customize any table's features.

Tip: If Publisher 2000's drop-down Table menu options appear as shadowed, and they are not active, add a table frame or click on the desired table within your Publisher document. Publisher activates the Table menu options by unshadowing those menu options.

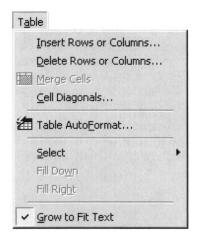

The Arrange Menu

As you become more sophisticated working with Publisher 2000, you'll be selecting the Arrange menu more and more. Some of Publisher 2000's important Arrange menu options include:

- **Layout Guides**   Select this option, and Publisher displays its Layout Guides dialog box, where you can enter custom specifications for margin grids and grid guides, the nonprinting framework for creating your document.
- **Ruler Guides**   With this convenient option, you add—or hide—horizontal and vertical ruler guides, which appear onscreen in nonreproducing blue. Choose these guides from the Arrange menu, shown here, to help you place text or graphic elements in the same location on each page.

Tip: Using the Group Objects command to link design elements is a strategic Publisher design feature, but just finding either command on the Arrange menu can drive you crazy! You have to know the "key" to controlling the Group Objects command to be able to use this handy feature. How? See Figure 2-21 for the secret to using the Group Objects command.

- **Group Objects and Ungroup Objects**   Perhaps the most important Arrange menu option is Group Objects (CTRL-SHIFT-G). You can group together two or more text or graphic objects, so that you can move or resize the objects as a single unit. After you have grouped objects together, you can ungroup them by opening the Arrange menu and selecting Ungroup Objects (CTRL-SHIFT-G). (See Figure 2-21.)
- **Align Objects**   Select this option to access the handy Align Objects dialog box. Use this dialog box to precision-align two or more text or graphic elements, relative to each other or to the page margins.

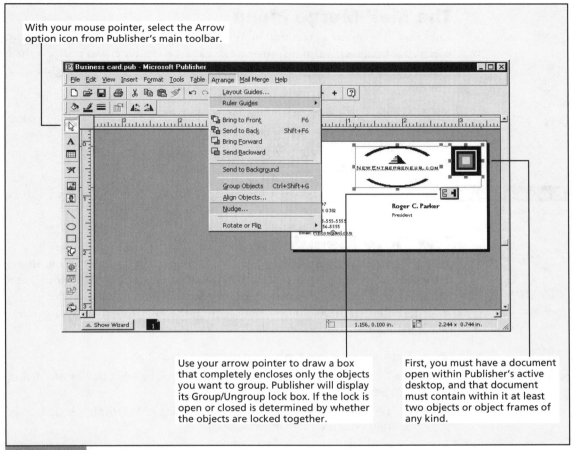

With your mouse pointer, select the Arrow option icon from Publisher's main toolbar.

Use your arrow pointer to draw a box that completely encloses only the objects you want to group. Publisher will display its Group/Ungroup lock box. If the lock is open or closed is determined by whether the objects are locked together.

First, you must have a document open within Publisher's active desktop, and that document must contain within it at least two objects or object frames of any kind.

FIGURE 2-21   Want to know the secret to making Group Objects and Ungroup Objects appear as options on the Arrange menu?

Before you can do anything with the Arrange menu's Group and Ungroup Object options, you have to perform a series of steps. In fact, if you try to locate these two menu options and you don't know how they operate, you might never find them!

Tip: If you're used to working with Microsoft Word, notice that one of Publisher 2000's "curve balls" is inconsistency with the File menu and the Page Setup dialog box. In Publisher, if you want to adjust margins, for example, select Arrange, Layout Guides. You also have to use the Layout Guides dialog boxes when you add columns and need to reorganize a document's object placement.

The Mail Merge Menu

Publisher 2000 offers a great deal of utility not only because creating documents is easy, but because it's also easy to print and address customer and prospect mailings. With Publisher 2000's Mail Merge menu options, as shown in Figure 2-22, you can:

- Create a database of customer names and addresses
- Import a database of previously created names and addresses
- Address brochures or newsletters or postcards to some or all of your customers and prospects

Cross-Reference: For more information on learning how to distribute your newsletters, see Chapter 14.

The Help Menu

Help is never more than a click away with Publisher 2000's Help menu, shown in Figure 2-23. Just press the standard F1 function key, and Publisher displays the animated, smiling Office Assistant, asking "What would you like to do?"

With Publisher 2000, you can choose from the following friendly, eager animated assistants:

- The familiar Clippit, the smiling paperclip
- The Dot, a somewhat hyperactive, bouncing red ball that can transform itself into any shape
- F1, a crustacean-looking robot, who is the first of Microsoft's 300/M series, but fully optimized for Office's work

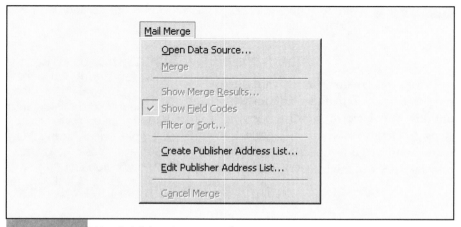

FIGURE 2-22 Use Publisher 2000's Mail Merge menu options to create and edit customer/prospect databases, or print addresses on brochures, newsletters, and postcards

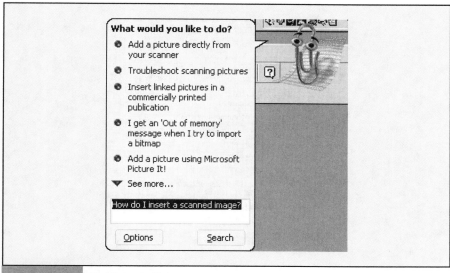

FIGURE 2-23   Publisher's Help menu

- The Genius, an older gentleman resembling a cross between several of my college professors and Einstein himself
- The brightly colored, groovy, musical Office logo
- Mother Nature, an Earth sphere that transforms itself into a variety of Nature's images, including the dove, the volcano, the flower, and the sun
- A cool cat named Links, who asks, "Did I see a mouse?"
- Rocky, the friendly barking retriever, as well as Man's and Office's best friend

In addition to these unusual characters, Publisher's Help menu offers access to a variety of types of assistance while you are creating, printing, and troubleshooting your document. These Help options are described in Table 2-2.

Option	Description
Microsoft Publisher Web Site	If you click on this item, your computer automatically connects you directly with the Microsoft Publisher Web Site (provided you are connected to the Internet). From this Web site, you can directly contact Microsoft's Publisher experts.
The Print Troubleshooter	The Print Troubleshooter uses printing-problem symptom descriptions to identify printing problem causes through Publisher's Print Troubleshooter, as shown in Figure 2-24.
Detect and Repair	This Help option inspects your Publisher 2000 program files and prompts you to perform preventative maintenance when necessary.

TABLE 2-2   Publisher 2000's Specific Help Menu Options

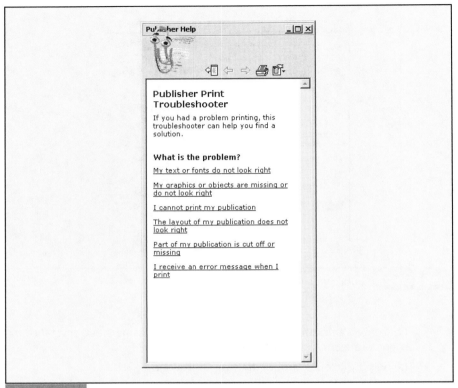

FIGURE 2-24   Publisher's Print Troubleshooter asks you whether your printing problem falls into one of six areas

Accessing Publisher 2000 Floating Shortcut Menus

With Publisher 2000, instead of using a mouse to activate the main menu's drop-down options lists, you have an alternative. Click your right mouse button on any object's border. Instead of being organized by category, these "floating" menus are organized by their immediate applicability to the task at hand. The menu that appears contains the commands needed to edit or format the text or graphic object, change your view of the screen, or search for Help.

Tip: If you want access to menu options associated with graphics, right-click on any edge of a graphics frame, as shown in Figure 2-26.

These context-specific menus often contain numerous nested menus that reveal even more command options. Figure 2-25 shows a "floating" menu for a text frame.

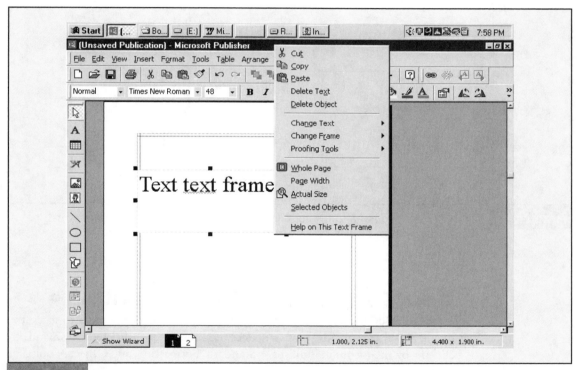

FIGURE 2-25   Right-clicking the edge of a text frame reveals a menu of commands associated with editing or formatting text. The nested menu options offer even more editing and formatting choices.

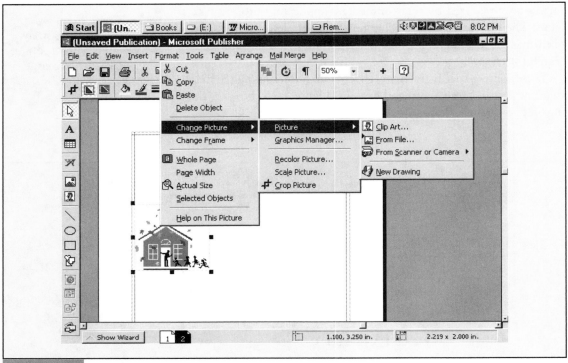

FIGURE 2-26   Right-click the edge of a frame containing a graphic when you want to reformat the object's contents or border, or replace the current graphic with another one

Using Publisher 2000's Toolbars

Publisher 2000's Toolbars eliminate the need to open menus in order to access frequently used commands. You can select the most frequently used commands by clicking on their icons in Publisher's Standard, Formatting, and Objects Toolbars.

Tip: *Tippages* are short phrases that explain the command associated with each Toolbar icon.

Exploring the Standard Toolbar

The Standard Toolbar icons duplicate frequently used menu options from the File, Edit, View, and Arrange menus. (See Figure 2-27.) Although at first you may not be familiar with the menu options associated with each icon, you will soon master the commands, because something Publisher calls *Tippages* appear when you place the insertion point over each icon and wait for just a few seconds.

1. Click the User Assistance tab.
2. Click the Show Tippages box to activate the feature.
3. Click the Reset Tips buttons to activate Tippages you may not have seen before.
4. Click again to deactivate the Tippages feature.
5. Click OK to close the tabbed Options box.

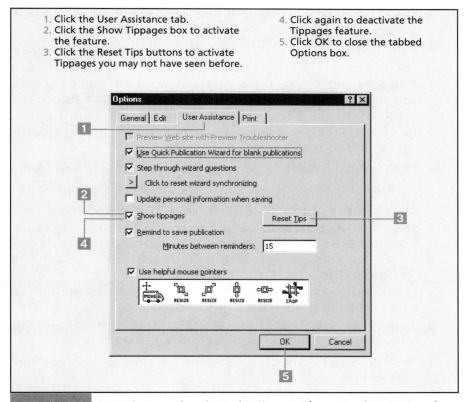

FIGURE 2-27   To activate or deactivate the Tippages feature, select Options from the Tools main menu

You can activate or deactivate the Tippages feature by choosing Tools | Options. Figure 2-27 shows the Options menu. Options from the Standard menu are shown in Figure 2-28 and explained here:

- **New**   Prompts you to save and close the current document and begin a new file.
- **Open**   Opens a previously created and saved file.
- **Save**   Creates a new file or updates a previously saved file.
- **Print**   Prints the document without having to go through the Print dialog box.
- **Cut**   Removes a text or graphic from the page and places it in your computer's memory.

- **Copy**   Leaves a text or graphic element on the page, but places a copy in memory so it can be added elsewhere in the document.

- **Paste**   Adds a previously cut or copied text or graphic element to your document at the insertion point.

- **Format Painter**   Applies the formatting characteristics—such as typeface, type size, background color, and so on—of one text or graphics element to another.

- **Undo**   Restores the appearance or contents of your document as if you had not executed the last command.

- **Bring to Front**   Moves layered text or graphic elements to the top level.

- **Send to Back**   Sends stacked text or graphic elements to the bottom layer.

- **Custom Rotate**   Places text or graphic elements at an angle on the page.

- **Show Special Characters**   Reveals formatting marks, such as spaces between words and end-of-paragraph symbols in your document. (Note: If Show Special Characters has already been selected, the icon becomes Hide Special Characters.)

- **Zoom**   Indicates the current magnification view of your document. Click the downward-pointing arrow to change the magnification level.

- **Zoom Out**   Shows more of each page of your document at a smaller size on your screen, providing an overall look of your document.

- **Zoom In**   Shows less of your document at higher magnification, permitting you to read text and focus on details.

- **Help**   Reveals the "What would you like to do?" dialog box, which invites you to type your question and search for the answers in plain English.

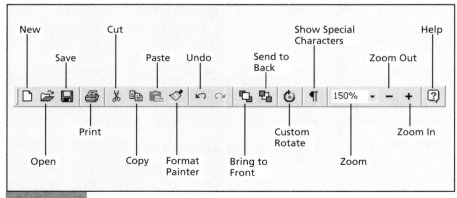

FIGURE 2-28   Use the Standard Toolbar for quick access to frequently used commands located in several different menus

Exploring the Formatting Toolbars

The icons shown in the Formatting Toolbar change according to whether you have a text, graphic, or table frame selected. For example, Publisher displays the Text Formatting Toolbar when you have selected a text object frame. Figure 2-29 shows the Text Formatting Toolbar, which contains the following options:

- **The Style Window**   Indicates the text style, or stored formatting characteristics, associated with the currently selected words. Clicking on the downward-pointing arrow reveals additional styles that may be applied to the text.

- **Font**   Reveals the name of the typeface the selected text is set in. Clicking on the downward-pointing arrow reveals other typeface options that may be applied to the text.

- **Font Size**   Indicates the size of the text in points. (An inch contains approximately 72 points.) Clicking on the downward-pointing arrow reveals additional type sizes, or you can enter a new size in the Font Size window.

- **Bold**   When grayed out, indicates that a heavier version of the font is currently being used. Otherwise, clicking on the Bold icon applies the bold version of the font.

- **Italic**   When grayed out, indicates that the italic, or slanted, version of the font is being used. Otherwise, clicking on the Italic icon chooses the italic version of the font.

- **Underline**   When grayed out, indicates that the words have been underlined. Otherwise, clicking on the Underline icon adds a line under the text.

- **Center**   Adds equal amounts of white space to the left and right of each word or line of type.

- **Align Left**   Creates text columns with a vertical left margin and an irregular right margin.

- **Justify**   Adds and subtracts word spacing within each line so that each line is of equal length, completely filled with text.

- **Align Right**   Creates text columns with a vertical right margin and an irregular left margin. Text aligned right is much harder to read than left-aligned text, because readers have to search for the beginning of each line.

- **Numbering**   Indents each paragraph and keeps track of the right number for each paragraph as text is added or deleted.

- **Bullets**   Indents each paragraph and adds a bullet symbol at the beginning of each. Bullet lists are used when the items in a list are of equal importance.

- **Decrease Indent**   Moves the left margin of an indented paragraph toward the left-hand margin.
- **Increase Indent**   Adds space between the left margin of each line and the beginning of each line of type.
- **Decrease Font Size**   Reduces the type size of the currently selected text.
- **Increase Font Size**   Increases the type size of the currently selected text.
- **Fill Color**   Adds a colored background behind the text.
- **Line Color**   Adds a colored border to each text object.
- **Font Color**   Changes the color of the selected text.
- **Line/Border Style**   Determines the thickness of the border around a text element.
- **Text Frame Properties**   Determines the offset, or amount of white space, between the text and the frame or object in which it is placed.
- **Rotate Left**   Changes a horizontal text object into a vertical text object with type reading to the top of the page.
- **Rotate Right**   Changes a horizontal text object into a vertical text object with type reading to the bottom of the page.

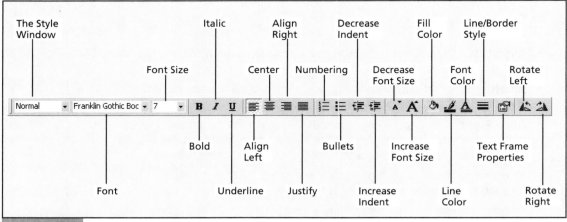

FIGURE 2-29   The Text Formatting Toolbar appears when you select a text object

Exploring the Graphic Formatting Toolbar

If you click on a graphic element, the Text Formatting Toolbar disappears and Publisher displays the Graphic Formatting Toolbar. (See Figure 2-30.) In later chapters, I'll explain these toolbars in greater length, but for now, here's a list of the Graphics Formatting Toolbar options:

- **Wrap Text to Frame** Separates adjacent text from the contents of a graphics frame, instead of adjusting to the shape of the illustration contained in the graphics frame.

- **Wrap Text to Picture** Allows adjacent text to follow the shape of the photograph or illustration, creating irregular text margins.

- **Fill Color** Adds color behind the illustration or photograph in the graphics frame.

- **Line Color** Creates a colored border around the illustration or photograph.

- **Line/Border Style** Determines the thickness of the border around a graphics object.

- **Picture Frame Properties** Determines the amount of space between a graphic and adjacent text.

- **Rotate Left** Flips the graphic 90 degrees to the left.

- **Rotate Right** Flips the graphic 90 degrees to the right.

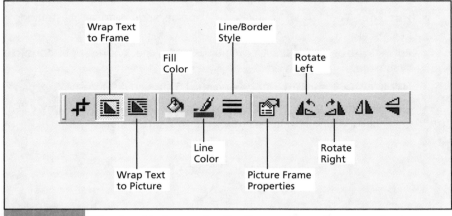

FIGURE 2-30 The Graphic Formatting Toolbar appears when you select a graphics frame, like an illustration or photograph

Exploring the Objects Toolbar

The Objects Toolbar contains the tools necessary to add or move text, graphics, tables, lines, squares, circles, and Design Objects in your document. Figure 2-31 shows the Objects Toolbar, which contains the following options:

- **Pointer Tool**   Selects any text or graphic object for deletion, formatting, resizing, or moving.
- **Text Frame Tool**   Creates a new text frame or selects a previously created text frame for cutting, copying, editing, formatting, moving, or resizing.
- **Table Frame Tool**   Creates a new table.
- **WordArt Frame Tool**   Adds graphic objects, such as logos, created by manipulating type and graphic elements.
- **Picture Frame Tool**   Creates a graphic object for importing an illustration or previously scanned photograph.
- **Clip Gallery Tool**   Adds one of the 16,000 clip art images that ship with Publisher 2000.
- **Line Tool**   Adds horizontal, vertical, or random-angle lines to your publication.
- **Oval Tool**   Creates rounded graphic objects.
- **Rectangle Tool**   Creates four-sided graphic objects.
- **Custom Shapes**   Creates a variety of arrows, stars, trapezoids, and other geometric shapes.
- **Hot Spot Tool**   Adds a link to a Web site address to an illustration or photograph.
- **Form Control**   Adds single or multiline boxes, check boxes, or buttons to a Web page.
- **HTML Code Fragment**   Adds a unique HTML element to your Web page.
- **Design Gallery Object**   Adds Web navigation bars, picture captions, calendars, logos, coupons, and accent bars to your publication.

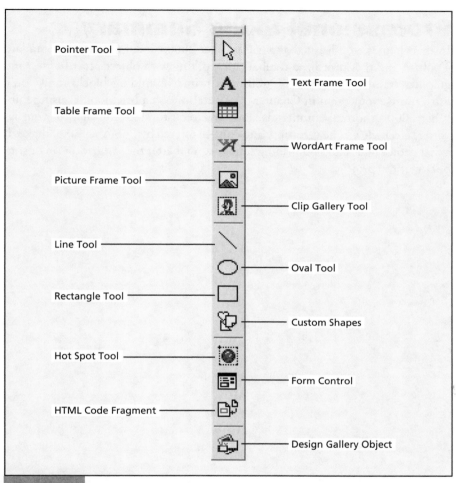

Pointer Tool

Text Frame Tool

Table Frame Tool

WordArt Frame Tool

Picture Frame Tool

Clip Gallery Tool

Line Tool

Oval Tool

Rectangle Tool

Custom Shapes

Hot Spot Tool

Form Control

HTML Code Fragment

Design Gallery Object

FIGURE 2-31 The Objects Toolbar contains the tools needed to add and select text, tables, and graphic and design objects

Professional Skills Summary

In this chapter, you learned about Publisher 2000's main menus, the Standard Toolbar, and the specialized toolbars for working with objects, text frames, and graphics frames. (Frames are Publisher's primary building blocks, and you'll learn more about them in Chapter 3.) You also took a brief look at using Publisher 2000's shortcut commands, and how to customize Publisher for your favorite screen view. The versatility and control offered by Publisher 2000 makes it a first choice in desktop publishing software, no matter the sophistication or simplicity of the project.

Introducing Publisher's Frames and Objects

In this chapter, you will:

- Understand Publisher's Foreground and Background View modes as integral document-creation tools

- Learn how frames and objects work together as Publisher 2000's primary document "building blocks"

- Learn more about using Publisher 2000's Object Toolbar to add, delete, or modify frames and objects—a prerequisite to using Publisher 2000's Wizards

An understanding of frames and objects is central to your ability to create attractive, easy-to-read documents with Publisher 2000. Even before you can understand how to use one of Publisher's Wizards, you must know the basics of text frames and objects. (Publisher is an "object-oriented program," in that frames and other objects such as pictures are used as preliminary building blocks for the document layout process.)

Working with Text Frames

Just as you cannot serve stew without a bowl, you cannot add words to a Publisher document without first creating a container—a text frame. (See Figure 3-1.) In this chapter, you'll learn the basics about frames and other objects, and how they relate to modifying and creating documents. Then, in Chapter 4, you'll put that knowledge to work when you use Publisher's Wizards.

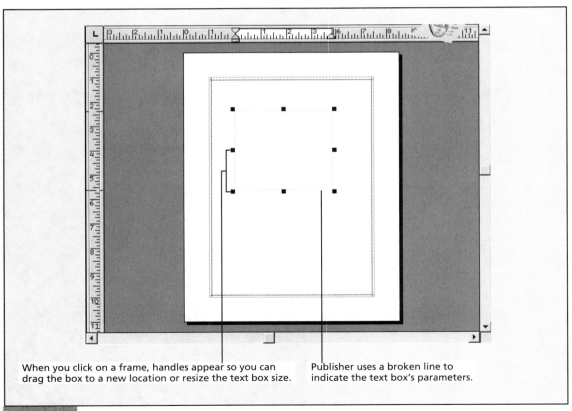

When you click on a frame, handles appear so you can drag the box to a new location or resize the text box size.

Publisher uses a broken line to indicate the text box's parameters.

FIGURE 3-1   A newly created, blank Publisher text frame waits for input

Learning About Foreground and Background Views

To understand how Publisher 2000 creates documents, you need to understand Publisher's Foreground View and Background View. (Previous versions of Publisher also operate by the same principle.) You must understand this design feature, and how to use it, to create professional-looking documents.

In the most basic sense, *Foreground View* is the standard page view, showing text and graphics in a manner similar to Word or any other word processing program. You will be doing most of your work in Foreground View, adding text and graphics to the various pages of your document.

Background View is where you add elements that will automatically appear on each page of your document. These elements include column guides and rulers as well as header or footer text (text that is repeated at the top or bottom of each page). Using Background View saves you time by automatically replicating these design elements on each page of your document, without you having to do anything extra.

Selecting Background View

Publisher 2000 normally opens displaying the Foreground View. To switch from Foreground View to Background View, first select View from Publisher's main menu, and select Go to Background (CTRL-M). Anything you add to your document while in Background View will appear on all pages of that document.

If you get confused about whether you are in Foreground or Background View, a quick check of the information at the bottom of the screen can verify this for you. When you are in Background View, the page numbers along the bottom of the screen are no longer visible. Instead, you will see a reversed L icon (for left page) or R icon (for right page). (See Figure 3-2.)

L▶ Tip: You can quickly move or *toggle* between Foreground and Background Views by using the CTRL-M keyboard shortcut.

Hiding Background Objects

From time to time, you may want to hide text or graphic objects that you have added in Background View. (You may want to eliminate header and footer information on pages containing large photographs, for example.) To hide objects created as part of the Background View on individual pages, select the View drop-down menu and select Ignore Background. Selecting this option hides text

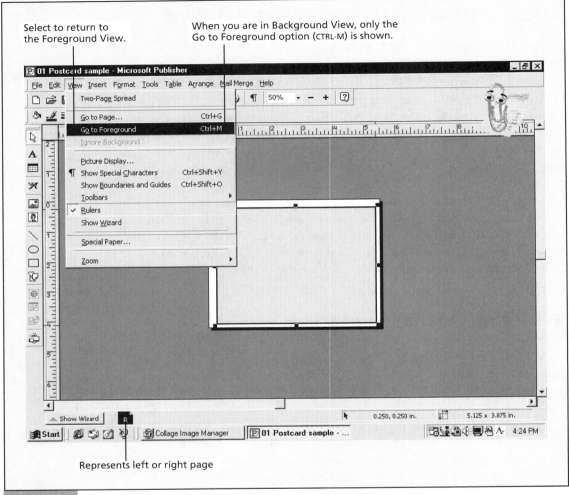

FIGURE 3-2   Reversed letters—white letters against a black background—indicate you're working in Publisher 2000's Background View

or graphic objects that you have added with the Background View feature. Note that if you are working on a two-page document, the Ignore Background dialog box will appear. With this dialog box, you can hide background elements on either the left or right pages, or both. (See Figure 3-3.)

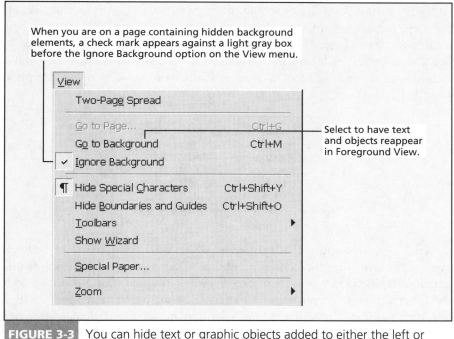

When you are on a page containing hidden background elements, a check mark appears against a light gray box before the Ignore Background option on the View menu.

Select to have text and objects reappear in Foreground View.

FIGURE 3-3   You can hide text or graphic objects added to either the left or right pages, or more pages of any document by selecting the Ignore Background option

Working with Objects

Microsoft Publisher 2000 is an *object-oriented program,* that is, a program that uses objects to create documents. In Publisher, objects are any element or item you use to create a page: text, headlines, photos, clip art, line drawings, tables, and so on. Before you can create anything on Publisher's opening blank page, you must first create the object using one of Publisher 2000's specially designed object tools.

Cross-Reference: We presented introductory information on the Objects Toolbar in Chapter 2. If you need to refresh your memory regarding this toolbar, see Figure 2-31.

The Objects Toolbar features eleven tools for working with different objects, with each object type fulfilling a different purpose in a document's composition. (Think of the single Publisher document as being analogous to a large box, with objects, such as text and photos, as smaller boxes contained within.)

If you click on Publisher's opening empty page, and begin to place any text on the page, Publisher displays a warning message, shown here, telling you to first create a text frame (object) in which to hold your text. Likewise, if you wanted to begin your Publisher document by adding a picture, you would first have to use Publisher's Picture Frame tool to create a picture frame (object) in which to place your desired picture.

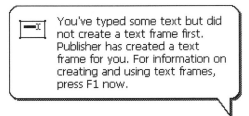

Working with software that is based on object orientation has several advantages. (Software other than desktop publishing software can also be object-oriented, with objects and tools specific to that software application.) Working with Publisher's objects, you can enjoy more versatility and power than possible with a non-object-oriented program. Objects let you move design elements around with ease—throughout a single-page document or a longer one—and you can resize the objects easily, as well.

Objects and the underlying concepts of object-oriented software are the foundation for Microsoft's Publisher application, and they make creating and using Microsoft's Wizards possible. When you are working with any Wizard—such as the Brochure Wizard or Newsletter Wizard—the Wizard places the necessary objects on the page in the desired design location, so you can concentrate on filling the objects with appropriate content.

Using Publisher's Tools to Insert Objects

The easiest way to insert most objects is to click the appropriate Object Tool in the Objects Toolbar (located on the screen's far left side) and, while holding down the left mouse button, drag to create the object to the desired size on the page.

Adding Text Frames

To create a text frame for a headline, caption, or column of text, click the Text Frame Tool in the Objects Toolbar. Position the insertion point at the upper-left corner of the area where you want to create the text frame and, holding down the mouse button, drag to the lower-right corner. Release the mouse button when the text frame reaches the desired size, as shown in Figure 3-4.

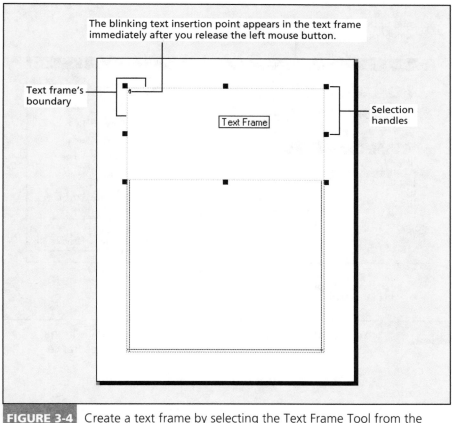

The blinking text insertion point appears in the text frame immediately after you release the left mouse button.

Text frame's boundary

Text Frame

Selection handles

FIGURE 3-4 Create a text frame by selecting the Text Frame Tool from the Objects Toolbar and dragging to proper size on the page

Creating Tables

Tables are ideal for organizing and presenting complicated information in easy-to-read columns and rows. Tables also make it easy to maintain exact spacing between text and graphic elements on a page.

To add a table, click Publisher's Table Frame Tool in the Objects Toolbar. Place the insertion point at the upper-left corner of the desired location for the table and, holding down the mouse button, drag toward the lower-right corner (or vice versa). Release the mouse button when the table is properly sized.

The Create Table dialog box appears when you release the mouse button, as shown in Figure 3-5. This tool permits you to enter or change the number of rows and columns in a table as well as modify its appearance.

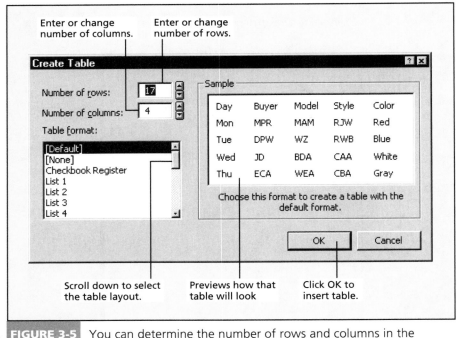

FIGURE 3-5 You can determine the number of rows and columns in the Create Table dialog box and choose its desired appearance

Creating WordArt Frames

> **Tip:** At any point, you can reedit WordArt text by double-clicking on the WordArt Object. If you do this, however, pay attention to the object's formatting to make sure that the text is still legible.

WordArt is a software program built into Publisher that permits you to manipulate text in distinctive ways. Use WordArt to create logos, titles, Web site buttons, and other distinctive text objects. WordArt loads immediately after you create a WordArt frame by placing the insertion point on the page and dragging to the desired size, as shown in Figure 3-6.

Adding Pictures to Your Publication

To add photographs to your publication, click the Picture Frame Tool. Place the insertion point at the upper-left corner of the desired area and drag to the lower-right corner. When you release the button, a prompt appears, instructing you to double-click the frame to insert the photograph, as shown in Figure 3-7.

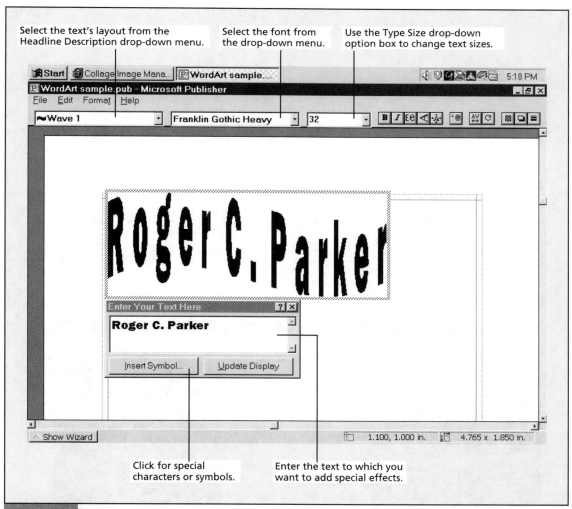

Select the text's layout from the Headline Description drop-down menu.

Select the font from the drop-down menu.

Use the Type Size drop-down option box to change text sizes.

Click for special characters or symbols.

Enter the text to which you want to add special effects.

FIGURE 3-6 Selecting the WordArt Tool automatically launches the WordArt program, which displays the WordArt options box for you to make your selections

Double-clicking the picture frame takes you to the Insert Picture dialog box, shown in Figure 3-8, which allows you to select the folder containing your scanned images or custom-created illustrations. When you reach the desired folder, a list of available files will appear. Selecting a file previews it in the sample window. To insert the file and close the Insert Picture dialog box, click the Insert button or Enter. Double-clicking the filename of the desired photograph or illustration also inserts the image and closes the dialog box.

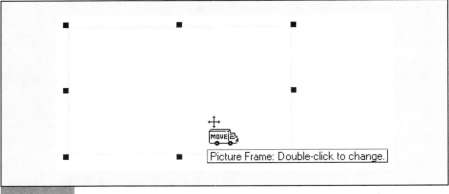

FIGURE 3-7 A Publisher prompt appears after you create a picture frame, instructing you to double-click it to insert a photograph

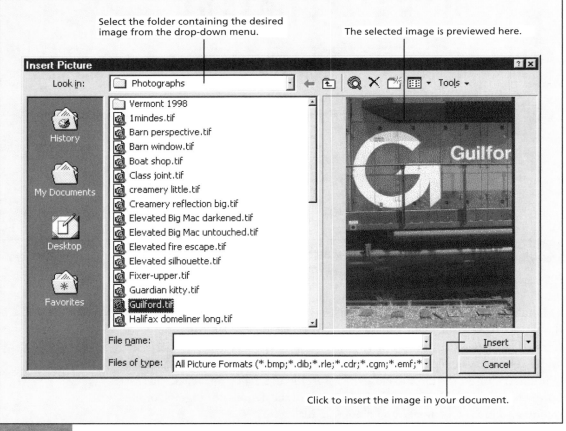

FIGURE 3-8 Double-clicking a newly created picture frame takes you to the Insert Picture dialog box

Inserting Clip Art

To insert one of the 16,000 clip art images that come with Publisher, click the Clip Gallery Tool and create a clip art frame. Immediately upon releasing the mouse button, the Insert Clip Art dialog box appears, as shown in Figure 3-9. You can search for desired clip art by either entering a description of the desired image in the Search for Clips window, or scroll through the list of available categories and click on one of the clip art categories illustrated to view more images.

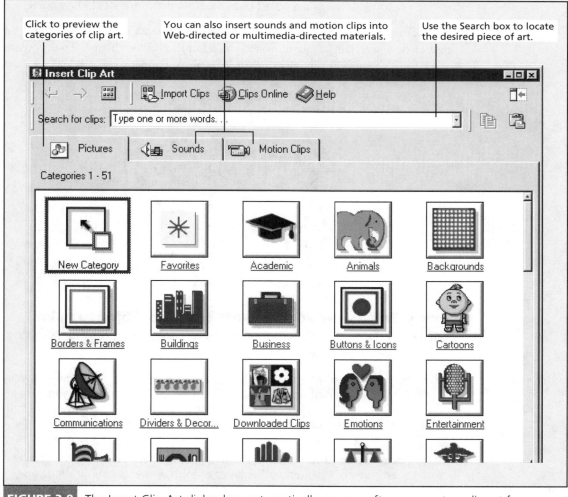

FIGURE 3-9 The Insert Clip Art dialog box automatically appears after you create a clip art frame

Using Publisher's Drawing Tools

The next three tools in the Objects Toolbar are used to create lines, circles and ovals, and squares and rectangles. Objects created with the Line Tool, Oval Tool, or Rectangle Tool can be constrained, or modified, by holding down either the CTRL or SHIFT key as you create a line, oval, or rectangle:

- Holding down the SHIFT key while using the Line Tool limits the line to either horizontal, vertical, or a 45-degree slant.
- Holding down the SHIFT key while using the Oval Tool creates a circle.
- Holding down the SHIFT key while using the Rectangle Tool creates a square.
- Holding down the CTRL key while creating a line, oval, or rectangle creates the object by drawing the object outward from the center or starting point.

Click the Custom Shapes Tool if you want to create an object that is neither an oval/circle or a rectangle/square. When you select the Custom Shapes Tool, you can select from a variety of triangles, trapezoids, arrows, banners, and other shapes.

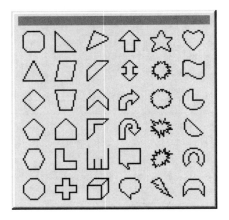

Using Publisher 2000's Web-Specific Object Tools

The next three tools in the Objects Toolbar are used when creating Web sites, and are discussed in greater detail in Chapter 8.

- **Hot Spot Tool**   Permits you to create an image map by assigning hyperlinks to portions of a photograph or illustration. (For example, if you have included a map of the New England states, clicking over the part of the map showing New Hampshire could take visitors to a page describing New Hampshire.)
- **Form Control Tool**   Allows you to add single-line text boxes, multiline text boxes, check boxes, and other types of form elements to your Web page.

- **HTML Code Fragment Tool**   Allows you to insert specialized instructions into your Web page, such as an instruction to insert a scanned photograph saved as a JPEG image instead of an image stored in Publisher's default GIF image format.

Inserting Design Gallery Objects

Clicking the Design Gallery Object Tool launches the powerful Microsoft Publisher Design Gallery. The Design Gallery allows you to select and insert previously formatted elements of page architecture, such as Attention Getters (shown in Figure 3-10), tables of contents, calendars, coupons, or rows of repeating elements such as boxes or dots. Objects are organized by category, or you can view them by design characteristic.

Most important, you can save and retrieve your own Design Objects—for example, custom-created newsletter elements such as department headers (Letters to

FIGURE 3-10   The Design Gallery makes it easy to retrieve and insert previously created layout elements, such as Attention Getters, as well as custom-created design elements

the Editor, The Editor Speaks, and so on). The next time you need to use one of the elements, you can insert it from the Design Gallery, rather than recreating it from scratch.

Moving, Resizing, and Deleting Publisher 2000 Objects

Once an object has been placed on a page, you can easily move, resize, or delete it.

To move an object, place the selection tool over it. When the "move" icon appears, hold down the left mouse button and drag to a new position. Holding down the SHIFT key while moving an object constrains the object, limiting it to either horizontal or vertical movement. (This prevents you from inadvertently drifting in more than one direction.)

To resize an object, click one of the selection handles shown in Figure 3-11 and drag in the desired direction:

- To proportionately increase or decrease an object created with either the Picture Frame Tool or the Clip Gallery Tool, drag one of the corner selection handles: A, C, E, or G. Dragging on a corner handle maintains the original height-to-width ratio.

- To proportionately increase a text frame or custom shape, hold down the SHIFT key while dragging one of the corner selection handles.

- To increase or decrease the size of an object around its center, hold down the CTRL key while dragging one of the corner handles.

- To stretch or compress an object created with the Text Frame Tool or the Custom Shapes Tool, click one of the inside selection handles (B, D, F, or H). This changes the proportions of the original object.

The correct method to delete an object—that is, remove it from the page—depends on the type of object and, if it's a text frame, whether or not the text frame contains text.

- To delete an object, select Edit | Cut, CTRL-X, or press the DELETE key. You can also click the Cut icon on the Standard Toolbar.

- To delete a text frame after text has been entered, select Edit | Cut, CTRL-X, or click the Cut icon in the Standard Toolbar. The DELETE key, however, will not work after text has been entered. If words are present in the text frame, the DELETE key will delete the character before the insertion point.

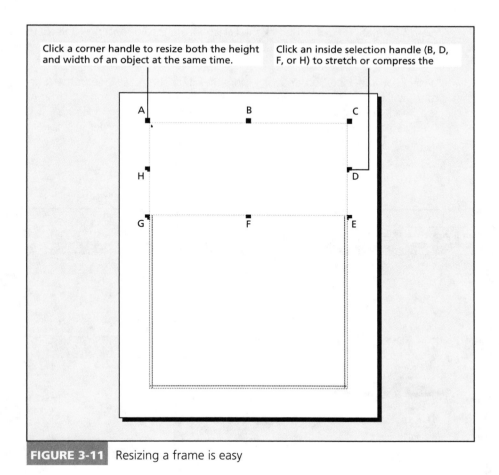

Click a corner handle to resize both the height and width of an object at the same time.

Click an inside selection handle (B, D, F, or H) to stretch or compress the

FIGURE 3-11 Resizing a frame is easy

Formatting Publisher's Objects' Contents

Efficient use of Publisher requires understanding the difference between formatting objects (or containers) and formatting the contents of the objects. Publisher permits you to separately format objects and their contents.

When you select a text frame or a clip art frame, any formatting you apply is applied to the object, not its contents. For example, you can:

- Select Format | Fill Color (or click the Fill icon from the Formatting Toolbar) to add a background to the object by selecting one of the fill color options, as shown in Figure 3-12.

- Select Format | Line/Border Style | More Styles (or select the Line Border/Border Style icon and More Styles in the Formatting Toolbar) to add a border of desired line thickness and color around the object, as shown in Figure 3-13. You can also determine whether the same or a different border will appear on each of the four edges of the object.

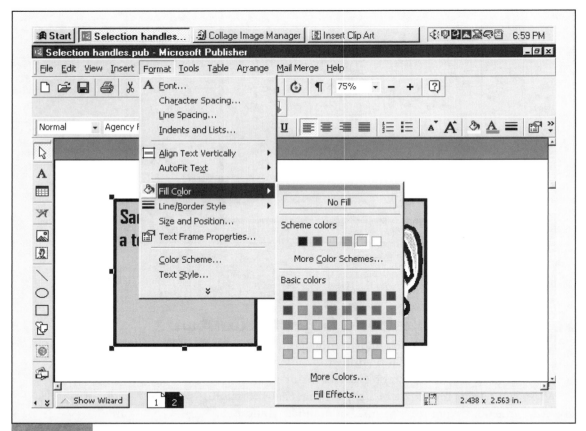

FIGURE 3-12   Select Format | Fill Color to add a background to a text frame, picture frame, or any other type of object

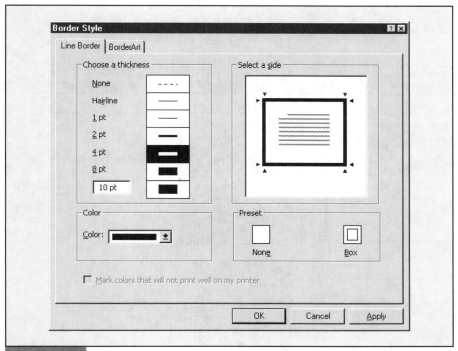

FIGURE 3-13   With the Border Style dialog box, you can add a solid-line border of almost any desired thickness and color around one or more edges of the selected object

Formatting—such as backgrounds and borders applied to objects like text frames, clip art frames, custom shapes, and picture frames—does not affect their contents. (See Figure 3-14.) To change the appearance (type size, typeface, or color) of text inside a frame, for example, you must first select the words you want to reformat by dragging (holding the left mouse button down as you high-light the words).

Professional Skills Summary

In this chapter, you learned about frames and objects, Publisher 2000's primary building blocks. In addition, we presented the basics about adding these elements to Publisher documents and how objects work within the framework

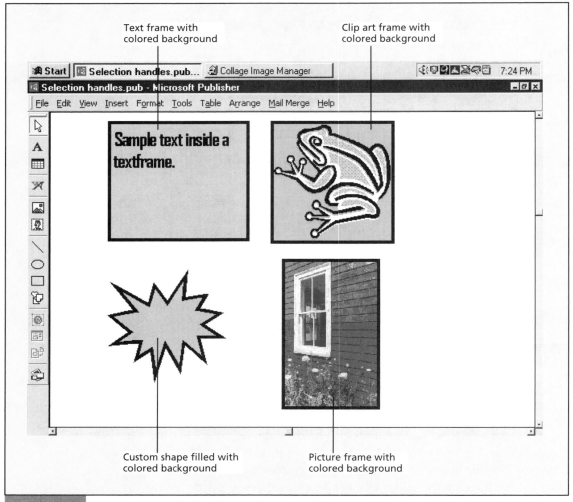

Text frame with colored background

Clip art frame with colored background

Custom shape filled with colored background

Picture frame with colored background

FIGURE 3-14 Formatting applied to objects does not affect their contents

of Publisher's object orientation. We also took a brief look at Foreground and Background Views, and how you can use these views to streamline your Publisher 2000 document creation. In the next chapter, you'll begin your document creation, with the help of Publisher 2000's Wizards.

chapter 4

Learning to Use Publisher's Wizards

In this chapter, you will:

- Learn how to use Publisher 2000's Wizards to create any type of document you may need

- Learn how to use Publisher's Design Master Sets to give all your documents a professional, uniform appearance

- Create a simple one-page flyer, called a Quick Publication, using a Publisher 2000 Wizard

- Apply your new Publisher knowledge to create other simple business items, such as letterheads with matching envelopes, and business cards

Publisher's strength in creating attractive, professional documents comes from its various Design Wizards. When you combine using these Design Wizards with Publisher's Design Master Sets, you have a fast and easy, user-friendly methods for creating almost any printed item you might need for your business, organization, or personal use. Publisher's Design Wizards and Design Master Sets let you concentrate on your document's *content* rather than its *appearance*.

First, we'll explain how the Publisher's Wizard creates the framework for a type of publication and guides you through the document-creation process through the use of questions and prompts. Then we'll explain how the Design Master Sets can be used to create complimentary sets of documents with the same look and feel (matching business cards, letterhead, brochures, catalogs, mailing labels, etc.).

Getting to Know Publisher's Wizards

Publisher 2000's distinguishing power comes from the inclusion of its new Catalog of Wizards, ranging from automating the creation of documents as simple as business cards to multipage catalogs. Publisher's Wizards are professionally created sets of automated, interactive instructions to take you through the complete document-creation process, regardless of which document you may need to create. Each of the Wizards contains numerous text frames, picture frames, and graphic accents. All you have to do to complete your document framework is click on the placeholder text (for example, "Heading") and replace it with the specific headline you want to use. (See Figure 4-1.) Good-looking results are guaranteed because the Wizards format the publication for you, choosing typefaces and type sizes, building white space into each page, and placing picture frames and graphic accents for maximum impact.

Publisher's Wizards use similar steps to create almost any document you might need. Whether the document is a simple business card or a multipage catalog, the steps are the same, although the documents vary significantly in their complexity. Some instructions may be different depending on the complexity of the document you are creating, but Publisher's Wizards use the same six basic steps to guide you in creating a finished product. Those six steps are:

1. From Publisher's Catalog, select a Wizard from the tabbed Publications by Wizard page, or choose a design from the tabbed Publications by Design page.

2. Follow the Wizard's instructions screen by screen as you work through the interactive, context-sensitive options the Wizard displays for you. These

instructions will guide you through selecting a color scheme and choosing a page size, as well as a page orientation.

3. Customize the Wizard layout to suit your preferences and needs.

4. Insert personal or business information, if needed.

5. Replace the Wizard placeholders with material relevant to your needs, including your own text and graphics elements, headings, messages you want to use, and any photos.

6. Proofread and then print the final product.

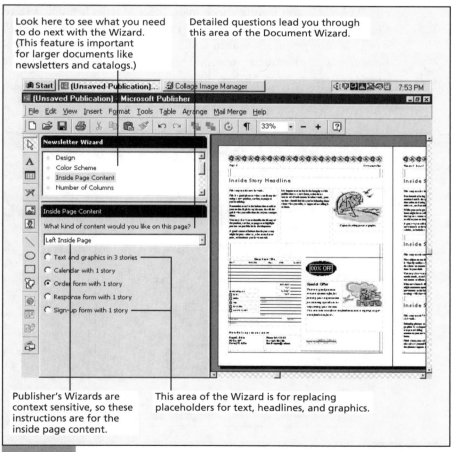

Look here to see what you need to do next with the Wizard. (This feature is important for larger documents like newsletters and catalogs.)

Detailed questions lead you through this area of the Document Wizard.

Publisher's Wizards are context sensitive, so these instructions are for the inside page content.

This area of the Wizard is for replacing placeholders for text, headlines, and graphics.

FIGURE 4-1 This Publisher Design Wizard creates a perfectly formatted newsletter, ready for you to fill in the blanks

Stepping Through Wizard Questions

Publisher offers two ways you can work with various Publication wizards: structured or unstructured. You can select either option from Publisher's Tools Options menu, but Publisher's default setting is to have the user step through each of the Wizard questions. In fact, with this option selected, you must follow Publisher's instructions or the program will not allow you to continue.

To change this default, you can use the Tools drop-down menu. Note, however, you must not have a Wizard active, or you cannot select this menu option.

Tip: If you deselect this option, you can answer only the Wizard questions you desire, in any order, allowing you to work at your own speed.

From the Tools main drop-down menu, select Options, and Publisher will display the Options dialog box. Select the User Assistance tab. As long as you leave a check mark before Step Through Wizard Questions, as shown in Figure 4-2, Publisher will not allow you to work on your publication until you have answered each of the questions the Wizard wants answered. This feature works similarly to the previous versions of Publisher.

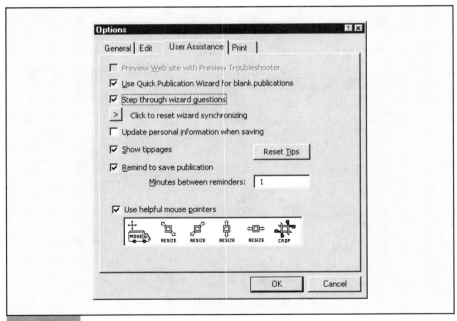

FIGURE 4-2 The Options tabbed dialog box

Creating Documents with Publisher's Catalog

Publisher's Wizards are accessed from Publisher's Catalog. If you are starting Publisher from the Windows Desktop, Publisher will display automatically the Catalog of Wizards. From Publisher's Catalog Wizard list, you may simply select the desired publication type from the list, shown in Figure 4-3. If you are already working within Publisher, you must select File | New from Publisher's main menu. Publisher will then display its Catalog, as shown in Figure 4-3.

Publisher's Catalog screen is the most important screen you will work with while using Publisher 2000, so let's take some time to understand it and how it relates to the rest of the document-creating software.

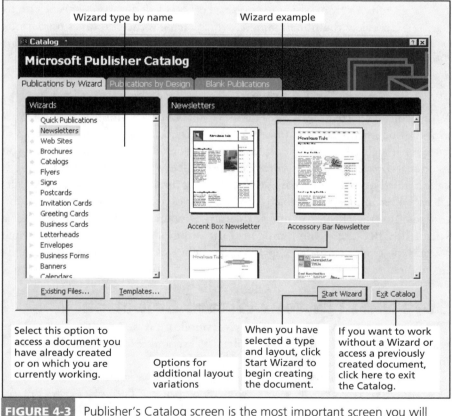

FIGURE 4-3 Publisher's Catalog screen is the most important screen you will work with in Publisher 2000

Step 1: Select Your Document Wizard

Publisher's Catalog has three methods by which you may access a document, and those methods are represented by the three tabs shown within the main catalog screen: Publications by Wizard, Publications by Design, and Blank Publications.

Options selected from the Publications by Wizard tab launch the interactive software that creates anything from a simple, one-page flyer to a complicated multipage catalog. Take a moment to browse through the list to see all of the types of documents for which Publisher can provide you a Wizard.

Tip: Using double-click as a method of selecting an option is a great timesaver available throughout Publisher. Whenever you are presented with options such as newsletter designs, double-click the desired option to select it and close the dialog box.

Notice that the content of Publisher's right screen window, which shows the Wizard pane, changes as you select a different Wizard. Each Wizard type, too, may offer a subset of selections. For example, the Wizard to create simple flyers has seven additional, more descriptive options from which to choose. To select a design you like, click on its preview thumbnail sample, which changes the example's border box (indicating that you have selected this example), and click the Start Wizard button.

Step 2: Modify Your Wizard Selection

When you've selected the Wizard example you want to customize, Publisher begins the document-creating process for that Wizard. Publisher will ask a series of questions, such as "What color scheme would you like to use?" and "Would you like a placeholder for the customer's address?" The Wizard will modify the publication based on your responses, so the resulting publication reflects your preferences. For example, if your goal is to increase sales to out-of-state customers, you can add an order form to your newsletter, or you can make your newsletter a self-mailer. Because of the numerous formatting options that accompany each Wizard, no two documents prepared will ever be exactly alike, unless you exactly make them so.

Step 3: Fill in Your Wizard Selection

The third step involved in preparing your publication is to replace placeholders with the specific headlines, photographs, clip art, and text to communicate your message.

With Publisher, placeholders are generic headlines, captions, body copy areas, or graphics areas you replace with your own choices. To replace a text placeholder, simply click on it and enter new text. When you enter the text, Publisher will choose a typeface appropriate for the publication design you have chosen. Publisher will also choose an appropriate type size for most headlines and "attention getters." Figure 4-4 shows text and graphic placeholders as the Wizard created and placed them. Publisher Wizards make creating good-looking publications easy by providing you with a preformatted framework that can be easily customized to your specific marketing goal.

Step 4: Printing Your Document

Once you have successfully filled in all the placeholders, you can print your document with either a printer attached to your computer or by using a commercial printer. Most Publisher users plan to manage the printing of their final documents. Others know from the start that their document will wind up in a commercial

Tip: Note that the text frame and graphic boundaries visible in Figure 4-4 are not visible if you move your cursor around on the page and work in other places. You can use the Hiding Boundaries and Guides option to preview your publication as it will look when printed, and all the "fill-in-the-blank" places will be consolidated into one page or document. To hide boundaries around individual frames after you see how selected areas fit together, select View | Hide Boundaries and Guides (CTRL-SHIFT-O). If you are working on a document with boundaries hidden, select View | Show Boundaries and Guides (CTRL-SHIFT-O).

FIGURE 4-4 Publisher's Wizards create text and graphic placeholders ready for you to replace with real information

printer's hands. From a feasibility standpoint, the decision of whether to use your desktop printer or a commercial printer doesn't matter, because Publisher delivers satisfactory results with either option.

However, if you know in advance that you will use a commercial printer to output your final document, you can benefit from asking questions as to how these businesses prefer files submitted to them, as well as seeking advice on color selection. Often, asking printers a few simple questions at the beginning of the project will simplify their task and guarantee a truly professional-looking final document.

Replacing Placeholders with the Right Information

Although you can enter text directly into Publisher and use its Line, Oval, and Rectangle drawing tools to create interesting graphic accents, in many cases you will be inserting previously created text and graphics files into your newsletter or brochure layout. You can use Word for Windows as your writing tool, make CorelDraw your image-creating tool, or utilize readily available clip art. The decision as to whether you should create the document in Publisher and then use other software packages to create the actual content is a dilemma reminiscent of the "Which came first: the chicken or the egg?" question.

You'll often find that creating your publication's content (graphics of any type from photos to line art, as well as text) ahead of time is the most efficient way to create a publication. Your newsletter may contain stories written by several contributors, or, if you are the author, you may find it easier to write all the stories for your publication ahead of time. Carefully consider issues like this one and how it will impact your document creation. These factors can help you determine whether you should create the document template with Publisher first, or create and gather all of the content prior to designing your document. Take into consideration, too, whether the document you are creating uses any shared graphics, such as a company logo, company-related photos, or standard text blocks that appear in every printed item a company or organization creates. Getting your hands on these items well in advance of any other activity is best. Once you see the elements you need to blend into the document, making decisions about how to proceed with the work will be easier for you.

Professional Pointer

For many novice desktop publishers, creating text in another program, such as Word or Microsoft Works word processor, and graphics with PC Paint, CorelDraw, or any other popular graphics software, and then importing these elements into a previously created Publisher document can be confusing. If I am the one creating all the document's content, I use the text and graphics processing features in Publisher, rather than importing material into Publisher from other programs. This way, I can control exactly how the material comes together. If, however, I'm using other peoples' materials, then, most likely, I will have to import text and graphics files into the final document. This necessity decreases the amount of control I have over the material.

Creating text from within Publisher works especially well with smaller documents up to about eight pages. If the document you are creating has more than eight pages, importing text and graphics files will probably be necessary. Be careful, however, because your documents gain increased number of pages. You'll have to develop some skill at keeping the pages and their contents in order in your head. It's a good idea to create a page-tracking method to keep from getting your pages mixed up.

Cross-Reference: For more information on working with multipage documents, see Chapters 5, 6 and 7.

Managing Text Replacement

Publisher offers you two ways to import text created with a word processor. The first option assumes that you have a document layout open that has an empty text frame waiting for text. This method, as follows, also works best with small text files or any graphics elements:

1. Make your word processing application active on your desktop.

2. Open the text file you want within your word processor.

3. Use your mouse to select the text within that file that you want to use in Publisher.

4. With the text you want still highlighted, select Edit from the main menu, and then select Copy from the drop-down menu (or use the shortcut key combination CTRL-C). This process copies the text you want to Window's Clipboard area.

5. Minimize your word processor and make Publisher active on your desktop.

6. Place your cursor in the text frame you created in your Publisher document.

7. From Publisher's main menu, select Edit | Paste (or use the shortcut key combination of CTRL-V). Publisher will now paste the material you copied to the Windows Clipboard into the existing text frame.

The second and faster option is as follows:

1. Click on the story placeholder in the Publisher document you created.

2. From Publisher's main menu, select Insert | Text File.

3. Publisher then displays the Insert Text dialog box, shown in Figure 4-5.

4. Use your mouse pointer to select the folder you want from the list of folders in the dialog box.

5. Make sure you've highlighted the correct file, and then click OK (or simply double-click on the filename). Publisher will insert the text file into the text frame.

Managing Graphic Images Replacement

The easiest way to replace a graphics placeholder in a Wizard-designed publication is to follow these steps:

1. Right-click on the Graphics placeholder. Publisher will display a floating drop-down menu with options that deal with manipulating graphics.

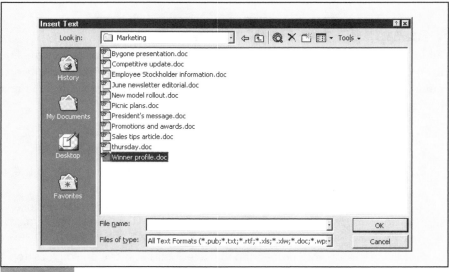

FIGURE 4-5   To insert a previously created text file into a Publisher text frame, double-click the filename as it appears in Publisher's Insert Text dialog box

2. From this floating menu, select Change Picture. Publisher will display a nested drop-down menu of options associated with changing pictures.

3. Select the Picture option and Publisher will display another nested drop-down menu, shown in Figure 4-6. From this list of options, you may select the graphics object you want to replace. Note that Publisher cascades floating drop-down menus to either the left or the right of the original menu, so that you'll have the best available view of the needed menu options:

- Select Clip Art if you want to replace the graphics placeholder with almost any type of clip art available.

- Select From File if you want to use a previously scanned photograph or previously created custom illustration in a graphics placeholder. With this option, you can browse through the various folders on your hard drive and preview your graphics files before you import them.

- Select the From Scanner or Camera option if you want to scan a snapshot or photograph that has not yet been saved as a file.

Tip: Use the right-click method when selecting a text or graphics placeholder so you have various menu options from which to choose. If you use the usual left-double-click selection method, Publisher assumes that you want to replace the graphic with another piece of clip art and then displays the Insert Clip Art dialog box, which may not offer you the command option that you need.

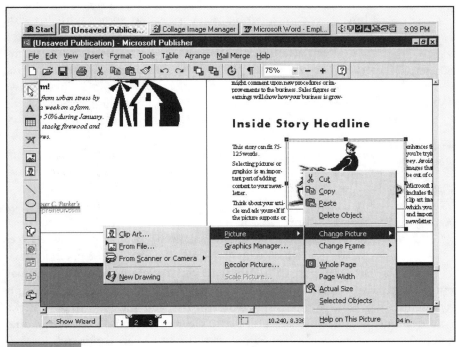

FIGURE 4-6 The best way to replace a Publisher graphics placeholder or element is to right-click on that item to access a series of nested drop-down menus that pertain to graphics

- Select the New Drawing option if you want to create an illustration (or line art) using Publisher's built-in AutoShapes and other drawing tools. When you select the New Drawing option, Publisher displays a floating AutoShapes toolbar.

New in 2000: Publisher 2000 comes with 16,000 pieces of clip art. You can also use clip art from third-party sources, or you can log on to Microsoft's Publisher Web site, where you can search for the type of graphic you want. The Web also offers third-party sites for downloading graphics, some of which may be animated.

Linking Text and Graphics Files to Publisher Documents

L ▶ Note: Because Publisher is an object-oriented program, the elements that create a document are technically called *objects*. Creators of software documentation and software-related books and magazines will often use the terms "object" and "file" interchangeably, without any consideration for maintaining consistency for the reader's sake. Don't let the technical term "object" intimidate you—they are simply text or graphics elements within your Publisher documents.

Although you can always use Publisher 2000's accompanying clip art and graphics files, you can also import previously created graphics files, or copy and paste files from other programs or third-party companies that sell clip art and photos ready for your personal or professional use.

You can also link objects from one software program to another. You can create links to Excel spreadsheets, illustrations created with drawing programs such as Microsoft PhotoDraw, scanned images modified with Adobe Photoshop or Microsoft's Picture It, or slides created with Microsoft PowerPoint.

Links can best be described as a way of connecting two objects of data (text or graphics files) together, although the objects are created in two completely different programs. Let's say, for example, that you are under a tight deadline to use Publisher to create a financial report, and you want to include an important graph of expenses. However, you have a problem because you haven't yet completed your Excel graph. You keep changing data in the Excel spreadsheet, which will, of course, impact how the graph looks.

As you lay out the report with Publisher, you have some sense of what that much-anticipated graph will look like (a bar chart), but you don't have the graph representing the final numbers yet. Don't worry. You still have time to make your deadline, because you use Publisher to create a placeholder for the graphic and link that placeholder by using Publisher's Insert Object command.

Object linking's big advantage is that the Publisher object will automatically be updated when the spreadsheet and related graph (objects) are edited in the original software, which in this case is Excel. In addition, you can easily launch the original software program from within Publisher if you want to modify the spreadsheet, scanned image, or illustration.

How to Create a Link

To link an object from another software program on your computer (or available on your network), create a Picture Frame and select Insert from Publisher's main menu. Then select Object from the Insert drop-down menu. Publisher will display the Insert Object dialog box, shown in Figure 4-7.

From the Insert Object dialog box, you have two ways to insert text or graphics files into Publisher documents. One way is for inserting objects that have not yet been created, and the other is for objects that have already been created and for which you have a file or can access the file through a network.

If the object you want is new, first select the Create New radio button. When you select this option, you can scroll through the various programs available on your computer and select the Object Type to which you want to link. When you select an Object Type, Publisher and Windows collaborate to start the other program to create the object—graphics or text file—that you need.

If you already have the object you need in file form (illustration, photo, or slide, for example), select the Create from File radio button. When you select this option, Publisher modifies the Insert Object dialog box so that it now has a Browse button and a Link option check box. If you click the Browse button, you can search your hard disk for the previously created object file you need. Once you find the needed object, click the Link check box to link the object to your Publisher document, as shown in Figure 4-8.

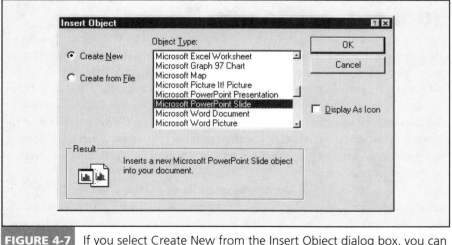

FIGURE 4-7   If you select Create New from the Insert Object dialog box, you can load another software program and create the object you want

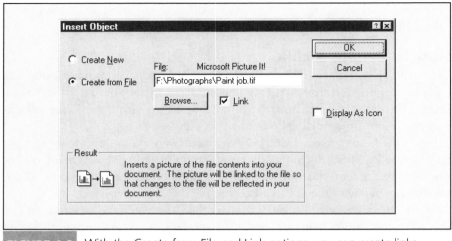

FIGURE 4-8 With the Create from File and Link options, you can create links
to previously created files, so the images in your publication will
automatically update if the files to which they are linked are updated

Cross-Reference: To learn more about working with clip art, illustrations, and
photographs, see Chapters 12 and 13.

Creating a Single-Page Publication with the Quick Publication Design Wizard

The best way to learn to use Publisher 2000 is to get to work creating a simple
one-page publication. This activity will provide you with a hands-on introduction to the many Publisher 2000 techniques you'll use again and again.

One-page flyers, like the one from the Quick Publications Wizard category,
are extremely valuable, but often overlooked, marketing resources. Flyers offer
an excellent way to communicate a simple message at very low cost. Because flyers have minimal text and graphics, they are ideal for last-minute communications such as announcing coming events, introducing new products, or advertising special promotions.

When you begin to run low on the quantity of a flyer, you can simply print
them on your desktop printer, especially if you have a color printer. You can also
prepare black and white masters, which you can take to a copy center for low-cost
duplication on colored paper.

Choosing Your Quick Publication's Design

If you have not yet started Publisher, start the program. The first thing you see will be the Microsoft Publisher Catalog. If you have already started Publisher, select File | New (or CTRL-N) to access the Catalog. Also, if the Standard Toolbar is visible, you can use it to access the Catalog by simply clicking on the New icon.

Publisher's Catalog has three tabbed options: Publications by Wizards, Publications by Design, and Blank Publications. The Wizard tab is the default, so it will be what you see first when you begin a new Publisher work session. Figure 4-9 shows the Publisher Catalog with the default Wizard tab visible.

Publisher lists the document types in its Wizards list. For our example, select the Quick Publications option, shown in Figure 4-9. Publisher's preview window

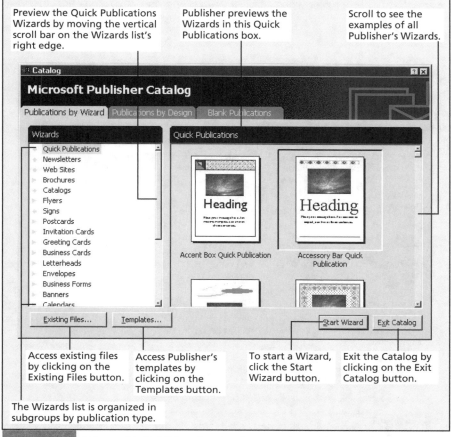

FIGURE 4-9 Microsoft's Publisher Catalog features the Publications by Wizard tab

automatically displays all the Quick Publications design options, as shown in Figure 4-10. For our example, select the Bars Quick Publication to start, and then you can further customize it. To start the Wizard, click on the design on the Bars Quick Publication example and then click the Start Wizard button. You can also select the Bars Quick Publication Wizard by double-clicking the sample in the preview window. Either method works equally well.

Read the Wizard's Introduction text. When you are ready to begin replacing text and graphics placeholders, click the Next button. Publisher's Quick Publication Wizard displays the next set of instructions in the process of completing the publication. In our Quick Publication Wizard example, the Wizard next presents the Color Scheme list from which you may select any of Publisher's 63 color combinations (including a Custom option). (See Figure 4-11.) These color schemes have been matched by professional designers to assist the "color-matching impaired," and to ensure that Publisher gives you the most professional-looking results possible.

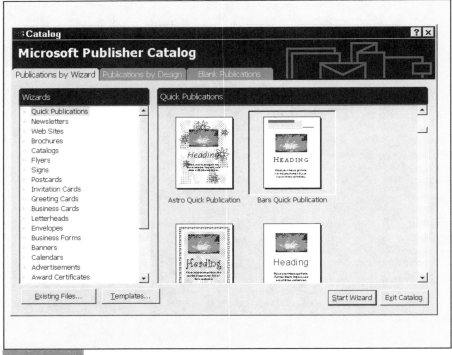

FIGURE 4-10   Publisher's Bars design selected from the Quick Publication Wizard category is ready for you to begin work

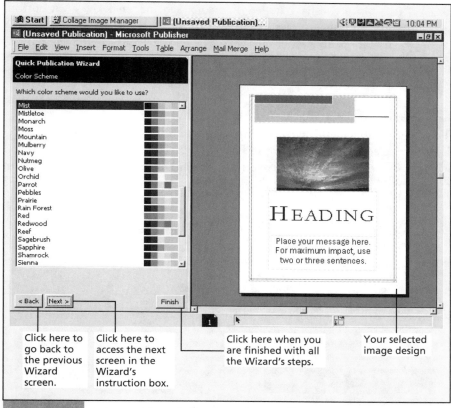

Start | Collage Image Manager | (Unsaved Publication)... 10:04 PM

(Unsaved Publication) - Microsoft Publisher

File Edit View Insert Format Tools Table Arrange Mail Merge Help

Quick Publication Wizard

Color Scheme

Which color scheme would you like to use?

Mist
Mistletoe
Monarch
Moss
Mountain
Mulberry
Navy
Nutmeg
Olive
Orchid
Parrot
Pebbles
Prairie
Rain Forest
Red
Redwood
Reef
Sagebrush
Sapphire
Shamrock
Sienna

HEADING

Place your message here.
For maximum impact, use
two or three sentences.

< Back   Next >   Finish

Click here to   Click here to   Click here when you   Your selected
go back to   access the next   are finished with all   image design
the previous   screen in the   the Wizard's steps.
Wizard   Wizard's
screen.   instruction box.

FIGURE 4-11 Select a color scheme from the Quick Publication Wizard's list to harmonize with the publication design you selected

If the number of Publisher's color scheme options overwhelms you, here are a few tips on how to decide which colors to use:

- If you are going to print a limited quantity of publications on your color ink-jet printer, you can choose just about any of the Color Schemes.

- Choose Black & Gray or Black & White if you are going to prepare a master that you will take to a copy shop for quantity distribution.

- Choose Black & White if your printer is only capable of 300 dot-per-inch resolution.

- Choose Black & Gray if your printer is capable of 600 (or higher) dot-per-inch resolution.

- Choose any of the color schemes if you are preparing files for commercial printing.

Tip: With Publisher 2000's Wizards, you can use the Back button at any time to change how you answered a question, which, in turn, changes the evolution of the publication on which you are working.

Tip: Publisher's Quick Publication Wizard's Blank design is ideal for printing flyers on existing letterheads.

Once you have settled on a color scheme, click the Next button. For the purpose of our example, which color scheme you select doesn't really matter, but you must select a color scheme before Publisher's Wizard will display the next set of instructions—choosing a page size for the example flyer.

Choosing a Page Size

The Quick Publication's next Wizard instruction screen in our example is the Page Size screen, which is shown in Figure 4-12. The Page Size screen asks you whether you prefer the portrait (vertical) or landscape (horizontal) orientation for your publication. Here's the distinction between the Portrait and Landscape options:

- Choose Portrait if you want your publication to be taller than wider—in other words, 8.5 inches wide and 11 inches tall.

- Choose Landscape if you want your publication to be wider than it is tall—that is, 11 inches wide and 8.5 inches tall.

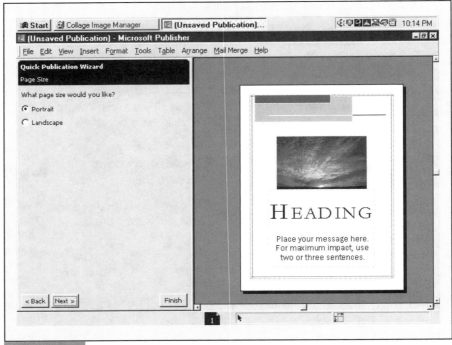

FIGURE 4-12   With the Quick Publication Wizard's Page Size screen, you can select either portrait (tall) or landscape (wide) orientation

Customizing Your Selected Flyer Wizard Layout

Once you have selected the publication's orientation (horizontal or vertical), click the Next button. The Wizard will then display its instructions for customizing your publication's layout. The Quick Publication Wizard's Layout screen, shown in Figure 4-13, is one of the most important of the series. Here, you can determine the contents of your publication by choosing the size and placement of the picture and message. Each time you select one of the options at the left, the window at the right changes to preview how your finished publication will look. You can choose from among 14 options listed in the Layout information box. (See Figure 4-13 for more details.) When you are satisfied with your choice, click the Next button.

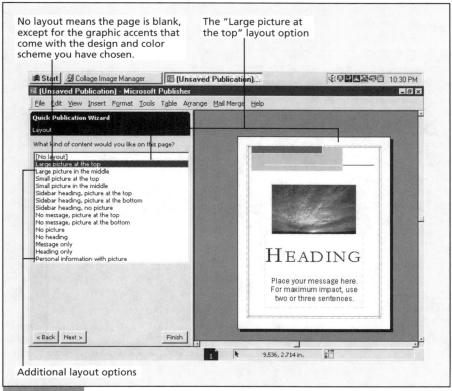

FIGURE 4-13   Use this screen of the Quick Publication Wizard to customize your publication's look

Inserting Personal Information

The Quick Publication Wizard's last step is the addition of your personal information, as shown in Figure 4-14. With this Wizard instruction screen, you can select the Personal Information set, if any, you want to include on your publication. Your choices include Primary Business, Secondary Business, Other Organization, or Home/Family.

Cross-Reference: For more information on Personal Information sets, see Chapter 1 and Chapter 2.

You have now completed all of the Quick Publication Wizard's instruction screens. If you want to go back through the screens to change any of your responses to Wizard questions, click the Back button. You can also use the Back button simply to review your responses to the Wizard options. When you are satisfied with all the information you have given to the Quick Publication Wizard, click the Finish button to complete the interactive part of the Wizard's actions.

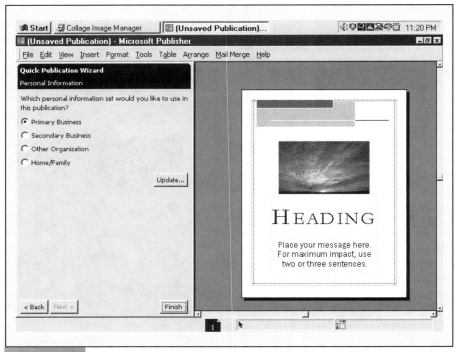

FIGURE 4-14   Click the Update button if you want to change the information in the Personal Information set you have chosen

Creating Your Quick Publication

Within a few seconds, Publisher displays the Quick Publication you selected, along with any additions or modifications you may have made while you worked within the Wizard. Figure 4-15 shows our example publication with all the changes and additions we made while working within the Wizard.

By default, the Publication Wizard remains visible while you work on your publication. The easy access to the Wizard and your selections makes refining your publication a much easier task. However, you may want to gain more working space, so you can click the Hide Wizard button at the bottom of the Wizard's instruction screen, which is visible in Figure 4-15.

L▶ Tip: Note that the Show Wizard button, with the upward-pointing green arrow, remains visible at the lower left of the Status Bar. (To display the Status Bar if it is not visible, select View from Publisher's main menu. Publisher will display a drop-down menu, from which you can select the Toolbars option and then the Status Bar option.)

Replacing Placeholder Text and Graphics

You are now ready to complete your publication and replace Publisher's placeholder text and graphics (objects) with the text and graphics you want included in your publication.

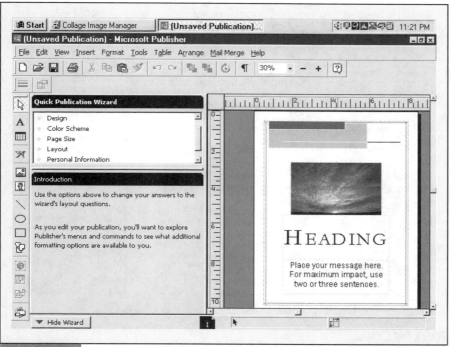

FIGURE 4-15 Once you click the Quick Publication Wizard's Finish button, Publisher displays the resulting document as you have specified

HEADING PLACEHOLDER   To begin the text and graphics replacement activity, start by selecting the word "Heading" on your publication, and then simply enter your desired heading text—a short phrase or headline that will grab your reader's attention. For our example Quick Publication, you can enter the phrase "Handyman's Special." Don't worry if the text you are entering momentarily disappears; it disappears because the type size is too large or the text you want to enter is too long to fit in the heading placeholder. After a few seconds, however, Publisher's AutoFit feature will reduce the type size so your heading will fit in the available space, as shown in Figure 4-16.

> **Tip:** Notice that you don't have to select the Heading text by dragging. A single click is enough to select placeholder text for replacement.

You can sometimes noticeably increase heading type size by eliminating Publisher's default text frame margins. Although the default margin is enough to keep text in adjacent frames from bumping into each other, sometimes the margins are too large.

Publisher's standard margin default is .04 inches, which doesn't sound like much, but it can be enough to cause trouble. To eliminate these default margins, first right-click the heading text frame, and Publisher will display a nested arrangement of floating drop-down

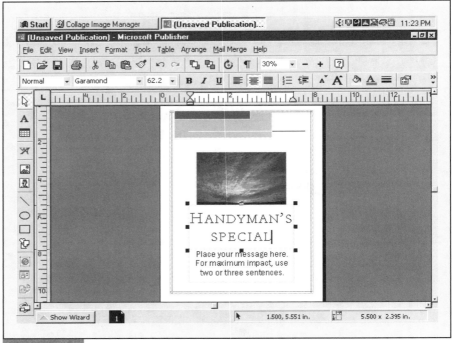

FIGURE 4-16   Publisher's AutoFit feature will make your desired text fit into the Heading placeholder

menus. From the first drop-down menu, select Change Frame, and the next nested drop-down menu will appear. From this menu, select Text Frame Properties, and Publisher will display the Text Frame Properties dialog box.

From the Text Frame Properties dialog box, replace Publisher's default .04-inch left, right, top and bottom margins with a 0-inch margin. Then click the OK option or Enter when you have made these changes. Note that if you use this technique, eliminating Publisher's default margins often changes line breaks and slightly increases heading type size.

The action of changing Publisher's default margins to 0-inch ones—when combined with some solid editing—often makes a significant change in the amount of available space you have in which to work.

PHOTOS   After you have successfully replaced the heading text, you need to replace the photo placeholder with a photo of your own. One way to replace the photo placeholder is to click on the placeholder, and then pull down the Insert drop-down menu. From this menu, select the Picture option. Publisher will then display the next layer of nested drop-down menu options. Select From File from the drop-down menu. An alternate method is to right-click on the picture placeholder, which will activate a set of floating drop-down menus relating to photos. Select Change Picture | Select Picture | From File. With either method you may choose, Publisher will display the Insert Picture dialog box, shown in Figure 4-17.

When Publisher displays the Insert Picture dialog box, browse through the various folders on your hard drive until you locate the folder that contains the photo you want to use. Select the photo's filename, and Publisher previews the photo you have selected. To insert the photo, double-click the filename, or click the Insert button.

MESSAGE PLACEHOLDER   The final step required to complete the publication is to replace the text placeholder that appears below the heading with the text you want to use to convey your message. As with the heading text, you don't have to select the text by dragging. Just click anywhere in the text frame, and Publisher will select all the words to be replaced. Replace the "Place your message here…" text with meaningful text that supports the message you want to communicate through your heading and photograph. Be sure to indicate what action you want readers to take—call your office, send you an e-mail, and so on.

Once you have completed replacing the text placeholder area with the text you want to use, your Quick Publication is finally complete. As with the heading text, Publisher will use the AutoFit

Tip: After the AutoFit feature fits your text to the available space, your text may be too small to read onscreen or in print. To better see the text onscreen, select View | Zoom | Selected Objects. (You can press the F9 key when in the Zoom menu for the last command.) You can also right-click the message text frame and choose Selected Objects.

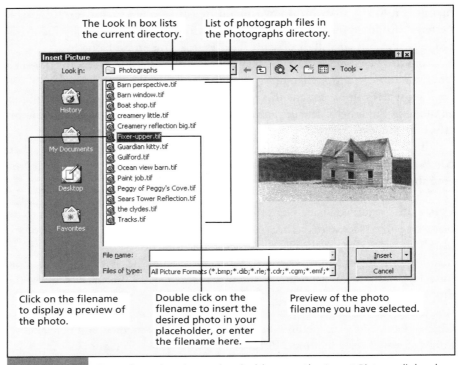

The Look In box lists the current directory.

List of photograph files in the Photographs directory.

Click on the filename to display a preview of the photo.

Double click on the filename to insert the desired photo in your placeholder, or enter the filename here.

Preview of the photo filename you have selected.

FIGURE 4-17 To replace the photo placeholder, use the Insert Picture dialog box to browse through all the photos you have on your hard drive until you find the photo you want to use in your publication

feature to choose the right type size to make your message fit the available space, as shown in Figure 4-18.

Professional Pointer

Additional solutions will become more and more obvious as you become comfortable working with Publisher 2000's various options. You can easily customize and build on Quick Publications created with the Design Wizard. For example, you might want to add text frames to the left and right of the photograph, and include detailed information in them.

FIGURE 4-18   Publisher AutoFits, or chooses, the right type size for your message

Creating a Visual Identity for Your Business or Personal Printed Items

Every firm and organization needs a strong visual identity. This identity begins with the philosophy and mission of the business or organization, and should continue through all aspects and activities of those entities. This identity should be clearly and obviously recognizable on every piece of paper that your prospects, customers, and employees see. If your business or firm has a Web site, this visual identity should also be present there.

Every business or organization's identity and philosophy should be the driving force in projecting the right image. Printed items created for that business or organization should consistently carry that desired image and identity. The identity should be flexible enough to successfully convey your image and identity on most types of printed documents, regardless of whether they are to be used for home or office. Your image as carried by your printed needs should be consistently of high quality and professionalism, regardless of whether you print the items on your ink-jet or laser printer or use a commercial printer when you need larger quantities than you can efficiently print with your desktop printer. And the most important consideration of all is if you can afford and maintain your image without compromise. After all, this image is built on the foundation of what your business or organization represents. So carefully consider how you want to create and maintain your image, and solidify it so you can succeed and grow.

With printed materials, letterheads are the starting point for creating a strong visual identity. Publisher 2000 Letterhead Wizard makes it easy to create a professional, unique visual identity, even if you do not currently have a logo (an electronic file consisting of your firm or organization's name formatted in a unique and distinct way). If your firm or organization does not yet have a distinct visual identity to present and reinforce its driving philosophy and purpose, now is the time to create one.

Choosing the Right Design

One good place to start creating your firm or organization's visual identity is with Publisher's Letterhead Wizard. Select File | New. When you see the Microsoft Publisher Catalog, select the Letterheads Wizard option from the Publications by Wizards list. Publisher immediately presents you with two options: Plain Paper or Special Paper.

Select the Plain Paper option if you are going to be preparing your letterheads on your office color ink-jet or color laser printer or are preparing artwork for duplication by a copy center or commercial printer. Plain Paper is also the appropriate choice if you want maximum design flexibility plus the ability to create a unified visual identity using Publisher's 20 Design Master Sets and the 30 different types of documents each can produce.

Select the Special Paper option if you plan on creating a business or organization's identity using papers preprinted with color accents, which are sold by companies such as Paper Direct.

L ▶ Note: Although Publisher's Special Paper Letterhead Wizards are designed to work only with certain papers that are sold by the supplier Paper Direct, you may prefer different paper designs from other special paper suppliers. Remember, though, that if you choose another supplier's special paper, you may have to experiment to get the Letterhead Wizard to work the way you want. You may contact Paper Direct for a free catalog at (800) 272-7377.

Cross-Reference: For more information on working with special papers, see Chapter 6.

Notice how the design options on the screen's right change as you select either Plain Paper or Special Paper. For our example, select Plain Paper.

Next, for our example, select the design called Punctuation. You can select this design by clicking on it, and then clicking the Start Wizard button. You can also start the Punctuation Letterhead Wizard by double-clicking on that design example. Once you have selected the Punctuation example, the Wizard follows the same steps to create this publication as it did for the Bars Quick Publication earlier in this chapter.

Adding Personal Information

Now that we have selected our Punctuation Letterhead Wizard, Publisher will display the Letterhead Wizard's introduction screen. Click Next to begin working on the example, and Publisher will display the instruction screen for selecting your color scheme, just as you did for the publication example earlier in this chapter.

After you have selected your color scheme, the Letterhead Wizard continues by presenting a screen that asks whether you want to include a logo. (This step is a slight departure from the Quick Publication Wizard.) Regardless of how you answer this question, the Wizard next displays the screen for entering your business, organization, or personal information, just as the Quick Publication Wizard did. When you have selected the information you want to include on the example letterhead (name, address, phone, fax, e-mail, and so on), click Finish.

After you select Finish, Publisher will display a Wizard screen with your beginning letterhead design showing on the screen's right, and four additional options from which you may select to further customize the Punctuation Letterhead example, as shown in Figure 4-19. These four options are Design, Color Scheme, Logo, and Personal Information.

Almost everyone in the business world today talks about having a logo. Although the term is widely used—and perhaps overused—a logo is simply an identifying symbol. Logos can act as identifying symbols for any entity ranging from prominent businesses to street gangs. If your business or organization already has a logo, you can insert it in file form into the Letterhead Wizard design. If your business or organization does not already have a logo, consider creating one using Publisher's Design Gallery.

Cross-Reference: For more information on creating a logo with Publisher's Design Gallery, see Chapter 12.

Sometimes you may want to add additional information from your Personal Information set, such as your firm's motto, or tag line, (for example, "Customer

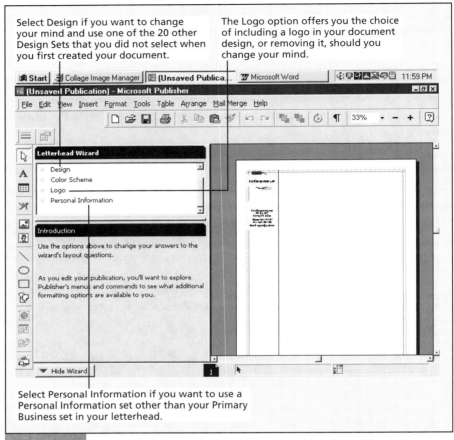

Select Design if you want to change your mind and use one of the 20 other Design Sets that you did not select when you first created your document.

The Logo option offers you the choice of including a logo in your document design, or removing it, should you change your mind.

Select Personal Information if you want to use a Personal Information set other than your Primary Business set in your letterhead.

FIGURE 4-19 The Letterhead Wizard permits you to modify four formatting choices (Design, Color Scheme, Logo and Personal Information) and preview the results

Tip: Select Personal Information | Insert Component if you want to create individual letterheads for different employees featuring each individual's name and job title.

Satisfaction Is King") to your letterhead. To add an element from your Personal Information set to your letterhead, select Personal Information and click Insert Component. You can then select the type of personal information you want to add, as shown in Figure 4-20.

Note that Personal Information components are not formatted or placed in any special location on the letterhead, as shown

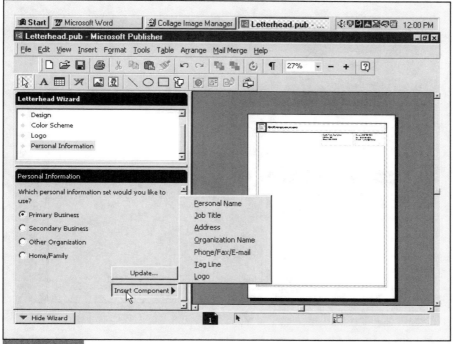

FIGURE 4-20 Click the Insert Component button in the Letterhead Wizard's Personal Information screen and select the type of information you want to add

in Figure 4-21. You must decide where you want to place them and choose an appropriate typeface and type size.

Click the border of the tag line and, when the Move icon appears, drag the tag line (or any other inserted Personal Information component) to the desired location on your letterhead. Once you've positioned the Personal Information item in the location you choose, you can then highlight the item and change its typeface, type style, and color, so it will coordinate with the rest of the letterhead you've created. To change the text attributes of the Personal Information item, select Format | Font, or right-click the text item you want to change and select Change | Text | Font. The result is shown in Figure 4-22.

Tip: The Wizard associated with each type of document chooses which categories of Personal Information components to include in each document. To insert additional categories of information, you can always select Personal Information followed by Insert Component.

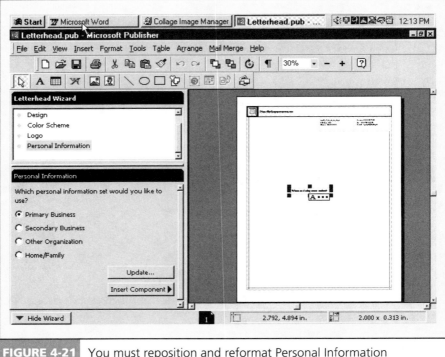

FIGURE 4-21 You must reposition and reformat Personal Information components, like the tag line (selected), visible in the middle of the letterhead

Depending on the size of your computer monitor, you may want to display just a portion of your letterhead in order to get a magnified view. Start by clicking the Hide Wizard button in the Status Bar below the Letterhead Wizard (or select View | Hide Wizard). Then select View | Zoom | Selected Objects, (or simply press F9) to magnify the screen to 100 percent. (You can also right-click the tag line and select Selected Objects.) If the Formatting Toolbar is visible, press the Zoom In or Zoom Out icon to fine-tune your view of the tag line and letterhead sizes.

Limitations of Personal Information Components

Note that the Letterhead Wizard does not reformat and reposition Personal Information components that you manually insert on your own. Publisher only repositions and reformats Personal Information components that it originally

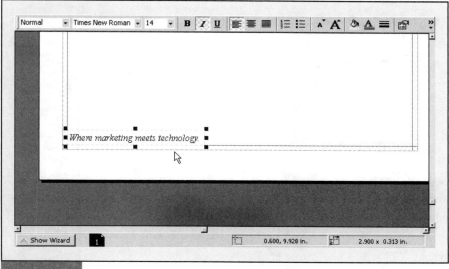

FIGURE 4-22   The tag line used on the letterhead is repositioned and reformatted

inserted into your letterhead when you first used a Wizard to create the document. These components typically include organization name, address, phone, fax, e-mail, and so on. To reposition or reformat Personal Information components that you have inserted without using a Wizard, you have to perform these changes individually.

Additional components you add to a letterhead, such as a tag line, personal name, or job title, remain static, even if you return to the Letterhead Wizard and select a different design or color scheme. This limitation might prove to be a problem, as the inserted component might interfere with some design options, as shown in Figure 4-23.

Choosing the Right Color Scheme

Just as with the Quick Publication example earlier in this chapter, the Letterhead Wizard gives you the option to select your desired color scheme. Even after the Wizard has generated your letterhead based on your responses to the Wizard's questions, you can always decide to change the selected colors again, and again, until you find the exact color combination you prefer.

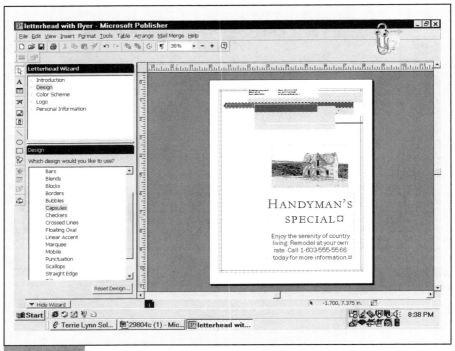

FIGURE 4-23 Because the Letterhead Wizard does not reposition or reformat Personal Information components you have added, they may cause problems if you go back and choose a different design option

Customizing Publisher's Design Sets

Tip: It's a good idea to jot down the color scheme used to create your letterhead, so you can apply it by name to your envelopes, business cards, labels, and other documents created with the same Design Master Set.

You can customize your letterhead even more by changing the Design Master Set's primary graphic accent.

The aspects you can change are:

- Accent Box: 5 variations
- Accessory Bar: 11 variations
- Linear Accent: 3 variations
- Marquee: 5 variations
- Punctuation: 3 variations

To customize one of these designs, select the graphic that gives each design its characteristic look and select View | Zoom | Selected Objects (or press

F9). You can also right-click the graphic and select Selected Objects. You'll know you've selected the right image when the Letterhead Wizard's wand appears in a gray box under the graphic, as shown in Figure 4-24. Clicking the Wizard's wand offers you several different options. Figure 4-24 shows the Contrasting Triangles option, while the following illustrations show the other four options.

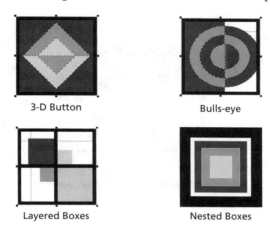

3-D Button

Bulls-eye

Layered Boxes

Nested Boxes

Click the Close button at the upper right of the Accent Box Creation Wizard when you have chosen the graphic you like the best. Once you change the graphic accent on a letterhead, you can add the modified graphic to Publisher's Design Gallery so you can use it with other Design Master Sets.

Cross-Reference: For additional information on Publisher's Design Gallery, see Chapter 2.

These modified graphic options can be saved as Design Gallery objects and shared between publications. Because you can save these modified objects, you can use the same modified Accent Box graphic that you used for your letterhead to create coordinated envelopes, shipping labels, and business cards.

To add the revised Accent Box (or any other) graphic to Publisher's Design Gallery, first click on the graphic object and then select Insert | Add Selection to Design Gallery. When Publisher displays the Add Object dialog box, shown in Figure 4-25, give the modified graphic object a name in the Object Name window. Then select a Category for the object. Click the OK button, or press Enter when you have finished.

Tip: In order to get a better feel for the available options, return to the Letterhead Wizard (by clicking the Show Wizard button or selecting View | Show | Wizard) and select Design. Select either the Accessory Bar, Linear Accent, Marquee, or Punctuation Design Master Set, and try out the different options available for each design.

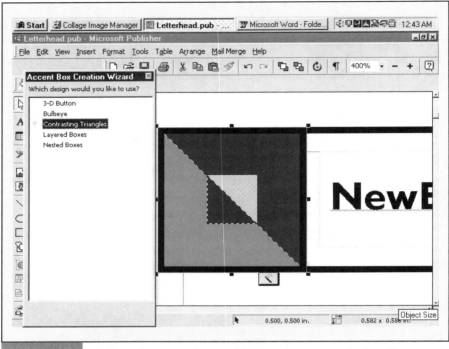

FIGURE 4-24 Clicking the Wizard's wand below the graphic displays five additional options. This is the Contrasting Triangles option for the Accent Box Design Master Set

Creating Matching Envelopes

Using Publisher's Envelopes Wizard to create envelopes to match your letterhead requires the same steps as the Letterhead Wizard. Of course, when you begin to create your matching envelopes, you have to select the Envelopes option from the Publications by Wizard list, instead of the Letterhead Wizard.

When you use the Envelope Wizard, there is one additional option than the Letterhead Wizard—the envelope size option. Publisher features two sizes of envelopes: the 3 5/8-inch by 6 1/2-inch size, which is known as a #6 envelope, and the 4 1/8-inch by 9 1/2-inch size, which is known as a #10 or business-size envelope.

Creating Matching Business Cards

Business cards play an important role in business communications. They reinforce personal meetings and add impact to mailings when you include them with brochures, catalogs, letters, and compliment (or thank-you) cards.

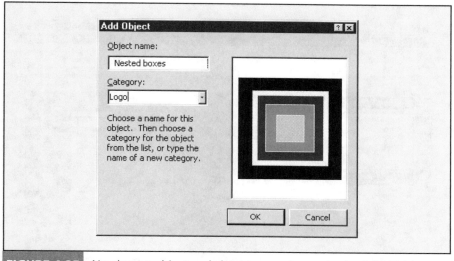

FIGURE 4-25 Naming an object and choosing a category in the Add Object dialog box makes it easy to retrieve and share the graphic

Using Publisher's Business Card Wizard to create matching business cards requires generally the same steps as those of the Letterhead and Envelope Wizards. From the Microsoft Publisher Catalog's list of Wizards, select the Business Cards Wizard, and then select the Plain Paper option, just as you did when you created matching letterhead and envelopes.

Select the same design you used for letterheads and envelopes, which in our example was the Accent Box design. To start the Business Card Wizard, double-click the Accent Box option, and then click the Start Wizard button. The Wizard will display instruction screens (Design, Color Scheme, Logo, and Personal Information) leading you through the Business Card creation process.

The Business Card Wizard offers an orientation option, which is different from the other Wizards we've used in this chapter. For your matching business card, you may choose between Landscape orientation—which is wider than tall—or Portrait orientation—which is taller than wide. Landscape orientation is the more common business card option, but Portrait orientation, shown in Figure 4-26, offers a refreshing departure from the conventional.

Print Tiling is another Business Card Wizard option. Print Tiling does not affect how your business card looks, but rather how many cards will be printed on a page. Select the Wizard's Print Tiling option if you plan to cut them apart after printing.

Tip: Your choice of Landscape or Portrait orientation for your business cards should be based on the design you have chosen as well as the relative length of your organization's name and address information.

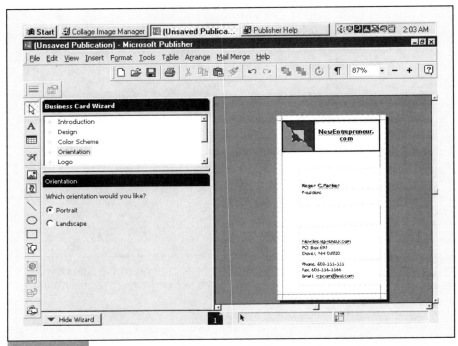

Portrait orientation for your business cards can offer a refreshing look that may distinguish you from other competitors

Click the Hide Wizard button after you have explored all the Business Card Wizard's options and observed how each option reformats the information inserted from your Personal Information set.

Professional Skills Summary

You can now see how easy it is to create great-looking documents with Publisher's Wizards and how quickly you can create a publication and a compelling visual identity with matching letterhead, envelopes, and business cards. Publisher's Wizards facilitate the entire document-creating process, from layout to printing.

After you have used Publisher 2000 for some time, feel free to get creative and customize or enhance any of the layouts the Quick Publications Wizard creates for you. For example, you might consider adding text frames with bulleted lists to the left and right of the photograph. Once you begin thinking creatively, using Publisher's Design Wizards as a starting point for design experimenting, there will be no stopping you!

Part II
Get to Work with Publisher's Wizards

Publishing Your First Newsletter

Even in the Internet age, print newsletters remain one of the most *predictably successful* ways to communicate your firm or association's message to a firm's clients, customers, employees, prospects, and stockholders, or an organization's contributors, members, supporters, volunteers, and the press.

It's hard to find somebody who doesn't enjoy the quick read that a four- or eight-page newsletter provides. Newsletters also succeed because they are tangible: they can be read anywhere, at any time. They can be shared with friends and saved for later reading. Newsletters provide enough space to fully develop your ideas.

Your value to your employer or organization will greatly increase, and your personal skill set will expand, once you become comfortable creating newsletters with Publisher 2000.

L▶ Tip: A single newsletter, of course, is rarely enough. Success depends on establishing an ongoing newsletter *program*. This requires newsletters with meaningful content that appear at consistent, predictable intervals.

Creating a successful newsletter program begins with carefully answering the questions the Publisher's Newsletter Wizard asks. As you answer the questions posed by the Newsletter Wizard, you're creating a framework that will guide you through the process of writing and creating your newsletter. First you'll create the look of your newsletter, and then you'll go back to replace Publisher's placeholders with the actual headlines, text, and graphics you want your newsletter to have.

Three Steps to Newsletter Success

Publisher 2000 greatly simplifies the creation and maintenance of an effective newsletter program. There are just three steps to success:

- **Step 1**   This step involves planning the contents of each issue, using Publisher's Newsletter Design Wizard to create a framework for your newsletter. This framework shows the location of the various articles and other graphic elements, such as calendars and order forms, you want to include in your newsletter. Save and print this rough layout, or "dummy," after completion. It provides a working guide for you as you write the copy and take the necessary photographs.

- **Step 2**   This step involves replacing Publisher's placeholder headlines and text and photo placeholders with the specific words you're going to use to communicate your message. By working from a rough layout, your job will be much easier because you'll have an idea of how much text needs to be written for each article. Most important, writing to fit the available space for each article encourages you to be concise. Layouts created by Publisher's Newsletter Design Wizard also encourage you to include several short articles in each newsletter, instead of a few long articles.

- **Step 3**   The final step involves fine-tuning your work, checking and re-checking content and formatting. Step 3 also involves improving on the framework that Publisher has created for you by adding refinements, such as subheads.

These steps, plus more details to help you perfect your newsletters, will be covered in the following sections.

Selecting Your Newsletter Layout

To begin work on a newsletter, select File | New (or press CTRL-N) if the Publisher Catalog is not visible on your screen. If you can see the Microsoft Publisher Catalog on your screen, click the New icon in the Standard Toolbar. You can scroll through the list of available newsletter designs by using the vertical scroll bar on the screen's far right, and double-clicking your preferred newsletter layout. A Publisher prompt, with a progress bar, will inform you that Publisher is creating the newsletter according to the design you selected.

Tip: Although you can select a range of magnification percentages to view your newsletter, I typically use the 100 percent option for the majority of my work. Once I'm satisfied with the general look of the document's individual elements, I switch to a magnification percentage that shows the entire page on one screen. I can then make some assessments about the overall look of the work I've done.

Cross-Reference: If you need to review the Publisher Catalog, see Chapter 4.

Publisher's Newsletter Wizard will first display its introductory screen, seen in Figure 5-1. This screen reminds you that you can fine-tune the design of your newsletter by clicking on one of the topics and choosing a different option.

You may want to start by increasing the size of how your selected newsletter layout looks onscreen, so you can more easily see the newsletter items on which you will be working. If you are working with the Standard Toolbar visible, click on the + or – icon, or enter a different measurement in the Zoom window. If you are not working with the Standard Toolbar visible, select View | Zoom and choose a desired degree of magnification.

By default, Publisher creates a four-page newsletter. This is often the most economical arrangement to work with because your newsletter can be printed on standard paper sizes. A single sheet of 11 by 17-inch paper, printed on both sides, can create four 8 1/2 by 11-inch newsletter pages.

Tip: The correct newsletter design is one that is most compatible with your company's or organization's other printed items. If you have previously created your letterhead and business cards with the Straight Edge Design Set, for example, you should use the Straight Edge design for your newsletter, too.

If you are satisfied with your newsletter design, you can ignore the Design option listed in the Wizard Newsletter's introductory instruction box. If you want to apply a different design, select a different Design option in the list under the Wizard's question, "Which design would you like to use?" Each time you select a different design, Publisher displays its working prompt to let you know the Newsletter Wizard is changing your design to what you selected. The Wizard immediately reformats the newsletter example on the right side of the screen.

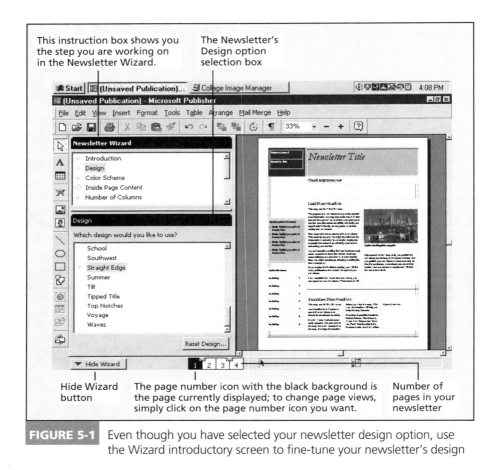

This instruction box shows you the step you are working on in the Newsletter Wizard.

The Newsletter's Design option selection box

Hide Wizard button

The page number icon with the black background is the page currently displayed; to change page views, simply click on the page number icon you want.

Number of pages in your newsletter

FIGURE 5-1 Even though you have selected your newsletter design option, use the Wizard introductory screen to fine-tune your newsletter's design

Next, you'll select your newsletter's color scheme. With the Newsletter Wizard's option of over 60 color scheme combinations (both for foreground and background graphic accents and headlines), click on one of the Color Scheme options.

Cross-Reference: For additional information on the Wizard's Color Scheme options, see Chapter 4.

Choosing Inside Page Content

To choose content for the two inside pages of your newsletter, here are the two beginning steps:

1. Begin by selecting one of the inside pages of your newsletter by clicking on the page 2 or page 3 icon, which are labeled in Figure 5-1. If you do not see

the Status Bar at the bottom of the screen, select View | Toolbars | Status Bar, and the bar should appear along the screen's bottom edge.

2. Next, click on Inside Page Content from the Wizard options listed in the Newsletter Wizard. Once you've selected an inside page, you can now choose from five different alternatives for each of the inside pages of your newsletter. The default, shown in Figure 5-2, includes a mixture of text and graphics for three stories. The best way to familiarize yourself with the Newsletter Wizard is to try out each of the Inside Page Content options.

Tip: It's a good idea to work with the Status Bar visible when creating newsletters with the Newsletter Wizard. You can easily hide or show the Newsletter Wizard, and you can easily select a desired page of your newsletter by simply clicking on it.

Newsletter Wizard Instruction box with the Inside Page Content option highlighted

The example response to the question above this field is to put the content on the left inside page.

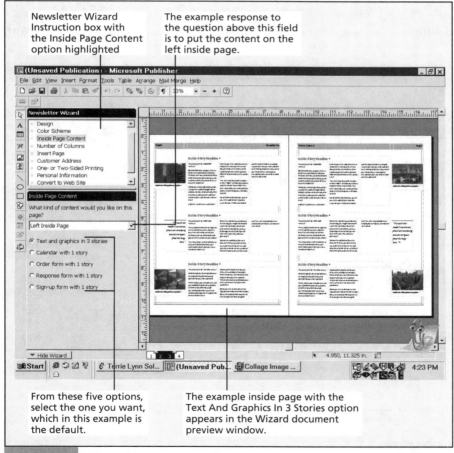

From these five options, select the one you want, which in this example is the default.

The example inside page with the Text And Graphics In 3 Stories option appears in the Wizard document preview window.

FIGURE 5-2 The default Inside Page Content Wizard layout creates three stories

The Calendar With 1 Story Option

When you click on the radio button option for the Calendar With 1 Story, the Newsletter Wizard changes to the newly selected layout—calendar at the page top and a text placeholder to the calendar's right, which is to be used to describe upcoming events. By default, the calendar displays the current month. Later in this chapter, in the section describing working with placeholders, you'll find out how to change the calendar to display any desired month. (See Figure 5-3.)

The Order Form With 1 Story Option

If you prefer the option for the Wizard layout that features an Order Form With 1 Story, click this option's radio button. Publisher's Newsletter Wizard immediately changes the preview example to show this new option, which places an order form on the bottom of the inside page, as shown in Figure 5-4. Along with

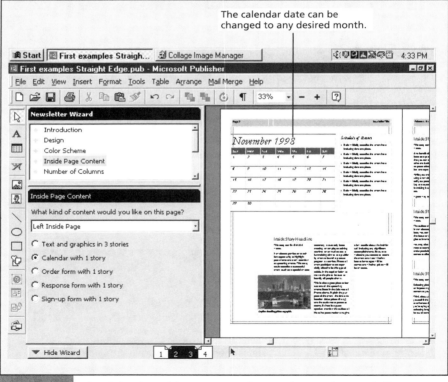

FIGURE 5-3 The Calendar With 1 Story Option can be used to easily list upcoming events of interest to readers

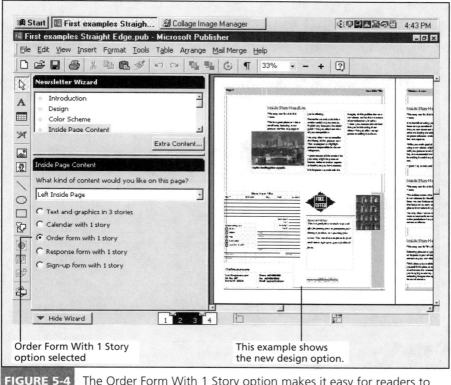

Order Form With 1 Story
option selected

This example shows
the new design option.

FIGURE 5-4   The Order Form With 1 Story option makes it easy for readers to
respond to your offers

the order form, this design option also has a space for customers to describe a special order. Both the order form and the custom order area make it easy for your customers and prospects to respond favorably to offers contained in your newsletter. There's space for readers to order several different products and to specify shipping preferences and credit card information.

The Response Form With 1 Story Option

When you use the Response Form With 1 Story option (see Figure 5-5), you have an easy and inexpensive way to solicit your readers' opinions. The response form provides a structured framework that asks your readers four questions and includes a comments box for a less structured response. Limiting responses to just three options (such as "Yes," "No," or "No opinion,") for each question both simplifies the response form (encouraging more readers to respond) and also simplifies compiling the results.

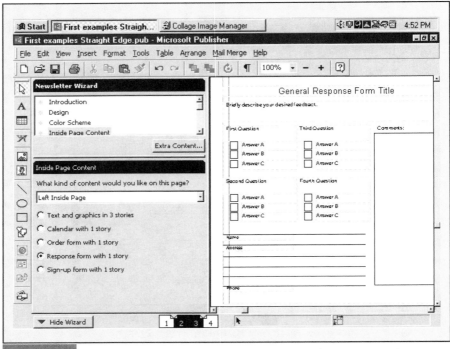

FIGURE 5-5 The Response Form With 1 Story option makes it easy and inexpensive to solicit your readers' responses

The Sign-Up Form With 1 Story Option

If you use the option that features a sign-up form, you are soliciting your newsletter readers to contribute for special purposes and to pay in advance to attend upcoming events. Editors of organizational newsletters can also use the Sign-Up Form With 1 Story, shown in Figure 5-6, to remind members of the various dues categories.

Determining Your Newsletter's Number of Columns

Return to the front page of your newsletter by clicking the Page 1 icon in the Status Bar at the bottom of your screen. Select Number of Columns. You can now

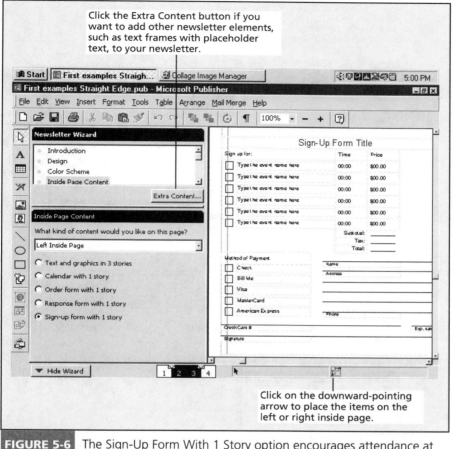

The Sign-Up Form With 1 Story option encourages attendance at upcoming events, and can be used to solicit contributions or remind members of dues

go through your publication, page by page, changing the number of columns you prefer.

Because your choice of columns greatly influences your newsletter's appearance, take the time to try out each of the four alternatives: single column, two-column, three-column, and a combination. Figure 5-7 shows an example of each option.

Tip: The Extra Content gallery provides a place for you to save and retrieve repeatable graphic elements, such as tables of contents and pull-quotes.

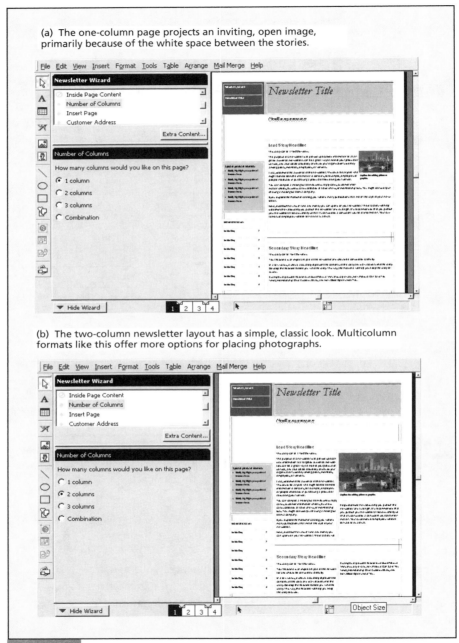

(a) The one-column page projects an inviting, open image, primarily because of the white space between the stories.

(b) The two-column newsletter layout has a simple, classic look. Multicolumn formats like this offer more options for placing photographs.

FIGURE 5-7 Publisher's Newsletter Wizard displays the various layout options: (a) one-column, (b) two-column, (c) three-column, and (d) a combination

(c) Each column layout example uses the same amount of text, but the three-column layout appears to offer higher word density.

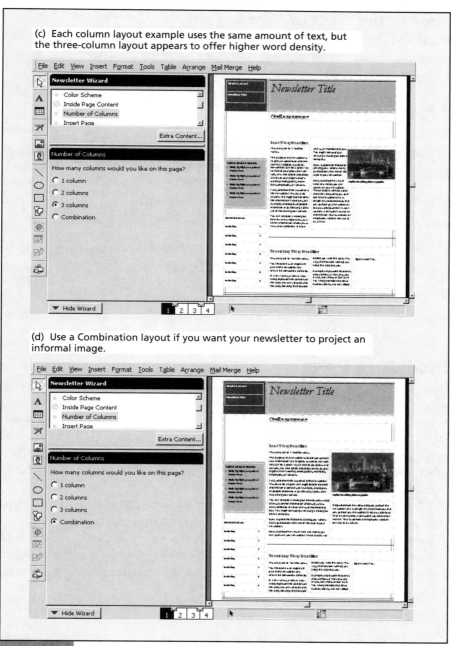

(d) Use a Combination layout if you want your newsletter to project an informal image.

FIGURE 5-7 Publisher's Newsletter Wizard displays the various layout options: (a) one-column, (b) two-column, (c) three-column, and (d) a combination *(continued)*

Making the Most of Your Layout

Regardless of which layout option you use, professional design artists have some important advice for all desktop publishers, whatever your level of expertise. Here are some of the more helpful ones:

- Alignment is one of the most important aspects of pleasing design.
- Multicolumn layouts present more options for placing photographs without creating text wraps. Text wraps occur when lines of text are carried over to the next line, to accommodate an illustration or photograph.
- Text wraps can play havoc with word spacing and hyphenation. In addition, text wraps slow readers down because they must adjust their reading speed each time line length changes.
- White space along the right edge of the right inside page forces the reader's eyes onto the articles on the page.
- You can create visual interest by using two different column layouts and using vertical instead of horizontal article placement. This asymmetrical arrangement of elements projects an energetic image, in contrast to more prevalent balanced or static layouts.
- Using two different column layouts can add visual interest to either the left or right inside page of your newsletter.

Inserting Pages

If you want to create a six- or eight-page newsletter (or even larger, if you desire), select Inside Page from the Newsletter Wizard. Publisher confirms that you want to insert additional pages by requesting that you click the Insert Page button and then displays the Insert Pages dialog box, shown in Figure 5-8. By default, the new pages will be inserted *after* the currently displayed pages, meaning that Publisher places the pages at the newsletter's end, so the new pages will be numbered 5 and 6.

Click the More Options button if you prefer to insert more than two pages, or if you want to insert the pages before, after, or between the currently displayed left inside page and right inside page. The Insert Page dialog box (singular, and not to be confused with the plural Inset Pages dialog box), displayed in Figure 5-9, also offers you further formatting options. With the Insert Page dialog box, you can:

- Insert blank pages.
- Create one text frame on each page.
- Duplicate all objects on a given page. The default is page 2, but you can duplicate the objects on another page by entering a different page number.

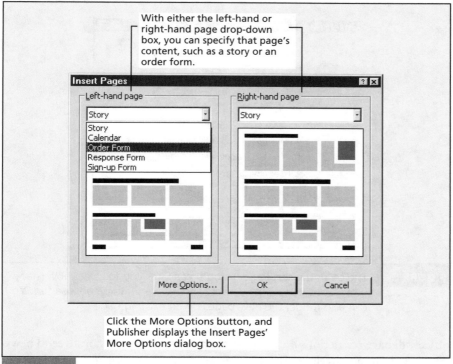

With either the left-hand or right-hand page drop-down box, you can specify that page's content, such as a story or an order form.

Click the More Options button, and Publisher displays the Insert Pages' More Options dialog box.

FIGURE 5-8 The Insert Pages dialog box permits you to choose the content of your new pages as you insert them

Adding a Customer's Address for Distributing Your Newsletter

One of the design considerations in newsletter creation is how you plan to distribute your newsletter. You have four basic options, and all four affect any newsletter's layout. Because of the impact, you need to decide how you will distribute your newsletter when you design it. The four distribution options for newsletters are:

- Hand it out in your place of business
- Fold and insert it in an envelope and mail it
- Fold your newsletter in half or thirds, and send it as a self-mailer
- Send it electronically as a Web-published newsletter

As is so often the case, the choice boils down to money and time. Newsletters inserted in envelopes arrive in better shape than self-mailers, and your local post

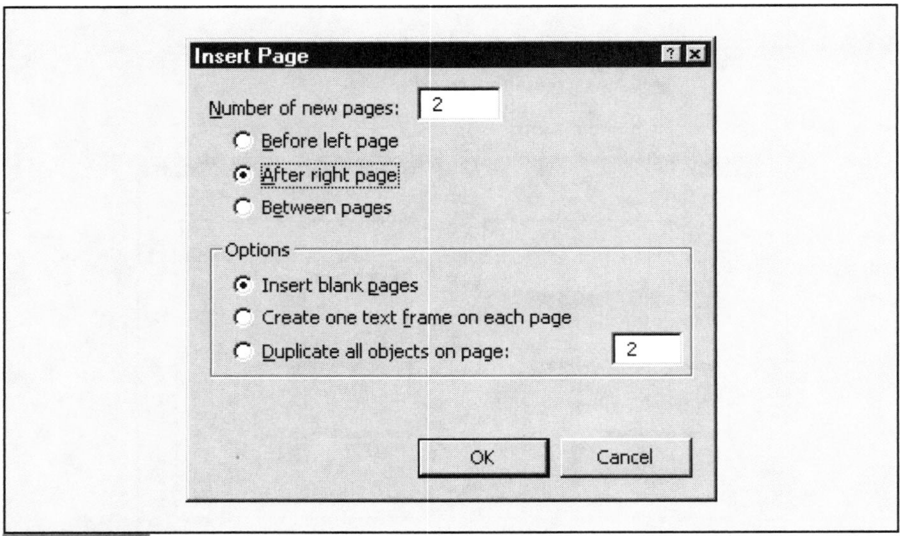

FIGURE 5-9   The second Insert Page dialog box allows you to select how many new pages you want to insert and where they will be inserted. You can also model the new pages on an existing page

office will have restrictions on the kind of paper to use if you want to send newsletters without an envelope. But it costs money to print and address envelopes, and it takes time to stuff the envelopes. Web publishing is very cost-effective, on the other hand, but may require more technical expertise (depending on how you do it). Also, if you distribute your newsletter via the Web, you are assuming that your target audience is Web-based.

For many newsletter publishers, self-mailers are the obvious, economical solution. By avoiding the costs and delays involved in printing and stuffing envelopes, you can get your message into the mail sooner—and possibly save enough money to afford to print extra copies.

Publisher features two ways to address self-mailer newsletters:

- You can address your newsletters as you print them on your desktop ink-jet or laser printer, using a subscriber or circulation name and address maintained in a Publisher-managed database. With this method, Publisher automatically inserts the reader's name, position, firm name, street name, city, state and zip code on each newsletter as it prints each newsletter.

- You can print address labels separately and place them on your newsletter.

Cross-Reference: To learn more about how Publisher can address each copy of your newsletter as it prints the final copies, see Chapter 14.

No matter how you distribute your newsletter, you'll probably want to add return address information to your newsletter—perhaps in an area within the newsletter known by professional periodicals publishers as the *masthead,* the top of the first page where the title of the publication is displayed. Additionally, you might leave space for a customer address panel somewhere on your layout.

To add address info to your newsletter, select Customer Address in the Newsletter Wizard's Information box, and click the Yes radio button. Publisher will add a customer address placeholder to your publication on the last page of your newsletter. Publisher's Newsletter Wizard inserts an address panel at the newsletter's top, as shown in Figure 5-10.

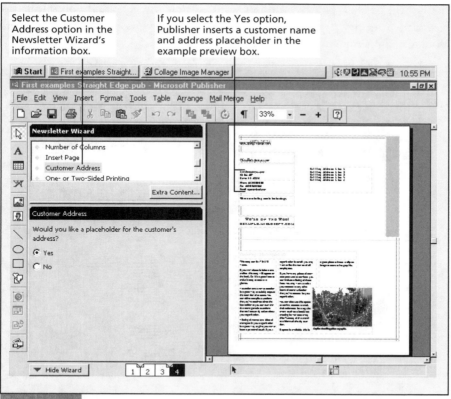

FIGURE 5-10 Use the option to add a placeholder for the customer's address if you want to distribute your newsletter as a self-mailer

More Newsletter Feature Options

Publisher's remaining Newsletter Wizard feature options pertain to fairly specialized choices.

One-Sided Printing

Do you plan to print single-sided or double-sided? Single-sided newsletters are typically designed for office or departmental communications. They are often printed on a laser printer and are stapled at the upper-left corner. Single-sided is Publisher's default printing option. This choice is also the correct one if you plan to have your newsletter commercially duplicated. Note, however, that if you select single-sided (or return to double-sided after having selected single-sided), a Publisher warning will appear explaining that Publisher will modify the pages of your publication to match the selected layout. Click Yes if you want to change the layout, or click No if you don't want to alter the layout. If you select single-sided printing, pages will be modified so that white space always appears along the right edge of each page, as shown in Figure 5-11.

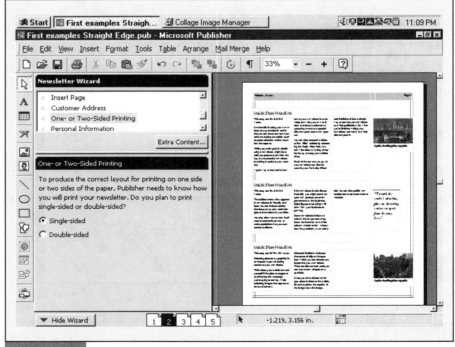

FIGURE 5-11 Publisher reformats newsletters intended for single-sided printing so that the white space appears along the right-hand edge of each page

Personal Information

Click on Personal Information if you want to insert information included in your Personal Information profile to your newsletter. Chances are, though, some information has already been added. If you have added a reply form, response form, sign-up form, or customer address, Publisher has already added your primary firm's name, logo, address, and contact information to the appropriate pages. Click the appropriate button if you want to include information stored with other Personal Information Sets, such as a Secondary Business, Other Organization, or Home/Family. If no information has been entered for these categories, Publisher will insert placeholder text for you to replace later.

Newsletter Look

If you are interested in creating a distinctively different newsletter, consider landscape (horizontal) page orientation. Select File | Page Setup. When you see the Page Setup dialog box, click on Landscape under Choose an Orientation. Publisher's Newsletter Wizard will automatically reformat your newsletter, adjusting column size and placement, to accommodate the new format.

Printing and Saving Your Layout

The last step involved in planning the design of your newsletter involves printing and saving your work. You need to print a copy of your newsletter layout so you can begin to think about the headlines and body copy you're going to fill in your layout placeholders. You can use the printed pages as a framework for penciling in ideas. To print your newsletter, select File | Print. Because this copy of your newsletter layout is for planning purposes only, use the draft option to print it.

Using your printed newsletter layout, you might want to pencil in the headlines, articles, and photo or graphics spots. For best results, limit your articles to between 125 and 150 words—this limit gives you enough space to develop most ideas. Second, most of the story placeholders that Publisher creates are designed to accommodate 125 to 150 words.

Saving Your Newsletter as a Template

Now that you have chosen a design, color scheme, number of columns, and inside page content, and replaced the newsletter title placeholder with your own title, you might consider saving your newsletter as a template. A template is a read-only file that must be saved under a different filename. Saving your newsletter as a template at this point makes sense because you're probably (hopefully!) not going to be choosing a different title for future issues of your newsletter.

Saving your newsletter as a template now, instead of later, offers you several important benefits:

- The major benefit is that you will be able to create future issues of your newsletter on the Newsletter Wizard's original layout. This is preferable to creating future issues on the working layout, as you may have modified it to accommodate the contents of the first issue—for example, you may have changed story length to accommodate overflow text, and so on.

- You'll also find it much easier to plan future issues by working with prints of your layout that include headline and text placeholders instead of being distracted by headlines and text you used in your first issue.

- Most important, by saving your newsletter as a template *before* you have modified the basic design by adding issue-specific text frames or graphics, the Newsletter Wizard will work much better when inserting pages and changing inside page content.

To save your newsletter as a template, select File | Save As. When the Save As dialog box appears, click the pop-up menu at the bottom of the screen and select Publisher Template. Enter an appropriate name, for example, "Empty 3 Col Small Biz newsletter," and click Save. Publisher will automatically save the file in the Templates folder.

To base a future publication on the template, select File | New, and click the Existing Files button when the Microsoft Publisher Catalog appears.

Note that after you have saved your newsletter as a template and reopened it at a later date, you will still be able to use the Newsletter Wizard. For example, you will be able to use the Newsletter Wizard's Inside Page Content feature to add a calendar, order form, response form, or sign-up form. If you didn't add a customer address, you will be able to now (and if you did add a customer address, you will be able to eliminate it).

Completing Your Newsletter

Congratulations! Now that your newsletter layout is done, you only have a bit more work to do. Using your pencil-marked draft of the layout, you will be able to complete your newsletter quickly.

All that remains for you to do now is to replace Publisher's placeholder text and photographs with text and photographs that support your company's or organization's message. Be forewarned, however, that no first-draft layout is going to work perfectly from the start. As you replace placeholders, you might need to make some changes to your basic layout, and—as I will show you—layout alterations can easily be done. If you work on completing your newsletter from your printed draft layout plan, you'll find that work will proceed quickly.

To complete your newsletter, you have only five short remaining steps:

1. Add title and issue information.
2. Replace placeholder headlines and text.
3. Handle overflow text.
4. Add photographs.
5. Apply the finishing touches.

Professional Pointer

Before you begin filling your Publisher placeholders, you'll find it extremely helpful to study other published periodicals. You can see examples (both good and bad, unfortunately) of what other layout designers have done with various elements, such as the title, issue number, and list of contributors' elements. Remember that you can gain insight and inspiration from others' work, but you cannot directly copy materials from any source without first seeking that source's permission to use the material for your own purposes. Such actions, called *plagiarism*, are both unethical and illegal. If you are unsure whether you are committing plagiarism, please seek clarification from a reliable legal source. If you are still in doubt about whether you need permission to use others' materials, take the conservative position and don't use the material. Innovate something on your own, and you will be worry-free about possible accusations of plagiarism.

Before you begin work on your newsletter's nameplate area (the place on the newsletter's front page that contains the newsletter's number and other issue-specific information), you may want to give yourself some additional working space. To temporarily hide the Newsletter Wizard, click the Hide Wizard button at the bottom of the screen. The newsletter instruction area will disappear, and you'll have additional space to create a strikingly attention-getting title. You'll also probably want to increase the size of the nameplate area by selecting View | Zoom | Select Objects, or simply press F9. (You can also right-click on the title area and click on the Selected Objects option from the floating drop-down menu displayed by Publisher.)

Now you can replace the Newsletter Wizard's title placeholder with your newsletter's title. First, click on the Page 1 icon to display the newsletter's first page on your screen. Click on the newsletter title placeholder. Now enter your newsletter title, and Publisher will automatically reformat the title in the typeface and type size most appropriate for the design you have chosen for your newsletter. Next, highlight "Volume 1, Issue 1" and replace it with the appropriate issue

Tip: Remember that the F9 function key lets you quickly toggle between selected objects and the previous view you had of your newsletter.

information. Finally, highlight the month and date placeholders and replace them with the date your newsletter is scheduled to arrive in your readers' hands.

When you are satisfied with your nameplate area, immediately save your work by selecting File | Save, or pressing CTRL-S. Then, switch to Whole Page view by selecting View | Zoom | Whole Page, or press CTRL-SHIFT-L, to see your newsletter evolving. (See Figure 5-12.)

Replacing Placeholder Headlines and Text

Scroll down your front page until you see the Lead Story Headline area. Click on the Lead Story Headline placeholder. Notice that the entire headline is selected when you click on the headline placeholder. Enter the headline you want. Next, click on the text in the adjacent article. Then follow these steps:

- If you have *not already written the article*, start typing. The text in the article placeholder will disappear and you can continue to write your article. Note that when you have finished typing in the first column, text will appear in the second column. This is because the Newsletter Wizard has linked the text frames.

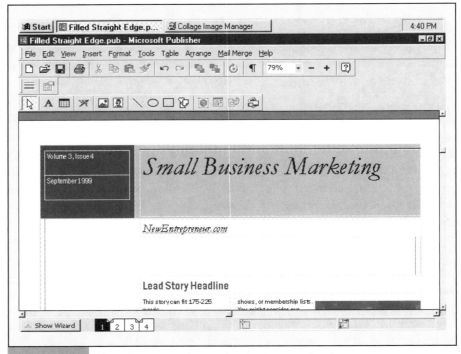

FIGURE 5-12   Your front page is now beginning to take shape

- If you have *already written* the article and saved it as a word processing file, select Insert | Text File. When the Insert Text dialog box appears, locate the folder containing the file for your story. Select the desired filename and click the OK button (or press ENTER), or double-click on the filename to insert it and close the Insert Text dialog box.

- If you want to use Word to write the story, taking advantage of Word's Normal view and other editing capabilities, select Edit | Edit Story in Microsoft Word.

If you are importing a previously created text file, there's a good chance that the file will be too long to fit in the space available in the Lead Story text frames. Publisher warns you of this, as shown in Figure 5-13, and asks whether you want to use the Autoflow feature to place the text in the next text frame. In the example shown in Figure 5-13, the next text frame unfortunately happens to appear under the headline for the next story.

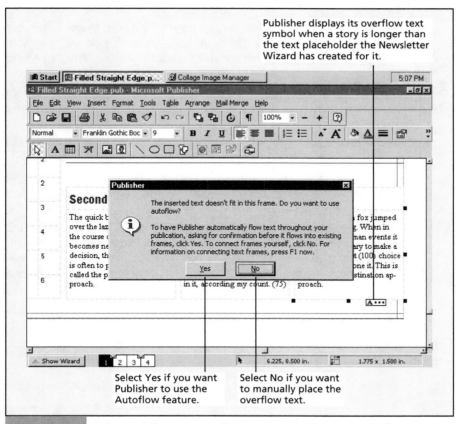

Publisher displays its overflow text symbol when a story is longer than the text placeholder the Newsletter Wizard has created for it.

Select Yes if you want Publisher to use the Autoflow feature.

Select No if you want to manually place the overflow text.

FIGURE 5-13 When Publisher cannot fit your story in the designated text placeholder, you will see this warning message

When you are fitting stories into text frames, you will rarely have stories that fit the text placeholders perfectly. To make stories fit the existing Newsletter Wizard text frames, you have some options. You can click the Yes button if you want Publisher to autoflow the text into the next text frame. If you select this option, you may have to make some simple, subtle layout changes, such as altering or deleting the next story's headline area. If you do not want Publisher to autoflow the text into the next text frame for you, you will have to place the remaining text into placeholders manually. This option is not difficult, and it gives you more control over the newsletter contents, but it does require slightly more expertise than simply using Publisher's Autoflow feature.

Managing Overflow Text

Resist the urge to allow Publisher to automatically flow the text to the next available frame. Consider, instead, several other solutions to fit the story into the text placeholder, some of which are:

- **Edit**   Go back to your word-processed story and check its length using your word processor's Word Count feature. If your story is just a bit too long (more than 175 to 200 words), you may be able to reduce it to length by eliminating unnecessary words or replacing long words with short words.

- **Subdivide the story**   This involves dividing a long story into two or more shorter stories. Often, problems of story length are based on a lack of story focus.

- **Change the layout**   This option involves removing one or more stories and increasing the size of the current story's text frames.

- **Eliminate photographs**   If the layout contains photographs placed within the text frames, removing the photographs might create the space necessary to accommodate the story.

- **Continue the story on another page**   This process involves linking the overflow text that can't fit into the desired text frame to be carried over to another text frame of your selection. The overflow text frame you choose may be on another page, so remember to add a "Continued on" notice on the page where the story breaks, and a "Continued from" notice to mark the text placeholder where the story continues. Without these directions, your readers will not be able to easily find where stories continue and end.

Note that the Overflow Text symbol disappears when you edit the text so that it fits the available text frame.

Continue working on your newsletter, replacing headline placeholders with appropriate text and replacing story placeholders with your stories. When you have finished replacing all your headline and story placeholders, save your work by selecting File | Save (or press CTRL-S), and print your in-process version of your newsletter by selecting File | Print (or press CTRL-P). Publisher will display the Print dialog box. Click OK and Publisher will print your newsletter.

LINKING TEXT FRAMES   One solution involves replacing a story on an inside page with text continued from the front page. Start by identifying the weakest story on an inside page. (Try to locate a story with less immediacy than the others, so you can run the story in the next issue of your newsletter.) To link a story to another text placeholder—rather than using Autoflow—follow these steps:

Tip: What you *don't* want to do is to reduce the type size of the story. Never use small text as a cure for poor editing. Readership goes down as type size decreases. Never make readers struggle to read your words. Reducing the type size in one article of your newsletter is also a sure-fire way to undermine your newsletter's appearance. Your newsletter will project a very unprofessional image if one or two of the articles are set in a slightly smaller type size.

1. Starting with the story you are replacing, begin by replacing the story's headline. Triple-click the headline and replace it with a one- or two-word summary of the headline used on the front page where the other article began. Add the word "continued" (in parentheses) after the keyword.

2. Click inside the first text frame of the story you're replacing and select Edit | Highlight Entire Story, or press CTRL-A. All the text in the frame will be selected (highlighted). Select Edit | Delete Text, or press the DELETE key. You can also right-click the selected text and select Delete Text.

3. Return to the first page and select the rightmost text frame (the one with the Overflow Text symbol), then select Tools | Connect Text Frames. When Publisher displays the Connect Text Frames Toolbar, click the Connect Text Frames icon (see Figure 5-14.)

4. The Connect Text Frame insertion pointer turns into what resembles a measuring cup, which indicates that Publisher has marked the text frame as ready to be connected to another frame, also shown in Figure 5-14.

5. Click on the page number of the inside page where you want to continue the story. Place the insertion point over the first text frame of the story, and you'll see that the measuring cup icon looks as though it's going to pour something into the newly selected text frame, as shown in Figure 5-15.

6. Click on the text frame and the overflow text from page 1 will appear in the story on the inside page, flowing into as many connected text frames as you have available in interior pages.

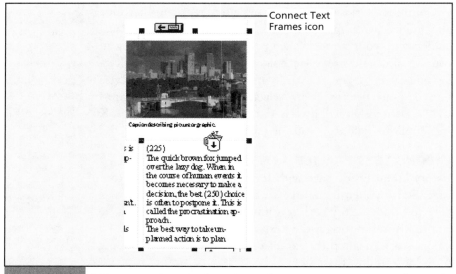

FIGURE 5-14 When you place the insertion pointer over an empty text frame, it turns into a pouring cup, indicating that the frame can be linked to a previous text frame

7. Note also Publisher's symbol that indicates the story continues to another page. Don't forget to add text to direct your reader to where the story continues.

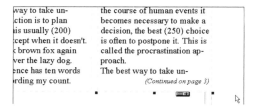

8. To add "Continued to" and "Continued from" directives, click on a text frame that is linked to an inside page, select Format | Text Frame Properties, or right-click the text frame and select ChangeFrame | Text Frame Properties. Publisher will display the Text Frame Properties dialog box, as shown in Figure 5-16. In the Options section of this dialog box, you will see options for wrapping text around objects and including Continued On Page or Continued From Page options.

RESIZING AND DELETING TEXT FRAMES   Another way to handle overflow text involves resizing stories. Often, you can increase the length of text

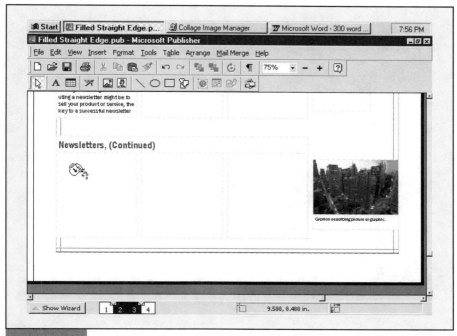

FIGURE 5-15   Text will "pour" to fill as many linked text frames as are available to complete the article

frames for one story by reducing the length of the next story's text frames. This section outlines only one of a myriad of text-fitting options.

Notice that the Text in Overflow symbol appears at the bottom of the right-hand text frame in the top story in Figure 5-17 ("Editing remains the key to success"), even though the story below it is so short that the text doesn't even extend into the third text frame.

The solution is obviously to increase the length of the top article and shorten the bottom article. This is a five-step process:

1. Start by adding rulers to your page, if they are not already visible, by selecting View | Rulers. Hold down the SHIFT key and drag a guide line from the horizontal ruler located along the top of the screen, as shown in Figure 5-18. (Alternatively, you can select Arrange | Ruler Guides | Add | Horizontal Ruler Guide and hold down the SHIFT key while you position the ruler.) This guide line will help you align the tops of the three text frames of the bottom article after you make the text frames shorter.

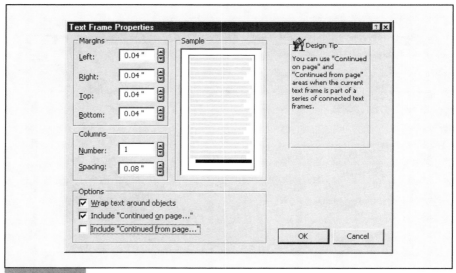

FIGURE 5-16 Use the Text Frame Properties dialog box to add story jump directions

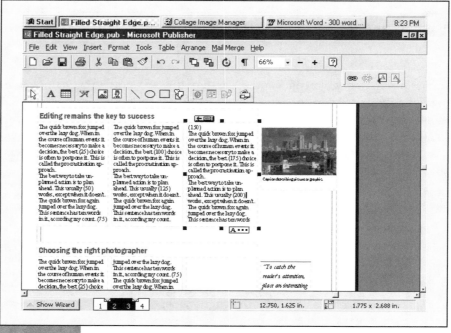

FIGURE 5-17 The top story contains too much text, as indicated by the Text in Overflow symbol, while the bottom article is so short that it doesn't extend into the third text frame

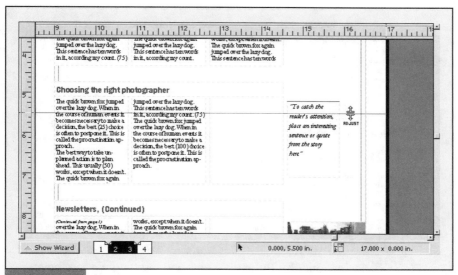

FIGURE 5-18 To accurately align the tops of the text columns in the bottom article after you reduce their height, hold down the SHIFT key and drag a guide line from the ruler

2. Drag the vertical ruler until it is next to the two text columns. Position the mouse pointer on the vertical ruler and wait for the two-headed arrow to appear. Hold down the SHIFT key while you click with the right mouse button along the bottom of the text frames of the top article. This action sets the measurement of the two columns to begin at the zero point now, which appears along the bottom of the top article. Now that you've established the top measurement to zero, you can now measure the distance between the bottom of the top article and the top of the text frame containing the headline of the bottom article. In the example shown in Figure 5-19, you can see that the articles are separated by 7/8 of an inch. This is an important figure, as you will want to maintain this distance when you change the heights of the text frames in the two articles.

3. Click on each of the text frames in the bottom article and drag the center top selection handle in the top center of each text frame down to the guide line. Then click along the edge of the Inside Story Headline text frame and, when the Move symbol appears, reposition the headline next to the top of the text frames of its story. Note how more of the text in the bottom story now appears in the third text frame after its columns have been shortened, as shown in Figure 5-20.

4. Hold down the SHIFT key while right-clicking the vertical ruler next to the top border of the Inside Story Headline text frame. This relocates the zero point along the top of the text frame. Hold down the SHIFT key and drag a

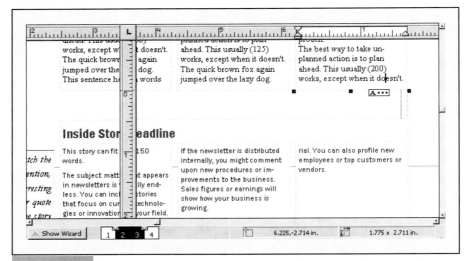

FIGURE 5-19   By repositioning the vertical ruler and resetting the zero point along the bottom of the text frames of the top article, you can see that the bottom headline is 7/8 of an inch lower

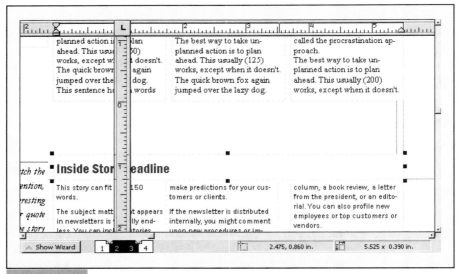

FIGURE 5-20   Reducing the height of the text frames in the lower story creates space for longer text frames in the top story

horizontal ruler guide from the horizontal ruler at the top of the page. (Or select Arrange | Layout Guides | Add Horizontal Ruler Guide.) Hold down the SHIFT key and drag the ruler into a desired position 7/8 of an inch above the top of the bottom headline text frame. This indicates how far down you should resize the text frames of the top story. (See Figure 5-21.)

5. Resize each of the text frames in the top story by dragging them down to the top guide line. This increases the size of the top article while maintaining proper spacing between the two stories, as you can see in Figure 5-22.

Tip: Note that the distance between the two stories may differ, depending on the Newsletter Wizard Design you have chosen. The crucial point, of course, is that you maintain consistent spacing between all of the stories in your newsletter. Readers will quickly note differences in story spacing and begin to subconsciously discount your message.

You'll probably find that some trial and error experimenting will be necessary to figure out how much you need to shorten one story and lengthen another. You'll probably have to repeat the preceding procedure a couple of times to determine the correct amount of space for each story. And, after changing the length of the text frames in each story, you'll still probably have to edit each story to ensure a perfect fit.

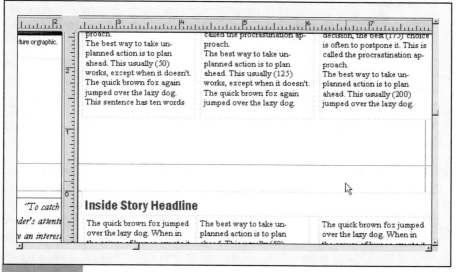

FIGURE 5-21 Adding a second ruler guide and repositioning it 7/8 of an inch from the top of the lower headline text frame preserves spacing between articles when you reposition the text frames in the top article

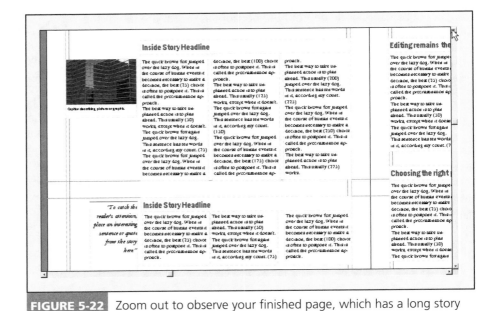

FIGURE 5-22 Zoom out to observe your finished page, which has a long story on top with a shorter story below. A comparison of the left page with the right page emphasizes the differences in story length

Tip: Always click the last text frame in each story after modifying text frames and editing story contents to make sure the Text in Overflow symbol does not appear at the bottom of the text frame.

After you have finished modifying story lengths, save your newsletter by selecting File | Save (or pressing CTRL-S). Save it under the title of the specific month it is scheduled to appear, for example, *Briefings Nov 2000*.

How to Keep Track of What Goes Where

When you're creating large documents—those with more than eight pages—it's a good idea to create a page-tracking method and a plan to follow to keep from getting your pages mixed up. In a four-page document, you'll probably be able to keep track of everything in your head, but that's not a very reliable approach. To keep you from losing your mind, you'll need to develop some skill at keeping the pages and their contents in order.

Once you have completed your layout, you need to print the layout pages with text and graphics placeholders to use as your "map," which in the old days of newspaper publishing used to be called "dummy layouts" or "mock-ups." Pencil in each placeholder what you intend to put in it. If you have to continue a story to another page, note this information on your map, too.

As a double-check, create a form within Publisher or Word to list all the items you want to include in your final document. Save this chart as a template and print one for each document on which you are working. Include the categories in the following bulleted list, and rank your items by the importance they'll have in your document. After you have created a few documents on your own, you may have additional categories you'll want to track, such as issue number, issue date, or theme, if the document on which you are working is a newsletter or catalog.

- Article ranked by number
- Article filename
- Article title
- Article author
- Article due date
- Accompanying graphics by filenames
- Accompanying photos by filenames
- Photo captions
- Page location/layout placement
- Notes for stories that continue to other pages, as well as notes for placement at the spot where the story picks up

Adding Photographs and Captions

After you have replaced the Newsletter Wizard's headlines and story text placeholders with your text, the next step involves replacing the Newsletter Wizard's placeholder photographs with your photographs. You may also want to add additional photographs.

Photographs play a key role in strengthening your message and setting each issue of your newsletter apart from other issues. Photographs are the first thing your readers are likely to look at when they receive each issue.

Go to the first page of your newsletter and click on the photo placeholders near the top of the page. Select Insert | Picture | From File (or right-click the photo and select Change Picture | Picture | From File). Publisher displays the Insert Picture dialog box, shown in Figure 5-23. Browse through the various folders on your computer until you locate the folder containing the photographs you want to include in your newsletter. To preview a photograph, click on its filename. To insert the photograph, click the Insert button (or press ENTER).

Tip: Double-clicking a photograph's filename in Publisher's Insert Picture dialog box inserts the photo and closes the dialog box.

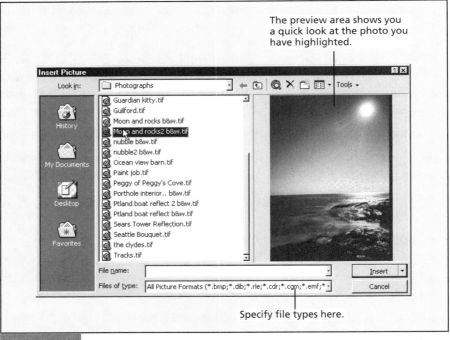

FIGURE 5-23   Locate the photograph you want to insert in your newsletter by browsing through the various folders on your computer. Preview the photographs by clicking on their filename

Note the problem illustrated in Figure 5-24. When you insert a vertical photograph in place of a horizontal photo placeholder, the photograph often appears too small. The problem is that Publisher's Newsletter Wizard has inserted a grouped Object containing a photograph as well as the caption for the photograph. The size of the Object remains the same, although the photograph changes to accommodate the height of the photograph and text wraps tightly around the photograph.

You have three simple solutions to this problem, which are:

- Replace the vertical photograph with a horizontal photograph
- Enlarge the Design Object until the photograph appears the right size
- Ungroup the Design Object so you can resize the photograph and reposition the caption

The easiest solution may be to replace the photograph with a horizontal photograph, if you have one. To replace the photograph, select the photograph and select Insert | Picture | From File (or right-click the photograph and select Change Picture | Picture | From File). The easiest way, of course, is to double-click the photograph.

FIGURE 5-24 Try to avoid replacing horizontal or square photo placeholders with vertical photographs, as size and spacing problems often result

Regardless of which method you use, Publisher again displays the Insert Picture dialog box, where you can select a replacement photograph. Notice how much better the horizontal photograph works, as shown in Figure 5-25.

Another option is to enlarge the photo placeholder Object by dragging one of the corner selection handles. The problem here is that the Object's size is determined by the caption, and in order for the photograph to appear of sufficient size, the caption might extend too far into the adjacent column, as shown in Figure 5-26. The caption may also become too "deep," bigger than you want from a proportional sense.

Tip: Save time by double-clicking a photograph when you want to return to the Insert Picture dialog box.

If you must use a vertical photograph, the best alternative might be to ungroup the photo placeholder Object and resize the photograph, but leave the caption alone. Here are the three steps to ungroup the objects and resize the photo:

1. To ungroup the photo placeholder, click the Ungroup Objects icon along its lower edge. You can also select Arrange | Ungroup Objects (CTRL-SHIFT-G).

2. Click the photograph and drag one of the corner selection handles in the desired direction, until the photograph is resized as desired.

3. Click one of the edges of the caption and when the Move symbol appears, reposition the caption below the photograph, as shown in Figure 5-27.

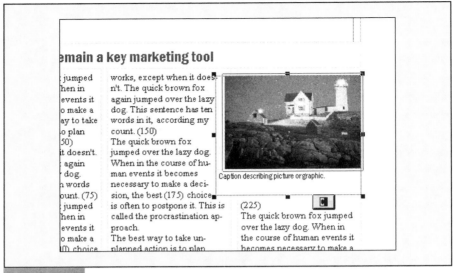

FIGURE 5-25   Horizontal photographs do a much better job of replacing horizontal photo placeholders than vertical photographs, as a acomparison with Figure 5-24 shows

FIGURE 5-26   Resizing the photo placeholder Object to accommodate a vertical photograph may cause the caption to extend too far into the adjacent column

FIGURE 5-27 Ungrouping the photo placeholder Object allows you to resize the photograph without changing the dimensions of the caption

After you have finished, highlight the caption placeholder and enter a caption that identifies the photograph and its significance.

Professional Skills Summary

In this chapter, you learned to use Publisher's Newsletter Wizard to create your first Publisher newsletter. You learned how to create your desired layout with the Wizard, and customize it to suit your personal preferences. After you settled on text and photo placeholders, you learned to fill in the placeholders with your own text and photos. You also learned some techniques for how to modify the layout to fit your desired content. Once you practice the steps outlined in this chapter and successfully create your first Wizard-based newsletter, you'll be able to use that knowledge to produce your first brochure.

Tip: Get in the habit of adding captions while adding photographs. You'll find it's much harder to go back later and try to remember why you included a photograph.

chapter 6

Creating Brochures That Sell

In this chapter, you will:

- Use Publisher 2000's Brochure Wizard to make basic formatting decisions

- Decide a brochure's size and how it will fold, which is central to the overall layout

- Determine how your distribution requirements will affect the brochure's design

- Decide whether to include special items in your brochure's design, such as reply or survey forms

Brochures are the most universally recognized item in business. You can use a brochure to present yourself, your service, your company, your product, and/or your organization. "Do you have a brochure?" is the second most-asked question in business, with "May I have your business card?" running first. Publisher 2000 has you covered either way—with coordinated designs, of course! In earlier parts of this book, we discussed business cards, and this chapter explains the Publisher brochure basics.

What Is a Brochure?

The average person may have never stopped to consider the technicalities of what a brochure is. One page, two, or more? Folded? How and where? Color? Photos? How is a brochure different from a flyer? A pamphlet? Aren't they the same names for the same things? If not, how do they differ?

Flyers, in contrast to brochures, tend to be informal and often time-dependent. They are more spontaneous in their appearance and creation, but that doesn't mean they don't play an important role. Brochures are often items that people keep to remind them of an activity, person, place, product, or service. Flyers may come and go, but brochures seem to last forever. The prices that brochures contain may go up, and the model numbers of items contained within change, too. But seeing *that* brochure with the name, address, and phone number was all someone needed to call *that* phone number to inquire about today's current information.

Generally, brochures are printed on better-quality paper than flyers, most likely because brochures will generally last longer. Common are the three- or four-fold designs that are easy to mail and also easier to produce by focusing on one major idea per panel. Designers plan to print both sides of a single sheet of paper folded to make brochures. You can hand brochures directly to prospects, mail them, or display them in literature racks. When complete, folded, stapled, or finished in a variety of ways, the most common size of brochure fits into a standard #10 envelope, measuring 4 1/8 inches wide by 9 1/2 inches long (10.4 by 24.1 cm.).

The Microsoft Publisher 2000 Brochure Wizard easily creates brochures that provide a framework for your message. And as with all of Publisher 2000's other Wizards we have worked with so far, all you have to do once Publisher's Wizard completes its activity is replace Publisher's placeholders with your specific text and visual objects.

Creating the Brochure That Suits Your Message

To create a brochure with a Publisher 2000 Wizard, select File | New if you are working on another document within Publisher 2000. If you need to start Publisher 2000 from the Windows desktop, remember that Publisher will first display its Catalog, so you can begin your work from this point. Publisher will display the Catalog Wizards list. Select the Brochures category to see the options shown in Figure 6-1. Publisher permits you to choose one of six different types of brochures. Which Brochure Wizard design you select will depend on how you want your brochure to look.

From the Catalog Wizards display list, you can scroll through the brochure options listed to see the designs previewed at right. Select the desired brochure,

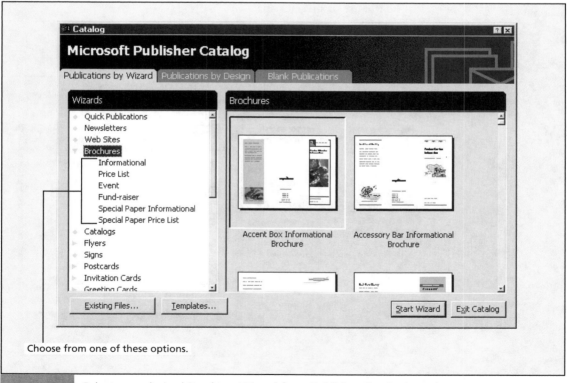

Choose from one of these options.

FIGURE 6-1   Select your desired Brochure Wizard from Publisher Catalog's options

and click on the Start Wizard button to begin working on your brochure. Publisher displays the Brochure Wizard's Introduction screen, as shown in Figure 6-2.

Reviewing Your Design Options

When you click on the Design option in the Brochure Wizard's options pane, Publisher's Brochure Wizard offers you six basic brochure design variations: Informational, Price List, Event, Fund-raiser, Special Paper Informational, and Special Paper Price List. With the Brochure Wizard's Design option, you can review both the front and back pages as you explore each of these variations. Each Brochure Wizard's interactive instructions contain graphic and text placeholders to guide you as you decide on your desired message and reinforce that core message with graphics.

Let's take a look at each of the four Brochure Wizard design variations that do not require the use of special paper.

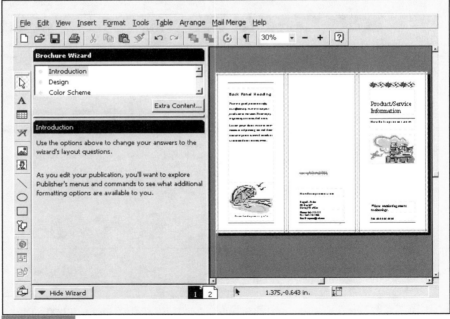

FIGURE 6-2   The Brochure Wizard's Introduction screen reminds you that you can fine-tune your brochure by addressing the questions associated with each of the Wizard's options

Professional Pointer

Special paper includes paper in a wide range of colors and special designs intended to work with design layout templates in the most popular word processors and desktop publishing software, such as Microsoft Word and Publisher 2000. Special papers, which come in various sizes including coordinated business cards and envelopes, are already printed in decorated, colorful themes. When you use a Design Wizard that is customized for use with a special paper, you don't have to add art or color. All you have to do is create the black printed text to show over the colored, themed special paper. The ink placement in combination with the template and the special paper's colors and designs offer incredibly creative and diverse options. Publisher 2000 has special designs tailored to work exclusively with certain types of special paper in Publisher's Wizards' Informational and Price List categories.

INFORMATIONAL   The first of six brochure layout options, the Informational Brochure Wizard design presents the text and graphics placeholders in a straight forward way. This Wizard easily and effectively presents your message in a simple three-column design. (See Figure 6-3.)

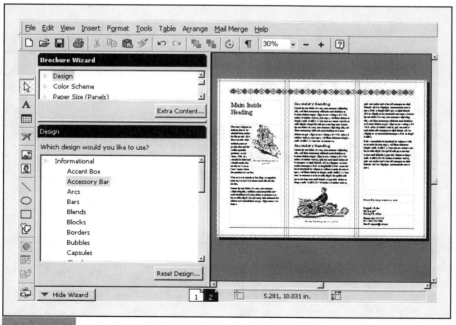

FIGURE 6-3   The inside spread of an Informational brochure contains space to describe and illustrate your message

PRICE LIST   Price List brochures replace the text placeholders typically found on the inside panels of Informational brochures with tables, as shown in Figure 6-4. These tables make it easy to maintain consistent spacing between items and their prices.

EVENT   Event brochures provide a framework for building attendance at a particular seminar on a particular date at a particular time, as the front panel placeholders in Figure 6-5 show.

FUND-RAISER   The front panel of a Fund-raiser brochure contains a simple title and a graphic placeholder designed to symbolize your organization's goals, as shown in Figure 6-6. It provides a framework for an attention-grabbing visual element that establishes an emotional appeal, which is reinforced by the text on the inside panels.

Selecting the Right Color Scheme

When you click on the Color Scheme option, the Brochure Wizard will ask you: "Which color scheme would you like to use?" Click on any of the pre-coordinated color scheme options, and your choice is previewed in the right pane of the Wizard's screen, as shown in Figure 6-7.

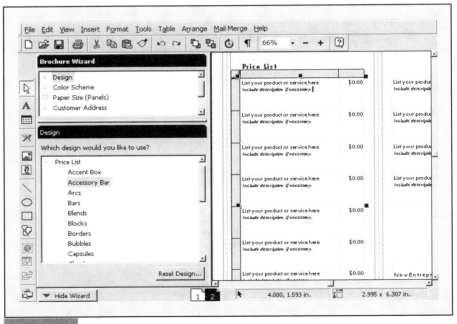

FIGURE 6-4   Tables on the inside panels of Price List brochures ensure good-looking results by maintaining consistent spacing

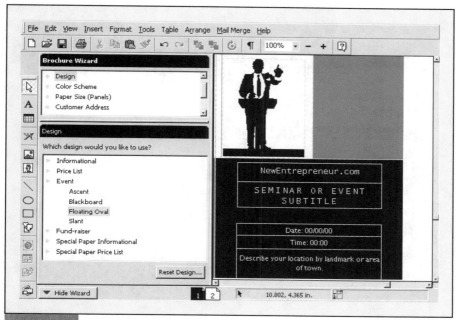

FIGURE 6-5 Event brochures contain placeholders for you to replace with the text and graphics describing a specific event

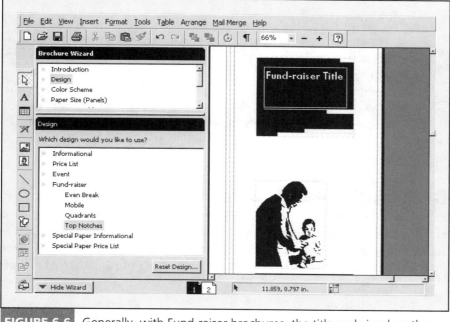

FIGURE 6-6 Generally, with Fund-raiser brochures, the title and visual on the front panel communicate a story, which is reinforced by details on the inside panels

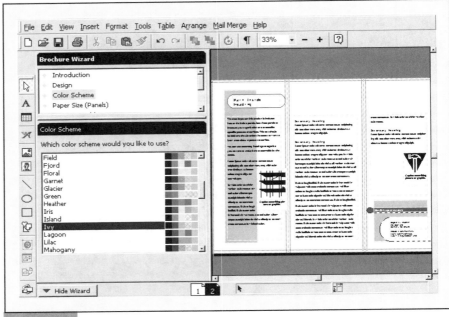

FIGURE 6-7   You can choose a color scheme from the pre-coordinated color scheme options

Tip: Take a few moments to try out different color schemes, especially if you're creating a Fund-raising brochure. Notice how your response to the same text and graphic placeholders changes depending on the color scheme you choose.

You have two approaches when you choose a brochure color scheme. If you have chosen the Brochure Wizard's Informational or Price List design variation, choose the same color scheme as the one you picked for your business card, letterhead, and other print communications. If you are using one of the other options, choose either the color scheme that's closest to your other marketing communications or choose a color scheme that projects the desired appropriate emotional image. The decision you make depends on the goal you hope to achieve with this specific brochure.

Choosing a Paper Size

Paper size is central to your brochure's layout. Your choice of paper size depends, in part, on how you plan to print your brochure. If you plan to print your brochure yourself on your desktop printer, consider the paper-size limitations of your printer. Your choice of paper size also determines the number of panels your brochure contains. (Panels are similar to pages, except that your reader will see all the panels on one side of a brochure at once, when the viewer unfolds the brochure.)

When you click on the Paper Size (Panels) option, Publisher offers two paper-size options. The letter-size default is for brochures printed on standard 8 1/2 by 11-inch paper. This size option creates a three-panel brochure with two folds. The second option is legal size (8 and 1/2-inch by 14-inch). If your printer can print legal-size paper, you may want to use this size option. (Note that most laser printers require a special paper tray to accommodate legal-size paper). Brochures printed on legal-size paper contain four panels with three folds, as shown in Figure 6-8. Each panel is slightly narrower with the legal-size option than with the letter-size option.

If you are preparing files for a commercial printer, of course, you can choose either option. However, you will need an ink-jet or laser printer with PostScript capability to print proofs in your office. (Publisher will automatically resize your legal-size brochure to fit on a standard 8 1/2 by 11-inch sheet of paper if you have a PostScript printer.)

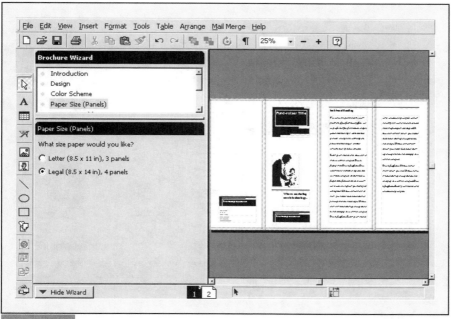

FIGURE 6-8   Legal-size brochures contain four panels instead of the three found on letter-size brochures

Making Your Brochure a Self-Mailer

As with flyers, newsletters, and other forms of printed communications, you can add an area to include the customer's address. Click the Customer Address option in the Brochure Wizard's options pane. The Brochure Wizard asks you if you'd like to have a placeholder for the customer's address. If you click Yes, your firm or organization's return address information plus a placeholder for the customer's mailing information will appear on the back panel of your brochure, as shown in Figure 6-9.

> **Tip:** If you are preparing files for a copy center or commercial printer, be sure to delete the Customer placeholder.

The Customer Address option is especially valuable when using the Special Papers Informational or Special Papers Price List design option, because you can have Publisher address your brochures as you prepare them.

Cross-Reference: For more information about having Publisher address your brochures, see Chapter 14.

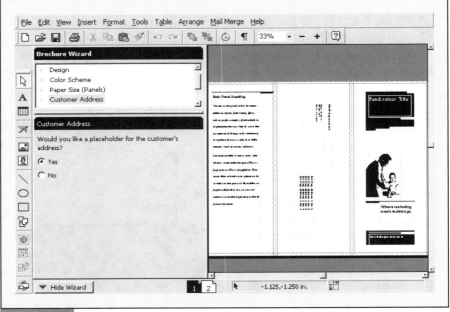

FIGURE 6-9 Selecting the Customer Address option converts your brochure into a self-mailer

Making It Easy for Readers to Respond to Your Offer

Click the Brochure Wizard's Form option, and Publisher will offer you three ways to make it easy for readers to respond to your order or give you the information you desire. These options are explained in the following sections. If you decide that you do not want your brochure to include any of Publisher's variations of the Form option, return to the Brochure Wizard's Form option selection screen and select None. Publisher will then remove any previously inserted Form choices.

Order Form

If you select the Order Form option, the Brochure Wizard reformats your brochure and adds an order form to the inside-right panel. Publisher displays a prompt that tells you to take a look at page 2 of your brochure to view the order form, shown in Figure 6-10.

Response Form

The Response Form option, shown in Figure 6-11, offers even more choices than the Form option. When you are sending Informational brochures to prospects, you can use a response form to make it easy for readers to request further information about specific products or services, and to gather information about your prospective clients and customers. This technique also creates a list for later telephone or in-person follow-up. If you are surveying your organization's members or supporters, you can use response forms to encourage them to express their opinions about important questions or express their concerns.

You are not limited to using the Response Form's four major questions. You can easily customize the Response Form by deleting the Comments box and copying and pasting two additional questions of your choosing to present your readers with six questions to which they may respond, as shown in Figure 6-12.

To replace the Comments box with two additional questions:

1. Click the Comments box and select Edit | Cut (or press CTRL-X or press the DELETE key).

2. Click the Comments text placeholder and select Edit | Cut (or press CTRL-X or press the DELETE key).

3. Place the insertion point above and to the left of the second question and—while you are holding down the left mouse button—drag down and to

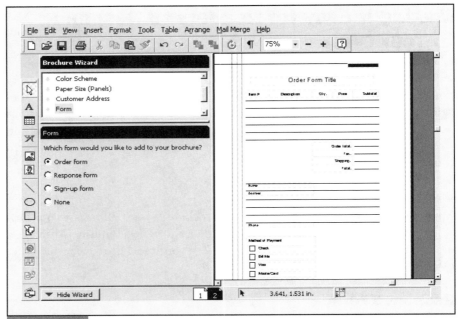

FIGURE 6-10 Order forms make it easy for customers to purchase any products you offer by mail

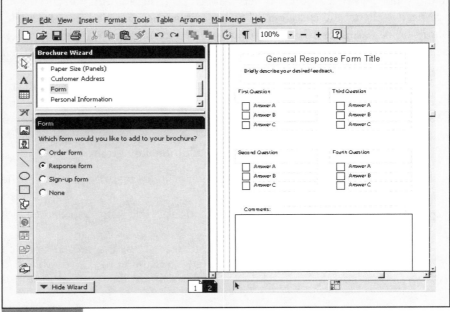

FIGURE 6-11 A response form makes it easy for readers to request further information or express their opinions

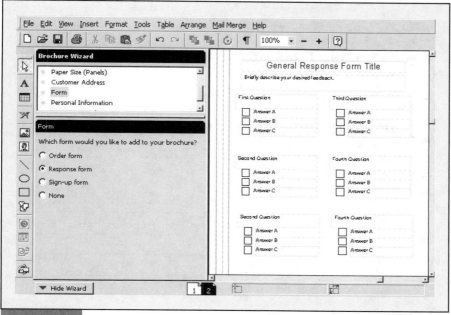

FIGURE 6-12 You can easily customize the Response Form by replacing the Comments box with two additional questions

the right of the fourth question, creating a marquee box around the lower two questions and responses.

4. Select Edit | Copy (or press CTRL-C or select the Copy icon in the Standard Toolbar).

5. Select Edit | Paste (or press CTRL-V or select the Paste icon in the Standard Toolbar).

6. Select the pasted copy of the questions. When Publisher displays the Move icon, drag the pasted text frames into the space recently occupied by the Comments box you deleted. Be sure to maintain consistent spacing between the three pairs of questions in this section of the layout.

Sign-up Form

The third option you can choose from the Brochure Wizard's Form options is a Sign-up Form. If you are preparing a membership brochure with different prices for different membership categories, or if you are promoting a daylong series of seminars and workshops, this brochure form option will work well. The Sign-up Form permits you to list six different events or price categories, which readers can respond to by simply adding a check mark next to the desired option, as shown in Figure 6-13.

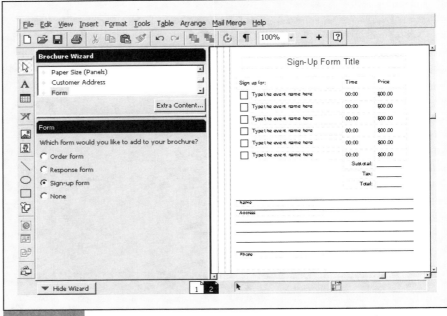

FIGURE 6-13   The sign-up form makes it easy for prospective members or contributors to indicate their desired level of participation

Adding Personal Information

If you want to add information contained with the Personal Information option as part of your Brochure Wizard creation, use the Personal Information option.

As with the other Wizards, the Brochure Wizard also allows you to insert the information you've entered into Publisher from your Primary Business (the default), your Secondary Business, Other Organization, or Home/Family.

Cross-Reference: For more information on entering varying sets of personal information, see Chapter 2.

Be warned, however, that if you later return to the Brochure Wizard and select a different Design option, your Publisher-inserted Personal Information components will not be reformatted to match the new design. Likewise, the Brochure Wizard will not recolor any inserted components, should you choose a different

Tip: You, not the Brochure Wizard, are responsible for formatting and properly placing inserted components. You must choose the proper typeface and type size for additional personal information added to your brochure. You also have to select and drag the components to their desired locations.

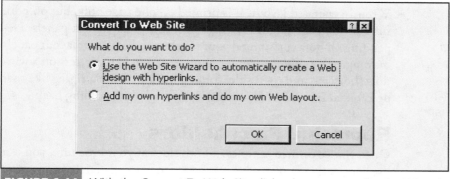

FIGURE 6-14 With the Convert To Web Site dialog box, you can let the Wizard automatically create your Web site or you can format the Web site and add hyperlinks yourself

color scheme. For these reasons, use inserted components with care and double-check your work before printing.

Converting a Brochure into a Web Site

The last option offered by Publisher's Brochure Wizard is the Convert to Web option. I don't recommend that you use this option at this point. If you want to make a Web site for your business or organization, there are many additional items for you to consider other than simply using the Brochure Wizard's Convert to Web option.

If you do want to use the Convert to Web option, however, complete your brochure's design and replace all the Wizard's text and graphics placeholders with your own information. Print and proof the completed brochure, and then select the Brochure Wizard's Convert to Web option. Click the Create button. Publisher displays the Convert To Web Site dialog box, as shown in Figure 6-14. You can use the Web Site Wizard option to automatically create a Web design with hyperlinks (the default), or you can create your own hyperlinks and your own Web layout with the material you've placed into the Brochure Wizard's text and graphics placeholders.

Completing Your Brochure

The Brochure Wizard has now created your brochure layout. All that remains is to replace the text and graphic placeholders with your specific information. Save and print your brochure at this point so you can get an idea of the graphics and amount of text needed to complete your brochure. Look at your just-completed

L▶ Tip: You should print out a copy of your brochure with placeholders *before* you start to add your own text and graphics. With a hardcopy in your hands that you can fold, it's easy to see exactly how your selected design will look.

Wizard-generated layout. It is printed on one page only, but on both sides of the page. With the two folds, this gives you six panels. Depending on how you wanted your brochure folded, your layout panels may logically progress in order of presentation like shutters on a window (both left and right sides folding inward), or in a zigzag like that of a folded fan (left side folding in and right side folding back).

Replacing Placeholders

Once you've printed samples of both sides of your brochure, you can use your design to plan where you want to place material of your own. To create some working space on your screen, first click the Hide Wizard button in the Status Bar, or if you cannot see the Status Bar, select View | Hide Wizard. In addition to giving yourself some additional working space, you can increase the front panel's size by altering the screen's Zoom level until you can comfortably read the text placeholders. Select View | Zoom and choose an appropriate Zoom level. If you are working with the Standard Toolbar visible, you can click the Zoom In icon as many times as you like. By cleaning your screen of unnecessary distractions, you can concentrate on creating your pencil-marked plan of the brochure's content based on the Wizard's design work.

Cross-Reference: For more information on creating a pencil-marked layout or plan to follow as you fill in your placeholders, see Chapter 5.

Creating an Attractive Front Cover

As you begin to replace placeholders, use the Status Bar Page Indicator icon to start working on your brochure's Page 1. Click the Page 1 icon in the Status Bar, or continue to click right-pointing arrow keys on the horizontal scroll bar until you can see your Brochure Wizard's title page, as shown in Figure 6-15. Note that the Brochure Wizard usually adds your organization's name and tagline to the front panel of most brochure designs, so you might see these objects on the pre-designed brochure title panel.

On your brochure's front panel, click the Product/Service Information placeholder. Note that a single click highlights all of the text. Enter the desired title. When you are selecting wording for a printed item as important as your brochure's title panel, be as concise as possible. Brochure Wizard's AutoFit feature will automatically choose the best type size for your title. The more words you include, the smaller the type size the Wizard will choose. If you use few, short, and direct words, Publisher's Wizard will be able to keep the type size large, for a greater visual impact on your brochure's first page.

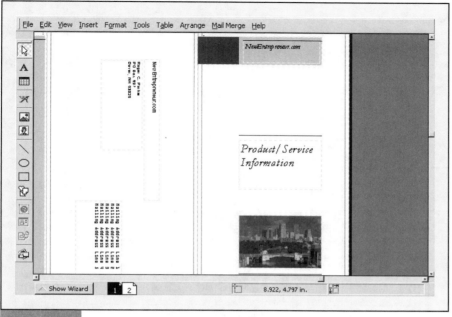

FIGURE 6-15 Your Wizard-created brochure front panel contains placeholders for your brochure's title and an appropriate visual element

You will also need to replace the text placeholders with your own text as you did with other Publisher Wizards. Remember that you can double-click a placeholder graphic and replace it with another piece of Publisher clip art. When you double-click the placeholder, Publisher displays the Insert Clip Art dialog box, shown in Figure 6-16, and will preview the available options.

If you prefer to use some other graphic item than clip art, you can right-click the graphic placeholder, and Publisher will display a graphics-context-sensitive floating menu. From this menu, select Change Picture | Picture | From File, and Publisher will display the Insert Picture dialog box, shown in Figure 6-17. From this dialog box, you can import a photo from another source, such as photos you may have taken and stored on disk. When you locate the file you need, double-click that option, or select it with a single click and then click the Insert button.

Once you have your graphics file replaced with your own written material and your photo is showing on your brochure's title panel, you will be able to see your brochure taking shape—becoming a personal expression, your business's expression, or your organization's expression. Note that each addition or modification makes the Brochure Wizard's work more your own creation. (See Figure 6-18.)

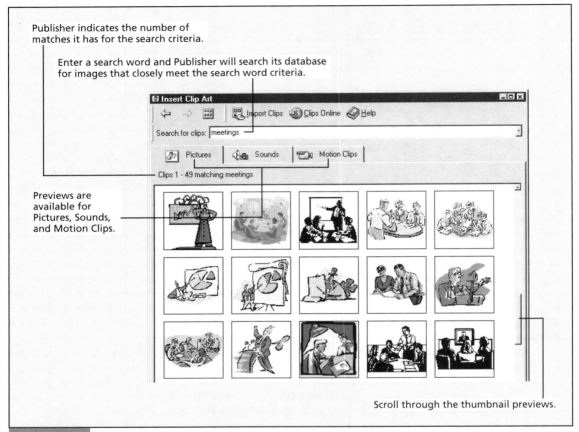

Publisher indicates the number of matches it has for the search criteria.

Enter a search word and Publisher will search its database for images that closely meet the search word criteria.

Previews are available for Pictures, Sounds, and Motion Clips.

Scroll through the thumbnail previews.

FIGURE 6-16 From the Insert Clip Art dialog box, you can search for clip art to find the exact image with which to replace the placeholder

Every time you modify the brochure, be sure to save the variations of your work, and you will need to remember to save the brochure when you have completed your work on the title panel.

Completing the Back Panel

Click the left-pointing arrow until the back panel of your brochure appears, as shown in Figure 6-19. The back panel is especially important, as it provides a quick summary to which many readers will turn, and they'll return to it later to reread after reading the inside panels.

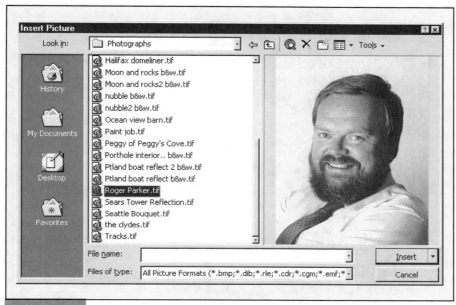

Use the Insert Picture dialog box to import a photo from anywhere on your computer or via scanner or disk file

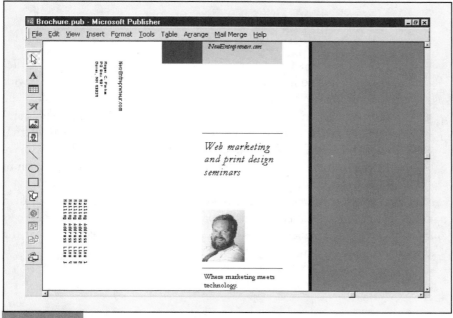

Each time you replace a text or graphic placeholder with your message and/or graphic, your brochure becomes a personal expression of your marketing goals

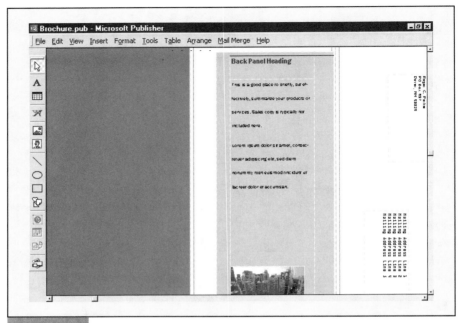

Use the back panel of your brochure to summarize the most important points communicated on the inside pages of your brochure

Tip: Notice, in Figure 6-20, how even generic clip art, such as the image of the Sydney, Australia, Opera House, can provide support for an idea.

Note, as when you have replaced Wizard placeholders in earlier chapters, all you need to do is click the placeholder and replace it with your message. Write as simply and to the point as possible. The shorter your sentences, the better. Edit to the bone. Be especially careful not to write more text than a text frame can accommodate. Watch for the Text In Overflow icon; that is your indication that you have written more text than the text frame can accommodate, as shown in Figure 6-20.

Now that your outside brochure panels are successfully filled with your own material, you need to complete the inside panels. Click the Page 2 icon to access your brochure's inside panels. Continue replacing the placeholder text for the headlines and body copy text.

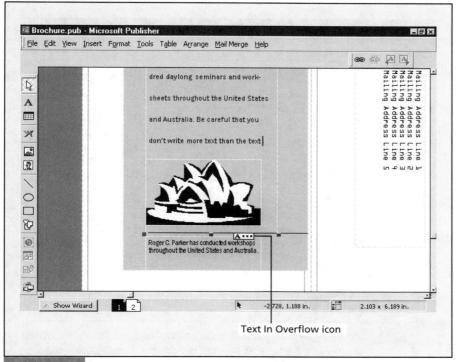

Text In Overflow icon

FIGURE 6-20   When replacing text placeholders, always check the bottom of the text frame to make sure the Text In Overflow icon does not appear

Resizing and Repositioning Graphic Placeholders

When replacing graphic placeholders with clip art or photographs, whenever possible choose a replacement illustration or photograph the same shape as the original placeholder.

Occasionally, you may need to resize and reposition a graphic placeholder after replacing it, as shown in Figure 6-21. The replacement photograph was not as tall as the original graphic placeholder. In addition, the short caption did not completely fill the space allotted for it, trapping white space between the caption and the text below it.

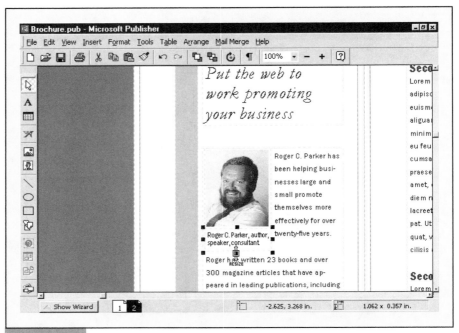

When replacing text placeholders, be alert for situations where the picture frame and caption need repositioning or resizing

The solution for that problem can be repaired with three easy steps:

1. Start by repositioning the picture frame and caption. Click on the picture frame. When the Move icon appears, drag the picture frame upward, so that the top of the picture frame will align with the top of the text frame.

2. Next, select the Ungroup Objects icon below the picture frame. This will permit you to resize the caption without inadvertently resizing the photograph.

3. Finally, click the caption and resize the text frame by dragging one of the lower selection handles upward.

Fine-tuning details results in a much better brochure, free of distracting gaps between photographs, captions, and adjacent text. Always be on the lookout for opportunities where repositioning and/or resizing are necessary. A few minutes' work can greatly improve the appearance of your brochure.

Customizing and Completing Forms

The last major step involved in completing most brochures is to customize and complete any forms you may have added with the Brochure Wizard.

To complete your form, simply replace the headline, "sign up for," and place-holder text.

Sometimes, however, the form may contain too many columns or too many lines, such as might occur if you use the Sign-up Form to indicate various categories of membership dues, as shown in Figure 6-22. The Time column is not needed, and there are only five dues categories for members.

To eliminate the unnecessary Time text frames, simply select them one at a time and select Edit | Cut or press CTRL-X. You can also right-click the text frame and select Cut.

Next, select the "Type the event name here" placeholder and, again, select Edit | Cut or press CTRL-X. You can also right-click the text frame and select Cut.

Tip: Do not select the text or use the DELETE key, because Publisher will then only cut the text, not the text frame itself.

Within a few moments, your form is completed and looks good, as shown in Figure 2-23, without requiring you to spend any unnecessary time spacing the text elements.

The Brochure Wizard always enters your firm or organization's name and address below forms. Depending on the particular design you have chosen, there may be space between the bottom of the form and your firm's address to add a text frame reminding members (or donors, and so on) to mail the form to you.

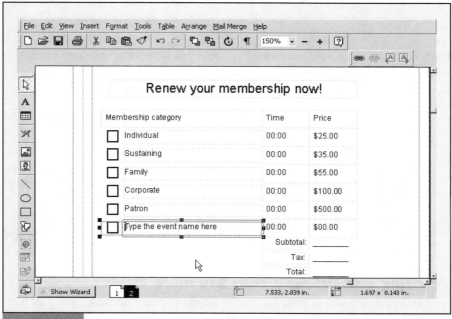

FIGURE 6-22 Some forms have unnecessary columns or lines

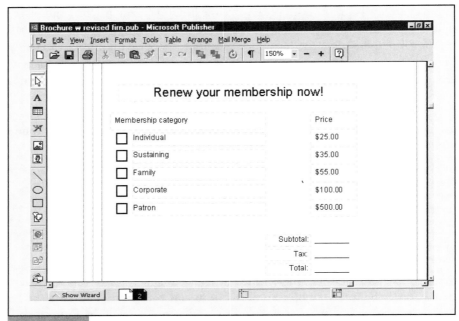

FIGURE 6-23   Eliminating the unwanted placeholders quickly results in a form custom-tailored for use as a membership builder

Even better, if all of your brochures are going to be sent at the same time, you might build immediacy into your offering, encouraging a positive response, by providing a deadline. Here are the four steps to add a reminder and a closer:

1. Select the Text icon in the Objects Toolbar and drag to create a text frame below your form.

2. Enter the desired text.

3. To format the text the same as your address, click on one of the words in your address and select the Format Painter icon in the Formatting Toolbar. (If the Formatting Toolbar is not visible, select Format | Pick Up Formatting.)

4. When the Paintbrush icon appears next to the insertion point, highlight the text you have just entered (or highlight the text and select Format | Apply Formatting).

Proofing and Printing Your Brochure

Save and print a proof of your brochure. Go through it and make sure you have not inadvertently omitted replacing one of the text or graphic placeholders.

Check your spelling one last time. Select Tools | Spelling | Check Spelling. Make sure that Publisher checks the spelling of every story (text frame) in your brochure, by clicking the Yes button when the prompt appears asking if you want to check the rest of your publication.

Pay particular care to the spelling of proper nouns. Avoid the temptation of absently clicking Ignore every time the same proper noun is encountered, because one of those times you may have misspelled it. Make sure you have added trademark symbols next to any brand names that may appear in your brochure.

Cross-Reference: If you are taking your brochure to a commercial printer for four-color printing, see Chapter 15.

Professional Skills Summary

In this hands-on chapter, I explained how to use Publisher 2000's Brochure Wizard to create a custom-looking brochure to fit a variety of important uses. Because creating a brochure calls for some experience to make the final result an effective one, we took a look at some of the core brochure-creating issues you need to consider that will help you as you make basic formatting decisions. For example, deciding how the brochure will fold—an issue that pertains directly to creating brochures—is a topic managed well by Publisher's Brochure Wizard. Also, deciding important issues regarding your brochure's distribution, or whether to include reply or survey forms, were examined from the vantage point of a professional advisor, since Publisher 2000's Brochure Wizard doesn't directly guide decisions for you. Once you have completed the materials covered in this chapter, you will have the knowledge to create a professional-looking brochure about any topic. Now that you've mastered brochure basics, we turn our attention to the task of creating a much more demanding publication—the catalog—with Publisher's Catalog Wizard.

chapter 7

Producing Your First Catalog

In this chapter, you will:

- Use Publisher's Catalog Wizard to create your catalog's design

- Decide how best to profile your products in your catalog

- Replace the Wizard's text and graphics placeholders with your own material

- Modify your catalog's design to suit your needs

New to Publisher 2000 is the Catalog Wizard, which dramatically reduces the work required to produce these multipage documents that used to have the capacity to cause a major headache.

Catalogs are difficult to design because of their complexity. Not only do they typically contain several pages, but each page is likely to contain a different mix of products. Moreover, catalogs often include several different page layouts: some pages contain just text, others one or two products, and still others many products.

The Publisher 2000 Catalog Wizard helps you get started by preparing a *dummy*, a practice page layout with placeholders showing the text and picture contents of each page. Printing this dummy helps you organize your project and see at a glance which text headlines, text, and captions need to be written, and which photographs or artwork need to be produced and organized. With a pencil and eraser, you can plan which products to place on each page and—when necessary—choose new layouts for various pages.

Cross-Reference: For more information on dummy layouts, see Chapters 5 and 6.

Reviewing Publisher's Wizards' Operations

Creating a catalog with Publisher's Catalog Wizard involves the same basic steps as the Wizards we have used in previous chapters (for flyers, newsletters, and brochures). The process for creating catalogs is different from other publications, however, because a catalog contains more pages and is more complex in its construction, with additional design elements such as cover page, back page, coupons, and so on. To accommodate a wide range of design needs, Publisher's Catalog Wizard offers 19 layout options for internal pages. The internal page design (or designs) you pick depends on the products you want to offer in your catalog, and whether you include graphics or photos. Publisher's Catalog Wizard can mix layouts on a page-by-page basis and offer you different designs to accommodate your needs.

In this chapter, we'll first review how the Wizard operates. Then we'll focus on elements that are different from the flyer, brochure, and newsletter examples, including creating a front and back cover for your catalog, mixing differing layouts, and keeping track of your design options while you fill in the Wizard's text and graphics placeholders. If, by chance, you haven't yet worked through the flyer, newsletter, or brochure Wizards, you may want to review the Wizard sections of Chapters 4, 5, and 6.

Maintaining Design Consistency

Before you begin your work with the Catalog Wizard, you'll want to consider the design of your other printed items, such as letterhead and business cards. If you have already designed any of these other publications, your decision about which design to use should be automatic. Consistency between documents is important, so when you're creating a catalog, select the same design you used to create other elements of your organization's visual identity. Synergy—where the whole is greater than the sum of its parts—results when all of your marketing communications project a consistent image.

Working Through the Catalog Wizard's Basic Options

The preliminary steps for starting the Catalog Wizard are very similar to the preliminary steps used with the flyer, newsletter, and brochure Wizards.

Tip: Chaos results if you choose a different Design set for every category of document you create for your firm or organization. Marketing success comes from projecting a consistent image throughout all of your marketing materials. If you use different Design sets for different categories of document, your firm will appear unprofessional and readers will discount your message—before they even begin reading.

1. If you have not yet started Publisher, start the application, and when Publisher displays the list of Wizard options, select the Catalog option. If you are working within Publisher already, select File | New. Publisher will then display the list of Wizard options; select the Catalog Wizard at this point.

2. Drag the vertical scroll bar up and down the right edge of the screen (or click in the area above or below the box) to sample the Catalog Wizard's various Design sets, as shown in Figure 7-1. These Design sets pertain only to the catalog's cover. You will select the design of inside pages in a later step.

3. Highlight your desired cover design and click the Start Wizard button (or double-click the desired design to close the Publisher Catalog dialog box and start the Catalog Wizard). Publisher will create a catalog with a default of 8 pages—with page 8 being the default back cover. You can add pages at a later point in the Wizard's catalog creation process. Once you click the Start Wizard button, Publisher will display the Catalog Wizard's Introduction, which will lead you through the Wizard's catalog-creating process.

4. Publisher will launch the Catalog Wizard and display the Color Scheme options list. Select the same color scheme as your other publications, if you have already created any. If the catalog is your first or only publication, you may select any color option you prefer. When you have selected your desired color scheme, click Next to advance to the next Wizard option.

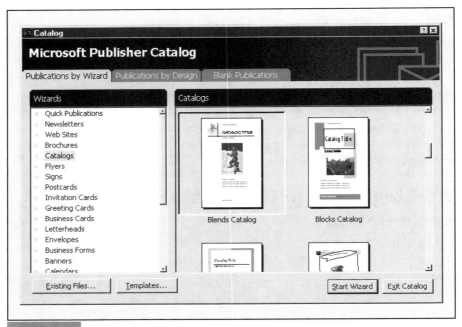

Select your catalog's cover page design from the examples in Publisher's preview window

5. The Wizard will ask you whether you want to add a placeholder for customers' addresses. If you select No, Publisher will display Personal Information Set screen instructions. If you select Yes, Publisher will create a customer address placeholder on page 8, the default back cover. If you plan to have more than 8 pages, Publisher will automatically move the customer address placeholder to the final page in your design, regardless of how many internal pages you add.

6. Publisher then displays the Personal Information Set (organization name, address, phone/fax/e-mail, and so on). At this point, you may choose any of the Personal Information Sets you may have entered for yourself, your business or other organization, or you may choose to not insert any Personal Information Set. Publisher also lets you update your saved Personal Information Sets. With this step, you can also add an additional Personal Information Component, such as a tag line, into your catalog.

7. Once you have completed the Catalog Wizard Personal Information Set step, click Finish to complete the introductory part of Publisher's Catalog Wizard. Publisher will generate an 8-page catalog featuring the cover design you've selected.

Reviewing Your Catalog Wizard Options

Once Publisher has created the design you've selected, the Wizard displays the catalog layout on the screen's right, and the entire list of design element options involved in creating the catalog, including options you have already selected and options you've yet to consider. Publisher redisplays some design options in case you want to change your mind about any of the selections you've made. Those Wizard options are:

- Design
- Color Scheme
- Inside Page Content
- Insert Page
- Customer Address
- Personal Information

Throughout the Catalog Wizard's interactive introduction, you have already made preliminary selections for Design (cover page only), Color Scheme, Customer Address, and Personal Information. If you would like to change any of these selections, click on that option, and the Wizard will redisplay the interactive instructions to guide you through any changes you want to make. You will next make selections to select inside page content and additional page insertions.

Determining Internal Page Contents

When you create a catalog, your inside page layout is just as critical as the design of your front and back cover. If you don't properly design your inside pages to best profile your products or services, your catalog won't do the selling job you need. Publisher provides you with 19 distinct inside page layout options, and does not place any limitations on which of these layouts you use. You can mix and match any of the options to give each of your products the best possible catalog exposure.

Select the Inside Page Content option from the Catalog Wizard. Note that before you can use the Inside Page Content option, you must be working on an inside page displayed in Publisher's work area. If you don't have an inside page displayed in the work area, Publisher will display a message prompting you to turn to an interior page.

You navigate through your catalog's pages by clicking on the Page Navigation icon along the screen's bottom. For instance, you'd move to page 2 by clicking on the 2–3 Page Navigation icon, as shown in Figure 7-2.

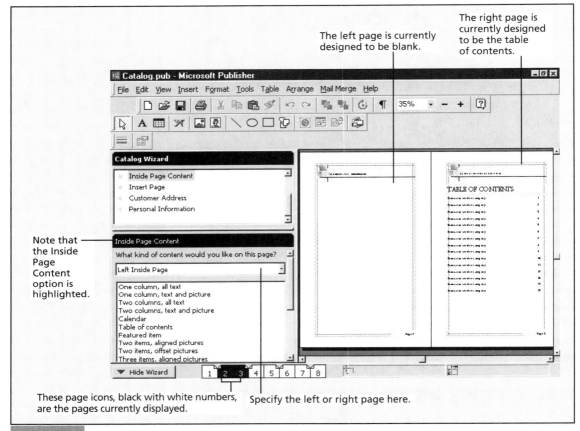

The left page is currently designed to be blank.

The right page is currently designed to be the table of contents.

Note that the Inside Page Content option is highlighted.

These page icons, black with white numbers, are the pages currently displayed.

Specify the left or right page here.

FIGURE 7-2   This two-page spread is ready for you to select designs for each side

The Inside Page Content screen allows you to specify either the Left Inside Page or the Right Inside Page, and select for each one a distinct design tailored for your needs on a specific page. Click the down arrow to choose between the left or right pages. Notice that Publisher offers so many inside page design options that Microsoft added a vertical scroll bar to this section of the screen to assist you in reviewing your options.

Selecting the right design for each page and the products it features is critical when you design a catalog, so before you begin to customize your catalog's inside pages, take plenty of time to familiarize yourself with each Inside Page Content design option. The following sections briefly describe each inside page design option, including advantages and disadvantages, where applicable. Examples of each inside page design option are shown in the following illustrations.

One Column, All Text Use this option for lengthy explanations, product introductions, and detailed descriptions, including product categories and applications. Use prior to the ordering form to explain ordering information, delivery, payment options, shipping fees, return privileges, and so on.

One Column, Text and Picture
This option offers a personalized introduction with a picture or seasonal identification, and best profiles horizontal pictures. Use this design for a category opener or to subdivide a catalog into sections, with text areas used to describe product benefits. You can wrap text around pictures for an informal look.

Two Columns, All Text Use this option for editorial or policy pages with short paragraphs. This design is more formal than the One Column, All Text design and provides a faster-reading option.

Two Columns, Text and Picture
Use this option for describing destinations, themes, events, or procedures. The narrow columns show off numbered or bulleted lists. This design is ideal for vertical and square photographs and features a good balance of text and photos.

Calendar   This option is good for posting scheduled events, especially a holiday shopping countdown. The calendar option is also good for use in seminar brochures, class schedules, or anything date-related.

Table of Contents   This option creates a quick-find item directory; great for quick overview; makes good road map for locating individual product listings.

Featured Item   Use this option to emphasize an important offering. This layout features a large picture placeholder for an image to dominate the page. Use this design when the product's picture speaks for itself. This layout offers a strong "retail feel" and sense of immediacy, and can be used with motivational phrases like "Special purchase," "Closeout," "Last chance," and "While Quantities Last!" This design works well opposite a table of contents page or a form page for maximum impact.

Two Items, Aligned Pictures
Use this option to present an organized, balanced image This layout works well with large photographs.

Two Items, Offset Pictures This design projects a "quiet" image and uses power of offset balance. Due to even distribution of white space, it offers a less dramatic look than the Aligned Pictures option.

Three Items, Aligned Pictures
This options works well with square or horizontal photographs, but it doesn't work well with vertical objects. The concentrated white space above and below the photographs draws the eye into the descriptive text. Your photo choices are limited, however, due to the design's narrowness.

Three Items, Offset Pictures
This option provides balanced page edges. It is less dramatic and less organized than the aligned pictures design. It also places product information farther from picture placeholders than the aligned option. A drawback is that the reader's eyes must move in the opposite direction than usual to read product information, from photo on the right to text on the left.

Three Items, Stacked Pictures
This option is good for combining horizontal and vertical photos, with a vertical photo on the top and horizontal photos at the bottom. This layout equally profiles all items on the page and creates visual interest. The design works well when facing an aligned photo design page. This design puts the "weight" at the page's bottom.

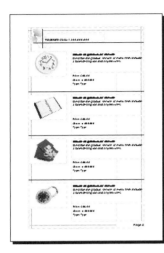

Four Items, Aligned Pictures

This option is good for creating an "open-looking" and organized feel. It offers a good balance because all objects are aligned with each other.

Four Items, Offset Pictures

This option offers dynamic, organized-looking pages. The design causes the reader's eyes to move unconsciously in "zigzag" direction, left to right, scanning the overall page.

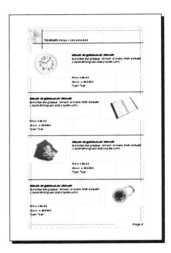

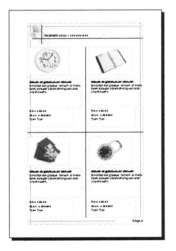

Four Items, Squared Pictures

This option offers a totally balanced presentation, projecting a "safe," static image. This option provides a "can't go wrong" design for use by those with limited design experience, time, or sense of adventure.

Tip: Avoid placing two Three Items, Stacked Pictures pages next to each other. The combination may create a two-page spread that is too horizontal and too balanced. The products in the bottom half of the page may dominate the two-page spread, as it will be very easy for readers to skim the bottom half of the page from left to right, inadvertently paying less attention to the products at the top.

Eight Items, No Pictures, One Column

This option is good for lists of events, such as concerts or seminars. The design naturally leads the reader's eyes across the page. The layout places additional emphasis on each item's price, order number, and keyword.

Eight Items, No Pictures, Two Columns

This option works well for listing retail locations, or for an inside back cover listing of miscellaneous products. It is a good layout for scanning items or columns because it relies on the column flow as a directional design element. This design projects a "classified ads" image.

Blank Page

This option offers a great space for creativity. This layout is good for featuring maps of your store location(s), a coupon, or advertisements of special, or limited-time offers.

Tip: Use care to not place two pages facing each other with both having the Four Items, Squared Pictures option. A two-page spread featuring this layout will be too static and balanced to attract much attention.

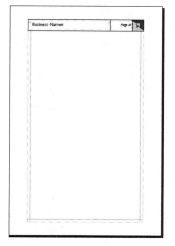

Form Page This option offers a spot for the reader to place an order. The form includes easy-to-fill-out spaces for entering order information, item descriptions, full shipping information, and credit card information.

Additionally, here are some important points to remember about some of the specific inside page design options with which you will want to work. Like any good Wizard, Publisher 2000's Catalog Wizard is capable of "magic." When working with any of the aligned pictures options—Two Items, Aligned Pictures; Three Items, Aligned Pictures; Four Items, Aligned Pictures—Publisher 2000 automatically reverses the page layouts depending on whether it is creating left pages or right pages. Pages with aligned pictures layouts work especially well when facing pages contain an unequal number of products. The white space around the photographs and the consistent width of the text frames containing descriptive text camouflage the fact that each page contains a different number of products.

Tip: Note that, in order to display the Inside Page Content examples as large as possible, most of this book's screens show only one page at a time, instead of facing pages (you might see a few exceptions). You would normally view the inside pages of your catalog as a spread, meaning that you would see both the left and right pages onscreen facing each other. To switch Publisher 2000's Catalog Wizard's default two-page view to a single-page view (and back), select View | Two-Page Spread.

Tip: Depending on the size of your computer monitor, you may run into a slight problem previewing all the options in the drop-down list after the Two Items, Offset Pictures option. By the time you reach the option list's middle, the drop-down menu at the top of the list, which allows you to apply the Inside Page Content to either the Left Inside Page or the Right Inside Page, is no longer visible. To apply Inside Page Content to either the Left Inside Page or Right Inside Page, you must scroll to the top of the list and select the desired option in the drop-down menu, then scroll down the list to reach the desired option. Don't assume that you are limited only to the options you can see at first glance in the drop-down list. Scroll through the options to ensure you are aware of all your choices.

Inserting Additional Pages into Your Catalog

Publisher's Catalog Wizard makes it easy to simultaneously add pages to your catalog and choose Inside Page Format for those pages as you add them. To insert pages, the Catalog Wizard must be visible. Click the Show Wizard icon at the screen's bottom left to display this Wizard, and once you can see the Wizard's list of options, select the Insert

Page option. Publisher will display the Insert Pages dialog box shown in Figure 7-3. You can also select Insert | Page from Publisher's main pull-down menus or press CTRL-SHIFT-N. Either method will cause Publisher to display the Insert Pages dialog box.

Click the More Options button to access the Insert Page options dialog box. Here you choose where you want the new page to be placed in relation to the current page, and if you want your new page to be blank, to contain an empty text frame, or to copy elements from another page you specify.

When you are satisfied with the Inside Page design options you've selected, click OK or press ENTER. Publisher then displays a warning that says you will be adding four pages to your catalog, instead of just the two for which you specified inside page designs. The addition of four pages is necessary because catalogs are usually printed in terms of four-page signatures. (A *signature* is a sheet of pages that is folded to create a publication. In this case, there are four pages of text in one signature.) The number of signatures you have in your catalog relates

Tip: Never choose page layouts in isolation. Always pay attention to the facing page's layout. Although you may have only one page at a time visible onscreen, remember that your readers will see both a left and right page when they look through your catalog. Certain page design combinations work better with each other than others, just as some page designs compete with each other when they are placed in an opposing order.

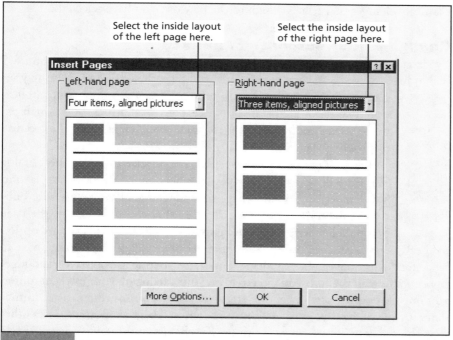

FIGURE 7-3 The Insert Pages dialog box permits you to choose desired inside page content for new pages as you insert them

Tip: Inserting pages should be done with care, only after you are convinced you have the budget to print and mail the extra pages. (Be careful that the extra pages do not push your catalog into the next postage category!) As you'll see in the "Deleting Pages and Retrieving Lost Content" section later in this chapter, it's a lot harder to delete pages than it is to add them.

directly to printing costs. Click the Yes button if you agree to insert four pages. Click No if you only want to insert two pages, even if it does increase printing costs. Notice, also, that Publisher automatically updates page numbers as pages are inserted (or, as discussed later, deleted).

Changing Your Mind Along the Way

At any point, you can change any Catalog Wizard options. For example, while working with a printout, or dummy, of your catalog, you may want to show fewer or more products on one of the pages, or you may want to insert some editorial information inside your catalog.

To change page content, click the Show Wizard button if the Catalog Wizard is not visible, or select View | Show Wizard from Publisher's main drop-down menu. Click the Page Navigation icon to display your desired two-page spread. Select the Catalog Wizard's Inside Page Content option on the screen's left, and the Wizard will display the interactive instructions for specifying Inside Page design. From the drop-down page list, select either the Left Inside Page or Right Inside Page. Then select the inside page design you prefer for that page. Publisher automatically changes that page's design to the new one you have selected.

Changing Your Catalog's Page Size

By default, the Catalog Wizard creates catalog pages 5.5 inches wide and 8.5 inches high. With these page dimensions, you have the option of printing your catalog on your PC's desktop printer. When proofing your publication, two pages are printed on each piece of 8.5-inch-by-11-inch paper. You are not limited to these sizes, however, at either the creation or proofing stages.

Tip: If you haven't already done so, be sure to save your catalog layout once you have chosen its design, color scheme, and inside page content.

You can create a catalog with pages of any size, and the Catalog Wizard will reformat your pages to accommodate your new layout. To change your catalog's page size, select File | Page Setup from Publisher's main drop-down menu. Publisher will then display the Page Setup dialog box, shown in Figure 7-4. Select the Special Size option to specify a non-standard page size. Remember that catalog pages do not have to be rectangular; they can be any shape you desire, so long as you have the budget to print and mail them. If you plan to print your catalog on your own computer, you must keep the overall page size small enough for your printer to accommodate. If you will have your catalog printed commercially, you can use sizes other than those that will work on your printer. To change your catalog's page size to a square format, for example, enter 8 inches in the Width and Height windows,

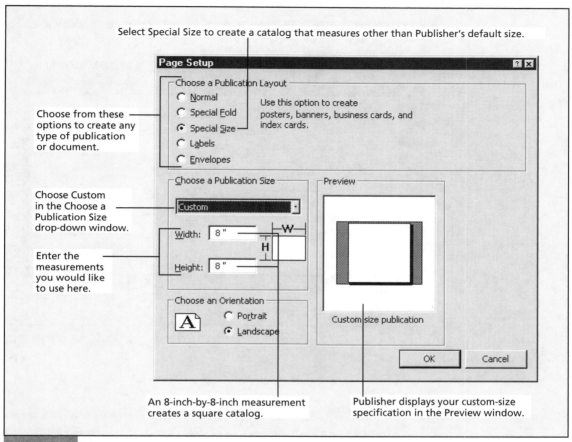

Select Special Size to create a catalog that measures other than Publisher's default size.

Choose from these options to create any type of publication or document.

Choose Custom in the Choose a Publication Size drop-down window.

Enter the measurements you would like to use here.

An 8-inch-by-8-inch measurement creates a square catalog.

Publisher displays your custom-size specification in the Preview window.

FIGURE 7-4 To create square catalog pages, enter 8 inches in the Height and Width windows

and click OK or press ENTER. If you are working with a square design, remember that Portrait and Landscape orientations will look the same in terms of page design, but where the page's top, bottom, left, and right appear will be determined by your orientation selection.

When you return to your catalog, the Catalog Wizard will have reformatted your pages to accommodate the new page size, as shown in Figure 7-5.

When resizing pages, remember that the Catalog Wizard can only resize (and reformat) objects that it originally placed on each page, which means that if you add any objects manually, resizing objects with Wizards will leave the manually added objects the size you originally created them. If you manually placed text frames, graphics, and Design Gallery objects on any pages, those pages and the elements you added to any pages will not be changed by changing your catalog's

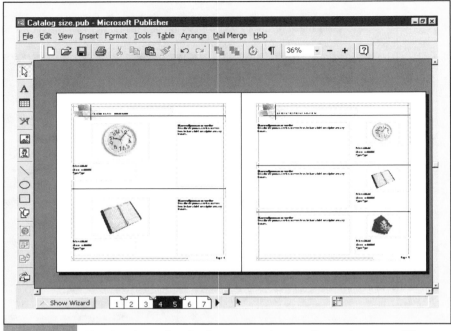

FIGURE 7-5   The Catalog Wizard reformats each page if you choose a different page size

page size. For manually added objects, you have to manually resize each object. This mix-match can cause some strange situations, like the one shown in Figure 7-5.

Completing Your Catalog

Once you have determined the design, color scheme, and inside page content for each page, and decided what products will appear on each page, the hardest part of creating your catalog is completed. All that remains is to replace the text and graphics placeholders on each page with the specific text and graphics you want in your catalog.

Creating Your Catalog's Front Cover

To complete your catalog's front cover, click on the page 1 Page Navigation icon in the Status Bar. Select the catalog title placeholder and replace it with your catalog title. Next, click on the text frame under the title placeholder. Select View | Selected Objects (or press F9) or right-click on the title placeholder. Publisher will display a context-sensitive floating drop-down menu. From this menu, select the Selected Objects option. When you make this selection, Publisher zooms this element to full-screen size so you can clearly see the words "Catalog Subtitle." Replace this placeholder with your desired subtitle. If you have no catalog subtitle, you can delete this text placeholder by clicking on it and selecting Edit | Cut from Publisher's drop-down main menu. If you delete this placeholder, you may also want to make some spacing changes on your page's design, depending on what kind of a gap is created by removing the subtitle placeholder.

Next, double-click the front cover graphics placeholder. Publisher will then display the Insert Clip Art dialog box, from which you can search for a replacement photograph or illustration. To locate a desired image, enter a text description in the Search for Clips window and press ENTER.

Cross-Reference: For more information on replacing graphics placeholders with selected clip art, see Chapter 12. For introductory information on replacing graphics placeholders, see Chapters 4, 5, and 6.

If you want to use a scanned image instead of clip art, click on the front cover photo placeholder, and select Insert | Picture | From File (or right-click the placeholder and select Change Picture | Picture | From File. Publisher will then display the Insert Picture dialog box, shown in Figure 7-6. Browse through the folders

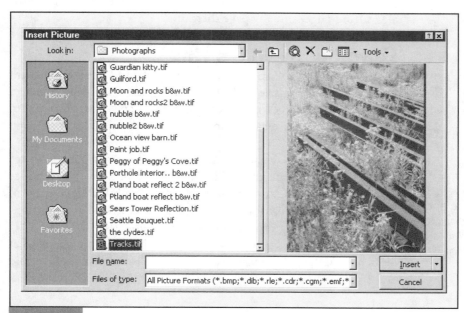

FIGURE 7-6 Use Publisher's Insert Picture dialog box to replace the cover page's graphics placeholder with a photo you have scanned in or gotten from another source

L▶ Tip: When replacing the front cover graphics placeholder, try to locate a photograph or clip art image that is oriented the same way, which means you would replace a vertical photo placeholder with a vertical photograph. If you replace a vertical graphics placeholder with a horizontal, or landscape, photograph, the photograph may be too small to display properly, or it may throw off the design of your catalog's front cover.

L▶ Tip: Don't forget that you can use View | Zoom to alter the magnification of any page or object to get the best possible view of your work. An even better alternative is to get in the habit of using the F9 function key to frequently toggle (or move back and forth between) a full-page view of your catalog and any text or graphics placeholders on which you may be working.

until you locate your desired photograph and double-click on its file-name to insert it in place of the placeholder. Click Close to complete the process.

Although changing orientation on your catalog's inside pages may be acceptable, you may not like its effects on your front cover, because the graphics placeholder is so much larger and the Wizard creates a front cover that contains only one graphic element.

Still working on your front cover, click the sidebar text placeholder, and press the F9 function key to magnify the placeholder so you can view the entire text placeholder. Replace the sidebar heading place-holder with a short phrase describing your catalog's contents. Then se-lect the "Briefly highlight your product of service here" bulleted text placeholder, and highlight the best-selling contents of your catalog in this place.

Complete the front cover of your catalog by clicking the date text placeholder at the page's bottom, and then enter either the catalog number or the date the catalog will circulate. You can delete the word "date," if you choose not to have one. If you don't want a two-line date, you may have to resize that text placeholder to make it smaller. When you have completed this process, your front cover will be com-plete. (See Figure 7-7.) Save your catalog after you complete your cat-alog's front page, and any page thereafter.

Learning by Observing

As a learning exercise, and so that you can familiarize yourself with how changes in the size and placement of text and graphic images make major differences in your catalog's appearance, you may want to click the Show Wizard button and select the Catalog Wizard's Design option.

Use the Page Navigator icons to display any inside two-page spread, and select different Inside Page Design options. You'll notice how each Design option you select projects a totally different image of your catalog, featuring different graphic accents, as well as reposition-ing and reformatting text and graphics placeholders.

Remember that as you use Publisher, and learn more about what looks best on the printed page, your design skills will also improve, and

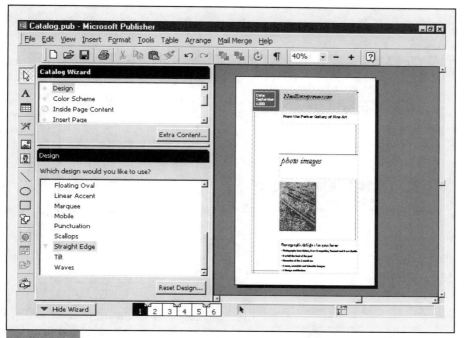

FIGURE 7-7 Once you replace Publisher's text and graphics placeholders, the catalog front cover now appears uniquely yours

you will begin to notice how subtle design changes will improve your designs, making your creations more attractive to your audience.

After formatting the front page of your catalog, save your publication again, and try out different Catalog Wizard designs just to see how different each design looks.

When you are finished previewing other designs, reapply the design you originally chose, or select Edit | Undo Wizard Action from Publisher's main drop-down menu (or press CTRL-Z) as many times as necessary to return the page on which you are experimenting to its original design.

Pay particular attention to the way that the size and alignment of the graphics influence the appearance of the finished page. In addition, notice the role that object alignment plays—especially how the vertical edge of the photograph is often lined up with the catalog title and subtitle, as shown in Figure 7-8. Note also that, with this design, the date and sidebar are deeply indented and aligned with each other.

Tip: Right-clicking on the screen anywhere except a graphic, text frame, or other object permits you to easily select Undo Wizard Action.

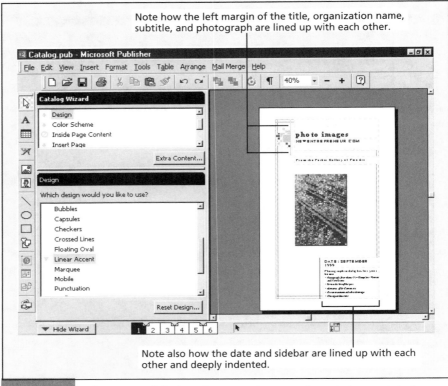

FIGURE 7-8 Alignment of design elements plays a major role in good design

Finishing the Inside Pages

Complete the inside pages of your catalog in the same way you completed the front cover. Begin by double-clicking on each graphics placeholder and—using the Insert Photograph dialog box—find your desired replacement photograph for each graphics placeholder. As you replace each text placeholder, press F9 whenever you click on a text frame to quickly magnify it large enough so you can easily write the replacement text. Press the F9 key again to return to your previous view, so you can watch your progress on the two-page spread. Don't forget to save your work as you complete each two-page spread.

Deleting Pages and Retrieving Lost Content

We've discussed adding, moving, and completing pages, but you may also have a need to delete some pages, regardless of whether you have completed them.

Deleting completed pages introduces several problems—along with several innovative Publisher 2000 solutions to handle them.

To delete a page of your catalog, click on the Page Navigation icon containing the appropriate page number in the Status Bar. Select Edit | Delete Page. The Delete Page dialog box appears and will ask you whether you want to delete one or both pages. Depending on which pages you want to delete, click on the Both Pages, the Left Page Only, or the Right Page Only radio button. Then click OK or press ENTER.

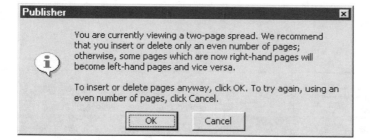

Because your catalog consists of two-page spreads, Publisher will warn you to delete two pages at a time, as the dialog box shown here shows. Otherwise, some right pages will become left pages, and vice versa. Click the OK button to acknowledge the warning and continue anyway, or click the Cancel button to return to the Delete Page dialog box where you can choose the Both Pages option.

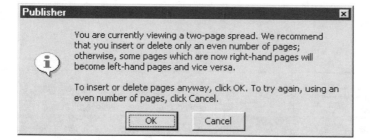

If you are working with conventional catalog page sizes (less than 8.5-by-11-inches), Publisher will also display another warning, shown here. This warning informs you that your current publication was intended for printing in multiples of four pages and that you should delete two more pages. Click the OK button, or press ENTER, to acknowledge the warning.

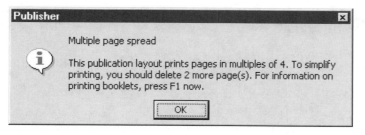

When you delete pages in Publisher, you are probably wondering what Publisher does with the deleted material. Is it gone forever? Moved to a clipboard for possible later use? What does happen to the content, the words and photographs contained on the deleted pages?

Click the Design Gallery Object icon in the Objects toolbar, or select Insert | Design Gallery Object from Publisher's main drop-down menu. Publisher then displays the Design Gallery, shown in Figure 7-9. Note the tabs that run along the top of the Design Gallery screen. The last tab, labeled Extra Content, is where Publisher saves deleted material until you manually delete it. Click on the Extra Content tab to see that Publisher has saved all the text frames and graphics that once appeared on the pages you deleted. All the content you added to the deleted page is now available for you to place on another page if you need to do so.

To place Extra Content text and graphics on a different page of your catalog, select it and click Insert Object. If you are positive that you will never want to re-use the text and graphics, you can delete each item one at a time. To delete the items, select each one separately and then click the Delete button. You can also opt to delete everything Publisher has stored in the Extra Content area by clicking the Delete All button. Click the Close button to exit the Design Gallery and return to your work.

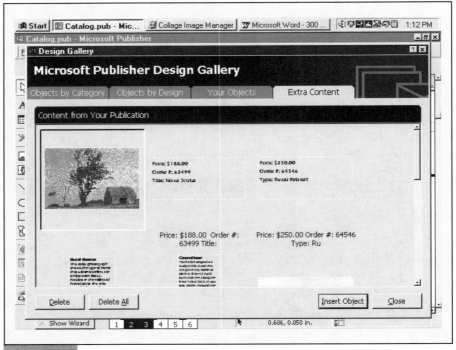

FIGURE 7-9 Publisher saves text and graphics previously added to deleted pages in the Extra Content area of the Microsoft Publisher Design Gallery

Professional Skills Summary

In this chapter, you have seen how easy it is to create a fairly elaborate and customized catalog with Publisher's Catalog Wizard. Also in this chapter, we took a look at 19 distinct inside page designs, and how they can work to best profile your products. We also reviewed how to replace the Catalog Wizard's text and graphics placeholders with your material. Finally, we discussed how to modify your catalog's design to suit your specific product needs, giving your catalog the most effective design to maximize your catalog sales potential.

Stick with us as we turn our attention toward harnessing the power of the World Wide Web—in Chapter 8 we'll show you how to build your first Web site with Publisher 2000.

Creating a Web Site

In this chapter, you will:

- Use Publisher's Web Site Wizard to create your Web site's design

- Decide how best to present your online message in your Web site

- Replace the Web Site Wizard's text and graphics placeholders

- Post your Web site to the World Wide Web

For all practical purposes, today's communication demands require any effective business or organization to have and maintain a Web site. With an effectively designed Web site, you can introduce your company, organization, or yourself to new customers, as well as keep current customers informed and enthusiastic about products, services, or information your Web site offers. For organizations, Web sites bond members and supporters, giving them an easy way to share their interests, experiences, and opinions. With a Web site, you can deliver your message in vivid color, complete with sounds and animation, at virtually no cost, using photographs and as many pages as you need to tell your story.

Individuals and families have also discovered the power of the Web to keep others informed about their activities and interests. It's hard to overestimate the power of the Web in its ability to permit you to communicate a lot of information.

Planning Your Web Site

Creating a Web site with Publisher's Web Site Wizard involves the same basic steps as the other Wizards we have used in previous chapters (flyers, newsletters, brochures, and catalogs). Creating Web sites is different, however, because Web sites are more complicated than paper-based publishing. To have and maintain an effective Web site, you need to be able to hook your creation to the Internet, and to ensure every link to and from your site works flawlessly. You need to make sure Internet surfers can find your Web site and load the Web site without an aggravatingly long wait. One additional complication is browser compatibility. Your Web site needs to be simple enough to display on older versions of Web browsers, as well as a variety of browsers. Although Publisher 2000 is designed to work with Microsoft's Internet Explorer, Internet users also use other browsers—Netscape Navigator is also a leading browser choice for many users. The Internet hosts other less well-known browsers that run with the UNIX operating system. When you design content for the Web, you need to understand that Internet users have many different computers, different operating systems, and different browsers, so you need to design your page to effectively communicate your message, while ensuring that anyone who accesses your site can load your Web page without any problems.

In this chapter, we'll first make a quick review of how the Web Site Wizard operates, and then we'll focus on elements that are different from our previous examples, including compatibility issues, creating links to and from your site, and keeping track of your design options while filling in the Wizard's text and graphics placeholders. If, by chance, you haven't yet worked through the flyer, newsletter, brochure, or catalog Wizard, you may want to review the Wizard sections of Chapters 4, 5, 6, and 7.

You'll also want to review the section in Chapter 7 called "Maintaining Design Consistency." Web sites, too, need to keep a consistent look and feel to coordinate with any existing printed materials—catalogs, brochures, letterhead, business cards, and so on—that you, your business, or your organization may already have.

Stepping Through the Web Site Wizard's Basic Options

As with the flyer, newsletter, brochure, and catalog Wizards, the preliminary steps for starting the Web Site Wizard are basically the same. If you have not yet started Publisher, start the application, and Publisher will display the list of Wizard options. Select the Web Site option. If you are working within Publisher already, select File | New. Publisher will then display the list of Wizard options. Again, select the Web Site Wizard.

Drag the vertical scroll bar up and down the right edge of the screen (or click in the area above or below the box) to sample the Web Site Wizard's various Design sets, as shown in Figure 8-1. Publisher will apply the design you select to the Web site's home page, as well as throughout any additional pages you may add to the Web site.

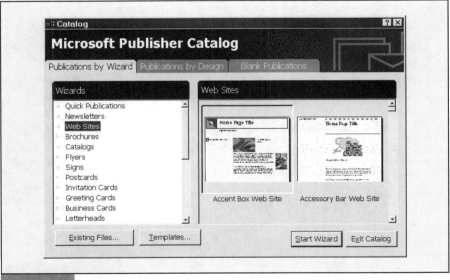

FIGURE 8-1   Select your Web site's home page design from the examples in Publisher's preview window

Highlight your desired Design and click the Start Wizard button (or double-click the desired design to close the Publisher Catalog dialog box and start the Web Site Wizard). Once you click the Start Wizard button, Publisher will then display the Web Site Wizard's introduction, which will lead you through the Wizard's Web site-creating process. When you start the Wizard, Publisher also creates and displays in the screen's work area a home page for your Web site, featuring the design you selected. (See Figure 8-2.)

Publisher's Web Site Wizard features several additional construction elements than the other Wizards with which we have worked. Each option is discussed in detail in the chapter sections that follow. Those Wizard options are:

- Design
- Color Scheme
- Form
- Navigation Bar
- Insert Page
- Background Sound
- Background Texture
- Personal Information
- Convert to Print

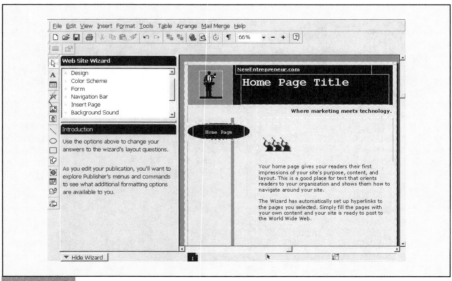

FIGURE 8-2 This example home page is ready for further customization

Choosing a Different Color Scheme

As with the other Wizards we've presented in earlier chapters, the first decision the Web Site Wizard will want you to make is to select a color scheme from the Color Scheme options list. Select the same color for your Web site as for your other publications, if you have already created any. If the Web site is your first or only Publisher 2000 creation, you may select any color option you prefer. With the Web Site Wizard, each color scheme employs a different combination of Web site foreground and background colors. As you preview various color options, be aware of how the design and colors interrelate. Remember, too, that you can always change the color scheme when you are completing your Web site. When you have selected your desired color scheme, click Next to advance to the next Wizard option.

Using the Wizard to Add Forms to Your Site

The most successful Web sites are those that facilitate a two-way communication with Web site visitors. What Web visitors have to say to you is as important as what you say to your visitors. Publisher's Web Site Forms options make it easy for Web site visitors to communicate with you and identify themselves (permitting e-mail follow-up at a later date). Forms convert your Web site from an "electronic brochure"—a term that describes Web sites that communicate in one direction only, from business to visitor—to two-way, interactive sites that permit visitors to communicate with you.

Forms are important because they help you establish a dialog with your Web site visitors. Survey forms let you find out who your Web site visitors are and what their information needs are. Using forms, you can fine-tune your Web site by finding out what visitors like about your site and what new information they would like to see added. Forms make it easy for visitors to request additional information, a telephone call, or a visit. Visitors to your Web site can use forms to sign up for a seminar or actually purchase a product.

Most important, forms make it easy for you to collect your visitors' names and contact information, so you can easily keep in touch with them. Once you have captured your visitor's e-mail address, you can—with their permission—send them e-mail notifying them when you have added new information to your Web site or new resources in which they might be interested. The ability to use e-mail as a low-cost (basically free) way to bring visitors back to your Web site is one of the most important aspects of a successful Web strategy—and it all begins with adding a form to your Web site.

Finally, forms help you evaluate your Web site by providing an easy way for visitors to provide feedback on various items, such as articles or reviews, displayed on your site. This helps you constantly improve your Web site in the coming months and years by eliminating unpopular articles or features and expanding and improving popular features.

With the Web Site Wizard, you can add three types of forms—order form, response form, and sign-up form—to your Web site, depending on the information you want your visitors to send back to you. If you don't need any of these three form designs, just click the None radio button option to remove or not include any form selection in your Web site. Here is a brief summary of each type of form Publisher 2000 features.

- **Single-line text boxes**   These boxes are intended for short text elements, such as first name, last name (entered separately so you can enter them in your database and sort alphabetically by last name), position (which gives you an idea of their income and buying power), name of business , street address, phone number, fax number, and e-mail address.

- **Multiline text boxes**   These text boxes offer visitors more space to enter information, such as "Best time to call" or "Comments." The more space you provide, the more you encourage a detailed response.

- **Check boxes**   These boxes give visitors a multiple-choice option. For example, in a section of your Web site asking about favorite outdoor recreation, you could include check boxes for "Hiking," "Kayaking," "Sailing," and "Swimming." Check boxes, which allow the visitor to choose more than one selection, are the appropriate choice because the individual could enjoy hiking as well as swimming.

- **Option buttons**   These buttons give visitors a choice between two or more mutually exclusive options. Although visitors may select multiple check boxes, they can select *only one option* from an option group, for example, "Are you left-handed?" or "Are you right-handed?" Other option groups might include: "Do you have a job?" "Are you self-employed?" or "Are you looking for work?" A final example: "Are you a vegetarian?" or "Do you eat meat?"

- **List boxes**   These boxes present visitors with a list from which to choose. Visitors can scroll through the list and choose one or more options. You control whether visitors are limited to just one or can choose several options from the list. List boxes can contain a list of approved state abbreviations to simplify submitting a Web site visitor's entry of his mailing address into your address form, or provide your visitors with a way to select favorite composer(s) from the list you have provided to accompany the list boxes format.

- **Command buttons**   These buttons include Submit for visitors to click when they have completed your form, and Restore for when visitors want to delete their responses and start all over again.

To modify the characteristics of a form control—whether you use a list, check box, button, etc.—select it, then select Format I Single-Line Text Box Properties, and the Wizard will display the exact type of form control required in the Format menu. You can also right-click the form control and select Single-Line Text Box Properties. Or you can directly access the correct form control Properties box if you double-click the form control.

To add a form to your Web site, click Form and select a desired type of form from the Form options.

Order forms provide a structured way for Web site visitors to purchase from you, supplying all necessary shipping information and indicating their preferred method of payment.

Response forms make it easy to survey your visitors to find out who they are, asking them to answer questions like what is their employment position within their firm or organization, how immediately they plan to buy items you offer, and what are their areas of interest. If you are preparing a Web site for an association, you can use response forms to poll your membership, giving members the opportunity to vote or express their opinions on important issues or elections. The response form also features a comments section where visitors have an opportunity to send their free-form text-based opinion in greater detail.

Sign-up forms are good to use for visitors to register for presentations or courses your Web site may offer. Regardless of whether the Web site accepts payment for these events, sign-up forms give you a quick way to determine visitor interest and attendance.

The Wizard offers an option for not adding any form. Selecting the None option will also delete a form from your Web site, if you have already added a form.

After you choose your desired form option, the Wizard will display a prompt telling you that it has added your form page to your Web site, and on what page it has added the form. Note that whenever you use the Wizard to add a form to your Web site, Publisher places the new form on the last page of your Web site.

> **Tip:** Double-clicking is the fastest way to go directly to a form control dialog box.

Using the Wizard's Order Form Design

If your goal is to sell a product or service through your Web site, select the first Form option, Order Form. The Wizard displays a message telling you the order form appears on page 2, and instructs you to go to that page to see it. Note that the Wizard adds the form to your Web site's last page, so if your Web site already includes three pages, the Wizard creates the form on page 4.

To view your form, click on the appropriate page number icon in the Status Bar along the bottom of the screen. The Wizard's order form design, shown in Figure 8-3, includes not only ordering and shipping information, but also method of payment, including space for visitors to submit credit card information. Note also that when you use the Wizard to add the order form to your Web

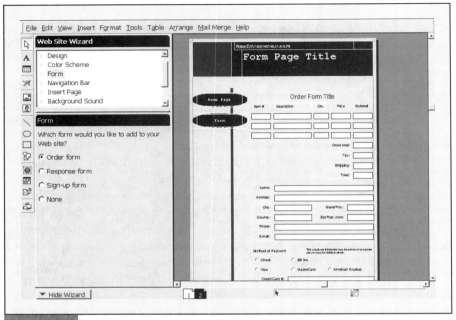

FIGURE 8-3 Publisher's Web Site Wizard order form gives you a way to become part of e-commerce

site, the Web Site Wizard automatically creates a form link to each previously existing Web site page.

For detailed information on Web site security issues and how to protect credit card information in your Web site, see *Internet: The Complete Reference,* Millennium Edition, by Margie Levin Young (Osborne/McGraw-Hill, 1999).

Using the Wizard's Response Form Design

Not all Web sites are intended to sell products. Perhaps you are responsible for an association or organization's Web site, and you want to solicit your members' feelings about important issues concerning them. If you need more of an information-gathering form, use the Wizard to add the Response Form option, shown in Figure 8-4. This form design provides placeholders formatted for four individual questions with radio button responses and a message window where each Web site visitor can voice comments, suggestions, and messages.

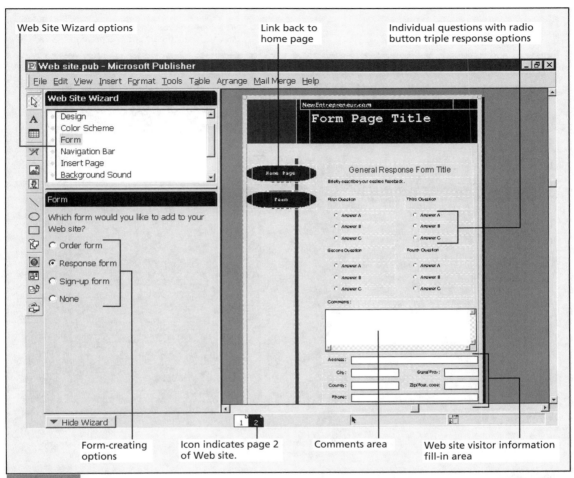

Web Site Wizard options

Link back to home page

Individual questions with radio button triple response options

Form-creating options

Icon indicates page 2 of Web site.

Comments area

Web site visitor information fill-in area

FIGURE 8-4 Use the Web Site Wizard's Response Form option to capture visitors' names, addresses, and individual messages

Using the Wizard's Sign-up Form

If you are even a bit creative, you will be able to find several uses for the Web Site Wizard's sign-up form, shown in Figure 8-5. Primarily designed for soliciting memberships, the sign-up form is also great for promoting special events—such as signing up for seminars that are offered at different times or on different days. Web site visitors can use the sign-up form to select a single option from the four placeholders with check box responses. Notice that the sign-up form also includes full payment and credit card information.

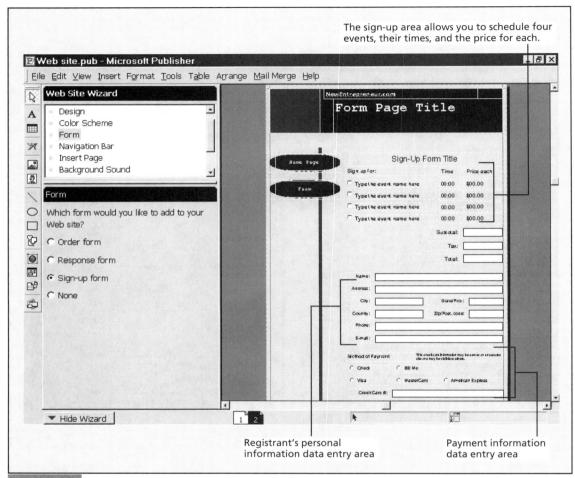

The sign-up area allows you to schedule four events, their times, and the price for each.

Registrant's personal information data entry area

Payment information data entry area

FIGURE 8-5   With Publisher's sign-up form, you can easily promote attendance at special events such as seminars, concerts, or plays

Modifying the Navigation Bar

Once you have used the Wizard to add any form designs you want, you then need to consider the navigation bar design options featured by the Wizard. The Wizard offers two navigation bar options: both a vertical and horizontal navigation bar, or just a vertical bar. (The Wizard also offers a None option, although I can't think of any instance when someone would create a Web site without a navigation bar.)

Select "Both a vertical and horizontal bar" if you want to combine navigation buttons at the top left of your Web site with text links along the bottom of each page. "Both a vertical and horizontal bar" is the preferred option because it makes it easy for visitors to go directly to a different page of your Web site after they finish reading a page. The two-bar technique offers your Web site visitors a convenient and fast way to access different pages of your Web site. With two navigation bars, visitors won't have to scroll their way back to the Web page top to access another page.

Select "Just a vertical bar" if you want to omit the text links along the bottom of each Web page. Note that the Web Site Wizard automatically creates links as you add new pages to your Web site, which I explain in more detail in the next section.

Adding Pages to Your Web Site

The Web Site Wizard's next option is to add any extra pages you might have planned. Make sure the Insert Page Option in the Web Site Wizard's steps area is highlighted, and that the Wizard's instruction area is displaying information that pertains to adding pages. Click on the Insert Page button. The Wizard displays the Insert Page dialog box, shown in Figure 8-6.

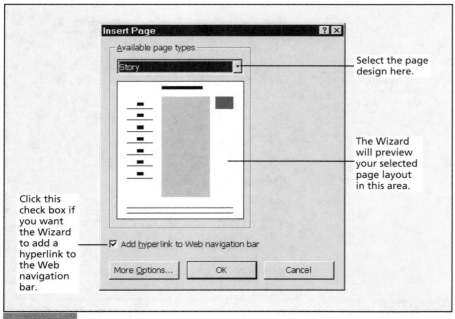

FIGURE 8-6   The Insert Page dialog box lets you add pages and specify the page type at the same time

Choosing the Right Page Design for Your Online Material

Use the Insert Page dialog box to add a page to your Web site and specify the design of the page (as shown in Figure 8-6). The Wizard offers you six design options for each page you add—Story, Calendar, Event, Special Offer, Price List, and Related Links. Click the More Options button to access the second screen of the Insert Page dialog box, from which you can specify where the new page will appear in your Web site, as shown in Figure 8-7.

By default, each time you add a new page, Publisher 2000 automatically adds a new link to the navigation bar (or bars, depending on your selection of navigation bars). When you replace the page title/headline placeholder with an actual page title, Publisher will insert the new title in the navigation button. Publisher also adds a text link to the bottom of each page, as shown in Figure 8-8, making it easy for visitors to visit another page of your Web site without having to scroll to the navigation bar at each page's top.

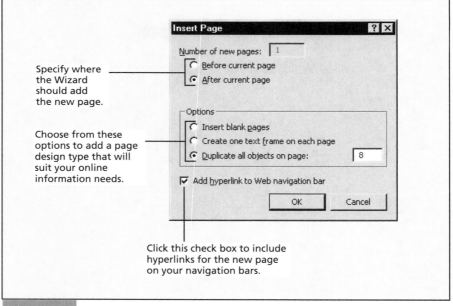

FIGURE 8-7 Click More Options to access the second page of the Insert Page dialog box

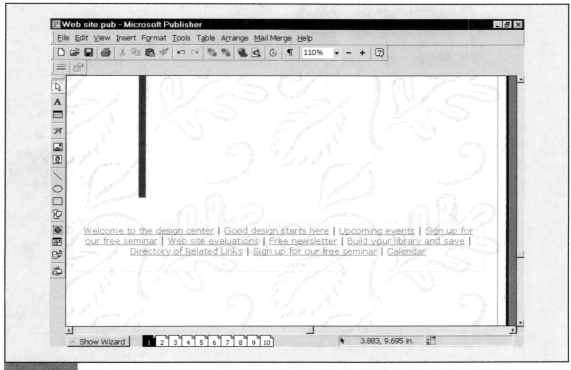

FIGURE 8-8   In addition to adding buttons to the navigation bar, Publisher also automatically inserts text links at each Web page's bottom

Notice the check mark next to "Add hyperlink to Web navigation bar." To add a new page to your Web site without adding a hyperlink to the navigation bar, deselect this feature by clicking the check box. For Web site visitors to reach this page, you will have to manually add a hyperlink to the page. (For more information on manually adding hyperlinks, see the section "Continuing Articles onto Additional Pages" later in this chapter).

To reveal the different options available, click the downward pointing arrow next to Story under Available Page Types, and select from the six design options. To add a page, select the page design you want applied to the new page from the drop-down menu and click the OK button (or press ENTER). Each of these page design options is designed for a range of specific purposes, although you may be able to modify any one of them to suit a different purpose. The followings sections give an overview of the page design options.

Story   Use this design primarily for text-based information. This design option also features pull-quotes and a small graphic object. The Story design will probably be your Web site's most frequently used format.

Calendar   Use this design to make it easy for Web site visitors to relate the date of an upcoming event to the month in which it appears. This option places a large calendar at the top of each page and provides space for you to briefly describe the events that occur on each date.

Event   Use this design to emphasize an upcoming event (for example, a concert, play, seminar, or speech). The design also features two placeholders for photos and a brief description under each, and a map at the page's bottom.

Special Offer   Use this design to feature limited-time events (such as promotions, sales events, or membership renewals) or to emphasize important introductory prices on new products or services.

Price List　Use this design to summarize your firm or organization's products, services, and prices. This design works well if you are a retailer, distributor, or consultant.

Related Links　Use this page for a variety of applications that may not be obvious at first. You can use it to list links to other Web sites in which your visitors might be interested. For example, if you are a manufacturer, you can include links to distributors and retailers who sell your product. Or, if you are producing a Web site for a national organization, you can insert links to your organization's local chapters. You can also include links to organization members' Web sites, your area's schools, departments within your college, and so on.

Deleting Pages

To delete a page you have added, select Edit | Delete Page. Publisher 2000 will warn you that deleting the page will also delete all objects on that page. Click the OK button to confirm that you want to delete the page. Click the Cancel button if you want to return to Publisher without deleting the page.

When you are deleting pages, Publisher will display a prompt informing you that the page you want to delete has hyperlinks to other page locations and that these links will be removed. Click the Yes button if you agree to delete the hyperlinks. Click No if you want the hyperlink to remain, even if you delete the page. Leaving the link can assist you if you are making major changes to your Web site in progress, but having links that go nowhere is not a permissible Web site design characteristic.

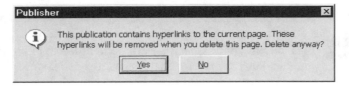

When you delete hyperlinked pages, Publisher 2000 automatically updates all hyperlinks and adds text and graphics from deleted pages to the Design Gallery. To view text and graphics from deleted pages, select Insert | Design Gallery Object, or click the Design Gallery icon, and select the Extra Content tab. When the Design Gallery's Extra Content window appears, as shown in Figure 8-9, you can review and, if desired, rescue text and graphic images from deleted pages and use them on other pages of your Web site.

Adding Sounds and Textures

Publisher 2000's Web Site Wizard also offers options to add background sounds and background textures to customize your Web site, adding an extra layer of uniqueness. The ability to augment your visual Internet message with sound makes any Web site a multimedia flare. You can use music or sound effects to introduce your Web site, or you can record your own spoken introduction the Web site will play each time a new page loads, or when your visitors click on your sound hyperlinks.

To add sound to your Web site, select Background Sound from the Web Site Wizard and click the Select Sound button. (At this point, you may want to make sure that your Web browser is configured to play sound and your speakers are working properly.) When the Web Site Wizard displays the tabbed Properties dialog box, select the Page tab, and click the Background Sound Browse button, as shown in Figure 8-10. When the Wizard displays the Background Sound dialog

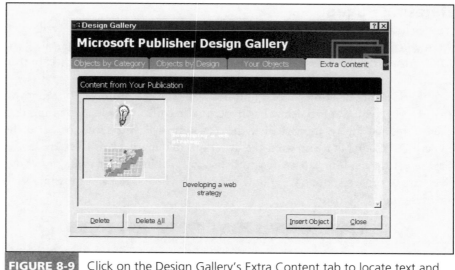

FIGURE 8-9 Click on the Design Gallery's Extra Content tab to locate text and graphics Publisher has saved from your deleted pages

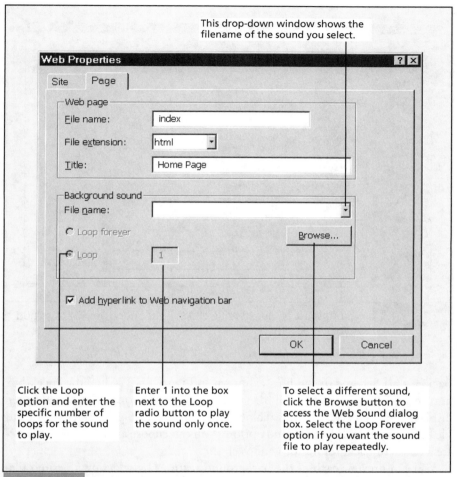

FIGURE 8-10   Click the Browse button to see a list of sounds from which you may add to your Web site

box, as shown in Figure 8-11, select the sound you want and click the Open button (or double-click on the filename, or click ENTER). With this selection, the Wizard redisplays the Web Properties dialog box. Click OK to complete adding sound to your Web site.

To give your Web site a creative look, you might want to change your solid background to a textured one. To replace a solid background with a textured background, select the Web Site Wizard's Background Texture option and click the Select Texture button. The Wizard will then display the tabbed Color and

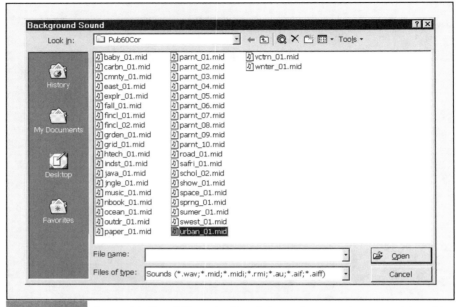

FIGURE 8-11 From this list of files, double-click on the sound you want to add to your Web site

Background Scheme dialog box, as shown in Figure 8-12. Click the check box next to the Texture option, and then click the Browse button. The Wizard then displays the Web Backgrounds dialog box, as shown in Figure 8-13. From this file listing of possible background options, you can choose an image that will create a textured background for your Web site.

You can preview each of the background textures by selecting a desired filename and clicking the Open button or by double-clicking the desired filename. This action redisplays the Color and Background Scheme dialog box (Figure 8-12), where you can preview both the overall look of the texture as well as view a sample at higher magnification.

Customizing Your Web Site's Background

You can further customize your Web site by clicking the Color and Background Scheme's Custom tab. With the Custom tab's options, shown in Figure 8-14, you can modify each of the colors used in your Web site's color scheme. Simply click on the downward pointing arrow next to the New color box and choose a

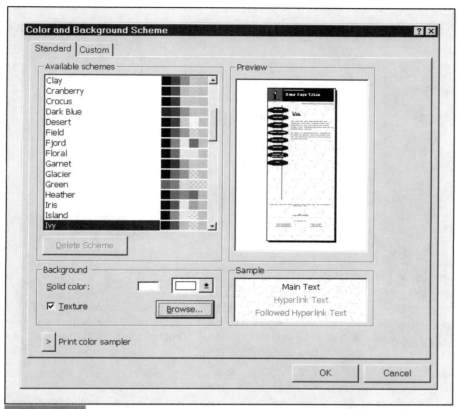

FIGURE 8-12 Use the tabbed Color and Background Scheme dialog box to add a texture to your Web page background

different Main, Accent, Hyperlink, Followed, or Background color. If the initial color palette that appears doesn't offer enough options, click the More Colors button for more choices.

Adding Personal Information

To automatically insert your firm or organization's information into each page of your Web site, click Personal Information from the Web Wizard's list of steps, and select whether you want to insert information previously entered into your Primary Business, Secondary Business, Other Organization, or Home/Family personal profiles, or enter new, different information.

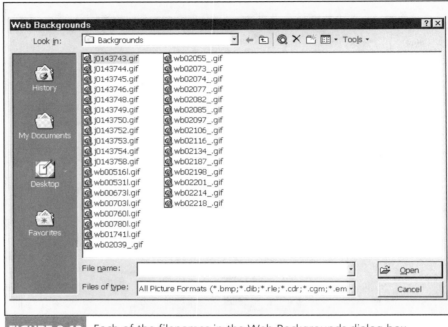

FIGURE 8-13   Each of the filenames in the Web Backgrounds dialog box represents a different texture

Click the Web Site Wizard's Personal Information update button if you want to change some previously entered information. Click the Insert Component button if you want to add additional information, such as your job title.

Producing and Previewing Your Web Site

Don't be too concerned if you feel you haven't added enough pages at this point of your Web site creation. You can add additional pages to your Web site at any point. In most cases, the information already entered will provide enough of a framework for you to begin working on adding your detailed information to your Web site.

At this point, you might want to click the Hide Wizard button in order to concentrate on your Web site and work at a higher magnification. You can always reveal the Web Site Wizard later, by selecting View | Show Wizard.

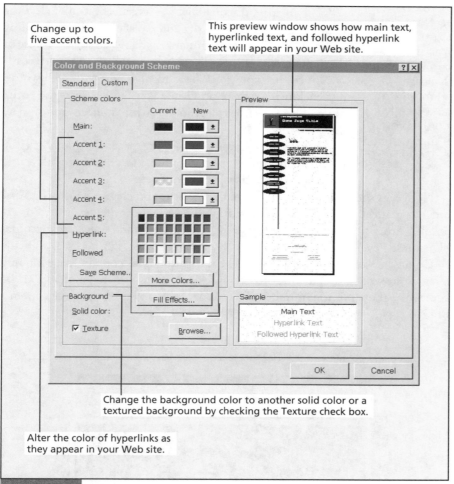

Change up to five accent colors.

This preview window shows how main text, hyperlinked text, and followed hyperlink text will appear in your Web site.

Change the background color to another solid color or a textured background by checking the Texture check box.

Alter the color of hyperlinks as they appear in your Web site.

FIGURE 8-14   The Color and Background Scheme's Custom tab permits you to fine-tune your color scheme by choosing different foreground, accent, and hyperlink colors

Adding Page Titles

The first step in completing your Web site is to go through page by page, replacing the default page titles with titles that reflect the information you want to display on each page.

Tip: Note that Publisher 2000 automatically chooses a title type size that will fit the available space. This may lead you to inadvertently include more words in your titles than can fit in the navigation links.

Click the page 1 icon along the screen's bottom. Select the Home Page Title placeholder and replace it with a welcoming message, or a title that summarizes your Web site's purpose or the benefit that visitors will enjoy by spending time with you.

Notice that you don't have to highlight the three words; just clicking anywhere on Home Page Title selects the entire phrase. Replace the placeholder with a more appropriate introduction.

After you are through changing page 1's title, click the page 2 icon. Again, select the title and replace it with a title that summarizes that page's contents.

Notice, as shown in Figure 8-15, that every time you change a title, the Wizard automatically updates all the navigation links to reflect the new title. For example, "Story title" becomes "Good design starts here" and "Calendar" becomes "Upcoming events."

Conciseness is, of course, a virtue. The navigation links contain space for only a few short words. If your titles are too long, the entire title may not appear. Be sure to use the minimum number of words necessary to "telegraph" the contents of each page.

FIGURE 8-15   Navigation links are automatically updated when you replace page title placeholders with text identifying the contents of each page

Replacing Placeholder Text with Your Message

Next, return to page 1 and replace the placeholder text and graphics with the words and visuals that communicate your message.

Notice how each text placeholder provides a description of the type of contents that should appear. Also note that clicking anywhere on a text placeholder selects the entire placeholder, so you can immediately begin typing (or insert a previously saved text file).

After you have replaced the text on your Web site's home (or first) page, click the page 2 icon and—again—enter the text you want to use to support the topic you promised in the page's top title/headline.

Proceed page by page through your Web site, until you have replaced all of the text placeholders with your firm or organization's unique message. Notice that Publisher automatically formats the type for you, choosing a serif or sans serif typeface for body type, depending on the Web Site Wizard design you have chosen. Publisher automatically chooses a type size appropriate for most Web browsers. (Remember, however, that your Web site visitors can change the type size by choosing a different font setting in their browsers.)

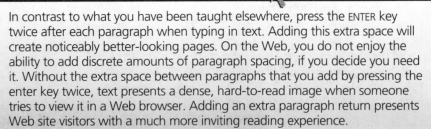

Professional Pointer

In contrast to what you have been taught elsewhere, press the ENTER key twice after each paragraph when typing in text. Adding this extra space will create noticeably better-looking pages. On the Web, you do not enjoy the ability to add discrete amounts of paragraph spacing, if you decide you need it. Without the extra space between paragraphs that you add by pressing the enter key twice, text presents a dense, hard-to-read image when someone tries to view it in a Web browser. Adding an extra paragraph return presents Web site visitors with a much more inviting reading experience.

Do not overlook the short text frames provided for pull-quotes, as shown in Figure 8-16. These short text blocks act like magnets, drawing your Web site visitor's eyes, and they can be used to deliver presales information or reinforce the importance of the adjacent text. (Most readers would rather read one or two sentences than a full page any day!) Simply click on the text placeholder—which selects all of the text within that placeholder—and write a short sentence summarizing the adjacent text. You can also copy and paste a sentence from the adjacent text into these short, attention-getting text blocks.

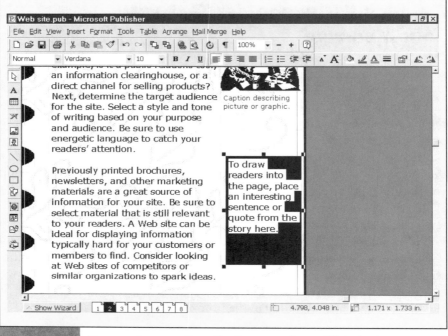

FIGURE 8-16 You can increase the effectiveness of your Web site by summarizing adjacent text in the short pull-quote text frames the layout provides

Avoid the temptation to resize these frames and add a lot of text. Shorter is always better when it comes to design elements like pull-quotes.

When completing your Web site, one of your tasks will be to update any calendars you have inserted. By default, Publisher 2000 creates the calendar inserted by the Wizard for the current month. In most cases, you're going to want a calendar for an upcoming month.

To display a different month in the calendar, select the calendar and click the Calendar Creation Wizard symbol at the bottom, as shown in Figure 8-17.

When you click on the Wizard's Calendar Creation option, the Wizard displays the Calendar Creation dialog box. Select the Dates option, and then click the Change Dates button. When the Wizard displays the Change Calendar Dates dialog box, select a desired month from the drop-down menu and select the year by clicking the up/down arrows, as shown next. When you have selected the month you want, click OK or ENTER. To close the Calendar Wizard and return to Publisher, click anywhere on your Web site's page.

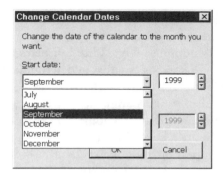

Setting Your Web Site's Forms' Submit Button Parameters

After you have replaced all your regular text placeholders, you need to make sure all the information you request on any forms you have included will be returned in a format that is meaningful and useful to you. Locate your first form page,

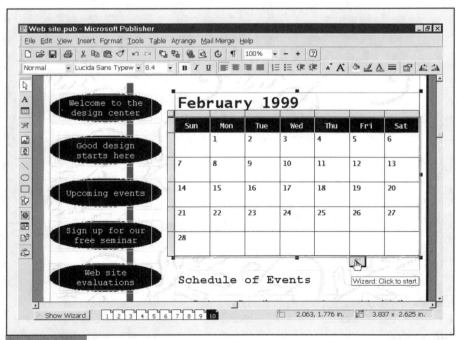

FIGURE 8-17 Select the calendar and click the Calendar Wizard icon to change the calendar to a different month

scroll to the page's bottom, and select the Submit button. Select Format | Command Button Properties (or right-click the Submit button and select the Command Button Properties option). The Wizard displays the Command Button Properties dialog box. This step is essential in determining how you will receive and handle information submitted by Web site visitors.

When the Wizard displays the Command Button Properties dialog box, you can rename the Submit button, if you choose. Click the Button Type option to deselect it. In the Button text box field, enter the new name you have chosen for the button, as it will appear on your Web site form. From this dialog box, you can also rename the button to be the Reset button, if you want. On your Web site form page, the Reset button will clear all information your Web site visitors have keyed into your form, letting them begin to fill in the form again.

Select "Save the data in a file on my Web server" if you operate your own server and you have installed Microsoft's FrontPage server extensions (version 2.0 or higher). In the Command Button Properties dialog box's Data Retrieval Information area, as shown in Figure 8-18, you can specify the name of the file in

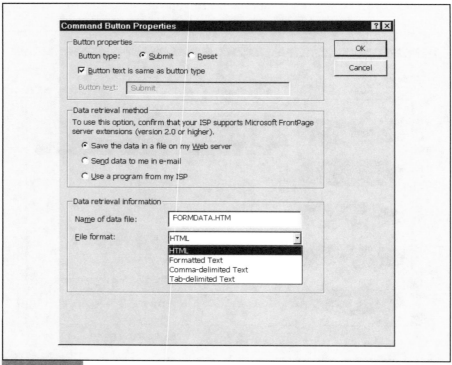

FIGURE 8-18 If you operate your own server, enter a filename where you want form information saved and choose a file format from the drop-down menu

which you want the form information saved, as well as the format in which you want to save the information. Enter your preferred filename in the Name of Data File box, and then select a file format from the drop-down menu. If you want to enter responses directly into a database, identify the file and select either Comma-delimited Text or Tab-delimited Text, depending on the database you use. You can select to have Excel work with Publisher automatically to save new names and addresses added to an Outlook or Access database, as well as compile survey results.

Select "Send data to me in e-mail," shown in Figure 8-19, if you do not expect to receive too many form responses and you are willing to copy the information from your e-mail to your database and e-mail address books (so you can respond in the future). This option is simpler to set up, but may take more time in the long run. If you choose this option, enter the e-mail address where you want form responses sent in the Send Data To This E-mail Address box and replace the someone@microsoft.com placeholder with your specific e-mail address. You can also enter new text to replace the Subject of E-mail default.

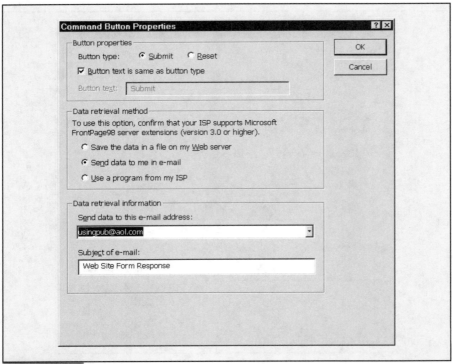

FIGURE 8-19   If the volume of anticipated responses is low, select the "Send data to me in e-mail" option

If you anticipate a high volume of responses, your Internet service provider (ISP) may be able to work with you setting up a data retrieval method that automates the process of compiling form responses, summarizing the information, and presenting it to you in the most useful manner. In this case, select the "Use a program from my ISP" option and identify the program in the Action box in the Data Retrieval Information area of the Command Button Properties dialog box, shown in Figure 8-20.

As you complete your Web site, make sure that you do not neglect to replace all placeholder text in any Web pages or forms you may have added, including order forms, response forms, or sign-up forms.

Continuing Articles onto Additional Pages

Whenever possible, limit your Web site stories to a single page. Shorter is always better. The story pages can accommodate approximately 375 words.

If an *essential* story is too long to fit on a single page and you *absolutely must* continue it on an additional page, here's what to do.

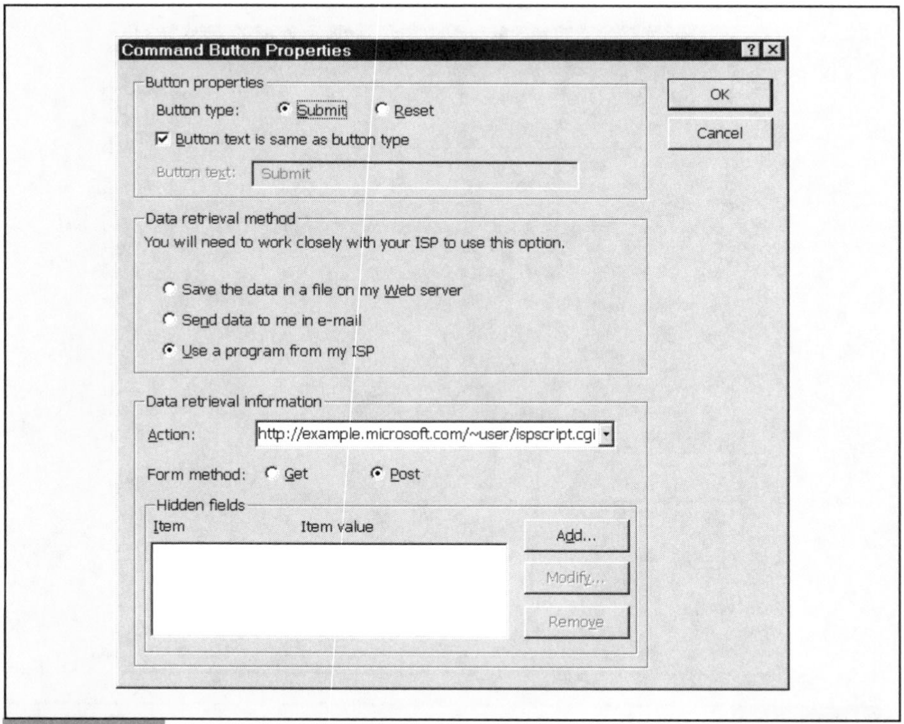

FIGURE 8-20 Your ISP may offer programs that will compile form results and forward them to you automatically or as requested

First select Insert | Page (or press CTRL-SHIFT-N). When the Wizard displays the Insert Page dialog box, click the More Options button. Click the radio button next to the Duplicate All Objects on Page option (which, by default, is the current page). Then deselect Add Hyperlink to Web Navigation Bar by clicking the check box next to this option, as shown in Figure 8-21. You need to make these choices so that the page on which you continue the article will resemble the page from which the article is continued. Be careful, too, to avoid adding a navigation link to the continuation page, which would then appear on every one of your Web pages. Visitors have no need to go directly to any Web site article continuation page. Click OK or ENTER when you have made these changes.

Publisher automatically will take you to the newly inserted page. Once you have seen the newly added page, you'll need to make several changes to this page's appearance, so visitors will know without a doubt that this page contains material continued from another Web page. Also, don't forget to add "Continued" to the end of the story on its page of origin, as shown in Figure 8-22.

Add a comma and "Continued" to the title at the top of the page. Select the navigation bar and remove it by selecting Edit | Cut (or press CTRL-X). Select and Cut (or DELETE) clip art and short text elements like pull-quotes. Place the insertion point within the text box, select Edit | Highlight Entire Story (or press CTRL-A). Then select Edit | Cut (or press CTRL-X) to remove the text. You have now readied the added page so you can continue the article from the first Web page.

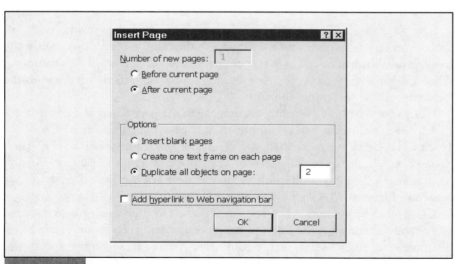

FIGURE 8-21 When the Wizard displays the Insert Page dialog box, select the Duplicate All Objects on Page option and deselect Add Hyperlink to Web Navigation Bar

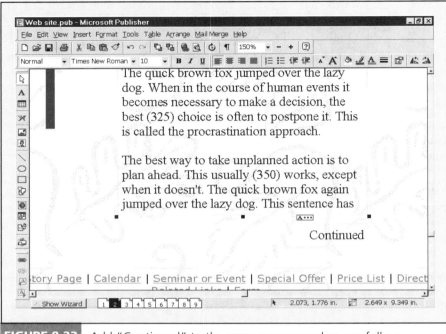

FIGURE 8-22 Add "Continued" to the page so your readers can follow your layout

Save your work (CTRL-S) and click the page number of the previous page. Select the text frame and shorten it by dragging the middle handle upward. In the newly available space, create a text frame and enter the word "Continued." Choose right alignment for the new text frame and align its right edge with the right edge of the text frame above.

Next, you must link the continuation page to the page where the article originated. Double-click the word "Continued" and click the Hyperlink tool, or select Insert | Hyperlink (or press CTRL-K). When the Wizard displays the Hyperlink dialog box, select Another Page in Your Web Site, next to the Create a Hyperlink To option. In the Hyperlink Information section, click the Next Page option, as shown in Figure 8-23. Click OK, or press ENTER.

Click on the page number of your newly inserted page to return to the page where you will continue the story. In the space above the text frame, create a new text frame and enter "Return to previous page." Select that text frame and, again, click the Hyperlink tool, or select Insert | Hyperlink (or press CTRL-K). When the Wizard displays the Hyperlink dialog box, select the Another Page in Your Web Site option, and this time select the Previous Page option, as shown in Figure 8-24.

Part I: Meet Your New Marketing and Publishing Department

How would you like to be your own marketing department and save hundreds or thousands of dollars otherwise spent in creative costs each year—without sacrificing quality or spending hours mastering complicated software? Images 1 and 2 show the professional-quality results you can create using Publisher 2000, Microsoft's latest version of its versatile desktop publishing software.

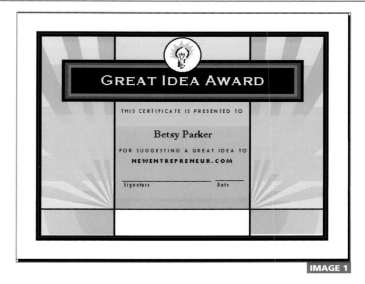

GREAT IDEA AWARD

THIS CERTIFICATE IS PRESENTED TO

Betsy Parker

FOR SUGGESTING A GREAT IDEA TO

NEWENTREPRENEUR.COM

Signature   Date

IMAGE 1

Looking for Exposure?

NewEntrepreneur. com provides the most professional and exciting print publications around and can come up with the right design for you.

Phone us up now!

NewEntrepreneur.com
PO Box 697
Dover, NH 0382

Osborne/McGraw-Hill
2600 Tenth Street
Berkeley, CA
94710

NEWENTREPRENEUR.COM

Product/ Service Information

Print & Electronic
Media Specialists

Tel: 555 555 5555

IMAGE 2

If you've been disappointed and frustrated in the past when you tried a new software application and found you had to become a "guru" to achieve minimally satisfactory results, you'll be pleasantly surprised about how little you have to learn to create professional-looking documents, ranging from business cards to complex, multipage catalogs. The Publisher Catalog allows you to create documents from one of Publisher's Wizards, existing Publisher files, or any of the document templates that are included in the product. The chapters in Part I get you going on your first project, showing you the basics needed to make great looking documents, and acquaint you with the many enhancements Microsoft added to Publisher 2000.

See Chapter 1, "What You Can Do with Microsoft Publisher 2000," for an overview of the many tasks you can accomplish with Publisher 2000. See Chapter 4, "Learning to Use Publisher's Wizards," for details on how to create your own professional documents.

IMAGE 3

One of the features new to Publisher 2000 is the Clip Art Gallery (Image 3). This feature offers you the opportunity to quickly spruce up your documents with an assortment of illustrations. You can enter keywords to search for just the right image and then easily drag and drop it into your document.

Another new addition is Publisher's ability to support the Pantone Matching System (PMS). Choosing a specific color number from the Pantone library ensures that you will get the exact industry-wide PMS color that you specified (Image 4). This guarantees the final printed product will match what you saw on your screen and envisioned when creating your publication.

See Chapter 1 for more details on Publisher 2000's enhanced capabilities and its compatibility with previous versions.

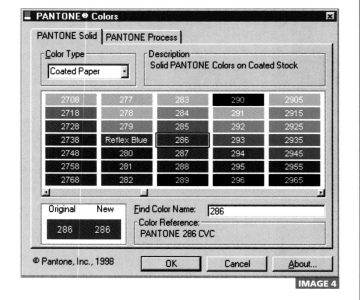

IMAGE 4

Publisher's Newsletter Wizard provides a variety of page designs and color schemes to help you capture the desired look and feel for your particular message. The newsletter templates allow different layouts, so your pages can contain a variety of elements—both 3- and 4-column text layout, for example, as well as space for mailing addresses and return address information on the back page. See Images 19, 20, and 21.

Chapter 5, "Publishing Your First Newsletter," provides the details for creating a newsletter, showing you how to use wizards to create a publication and how to alter a wizard's layout to meet your particular needs.

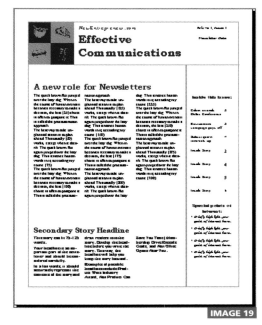

IMAGE 19

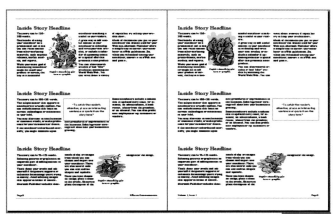

IMAGE 20

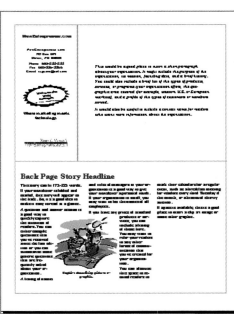

IMAGE 21

The Brochure Wizard gives you the tools to easily create a brochure that integrates with other publications you may have produced; you can also create an independent design that best serves your purposes. Your brochure can incorporate a variety of different elements, as shown in Images 22 and 23.

Chapter 6, "Creating Brochures That Sell," shows you how to determine a brochure's size, how it will fold, and your distribution requirements—all elements that will affect the brochure's design.

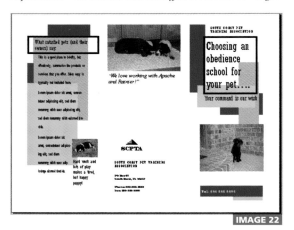

IMAGE 22

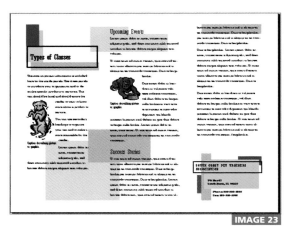

IMAGE 23

IMAGE 24

Publisher's Catalog Wizards make catalog creation a virtual snap. You can easily pull together various clip art selections, photographs, and text to build an attractive presentation for your products and services. Without the Catalog Wizard, you'd likely spend hours just determining your page layout and figuring out how to display your products and ordering information. Images 24, 25, and 26 show the results of using the Catalog Wizard to produce crisp, clean documents that highlight what you offer.

Chapter 7, "Producing Your First Catalog," provides the details on using the Catalog Wizard to produce exactly the look you're after, and gives tips on choosing the right layout to best profile your products.

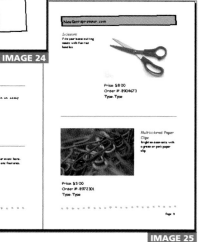

IMAGE 25

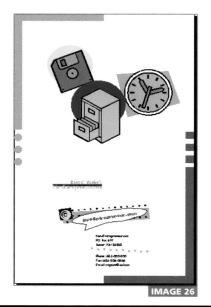

IMAGE 26

While Publisher offers templates and Wizards that help you create short documents, such as matching business cards and letterhead, you can also create much larger documents with ease. For instance, if you're writing a grant proposal that requires footnotes, 2-column text, varied margins for different sections, and a table of contents, Publisher provides the tools for this. Or maybe you're writing an instructional booklet which gives step-by-step directions for how to assemble the wooden Adirondack chairs that you built, and you want to add some pizzazz to your booklet's pages. With Publisher 2000, you can add a subtle image behind your text to add interest or add a watermark to highlight a document's confidential nature (Images 27 and 28).

Chapter 9, "Using Publisher to Create Long Documents," shows you how to set margins and columns, add borders to each page, and add a table of contents.

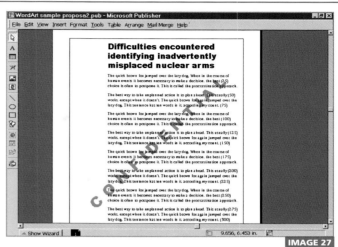

IMAGE 27

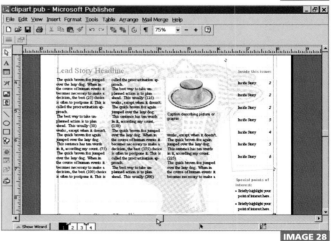

IMAGE 28

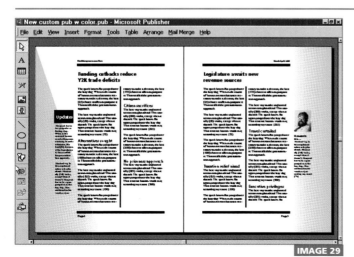

IMAGE 29

Once you have practiced with the predefined Publisher templates and Wizards, you may want to further explore Publisher's capabilities and create documents that are not based on a template. You can easily pull together a professional-looking document of your own by using Publisher's capabilities. Perhaps you've designed a brochure and would now like to add a color that matches your firm's logo—you can use Publisher's Background color panels feature to easily dress up the pages of your brochure and call attention to the content, as shown in Image 29.

Chapter 10, "Creating Publications Without Wizards," discusses the pros and cons of creating documents from scratch.

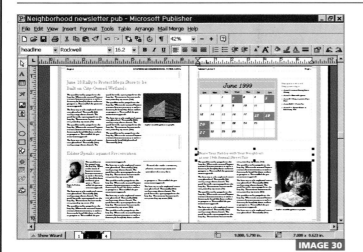

IMAGE 30

If you've created a brochure or newsletter which successfully captures the spirit of what your organization is all about (Image 30), or that profiles products and services you offer, you can work with Publisher to turn that document into a Web site, establishing a cohesive online presence that mirrors your print publication. For example, Publisher can build a home page for your newsletter (Image 31) and establish links to any of the content from other issues. As you can see, the Web page contains links to the newsletter's calendar and featured articles.

IMAGE 31

If Publisher can't fit all of your content on the Web site, the material is saved for you under an Extra Content tab (shown in Image 32) so you have the option to create additional pages to accommodate the extra material.

Chapter 11, "Creating Web Sites from Print Publications," details how to create a Web site from an existing publication, and shows how Publisher's Web Wizard takes your print content, whether that is a brochure or a newsletter, and creates an online presence from this material.

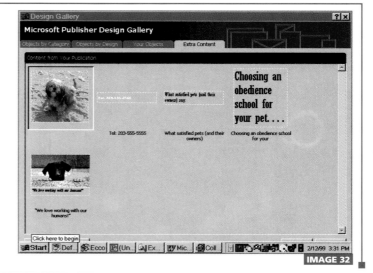

IMAGE 32

With PhotoDraw, you can make simple modifications to your photos and turn them from flat, motionless images into vibrant images that seem to move on the page. The paintbrush effect applied to the photo shown in Image 45 illustrates how simple circular motions that emphasize the subject's focus can quickly liven up the picture.

IMAGE 45

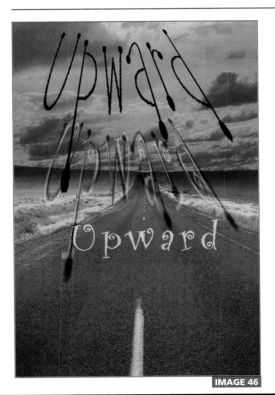

IMAGE 46

While applying effects to your photos can add implied motion to the images, you can achieve some of the same results with text. If you want to add life to an otherwise flat document, you can use images that depict motion. Then, you can add text effects to further the sense of movement, as shown in Image 46.

Chapter 13, "Making the Most of Photographs in Print and Online," details how you can add life to your existing photographs, and turn them from ordinary images into image-and-text combinations that deliver a message or simply make your Publisher documents more interesting.

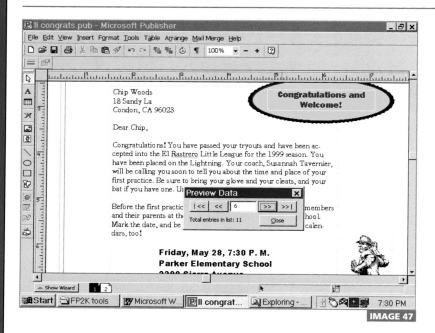

Not only does Publisher help you to create professional newsletters, flyers, and brochures, but you can also add addresses from the records in your database. Use a wizard to walk through the mail merge process and preview your data along the way, as shown in Image 47.

In addition to the helpful mail merge features, Publisher 2000 also allows you to either print the document yourself or, for more sophisticated jobs, to use a commercial printer. To make the commercial printing venture as easy as possible, Publisher includes a variety of wizards to help you prepare your files, including the size and location of each graphic element. These details, shown in Image 48, ensure that your printer can easily reproduce your document and provide the finished product without any snags or difficulty.

Chapter 14, "Addressing Postcards, Newsletters, and Brochures," and Chapter 15, "Choosing Between Desktop and Commercial Printing," wrap up the book. In these chapters you learn how to use a database of names and addresses to address your publications, how to choose whether a commercial printer is best suited for your print job, and, if so, how to prepare your documents for printing at a commercial printer.

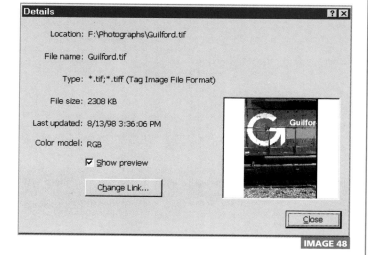

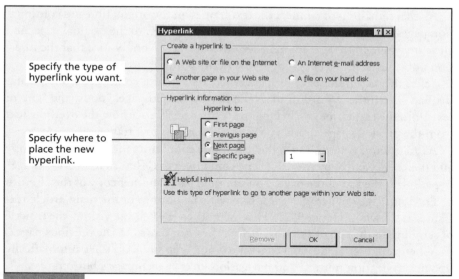

Specify the type of hyperlink you want.

Specify where to place the new hyperlink.

FIGURE 8-23 When the Wizard displays the Hyperlink dialog box, select the Another Page in Your Web Site and the Next Page options

New text frame containing the added hyperlink

FIGURE 8-24 On the page where your story continues, create a new text frame containing a hyperlink to the page from which the story is continued

All that remains is to connect the text frames on the origination and continuation pages, so that text will flow between them. Return to the original page, and click anywhere in the text frame. Select the Connect icon. Notice that the insertion point turns into a cup with a downward-pointing arrow.

Select the page number of the page where the article is continued from the Status Bar. When the Wizard displays the newly inserted page, "pour" the "cup of text" into the text frame by clicking the text frame. Notice how the overflow text from the previous page appears in the second page's text frame.

As an option, you can resize the text frame containing the continuation copy and then select and copy the text frame containing the "Return to Previous Page" hyperlink at the top of the page. You can then paste another copy of the "Return to Previous Page" hyperlink text frame near the bottom of the main article text frame, as shown in Figure 8-25. This method saves Web site visitors the trouble of scrolling to the top of the story before they can return to the previous page.

When you insert additional pages into your Web site, Publisher automatically updates navigation buttons and navigation links at each page's bottom.

Inserting Clip Art and Photographs

After you have added headlines, text, and pull-quotes to your Web site, return to your Web site's first or home page, and concentrate on replacing placeholder clip art with illustrations and photographs more appropriate for your specific message.

To replace a clip art placeholder with your own art, right-click on the placeholder and select Change Picture | Picture. The Wizard will display a series of nested drop-down menus. Select from these source options: Clip Art, From File, or From Scanner or Camera, as shown here. Select New Drawing if you want to create a drawing using Publisher 2000's AutoShapes.

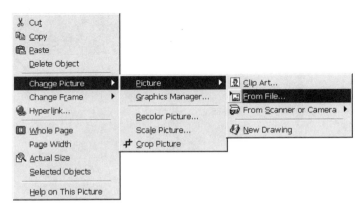

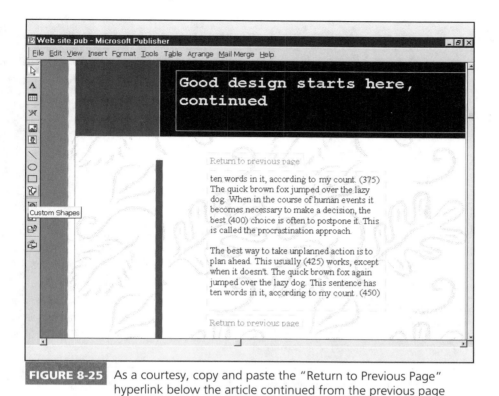

FIGURE 8-25 As a courtesy, copy and paste the "Return to Previous Page" hyperlink below the article continued from the previous page

To resize a photograph, drag one of the corner handles. Publisher 2000 will maintain the photograph's original height-to-width ratio and proportionately increase or decrease the artwork's size.

Avoid the temptation to include large visuals in your Web site. The larger the visual, the longer the Web site takes to load on your visitor's computer. Always keep visuals, especially photographs, as small as possible.

Feel free to reposition the placeholder visuals. For example, Figure 8-26 shows an awkward-looking photograph, because the individual is looking to the left.

If you drag the visual object to the right side of the Web page, the photograph looks into the page, creating a page with better balance, as shown in Figure 8-27.

Previewing and Posting Your Web Site

You can check the work you've done on your Web site while continuing to work on it, replacing placeholder text and visuals with the words and photographs that communicate your message. Once you have replaced all the text and graphics placeholders, you can perform a more exhaustive test of your Web site by using

FIGURE 8-26 Avoid photographs "looking off the page," like this left-facing photograph in the Web Site Wizard's default position along the page's left-hand margin

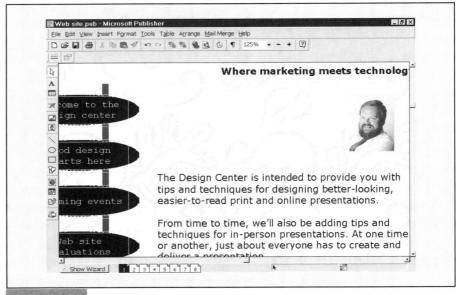

FIGURE 8-27 Repositioning visual placeholders often creates better-looking pages, depending on the photograph or illustration you have chosen to use

Publisher's Design Checker. Once you have checked your Web site with the Design Checker, all that remains for you to do is to post your Web site to the ISP who will be hosting your Web site.

Previewing Your Site While Working on It

At any point while you are working on your Web site, you can preview it by either clicking the Standard Toolbar's Web Page Preview icon, or selecting File | Web Page Preview (or pressing CTRL-SHIFT-B).

You'll benefit from another important advantage when you use the File | Web Page Preview option, rather than clicking the Web Page Preview icon. When you use File | Web Page Preview, the Wizard will display the Web Page Preview dialog box.

With the Web Page Preview dialog box, you can preview your entire Web site or—more importantly—just the current page. Previewing just the current page is much faster, although you cannot navigate to other pages or check to make sure that all hyperlinks are working properly.

If you click the Web Page Preview icon, the Wizard will display another version of the Web Page Preview dialog box. This dialog box will tell you that Publisher is launching your Web page browser, and creating and saving an HTML copy of your Web site to your computer's hard disk. The progress bar informs you of the Web Page Preview feature's progress.

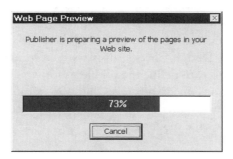

You should get in the habit of frequently previewing your Web site as you work on it. Publisher automatically resaves the current version each time you preview the Web site. If you frequently preview your Web site with the Web Page Preview feature, you'll ensure that the order of the information you are presenting is logical and that all your navigation links are working. Checking your navigation links' operation is especially important if you insert "continuation" pages that do not appear on the automatically Wizard-created navigation bar.

Your Web site is likely to present a completely different image when you view it in your Web browser than when you view it in Publisher 2000. The type will be different (probably larger), and mistakes will be more obvious.

Frequent previews also remind you of the importance of keeping visuals, such as scanned photographs, as small as possible. In addition, frequent previews help you locate clip art or text placeholders that you overlooked deleting or replacing with your message.

Using Publisher's Design Checker

With Publisher 2000's Web site Design Checker, you can fine-tune your Web site before posting it to the World Wide Web. To avoid unpleasant surprises—such as a Web site that takes too long to load into anyone's browser—select Tools | Design Checker. When Publisher displays the Design Checker dialog box use it to check your entire Web site, or just one or more pages at a time, as you complete them.

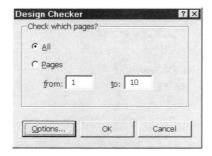

When you are using Publisher's Design Checker, click the Design Checker's Options button. The Design Checker displays the Options dialog box, shown next. Use this dialog box to define the problems for which the Design Checker will search. The Options dialog box saves you time because it avoids indicating problems of which you are already aware, but have decided to leave as is, such as graphics elements that take too long to load.

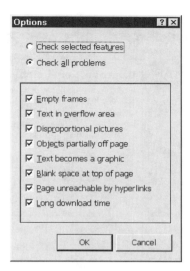

Each time the Design Checker encounters a problem, it selects the offending frame, indicates the design problem, and suggests a solution. By clicking on the appropriate buttons, you can select the Ignore option to ignore that individual problem, Ignore All to ignore all the instances of the problem, or Continue, which, in many cases, guides you through the task of fixing the problem.

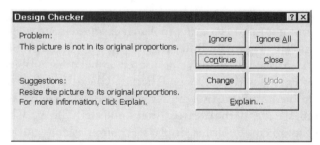

After you click the Continue button, the dialog box will display the Change button. If you click the Change button, Publisher will correct the problem it has detected, using the solution it has suggested.

If you are unsure how to fix any particular problem, click the Explain button. This action launches Publisher's Help and takes you directly to the page explaining how to solve the problem, as shown in Figure 8-28. Once you've solved this

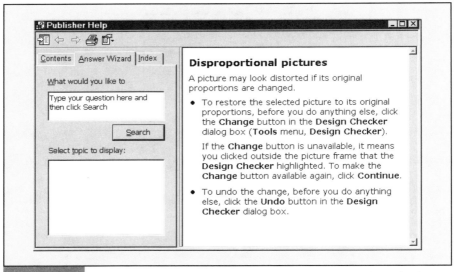

FIGURE 8-28 Clicking the Explain button launches Publisher's Help and selects the topic that addresses the problem the Design Checker has identified

problem, again click the Continue button to view the next problem. The Design Checker will continue to explain each problem it encounters and suggest solutions.

As the example in Figure 8-28 shows, you can solve some problems without leaving the Design Checker, while you must remember other problems and solve them after you have closed the Design Checker. Click the Ignore button if you encounter a problem you must solve after you close the Design Checker.

On the Web, speed is of the essence. After Publisher's Design Checker identifies an obvious problem, Publisher displays a prompt asking your permission to test whether your Web site will download quickly. Because this test can take a few seconds, Publisher gives you the option to select the Yes button if you want to test downloading speed, or No if you want to skip this test. (You might want to skip any particular test for problems you want to fix outside of the Design Checker, such as overlapping text frames.)

If you click the Yes button, the Design Checker will proceed through your Web site, checking the downloading speed of every graphic. Whenever the Design Checker encounters a graphic that will require an unusually long time to download, it will select the graphic and identify it, and suggest that you resize it or delete it, as shown next.

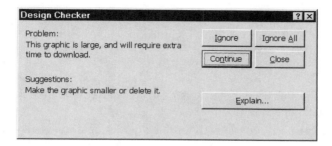

Posting Your Web Site

You have two ways to post your Web site to the Web. First, you can save your Web site to your computer's hard drive as an HTML document, and use the File Transfer Protocol (FTP) software that you can obtain from your ISP or off the Web. Use the FTP software to upload your Web site to your ISP's computer. Second, you can use the Publisher Web Site Wizard to guide you through the process of uploading your Web site directly to your ISP's computer.

Before making a choice, you may want to check with your ISP and ask them which option the ISP's operators prefer.

The first step is to save your Publisher files as a Web site on your hard drive. Before saving your Web site to your computer's hard drive, you should create a folder where you want all of the files associated with your published Web site to be placed. Saving your Web site to your hard drive creates numerous files—one for each navigation button and graphic file, as well as one for each page—and you're going to have to gather all of them together and submit them to your ISP. To simplify this process, you might want to create a "Published Web Site" folder in which to store these files.

After you have created and identified a destination folder, select File | Save As Web Page. Publisher will display the Save As dialog box, from which you can specify the previously created folder where Publisher will store all the files associated with your ready-to-be-published Web site.

Publisher's Save As Web Page dialog box displays a progress bar that confirms it is converting your Web site into the HTML format necessary for posting the Web site on the World Wide Web. At the same time, Publisher is converting illustrations and WordArt graphics to the .gif format.

Testing Your Web Site Forms

If you included any of the Web Site Wizard's forms in your final Web site design, testing the operation of those forms is important to make sure they function properly, returning the desired information to you. To test your forms, follow these steps for each form you have included in your Web site:

1. Copy each individual form—one at a time—on one of your Web site's un-linked pages.

2. Use your Web browser to submit each form to you, as though you were encountering each form on the Web.

3. Enter into each spot on each form the type of data you want to gather from your Web site visitors. Use as many variations and combinations of data input as you can possibly create to test your individual data entry areas, as well as the performance and integrity of each form you've added to your Web site.

4. Verify that you have received all the test data you entered and sent by way of the forms. If you discover any problem or inconsistency with the test data you sent and the test data you received, contact your ISP to ensure that the data you want to gather via your Web site is being collected in the required format, and that the ISP is handling the data consistently with your data-gathering expectations.

The Web site Design Checker will interrupt its own progress, however, if it encounters a form in your Web site for which you have not specified to Publisher how to handle its responses. When the Web site Design Checker finds this type of problem, Publisher displays a prompt, shown here, asking you if you want to specify how Publisher should handle that individual form's responses. Click the Yes button if you want to fix the problem now; click the No button if you want to continue saving the files in HTML and .gif format for your Web site.

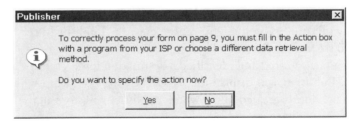

Note that you will have to follow this design checking process for every form you have included in your Web site; perfecting this process—and all your Web site's important data collection points—can take some time.

If you choose to supply the missing information, Publisher's Command Button Properties dialog box will appear, allowing you to define how you want responses from your form to be handled, as in Figure 8-29.

Return to the Windows desktop and select the folder where you have saved your Publisher file as a Web site. Notice that there are separate files for each page,

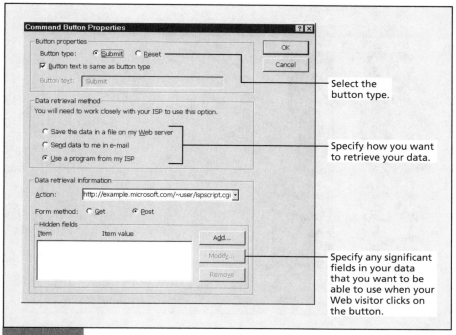

FIGURE 8-29 The Command Button Properties dialog box allows you to define how you want responses from your form to be handled

each navigation button, and each graphic, as shown in Figure 8-30. Select Edit | Select All (or press CTRL-A) to select all the files when you're ready to upload them to your ISP using FTP, as we discussed in a previous paragraph.

After your Web site has been saved to your hard drive, Microsoft's Web Publishing Wizard, which ships with Internet Explorer 5.0, guides you through the process of uploading your Publisher files to your ISP. Remember that whether you can use Web Wizard's uploading utilities depends on your ISP's hardware and software, so always check with your ISP to get exact instructions for posting your Web site to the Web.

Select Start | Programs | Internet Explorer | Web Publishing Wizard. Internet Explorer's Web Publishing Wizard will guide you through the steps involved in establishing a two-way communication between your computer and the ISP of your choice.

If the Web Publishing Wizard does not appear in your Program menu, you must reinstall Internet Explorer 5.0, but when you install it this time, select Custom Install | Add a Component | Customize your Installation | Web Publishing Wizard.

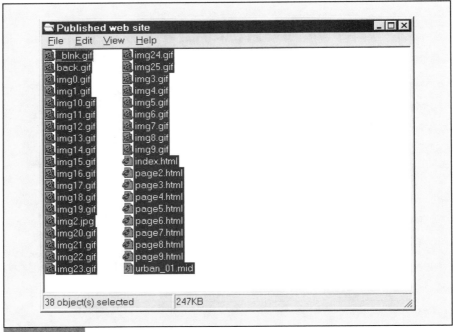

FIGURE 8-30   Use Edit | Select All (or press CTRL-A) to select all the graphic and HTML page files for uploading to your ISP

After you install Microsoft Internet Explorer 5.0's Web Publishing Wizard, start the Wizard, and it will guide you through the process of uploading your Web site to the ISP you have selected.

Professional Skills Summary

In this chapter, we took a look at using Publisher's Web Site Wizard as the tool to create your first Web site—today's primary lifeline to the "cyber world" for any professional, business, or organization. In addition to using the Wizard to create a tailor-made site for you with reliable links to and from other URLs, we also presented instructions on adding order forms, membership forms, or response forms to your Web site for taking orders, soliciting memberships, or gathering general feedback on your site. When compared with other Web site-authoring tools, Publisher 2000's Web Site Wizard offers you professional-looking results with a super-easy user interface to get the job done. No one—not even the most magical of Web wizards—will suspect that you created your customized Web site with a simple desktop publishing tool!

Part III

Polishing Your Basic Publisher 2000 Skills

chapter 9

Using Publisher to Create Long Documents

In this chapter, you will:

- Create a structure for long documents
- Choose layout sizes and folds
- Use text styles to speed document formatting
- Create section dividers
- Create a table of contents

Examining Long Documents' Unique Needs

Long documents (generally more than 10 pages), such as proposals, position papers, and instruction booklets for assembly or processes, present their own set of unique challenges.

With Publisher, you'll find it easy to create long, multipage documents by automatically inserting page numbers and header/footer information on each page, as you create additional pages. A *header* is additional information, such as titles and page numbers, that appears at each page's top, outside the top page margin you set for the page. A *footer* is additional information—again, such as titles and page numbers—that appear at each page's bottom and outside the bottom page margin you sent for the page. You can also speed your work on long documents by using text styles to quickly format the pages you add, thereby creating a desired information hierarchy. If you think back to your days in high school or college, your English teachers hounded you about mastering outlines to write the perfectly organized term paper. With long documents, like those discussed in this chapter, an information hierarchy is nothing but a more sophisticated term for an outline. Adding different styles to the different outline levels creates a more professional-looking presentation and helps the reader get a handle on how the information levels are related.

New in 2000: Publisher now has additional capabilities to handle multipage documents that enable you to have your long document easily and cost-effectively printed by a commercial printer. With these added features, you can take advantage of the "economies of scale," when you have your long documents professionally printed on large sheets of paper and cut apart.

Choosing Sizes and Folds for Long Documents

If you want a successful publication, regardless of length, your first step should always be careful planning. The most important question to address is how many copies of the final, printed document you will need. The number of final copies you need will influence your document's size and whether you will choose one- or two-sided printing.

If you are preparing a proposal or position paper and require fewer than 50 or 100 copies, you will probably print a master copy on high-quality glossy paper using your office ink-jet or laser printer and take it to a commercial copy center for quantity duplication, collation, and stapling or binding. This option is also your best choice if single-color printing is sufficient. You can also print copies on your existing letterhead. If you have a color printer, adding color to your limited-quantity print run is easy and completely do-it-yourself.

If you're preparing an instruction booklet or employee benefits manual, for instance, and require more than 100 copies, you'll probably choose two-sided printing. If you need quantities of more than 100, this job is best done by a commercial printer because of economy and quality issues, not to mention printing speed. With two-sided printing, you can still incorporate color into your design. You can also use folds to maximize your publication's information density.

To start creating your long document, select File | New. When you see the Publisher Catalog, click the Blank Publications tab.

Select the Blank New Page option, and select the Full Page option, if you are preparing a proposal or position paper to be printed on your office printer or taken to a copy center for duplication. Next, click the Create button to begin working on your publication.

Scroll down to Blank Book Fold and select Book Fold if you want to prepare a two-sided booklet or pamphlet to be taken to a commercial printer, as shown in Figure 9-1. Click the Create button to begin your work.

Publisher will display a prompt like the one shown in Figure 9-2, that reminds you that two-sided publications are typically printed in four-page groups called *signatures*. Click the Yes button to confirm that you want to insert an additional three pages.

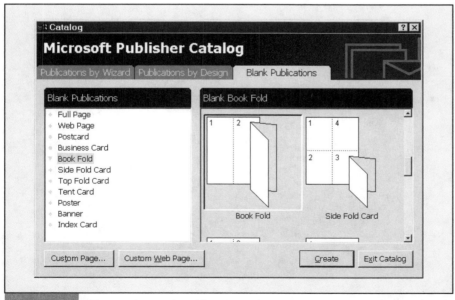

FIGURE 9-1   Choose the Book Fold option when you want to prepare a two-sided pamphlet or instruction book

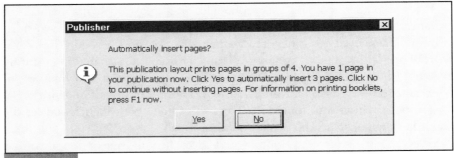

FIGURE 9-2 Publisher's "Automatically insert pages?" prompt reminds you that two-sided publications are typically printed in four-page signatures

If you are creating a publication that will ultimately be a two-sided publication, select File | Page Setup, which will give you an opportunity to fine-tune your page setup. Publisher displays the Page Setup dialog box, as shown in Figure 9-3. Locate the Choose an Orientation area and select Landscape. Then click OK or press ENTER to close the dialog box.

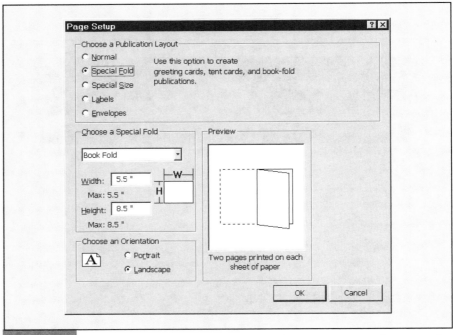

FIGURE 9-3 Select the Landscape option in the Choose an Orientation area of the Page Setup dialog box when creating books and pamphlets

When Publisher redisplays your publication, you'll immediately notice that something's amiss. Publisher's default one-inch margins, which might be appropriate for full-sized publications, are definitely too generous for pages printed with a book fold on 8.5-by-11-inch paper, as shown in Figure 9-4.

Choosing Margins and Column Arrangements

To set up an appropriate framework for your publication, select Arrange | Layout Guides. With Publisher's Layout Guides dialog box, shown in Figure 9-5, you will make several decisions that are central to creating good-looking documents, whether the final document is a single-sided publication, such as a proposal, or a two-sided publication, such as a book or pamphlet.

First, start by selecting the margins you want for your document. If you are creating a single-sided publication, you can accept the default one-inch margins or reduce the margins, whichever you prefer. Consider how you want your document's pages held together. If you are going to put three holes into your document to hold it in three-ring binders, you might want to increase the left margin to allow for adequate hole-punching space. However, if you are creating a two-sided publication, you will probably want to reduce the margins to a more proportional measurement. Adding a little extra margin to page tops creates a more inviting page.

Tip: If you are working with the Quick Publication Wizard, select Page Size | Page Setup to locate the Page Setup dialog box.

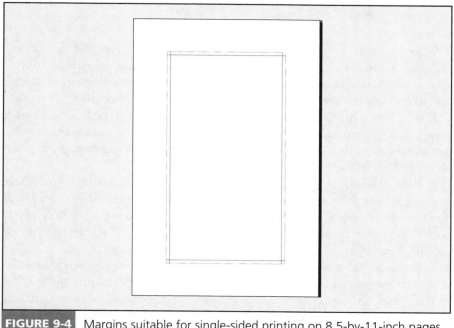

FIGURE 9-4   Margins suitable for single-sided printing on 8.5-by-11-inch pages are too generous for pages printed using a book fold

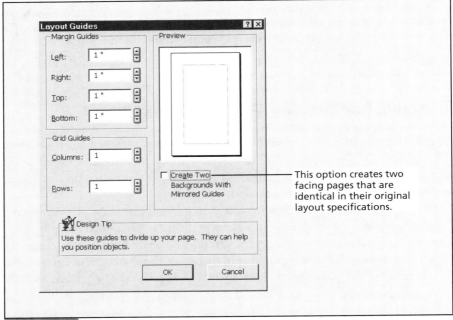

This option creates two facing pages that are identical in their original layout specifications.

FIGURE 9-5   Use the Layout Guides dialog box to set up desired publication margins and columns, as well as create different left and right background pages

Next, locate the Layout Guides dialog box's Grid Guides area and choose your preferred column arrangement. When you specify the number of background columns with these grid areas, be aware that your publication's foreground doesn't necessarily have column layouts that relate directly to text placement.

If your final publication is a single-page document printed on 8.5-by-11-inch paper, such as a business proposal, your two most common options are two columns and three columns. You also have the same basic options to apply to pamphlets and books.

A two-column arrangement for your publication offers you maximum text density plus an opportunity to use a single, wide column of text to introduce each new section, as shown in Figure 9-6. The two-column format projects a symmetrical, classic, conservative, "all-business" image. Its primary disadvantage is that it is difficult to insert visuals—charts and graphs—into the layout.

An asymmetric, three-column arrangement offers a more open page in addition to far more flexibility, as shown in Figure 9-7. The first column to the left is used to build white space into each page as well as accommodate visuals, such as charts and graphs, and text, such as short quotations or ancillary information. A single column of text spans the second and third columns. This arrangement projects a more contemporary image.

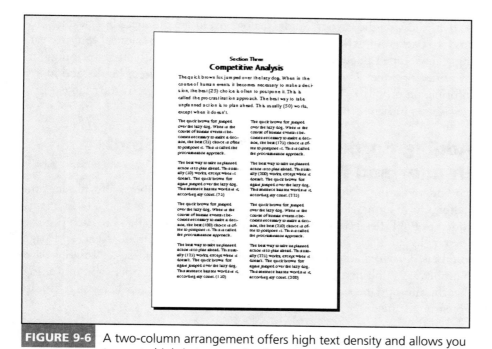

FIGURE 9-6 A two-column arrangement offers high text density and allows you to create high-impact section introductions

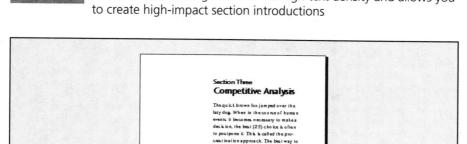

FIGURE 9-7 A three-column arrangement creates an open feeling and provides space for visuals and short text elements

Before leaving the Layout Guides dialog box, locate the check box next to Create Two Backgrounds With Mirrored Guides. Leave this box alone if you are creating a single-sided publication. Check this box, however, if you are planning on two-sided printing. This option permits you to place different header and footer information on the backgrounds of each left and right page, as the changed Preview shows in Figure 9-8.

Adding Borders, Page Numbers, and Header and Footers

To add repeating elements, such as borders, page numbers, and header and footer information, select View | Go to Background (or press CTRL-M). Elements added to Publisher's Background View are automatically added to each page.

Start by adding a border using Publisher's Rectangle tool. Next, add page numbers. Create a text frame at the desired location and select Insert | Page Numbers. A Publisher prompt appears pointing to the number sign, indicating that the appropriate page number will be added to each page when you return to Foreground View.

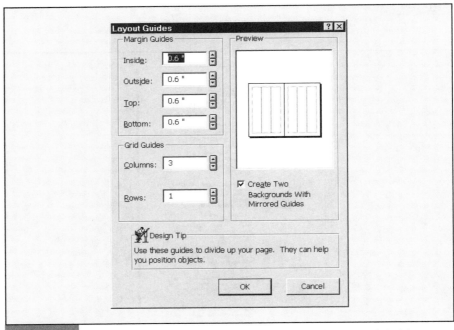

FIGURE 9-8   Checking the Create Two Backgrounds With Mirrored Guides option permits you to add different header and footer information to the left and right pages of two-sided publications

Finally, add any other repeating information you want added to each page. If you are preparing a proposal or formal report, you might want to include the client's name or the title of the report. If you are preparing a pamphlet or instruction book, you might want to include the publication title.

Use Publisher's text formatting tools to select a desired typeface, type size, and alignment. Alignment is particularly important. Elements placed along the right edges of each page should be right-aligned, and elements added to the left edges of each page should be left-aligned, so that your text lays out attractively.

To work as efficiently as possible when creating multiple header elements, drag a guide from the ruler to "hang" titles and page numbers, as shown in Figure 9-9. This assures that all four titles and page numbers (on facing pages) will be properly aligned.

Cross-Reference: For introductory information on using guides, see Chapter 2.

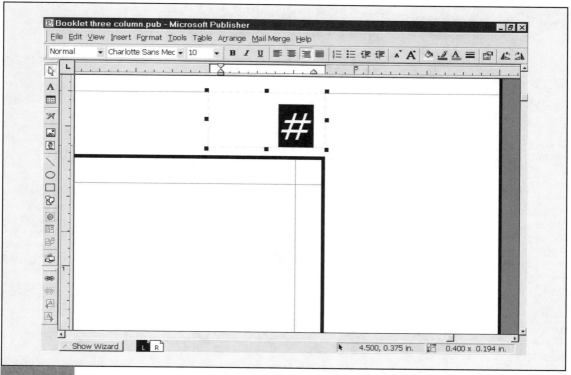

FIGURE 9-9 To assure accurate alignment of headers and page numbers, drag a horizontal guide from the ruler and "hang" the header's text frames from it

To speed formatting of header and page numbers, create and format one text frame, and copy and paste it into the other locations, making sure that you adjust alignment to compensate for either left or right placement.

Select View | Go to Foreground when you have finished adding and formatting repeating elements. Notice the difference that borders—especially those that go around an entire page—headers, and page numbers make, as shown in Figure 9-10.

L▶ Note: If you have been working with a multicolumn layout, as previously described, select Arrange | Layout Guides. When Publisher displays the Layout Guides dialog box, choose the 1-column option.

Maximizing Long Document Layout with Text Styles

One of the best ways to speed the preparation of long documents containing a definite information hierarchy is to use text styles to automatically indent headings, subheads, and text.

This technique improves the appearance of your publication by automatically building white space into each page. Equally important, you can let Publisher automatically insert new pages and create new text frames when importing word processor text.

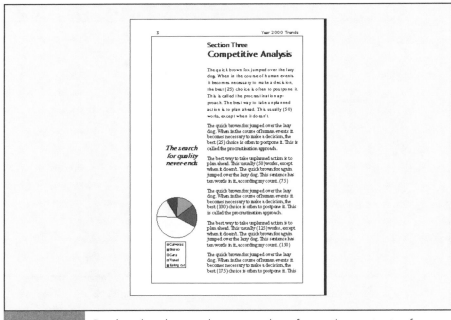

FIGURE 9-10 Borders, headers, and page numbers frame the contents of each page

Creating an Indent Body Text Style

The first step is to create a Normal text style that, in addition to specifying the typeface, type size, line spacing, and hyphenation for the bulk of your document, indents the text a desired distance from the left margin.

Create a text frame the full width of the page. Import or enter enough body copy to cover that entire page. Select Format | Text Style | Create a New Style. When Publisher displays the Create New Style dialog box, enter a desired name, such as "Indented body copy," as shown in Figure 9-11.

Then format the text by clicking the appropriate buttons:

- Click the Character Type and Size button to select a desired typeface and type size.
- Click the Line Spacing button to fine-tune line spacing and enter additional spacing between paragraphs (if desired).
- Click the Character Spacing button if you want to fine-tune letter spacing.
- Click the Tabs button to determine the location of any necessary tabs.
- Most importantly, click the Indents and Lists button. Publisher will display the Indents and Lists dialog box. Locate the Left indents and enter the distance you want to indent the left margin of the text, or click the up/down arrows.

A deep left-hand indent will add white space to each page and create space for you to hang headings and subheads. You can preview the relative depth of the indent in the Sample window, as shown in Figure 9-12.

Before leaving the Indents and Lists dialog box, choose a desired text alignment from the Alignment drop-down menu, and click OK or press ENTER. Click

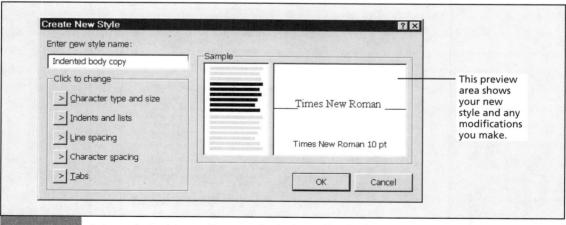

FIGURE 9-11   Enter a desired text style name for indented body copy in the Enter New Style Name box, and click the appropriate buttons to format the style

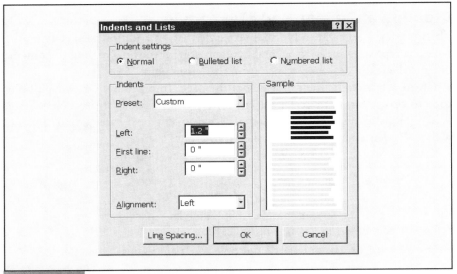

FIGURE 9-12   Enter a deep left indent for body copy in Publisher's Indents and Lists dialog box to create space to hang headings and subheads

OK to close the Create New Style dialog box and return to your publication. Notice the deep left indent shown in Figure 9-13, providing space for headings to be hung to the left of the text.

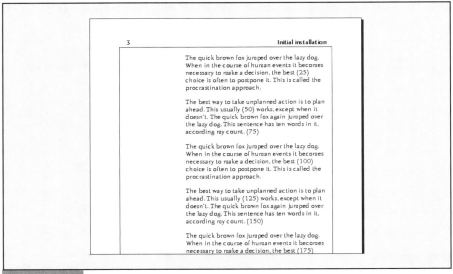

FIGURE 9-13   A deep indent adds white space to each page and provides space to emphasize headings and subheads that extend to the left of the text

Creating Hanging Indent Styles

Following the same procedure, you can create styles for as many subhead levels as your document requires. Each heading level should be visually distinct so readers can gauge its relative importance at a glance. Primary, or Level One subheads, for example, should extend further to the left than secondary, or Level Two, subheads. (This means you enter a narrower left indent in the Indents and Lists dialog box.) You can begin to create these subhead levels by selecting Format | Text Styles and clicking the Create A New Style button.

You can also visually indicate importance by using a larger type size for Level One subheads and adding extra line spacing above them.

When you're through, readers should be able to scan each page at a glance and identify the relative importance of each topic, as shown in Figure 9-14.

Creating Section Dividers

It's often difficult to add visual interest to single-sided publications, such as position papers, proposals, or reports that will be photocopied or printed in one color on a laser printer. Even if you use typographic formatting to make each heading and subhead visually distinct, it's hard to make each section heading noticeable. It's also harder to project a specific impression in the absence of color.

Publisher's WordArt can help you create distinct section headings. These section headings can add a unique touch to your publication as well as improve its

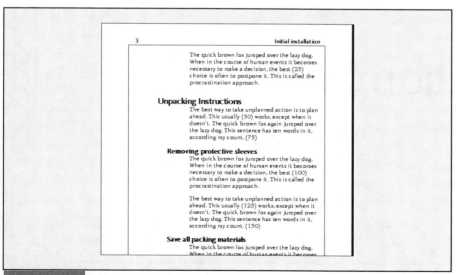

FIGURE 9-14   Different type sizes and line spacing, as well as different left indents, make it easy for readers to easily separate Level One headings from Level Two headings

usability. WordArt section dividers can be as simple or as elaborate as desired. Most important, they can be saved to the Publisher Design Gallery and easily re-used as needed.

For a simple section divider suitable for a three-column publication, create two WordArt objects, as shown in Figure 9-15. Notice that the right WordArt frame extends to the right margin. Choose a bold, heavy sans serif typeface and use a specific type style (for example, 16 points). Choose left alignment for both WordArt objects.

To format the WordArt objects into section dividers, select the right WordArt object and change the character fill to white.

Click outside the WordArt frame to close WordArt and return to Publisher. When you return to Publisher, right-click the right WordArt object and select Change Frame | Fill Color | Black.

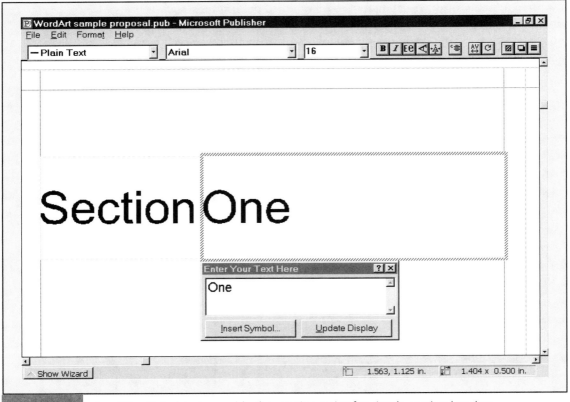

FIGURE 9-15 Two WordArt objects provide the starting point for simple section headers

Again, right-click the right WordArt object, select Change Frame | Line/Border Style | More Styles option. When Publisher displays the Border Style dialog box, highlight the 8-point line option, and click the left edge of the Select a Side sample, as shown in Figure 9-16. This step is necessary in order to separate the text in the two WordArt objects.

Right-click the left WordArt frame and select Change Frame | Fill Color | Fill Effects. When Publisher displays the Fill Effects dialog box, shown in Figure 9-17, click Tints/Shades, and locate the Color section's Base Color drop-down menu. Use the horizontal scroll bar to locate the rectangle that indicates a 40 percent tint, and double-click on it, or highlight it and click OK or press ENTER.

When you are finished, you will have created a distinct section header that can be immediately added to your document. Hold down the SHIFT key while selecting both WordArt objects and click the Group button, as shown in Figure 9-18.

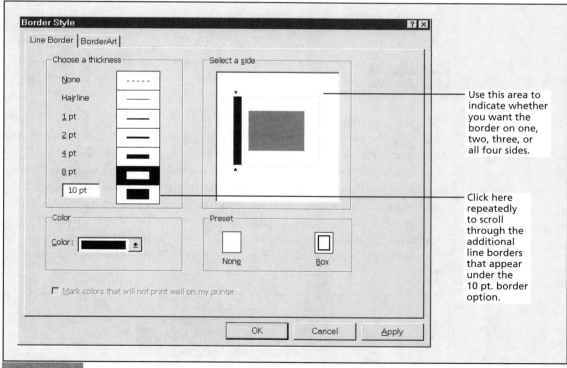

FIGURE 9-16   Adding an 8-point border to the left edge of the right WordArt object provides necessary text separation

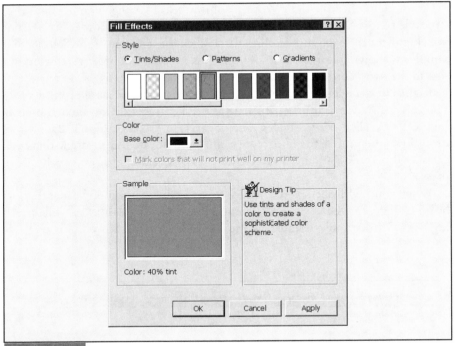

FIGURE 9-17 Select a 40 percent tint of black from the Fill Effects dialog box for the left WordArt object

This locks the two objects together, so you can easily move them around your document, or copy and paste them to the Publisher Design Gallery.

Even after the objects have been grouped, copied, and pasted, you can still select the right object (by double-clicking on it) and edit its content. Note how much this simple design touch adds to the document it is placed in, as shown in Figure 9-19.

If appropriate, you could use the same techniques to create consistent, attention-getting headings and subheads through your proposals and reports. In this case, you might want to select WordArt's Best Fit type option so that the right type size would automatically be chosen.

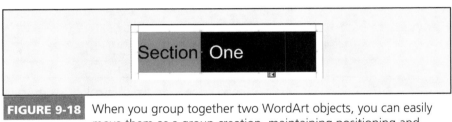

FIGURE 9-18 When you group together two WordArt objects, you can easily move them as a group creation, maintaining positioning and spacing within the object

FIGURE 9-19   Note how much attention the black and gray WordArt object adds when used to emphasize new topics

Adding a Watermark to Your Long Document

WordArt can play yet another role in creating long documents, that of adding watermarks to the background of each page. Although watermarks can consist of lightly screened visuals, such as your firm's logo or a signature graphic, you may want to create watermarks containing warnings regarding the distribution of your document. To create a watermark, follow these steps:

1. Select View | Go to Background.

2. Create a WordArt object that contains the watermark design warning you want.

3. Then select a strong sans serif typeface for your specific watermark message.

4. Use the Best Fit type size option, but customize the option by using the Spacing Between Letters tool to set the spacing to the Very Loose option.

5. Select the shading tool, and choose a lightly tinted black or red.

6. Click outside your document to close WordArt.

7. Resize the WordArt object to meet your requirements.

8. Select Arrange | Rotate or Flip | Custom Rotate to place the watermark warning at a 45-degree angle. Remember that when you are creating a watermark, you want one that will be bright enough for recipients to notice, yet not so bright that it will interfere with the text on the document in front of the watermark, as shown in Figure 9-20.

FIGURE 9-20   Create a WordArt warning, then resize and rotate it by using Publisher's tools

To check to see whether your watermark shows through the text on the document in front of it, right-click the text block, and select Change Frame | Fill Color | No Fill. Because you have no precise way to assess the watermark's color saturation, you may have to return to Publisher's Background View and fine-tune the WordArt shading to ensure you have created a noticeable watermark that doesn't interfere with easy reading, as shown in Figure 9-21.

Adding a Table of Contents

You can save a lot of time creating a table of contents for a long document by inserting one of the pre-formatted tables provided with Publisher 2000. Using a pre-formatted table can save you a lot of formatting time and provide the various spacing elements that are part of a good-looking table of contents.

Start by selecting Publisher's Table Tools and dragging to create a table of contents close to the size you think you'll need. When you release the mouse button after dragging, Publisher displays the Create Table dialog box. Scroll through the list of options almost to the list's end, to the listing for Table of Contents 1, as shown in Figure 9-22. Select the Table of Contents option that most closely suits your final table of contents design, and click OK or press ENTER.

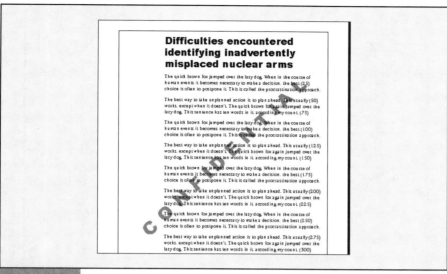

FIGURE 9-21 The perfect watermark is bright enough to be noticed, yet not so distracting that it interferes with reading the text placed over it

Enter text into the cells of the table of contents. Notice how the cells automatically expand to accommodate multiline content, as shown in Figure 9-23.

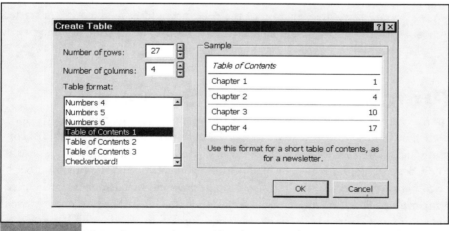

FIGURE 9-22 Save time creating a table of contents by using one of Publisher's pre-formatted tables

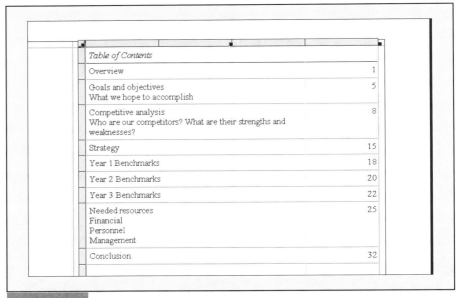

FIGURE 9-23 Publisher's table of contents option automatically maintains correct spacing and alignment between elements, even if some topics contain more text than others

Tip: After you format your table of contents, save it to your publication's Design Gallery, so you can reuse it in a later publication.

After you enter and edit all the necessary information, format the text using separate text styles for main headings, page numbers, and supporting text. Use Publisher's Table Tools to add or delete unnecessary rows. In a fraction of the time it would have taken if you started from scratch, you'll have created a good-looking table of contents, as shown in Figure 9-24.

Professional Skills Summary

In this chapter, we took a look at several of the special requirements of long documents, including using text styles to speed text formatting, creating a table of contents, and adding section dividers. We also discussed how to choose page sizes and folds, depending on the type of final printing you choose and the final number of documents you need. With Publisher's long-document management features, creating multipage documents is easy, speedy, and efficient. In the next chapter, we'll discuss how to create publications without using Publisher's Design Wizards.

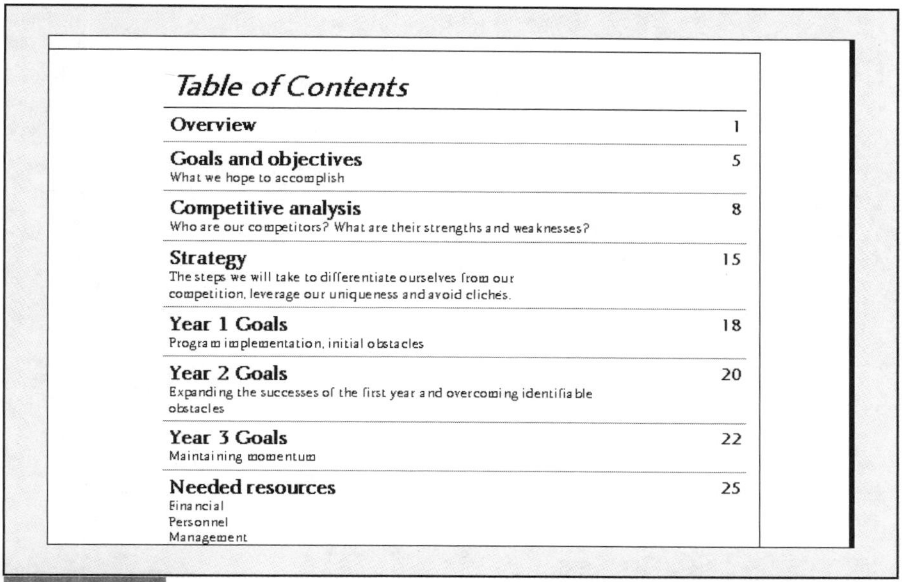

Table of Contents

Overview	1
Goals and objectives What we hope to accomplish	5
Competitive analysis Who are our competitors? What are their strengths and weaknesses?	8
Strategy The steps we will take to differentiate ourselves from our competition, leverage our uniqueness and avoid clichés.	15
Year 1 Goals Program implementation, initial obstacles	18
Year 2 Goals Expanding the successes of the first year and overcoming identifiable obstacles	20
Year 3 Goals Maintaining momentum	22
Needed resources Financial Personnel Management	25

FIGURE 9-24 The completed Table of Contents conveys a very organized and professional image

chapter 10

Creating Publications Without Wizards

In this chapter, you will:

- Explore the advantages and disadvantages of creating documents from scratch

- Choose your document's size, layout, and folds

- Create your document's structure

- Add repeating page elements

- Add color backgrounds and accents

- Insert Design Gallery Objects

Creating a publication from scratch is like working with a blank sheet of paper. You enjoy maximum opportunities for creative design. This freedom comes with a price, however. Before you decide to create a document from scratch instead of using a Wizard, you should make sure you have the available time. This chapter discusses some of the issues you should consider.

When to Work from Scratch

Sometimes, the right type of Wizard-designed publication doesn't exist. You might want to create a formal proposal document or a multipage instruction book for which there's no Publisher Wizard.

Another reason you might want to create your own publication is because your new publication has to match the size, shape, or layout of your firm or organization's existing publications. If you start with a blank publication, it may be easier to replicate existing brochures and newsletters to reinforce your firm's visual identity.

Document content is also a consideration. In general, Publisher's Wizards are best suited for creating documents containing numerous short text features. Notice the relatively short articles characteristic of newsletters created with the Newsletter Wizard in Chapter 5, for example. If, on the other hand, your documents typically contain a few long articles, you might be better off creating your own newsletter design from scratch.

Tip: After creating a custom document, save it as a template, so you can reuse the basic format over and over again.

Finally, you might not like the looks of Wizard-created documents, or just might want to create a look that's totally different. There may be the nagging suspicion that your readers might recognize the origin of your publication in one of Publisher's Design Wizards. There's also the personal satisfaction that comes from being able to say, "I did it my way!"

Disadvantages of Creating Documents from Scratch

Time and consistency are the primary disadvantages of creating documents from scratch.

It simply takes more time to create a document from scratch. Partly, the extra time required comes from having to lay out and format all the pages yourself, placing text columns and choosing the right typeface, type size, and type style for each element of page architecture. You also have to add repeating elements, such as graphics (borders and vertical rules between columns) as well as page numbers.

It also takes more time to complete documents started from scratch. One of the recurring themes of the previous chapters is that Publisher's Wizards not only make it easier to create a family of well-designed documents, but also help you develop your message and determine your publication's content. (In many cases, such as catalog creation, once the Wizard has created the format for the publication, it becomes relatively easy to replace the text and graphic placeholders.) You sacrifice this guidance, however, when you start a document from scratch. As a result, you need to have a much better idea of the content of your publication before you begin work.

Creating your own documents makes it very easy to inadvertently sacrifice consistency. Rather than seeing each document as a part of a family of different document types, "creativity" might get in the way, and you might inadvertently create a series of documents with only a passing resemblance among them.

You have to balance the pros and cons of using Wizard-based documents versus using custom-created documents fine-tuned to your marketing needs.

Choosing Document Size, Layout, and Folds

There are two ways to create a publication from scratch:

- One option is to click the New icon in the Standard Toolbar (or use the CTRL-N keyboard shortcut). When Publisher displays the Quick Publication Wizard, click the Hide Wizard button.

- The other option is to select File | New. When Publisher displays the Catalog dialog box, select the Blank Publications tab. Select the type of document you want to create from the list of Blank Publications on the left, as shown in Figure 10-1. Preview the various publication types on the right. Select a desired option and click the Create button. (You can also double-click the desired option to close the Microsoft Publisher Catalog and begin working on your document.)

- Select the Full Page option from the list of Blank Publications if you want to print each page of your publication on one side of an 8.5-by-11-inch sheet of paper.

- If you want to choose a different page size or orientation, click the Custom Page button at the screen's bottom. Publisher will then display the Page Setup dialog box, shown in Figure 10-2, where you can determine a desired page size as well as create a landscape, or horizontal, publication (one that's wider than it's tall). Click OK or press ENTER to close the Page Setup box.

Publisher determines maximum page size according to the printer you have currently selected. To select a different printer, perhaps one that can output 11-by-17-inch tabloid-sized publications, select File | Print Setup. Publisher will display the Print Setup dialog box. The Print Setup dialog box permits you to

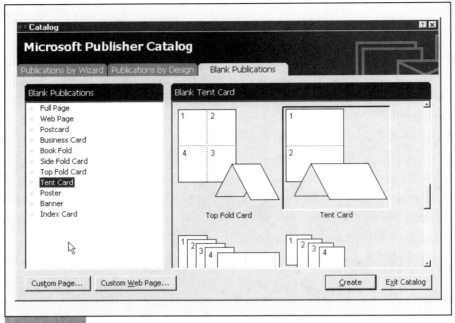

FIGURE 10-1 Use the Blank Publications tab in the Microsoft Publisher Catalog to select a desired document type

determine which paper tray your printer will use (if your printer has more than one), as well to prepare documents for printing by a commercial printer. You may want to select a different printer if:

- You want to print your newsletter on legal-sized paper (8.5-by-13-inch paper).
- Your office printer is capable of printing tabloid-sized (11-by-17-inch paper).
- You are going to take your project to a commercial printer for imaging.

When Publisher displays the Print Setup dialog box, click the Name window and choose a different printer or output device.

- If your office printer has more than one paper tray attached, click the Size window and select a different paper size.
- If you are taking your files to a commercial printer, select MS Publisher Imagesetter from the Name window. This feature offers the greatest variety of paper sizes.
- Click OK or press ENTER to close the Print Setup box.

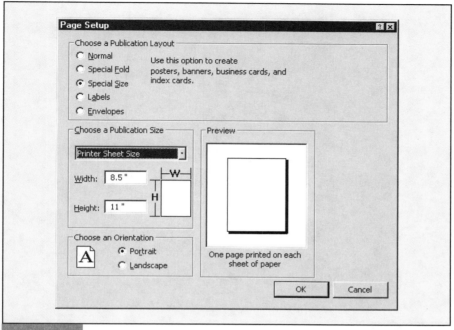

FIGURE 10-2 Use the Page Setup dialog box to select a different page, page size, and orientation

Creating Your Document's Structure

Margins and grids are the fundamental tools designers use to organize the contents of each page of a document. Margins refer to the distance between the edge of the paper a page is printed on and the live area of each page—the area containing text and graphics.

Grids consist of nonprinting lines that control column size and placement. Grids promote page-to-page consistency by remaining the same, regardless of how the contents of each page change. You can also add additional nonprinting guidelines that will appear on each page, helping you precisely position text and graphics.

Specifying Margins

Publisher's default margin specification—one inch on all sides—is too generous for most publications. To change the margins to a different setting, select Arrange | Layout Guides. This reveals the Layout Guides dialog box, shown in Figure 10-3.

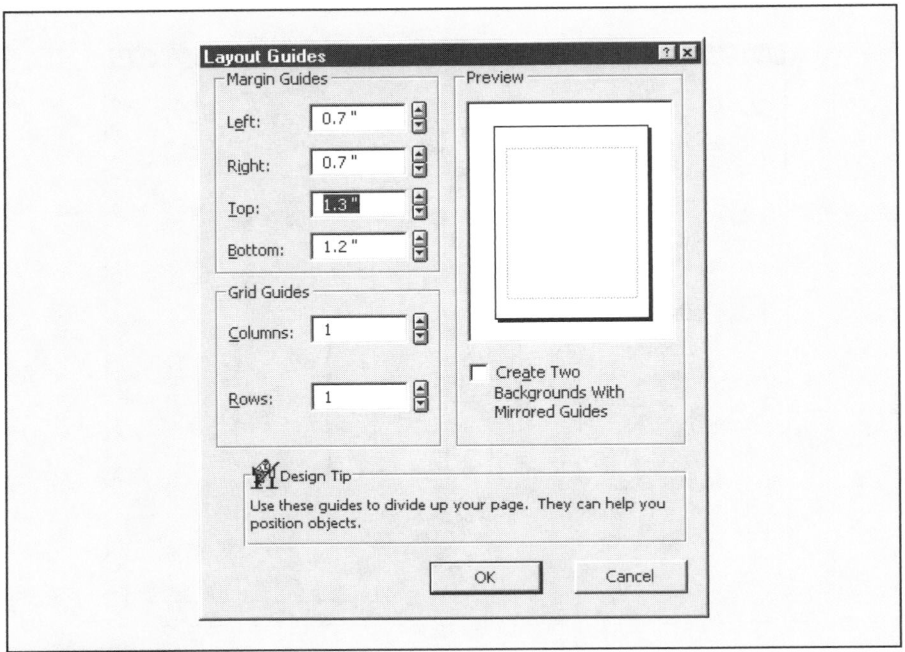

FIGURE 10-3 Change Publisher's default generous margins by using the Layout Guides dialog box

Tip: One reason you may want to include extra white space at the top and bottom of pages is to place text and graphics in the header and footer of each page. *Header* refers to the space between the top of a column and the top edge of a page when printed. *Footer* refers to the space between the bottom of a column and the bottom edge of the printed page. Page numbers are also frequently added to the header and footer area of each page, as well as newsletter issue dates and section/chapter information in longer documents.

Enter the desired margin measurements in the Right, Left, Top, and Bottom windows of the Layout Guides dialog box. You can also click the up and down arrows next to these windows to scroll through and select pre-set margin measurements. As you replace the default margins, you can observe the effects of your changes in the Preview window at the right.

Creating a Column Grid

Few documents consist of a single line of text extending from one margin of the page to another. Readers find long lines of type extending from margin to margin difficult to read. It is also difficult to size and place graphics in documents containing a single column of text.

The solution is to create a background column grid. This background grid should remain consistent from page to page, even though the exact size and placement of columns on each page may change.

To add a background column grid, select Arrange | Layout Guides. When the Layout Guides dialog box appears, enter the desired number of columns in the Columns window, as shown in Figure 10-4, or

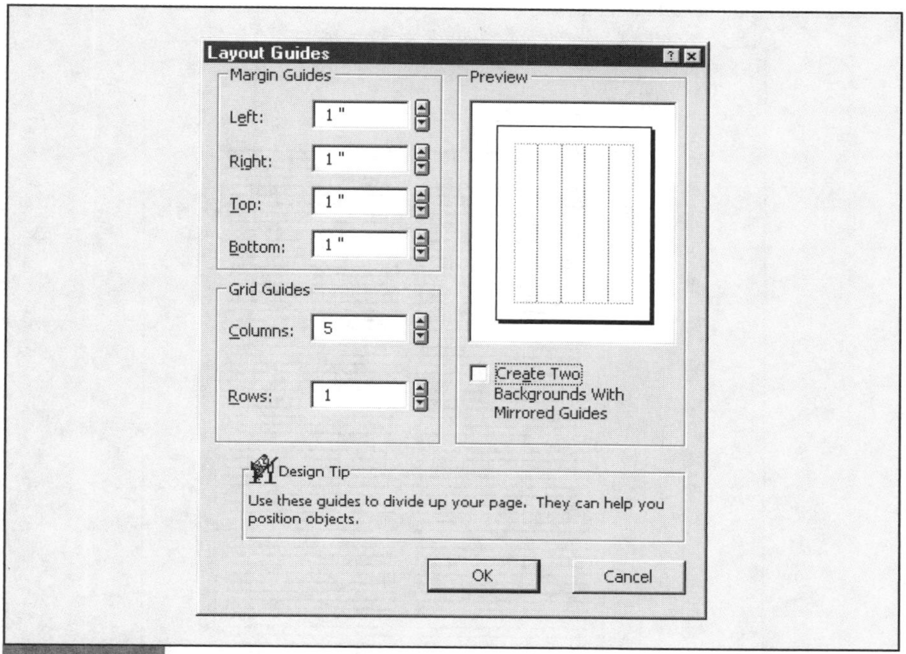

FIGURE 10-4   Enter a desired number of column grids in the Layout Guides'
Columns window or click the up or down arrow

click the up or down arrow. Grid columns control the horizontal placement of text and graphics in your document.

Which Is Best: Grid or Text Columns?

Columns created by adding Column Guides in the Layout Guides dialog box do not necessarily have to equal the number of text columns on a finished page.

The best example of this is a five-column grid. A five-column grid does not mean you will be placing five narrow columns of text on each page. Rather, the five-column grid offers you several alternative ways of placing text on the page.

The most common alternative is to leave the outer column of each page blank and create two text frames, each one spanning two columns, as shown in Figure 10-5. Later, you can go back and place graphics and short text elements in the narrow, outside column. This arrangement builds white space into every page and provides a great deal of flexibility for placing graphics.

Tip: You can save time by creating a column grid for your document for both the left and right pages with one visit to the Layout Guides dialog box. To create mirrored pages, locate the Create Two Backgrounds with Mirrored Guides check box below the Preview window. Click this option if you want the same margins and grid options to be applied to both pages.

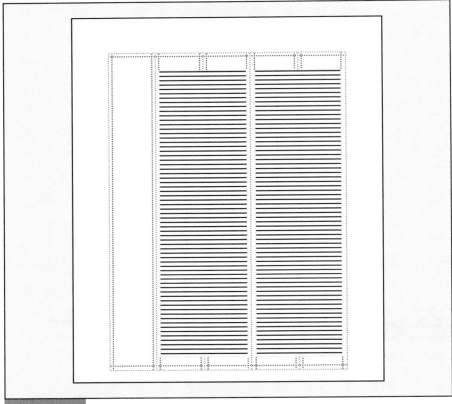

FIGURE 10-5 Two text frames, each spanning two columns, plus a narrow column of white space

Another common text arrangement based on the five-column grid involves a three-column text frame next to a two-column text frame, as shown in Figure 10-6.

Finished pages based on the five-column grid typically present a clean, contemporary, and easy-to-read image.

Controlling Vertical Object Placement

There are two ways to control the vertical placement of text and graphics. One way is to select Arrange | Layout Guides, and then replace the default in the Rows window with a desired number of rows, as shown in Figure 10-7. The more rows you add, the more opportunities you have to create page-to-page consistency by aligning text and graphics on each page.

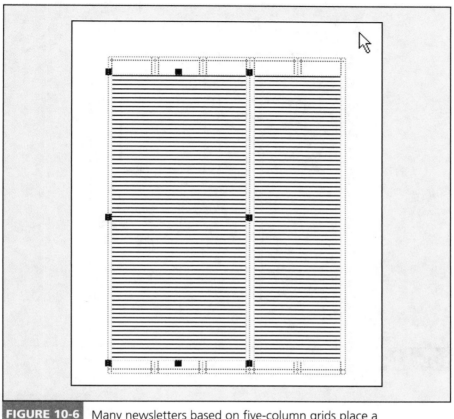

FIGURE 10-6 Many newsletters based on five-column grids place a three-column text frame next to a two-column text frame

Another option is to add horizontal guidelines at specified locations, such as the tops and bottoms of text columns. By adding a horizontal guide along the top of your pages, and aligning the top of your text frames to this line, you can add a *sink*, or consistent amount of white space, to the top of each page. You can also build white space into the bottom of each page by aligning the bottom of text frames to a horizontal guide along the bottom of each page, as shown in Figure 10-8.

To add horizontal guides to your document:

1. Select View | Go to Background (or press CTRL-M).
2. If you cannot currently see the rulers, select View | Rulers.

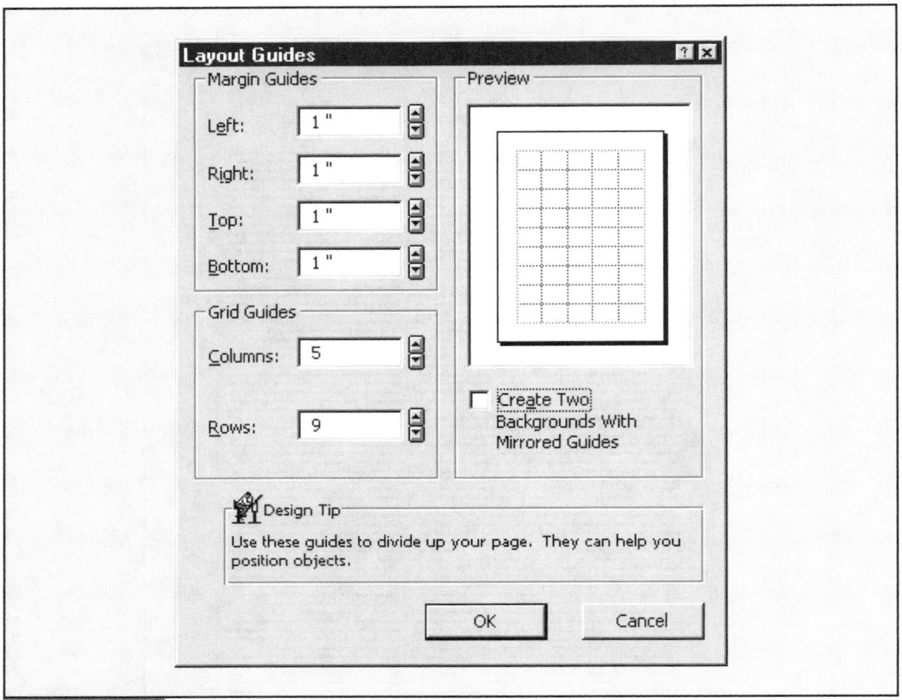

Layout Guides

Margin Guides

Left: 1 "

Right: 1 "

Top: 1 "

Bottom: 1 "

Grid Guides

Columns: 5

Rows: 9

Preview

☐ Create Two Backgrounds With Mirrored Guides

Design Tip
Use these guides to divide up your page. They can help you position objects.

OK   Cancel

FIGURE 10-7 You can add flexibility and page-to-page consistency to your documents by vertically subdividing your pages into rows

3. Hold down the SHIFT key and click on the horizontal ruler, then drag a horizontal guide a desired distance near the top of the page. Repeat and drag a second horizontal guide to the desired location near the bottom of the page. (If rulers are not visible, select Arrange | Ruler Guides | Add Horizontal Ruler Guide. The guide will appear in the middle of the page. Click the guide, and hold down the SHIFT key while you are dragging it to the desired location.)

You might even consider adding a third line, closer to the top of the page, to "hang" headlines on, as shown in Figure 10-8. Secondary features can be "hung" from a horizontal guide located approximately one-third of the way down from the top of the page.

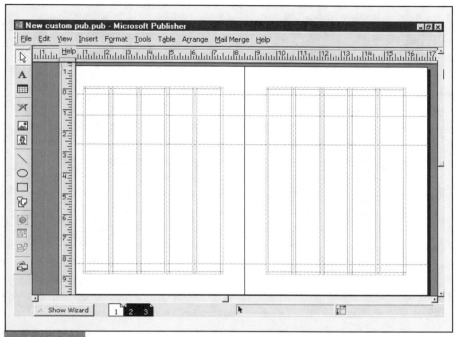

FIGURE 10-8 Use the horizontal guides to define the tops and bottoms of text frames placed on the page

To preview how your publication will look when printed—that is, to hide the margins, column grids and horizontal guides—select View | Hide Boundaries and Guides (or press CTRL-SHIFT-O). The underlying structure of the page becomes apparent when the grids and guides are hidden.

The resulting publication, with text frames aligned on a five-column grid with four horizontal guides, creates a very "open" document with easy-to-read headlines, plenty of white space on each page, and the page-to-page consistency necessary to project a professional image. Note the generous amount of white space surrounding the headlines and the symmetrical placement of text and graphics in the narrow columns, as shown in Figure 10-9.

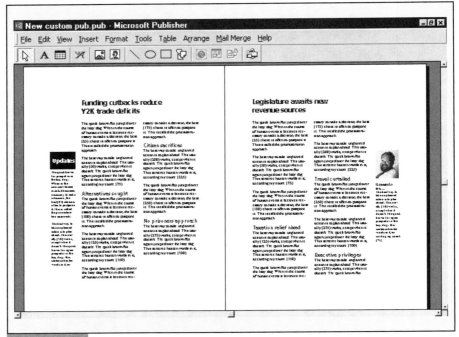

FIGURE 10-9 Using grids and horizontal guides creates a publication that projects an inviting, professional image

In a similar fashion, a pair of vertical guides offers an easy way of aligning headlines and subheads hung to the left of the text column with a page number located at the bottom of each page, as shown in Figure 10-10.

Adding Repeating Page Elements

Multipage documents, such as newsletters and training manuals, typically contain several types of text and graphics that are repeated on each page. This information is often placed in the headers or footers of each page, although sometimes the information appears in the background of each page.

Adding Rules and Borders

You may have noticed that the tops and bottoms of the two-page spread shown in Figure 10-9 appear somewhat empty. The tops and bottoms of each page lack definition; they appear unfinished. Horizontal rules would help define each page, as well as emphasize the white space at the top and bottom of each page.

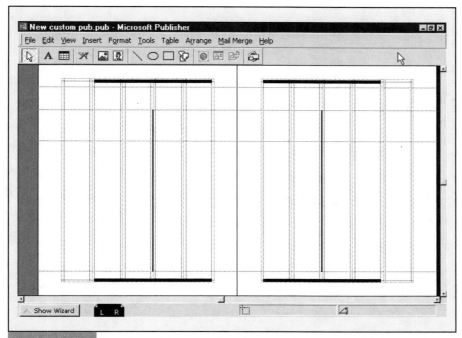

FIGURE 10-10 Vertical subheads make it easy to align text frames containing headlines, subheads, and a page number hung to the left of the text column

To add top and bottom borders, select View | Go to Background | Select View | Show Boundaries and Guides.

Use Publisher's Line Tool to create a horizontal rule two-columns wide, spanning the two text columns on the page's left side. Select the line and select Format | Line/Border Style | More Styles. When Publisher displays the Line dialog box, shown in Figure 10-11, enter **12 pt** in the Line Thickness window. Click the OK button (or press ENTER). (If you can see the Formatting toolbar, select the Line | Line/Border | More Styles to reach the Line dialog box.)

Copy and paste the line four times, repositioning the lines above and below the text columns.

Select the Line tool again and create a vertical line between the third and fourth columns on the left page. Select Format | Line/Border Style | More Styles, and enter **6 pt** in the Line Thickness window. Copy and paste a second line between the first and second columns on the right page.

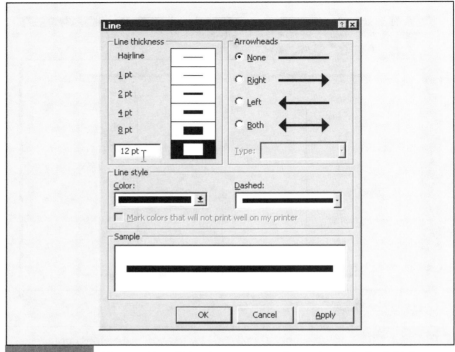

Use the Line dialog box to create lines of any desired thickness

When finished, there will be four lines visible in the Background View of each page.

Select View | Go to Foreground (or press CTRL-M). Then select View | Hide Boundaries and Guides. The horizontal and vertical lines now define the text columns and guide the reader's eyes inside the page, as shown in Figure 10-12. (Turn back to Figure 10-9 and see how much the lines add to the page's appeal.)

Adding Page Numbers, Date, and Time

To add page numbers to each page, go to Publisher's Background View (CTRL-M) and create a text box where you want the page number to appear. Then, select Insert | Page Numbers. Publisher will insert a symbol (#) indicating where the page number will appear when you return to Foreground View. Publisher will also display a prompt to inform you that the symbol you have added will be replaced by a page number when you go to Foreground View.

While you are in Background View, format the page number however you like by highlighting the # symbol and choosing a desired typeface, type size, and

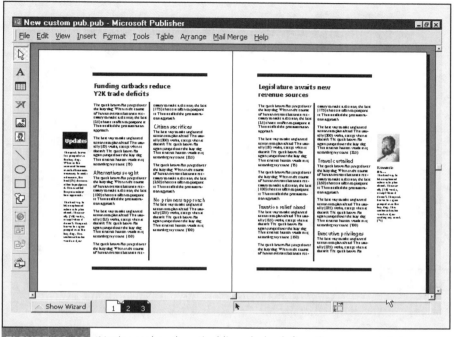

FIGURE 10-12 Horizontal and vertical lines help define the pages and draw attention to the white space surrounding the headlines

alignment. Note that you can also insert the word "Page" in front of the # symbol, so that the page number will be identified by the word "Page."

Page

The # symbol will be replaced by an actual page number when you return to Foreground View.

Depending on the type of publication you're creating, you may want to insert the date and time. This will be automatically updated each time you print your publication. To insert the date and/or time:

1. Select View | Go to Background (or press CTRL-M).
2. Select the Text Frame Tool, and drag to create a text frame.
3. Select Insert | Date and Time. When Publisher displays the Date and Time dialog box, select the format in which you want the date and time to appear, as shown in Figure 10-13. Check the Update Automatically option if you want the date and time to be updated every time you print your document. Click OK or press ENTER.

Tip: While you're in Publisher's Foreground View, a prompt will appear if you try to select an object on the Background View, reminding you that you must go to the Background View to select the object.

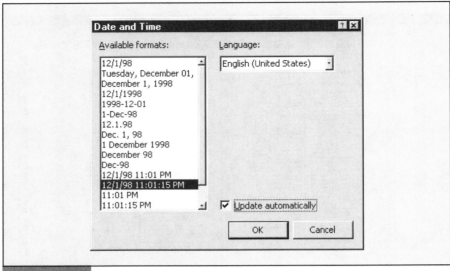

Select the desired format for the date and/or time, and check Update Automatically to update the date and time every time you print

Tip: Before you take your publication to a commercial printer for quantity duplication, be sure you return to the Background View and delete the text frame containing the date and time!

The advantage of adding the printing date and time to your publication is that you can easily keep track of the various drafts and proofs of your document that you're likely to print before taking your publication to a commercial printer.

Adding Text and Graphics to Headers and Footers

To add text or a graphic to every page of your publication, select View | Go to Background (CTRL-M). Anything you add to the Background View will appear on every page. Information typically added to the Background View includes:

- Publication title
- Section or chapter information
- Issue date
- Your firm or organization's logo

Often the best results are obtained when text (such as titles) and graphics on left page headers and footers are left-aligned, and text (such as issue dates) and

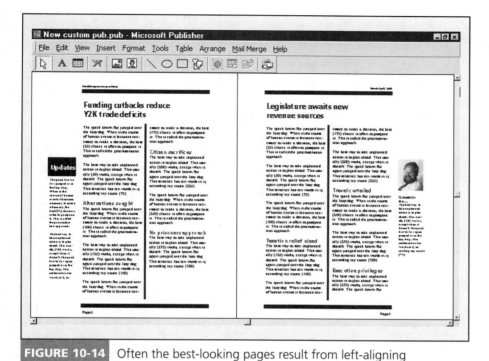

FIGURE 10-14 Often the best-looking pages result from left-aligning repeating elements on left pages and right-aligning elements on right pages

graphics on right page headers and footers are right-aligned. This alternating alignment reinforces the framing effect of each page, as shown in Figure 10-14.

Adding Color Backgrounds and Accents

Just as you can add text and graphics to Publisher's Background View, you can also create striking publications by adding color panels to the background. By positioning the panels in the same place on each page, you can easily give your publication a unified appearance.

The primary thing to watch out for, of course, is that these background colored accents remain accents and do not become so prominent that they make it difficult to read text and graphics placed on the Foreground View of each page. A variety of effects is possible, including triangles and rectangles that bleed to the outside edges of each page.

To add a color panel to the background level, Select View | Go to Background, and then follow these steps:

1. Select the custom shapes icon from Publisher's Objects Toolbar. When Publisher displays the Custom Shapes, select any shape you desire, such as the right angle triangle:

Right angle triangle

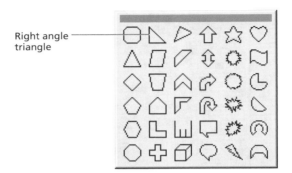

2. Drag to create a triangle from the top left edge of the left page to the approximate middle of the bottom of the page, as shown in Figure 10-15. Allow the edges of the triangle to extend to the edges of the page at the top, side, and bottom. The figure shows one triangle on each side.

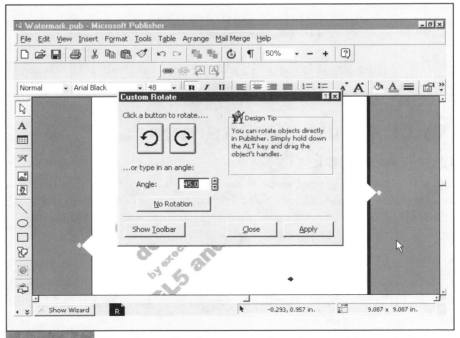

FIGURE 10-15 Dragging a triangle that extends to the top, side, and bottom edges of the left background page

3. With the triangle selected, click the Formatting Toolbar's Fill icon, and then select Fill Effects, or you can select Format | Fill Color | Fill Effects. You can also do the same thing by right-clicking the triangle and then selecting Change Shape | Fill Color | Fill Effects.

4. When Publisher displays the Fill Effects dialog box, click Gradients, and choose a desired gradient pattern for transitioning one color to another. Use the horizontal scroll bar to reveal additional choices. (There are many.) For more options, click the down arrow next to the Base Color box, and choose one of the color scheme colors. For even more options and combinations, click the down arrow next to the Color 2 box, and select a second color (perhaps white). Each time you make a choice, you can observe the variation of the effect in the Sample window, as shown in Figure 10-16. (You could play with creating new variations of these effects all day!) When you have selected an option to use, click OK or press ENTER.

5. You might want to remove the border because it places too much emphasis on the transition. Without the border, a potentially distracting element is eliminated from your creative work. Select the triangle, and then select Format | Line/Border Style | None, or select the triangle and click the Line/Border Style icon, and then select the None option. You can also right-click the triangle, and select Change Shape | Line Color | White.

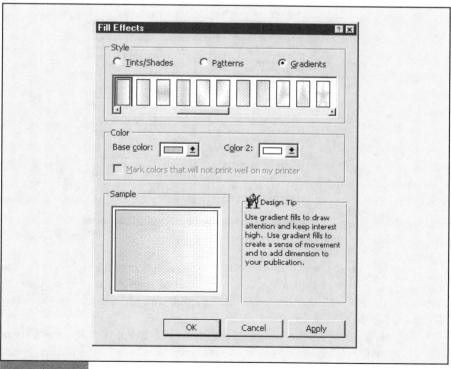

FIGURE 10-16   Click the Gradients button and select a Base Color, Color 2, and the desired direction for the color transition

L▶ Tip: Always
remember to remove
borders from shapes
containing gradient fills.
Otherwise, the borders
will undermine the
gradient of the fills.

Avoid Obscuring Your Text with Design Elements

If you add color panels to Publisher's background, you should be on the lookout for a few problems. Be careful about adding new graphics, such as custom shapes, that will appear in front of existing graphics. Notice here how the triangle obscures a portion of the horizontal line along the page bottom.

The solution is to use the mouse to select the newly created graphic, then send it to the background by clicking Arrange | Send to Back, or simply by pressing SHIFT-F6. (You can also right-click the graphic and then click the Standard Toolbar's Send-to-Back icon.)

If you place a text frame, such as a page number, in front of a custom shape you've created, Publisher may place a white box around the page number, which detracts from the custom shape, as shown in Figure 10-17.

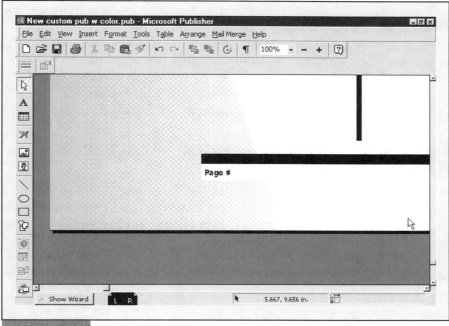

FIGURE 10-17 When you place text frames in front of custom shapes, white space may surround the text frames

To cure this problem, select the text frame and click the Formatting Toolbar's Fill icon, then select No Fill. You can also click the text frame, and select Format | Fill Color | No Fill, or right-click the text frame and select Change Frame | Fill Color | No Fill.

After you add custom shapes to your background and return to the Foreground View, you may find similar problems. Again, the solution is to right-click text frames, hide the background objects, and then select Change Frame | Fill Color | No Fill (or click the Formatting Toolbar's Fill Color icon, and select No Fill).

To give the right page a customized design look:

1. Select the Rectangle tool from the Objects Toolbar and create a rectangular box touching the top, bottom, and right edge of the page.

2. Right-click the rectangle and select Change Rectangle | Fill Color | Fill Effects. When Publisher displays the Fill Effects dialog box, click Gradients. Choose your Base Color and Color 2, then select your desired gradient direction. Click OK or press ENTER when you have finished.

3. Select the rectangle and then select Format | Line/Border Style | None, or select the rectangle, and then click the Line/Border Style icon, and select None. You can also right-click the rectangle and select Change Shape | Line Color | White. Click OK or press enter when you have finished, removing the border and eliminating the distracting element.

When you have completed these steps, your publication's Background View should resemble Figure 10-18.

Select View | Go to Foreground (or press CTRL-M). When you again see the Foreground View, the color accents you've placed on the background will frame the left and right pages, as shown in Figure 10-19. Repeated on the various types of documents you create, these accents will go a long way toward creating a unique visual look unifying the various types of publications you create.

Save Your Custom-Created Background Design Elements

In order to speed up production and reinforce your firm or organization's visual identity by maintaining strict document-to-document consistency, you can add custom-created background design accents to Publisher's Design Gallery. This makes it easy to reuse these elements again.

To add custom-created background design elements to the Design Gallery, select View | Go to Background, and select the desired shape or rectangle. Then

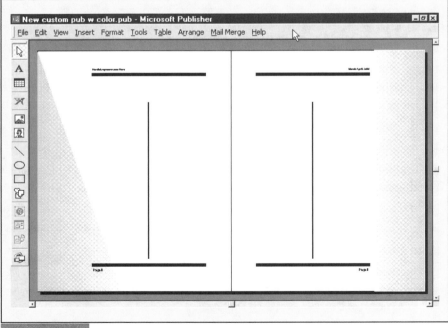

FIGURE 10-18   This Background View shows two completed color panels that will appear behind every two-page spread

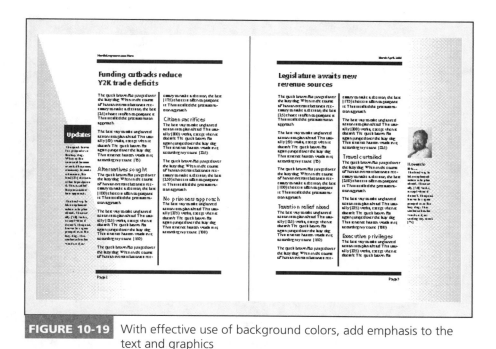

FIGURE 10-19 With effective use of background colors, add emphasis to the text and graphics

select Insert | Add Selection to Design Gallery. When Publisher displays the Add Object dialog box, enter an object name and the category of the object in the appropriate window, as shown in Figure 10-20. Click OK or press ENTER when you have finished. Repeat this process to store any design objects you create.

To confirm that the elements have been added, click the Design Gallery icon, or select Insert | Design Gallery Object. Click the Your Objects tab. Saved objects will appear, as shown in Figure 10-21.

Using Previously Saved Custom Design Objects

To reuse a previously saved custom Design Object, click the Design Gallery icon in the Objects Toolbar and select Your Objects. The Categories preview pane will probably be empty. Click Options | Browse.

When the Other Designs dialog box appears, locate the publication containing your custom Design Object. Double-click the filename. The Microsoft Publisher Design Gallery will appear showing Your Objects.

Select the desired object and click the Insert Object button, or double-click the object to insert it, and close the Microsoft Publisher Design Gallery. Reposition and resize the object as necessary.

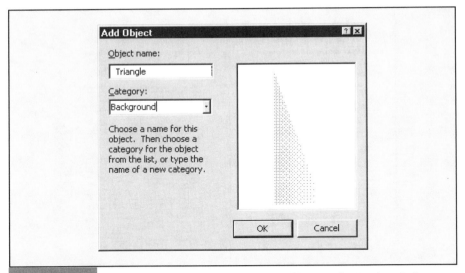

FIGURE 10-20   Adding a custom-created design object to the Design Gallery makes it available for use in other publications

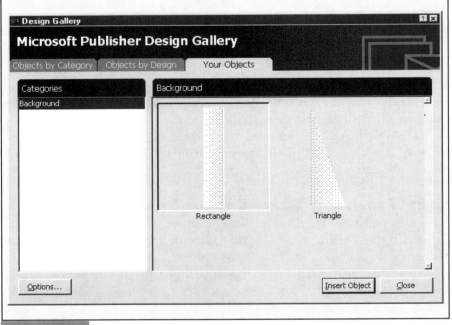

FIGURE 10-21   Click the Design Gallery icon and select Your Objects to confirm that your custom-created objects have been saved

Choosing Custom Publication Colors

When you're creating custom publications, always choose colors from Publisher's color schemes. This will make it easier to change or fine-tune your color choices at a later date.

By assigning colors from Publisher's color schemes, you save time and enjoy maximum flexibility. If you limit yourself to the five colors available with each color scheme, you are assured that the colors will work together. More important, you will be able to make major changes in the appearance of your document simply by choosing a different color scheme.

If you are creating a custom Web document, you are also assured that your Web site will appear at its best on the widest range of hardware platforms and software browsers. Each of the colors used in Publisher's color schemes are "Web safe" in that color scheme colors are limited to the 216 colors that reproduce well on all hardware and software platforms.

Inserting Design Gallery Objects

Even when you're creating your own custom document, Publisher 2000 can save you time by permitting you to insert several types of Design Gallery Objects in your publication. Design Gallery Objects include pre-formatted calendars, reply forms, and picture frames with captions.

After inserting Design Gallery Objects in your publication, you can resize and modify them as needed.

Adding Picture Frames and Captions

Picture frames are one of the most important types of Design Gallery Objects you can add to your publications. Design Gallery Object picture frames not only create an attractive framework for your photographs and captions, but—most important—they *lock caption and photograph together,* permitting you to move them as a single unit around your publication.

Design Gallery Object picture frames also ensure consistency so that each photo and caption throughout your publication—or family of publications—looks the same.

To insert a Design Gallery picture frame into your publication, click the Objects Toolbar's Design Gallery Object icon, or select Insert | Design Gallery Object. When Publisher's Design Gallery appears, select Picture Captions from the Objects by Category pane, as shown in Figure 10-22.

Scroll through the various types of picture frames and captions until you come to a design you like. Notice that some options surround both photograph and caption with a thin frame, while others use a thicker frame. Sometimes the

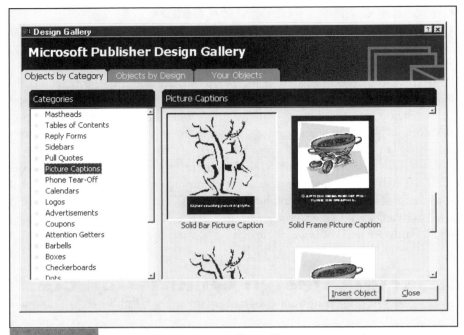

FIGURE 10-22   The Publisher Design Gallery offers numerous picture caption options

captions are reversed out of a black background; in other cases, the captions appear next to the photograph.

Select the picture caption option you like and click the Insert Object button, or double-click the desired selection to insert it, and close the Design Gallery.

Copy and paste as many picture captions as you need in your publication. Sometimes it's easier to add picture captions as placeholders when laying out your publications. Other times it's easier to return to the Microsoft Publisher Design Gallery each time you want to add another picture caption.

Position the picture caption as desired. Resize it if necessary by holding down the SHIFT key while dragging one of the picture placeholder's corner handles. Note that the caption and visual are resized together, because they have been grouped.

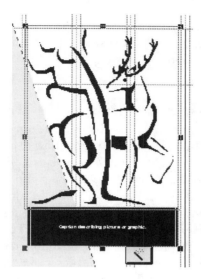

Right-click the placeholder graphic, and select Change Picture | Picture | From File. When Publisher displays the Insert Picture dialog box, locate the folder containing the desired photograph, and double-click its filename. If the photograph is too narrow to fit the picture frame, it will be surrounded by distracting bands of white space on either side.

To eliminate the distracting white space, select the picture caption and then select Arrange | Ungroup Objects (CTRL-SHIFT-G). Publisher will display a warning, verifying that you want to ungroup the object. Click the Yes button. You can now click on the photograph and resize it, so that its width will match the caption.

Hold down the SHIFT key and select the photograph and caption. You can now regroup the objects—in case you need to move or resize them—by selecting Arrange | Group Objects or by pressing CTRL-SHIFT-G.

Adding Calendars and Forms

Calendars and forms are another category of Design Gallery Objects you may want to insert into custom-created documents. Calendars and forms can be extremely tedious and time-consuming to create. By inserting a Design Gallery calendar or form, you can spend more time on customizing it and fine-tuning your message and less time setting up the basic structure of your document.

One of the most important Design Gallery Objects features is that they can be instantly resized by dragging one of the selection handles to fit your column grid.

Publisher will automatically resize the lines to length without you having to do any tedious fine-tuning. If you've ever worked with forms before, you'll appreciate how much time this feature saves you.

Professional Skills Summary

In this chapter, we examined the ins and outs of creating your documents without using Publisher's Wizards. We talked about how to choose your document's size, layout, and folds, if it needs them. We then spent plenty of time explaining how to create your document's structure, which is a difficult task to master manually, but is handled well by Publisher's Wizards. In addition, Publisher's Wizards are also great for creating document uniformity—something you'll have to do on your own if you create documents from scratch. To make this job a bit easier, we included in this chapter specifics about adding repeating page elements, adding color backgrounds and accents, and inserting Design Gallery Objects. Creating a Publisher document from scratch takes more effort, but the results can be wonderfully rewarding.

chapter 11

Creating Web Sites from Print Publications

In this chapter, you will:

- Prepare your existing printed source document's graphics and photos for use on a Web site

- Convert an existing brochure and newsletter into your Web site using the Convert To Web Site option

- Modify the newly created Web site to work best for the Web's specific requirements

- Learn the "cut and paste" method for quickly converting either a Web site to a print document or a print document to a Web site

Publisher includes tools to create a Web site from a print publication. If you play entirely by Publisher's rules, you may be able to get good results in attempting this transformation. To successfully transform a printed publication into a working Web site, you must use a printed publication created only with one of Publisher's Wizards, and you cannot have altered that source printed publication in any way whatsoever.

There's yet another limitation, based on the way Web sites are organized. For navigational purposes, a Web site must have a home page. Publisher will create one for you, in addition to transporting whatever pages exist in your printed publication to your newly created Web site. Even under the best of circumstances, when your transformation from print to Web is complete, you'll still have a lot of handwork to do. Later in this chapter, we'll take a look at a method to create a Web site from a publication that, while tedious, produces better results.

Why Use Your Print Publications as a Source?

If you've never created a Web site, you can save yourself significant time by starting with a print publication you have already created with a Publisher Wizard. The Wizards make many design decisions for you, and if you use Publisher's Wizards to create all your company's printed needs, the result will be both professional-looking and consistent. Using an existing printed publication created with one of Publisher's print Wizards is probably the quickest and easiest way to establish a Web presence. This method may still be the best one for you, even if later you decide to start over and create a new Web site from scratch or with Publisher's Web Wizard.

Creating Your Web Site from a Brochure

For this exercise, take a look at the brochure called "Choosing an Obedience School for Your Pet," which is a Wizard-created informational brochure using the Blocks design and the Tropics color scheme. (See Figure 11-1.) The brochure's inside content, shown in Figure 11-2, has a main heading and two secondary headings. (A separate article appears on the inner fold of the outside cover.) Except for the replacement of clip art with more appropriate selections and, in two instances, scanned photographs, the Wizard's brochure design is unchanged, and the only variation in layout is the addition of a photograph on the brochure's back fold.

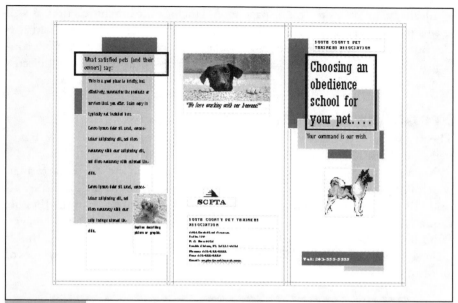

FIGURE 11-1   One of Publisher's Wizards created this brochure, with the exterior unaltered in any way, except for the addition of an extra center photo

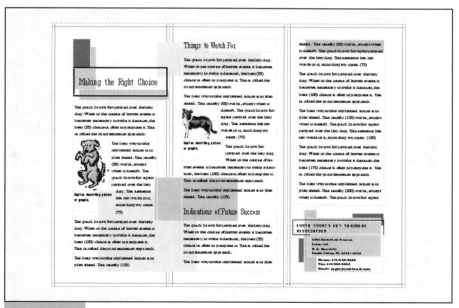

FIGURE 11-2   The brochure's inside contains three sections, each with an illustration

Ideally, your Web site's home page should include the brochure's title, as well as a listing of each subhead for each subsidiary page, as well as the inner-fold article. But don't count on it. The transformation process from print to Web content may not turn out as you would suspect. Much of this chapter will discuss how to correct problems that occur as a result of the print-to-Web process.

Preparing Your Graphics

The first step in preparing your print publication for conversion to the Web is to make sure your images are ready.

Most of Publisher's clip art that isn't photographic is in the WMF file format, which Publisher changes to GIF images for Web use. Most of the photos are already JPGs. If you want to make sure that any particular photo is of the JPG file format, right-click on the image and choose Change Picture | Graphics Manager. Publisher will then display the Graphics Manager dialog box, shown here. In this dialog box, you can see your Web site's entire list of the filenames and file types of all the pictures.

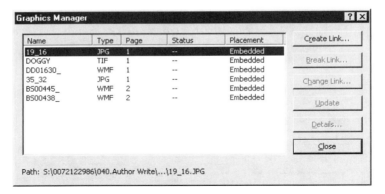

If you have photos that aren't JPGs, take the following steps to convert them to JPGs for more efficient Web use:

1. Click on the picture.
2. If the picture you have selected is marked as Grouped with its surrounding objects, you will have to ungroup it by choosing Arrange | Ungroup Objects. Once the picture is ungrouped, you can check its file type.
3. Click on a blank space, then click on the picture again to select it.
4. Choose Edit | Copy.
5. Open PhotoDraw, by clicking on the Drawing icon.

6. Choose Edit | Paste to paste the image into PhotoDraw.

7. Choose File | Save For Use In | On The Web. PhotoDraw will display the Save For Use In Wizard dialog box, shown here. You get a choice of the file format in which to save the file. Give the file a distinct name.

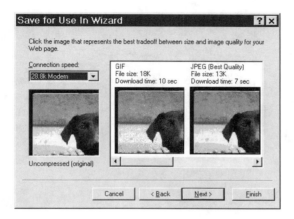

8. Click whichever of the two images in the white box on the right shows the smaller file size, then click Next.

9. Click Finish | Save.

10. From within Publisher, right-click on the image you started with, and choose Change Picture | Picture | From File.

11. Browse for the new version of your image, and then click on the distinct file-name you gave the file in Step 7, and click Insert.

12. If you need to regroup the picture with the objects surrounding it from which you ungrouped it in Step 2, hold down SHIFT and click on the picture's caption, then choose Arrange | Group Objects.

13. Repeat the procedure for any other photos in your brochure.

Creating a Web Site from a Print Publication

To create a Web site from a print publication, choose File | Open and select the source document from which you would like your Web site created. Publisher will open your document file in the right window and activate whichever Wizard you used to create the source document, in this case the Brochure Wizard, as shown in Figure 11-3. Note the last item on the Brochure Wizard Options list, which is Convert To Web. Select this option, and Publisher will display the

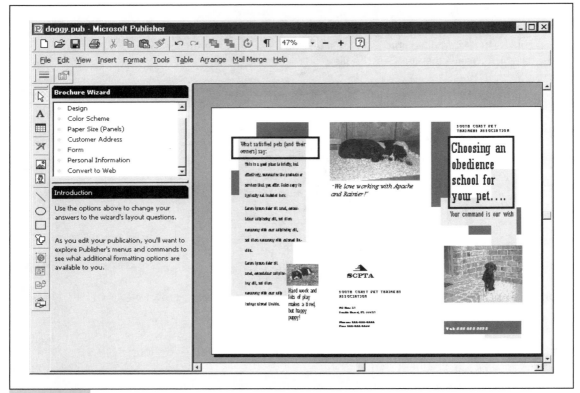

FIGURE 11-3 The Brochure Wizard contains an option to convert the document into a Web site

Convert To Web Site dialog box, shown here. Select the option to allow the Web Site Wizard to automatically create a Web design with hyperlinks.

When the Web Site Wizard conversion option completes its work, Publisher displays the newly converted Web site home page in the screen's right window, as shown in Figure 11-4. Notice, also that Publisher automatically changed the Brochure Wizard to the Web Site Wizard as soon as it converted the brochure to a Web site.

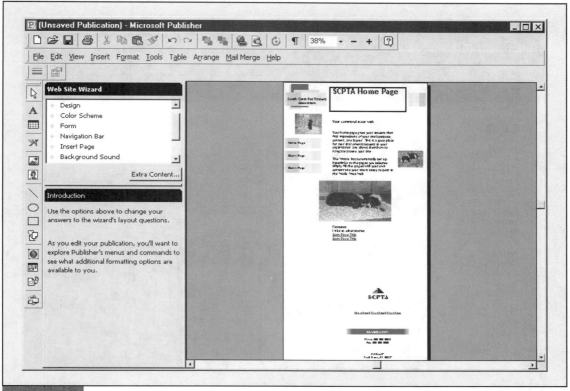

FIGURE 11-4   When Publisher completes the conversion of your brochure to a Web site, it displays its best effort at creating a Web site

Alternatively, you can begin the work of converting one of your printed documents to a Web site selected from Microsoft Publisher's Catalog. Select Web Sites from the list of Publications By Wizard, then click the Existing Files button to access the source document file you want to use as your converted Web site foundation, as shown in Figure 11-5. Publisher will display the Open Publication dialog box, shown in Figure 11-6, from which you may select the desired document file. Remember, though, the source file you convert to your Web site must be a document originally created with one of Publisher's Wizards and cannot contain any modifications. Once you have selected your source document file, Publisher displays the document in the right window, and the Wizard you used originally to create the document in the left window, as was shown in Figure 11-3. Notice the Wizard's final option is Convert To Web. Select this option and Publisher will display the Convert To Web Site dialog box. Select the first option, which allows Publisher to create the Web site's hyperlinks for you.

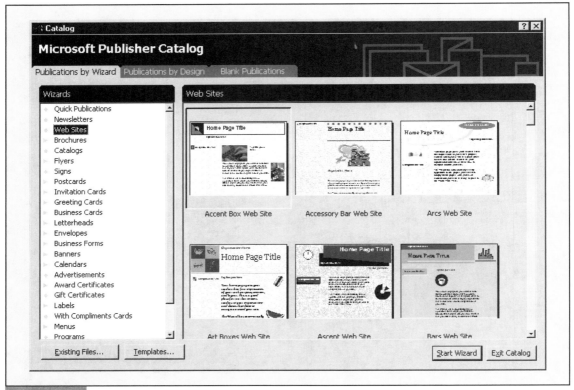

FIGURE 11-5   Click the Existing files button to see a list of all your Publisher documents eligible for conversion to your Web site

Using the Convert To Web Site option from within the source document's original Wizard may give you a usable result with some types of publications, but certainly not with a brochure. If you choose this option, you end up with a two-page Web site—one page for each side of the brochure. The pages do not feature any links to get from one page to the other. Moreover, if the style you used for your source document has any form of graphics behind the text as a background, all your text will be converted to graphics. As you no doubt know, graphics cause a Web site to download considerably more slowly than text, and your readers probably won't like waiting. However, if you need to create a Web presence quickly, this method is probably the simplest procedure. All you have to do is create hyperlinks between the two pages, which you'll learn how to do before this chapter's end.

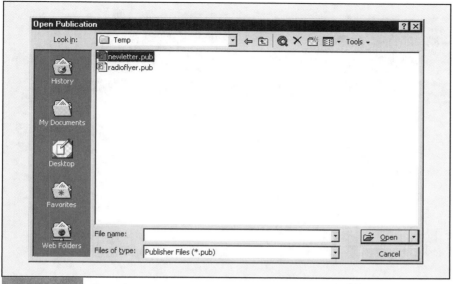

FIGURE 11-6   Select your desired source document from the Open Publication
dialog box

Cross-Reference: For more information on using photographs, see Chapter 13.

Surveying the Conversion Process Results

As was shown in Figure 11-4, your converted Web site is nowhere near the shape
it needs to be usable on the Web. Notice that the resulting page has a lot of white
space—in fact, too much white space. The brochure's left border became the
Web site *navigation bar,* with buttons that link to the other pages in your site.
The conversion process has left the brochure's right border reserved for graphics,
and text appears in a narrow column in the middle area. The arrangement will fit
in a browser window on a system using a 640 × 480 pixel-screen, which means
the resulting Web site will not have a second navigation bar on the screen's bottom. To enhance the layout, you might want to make the left border a bit narrower and the text box a bit wider. This small change puts your text closer to the
browser window's top, and on a Web site, the less scrolling your visitors have to
do is preferable.

Notice also that the Wizard now has a new button labeled Extra Content. In
most conversion instances, some source document objects are not copied to your
newly converted Web site. Click the Extra Content option, and Publisher will
display the tabbed Design Gallery, shown in Figure 11-7. Click on the Extra

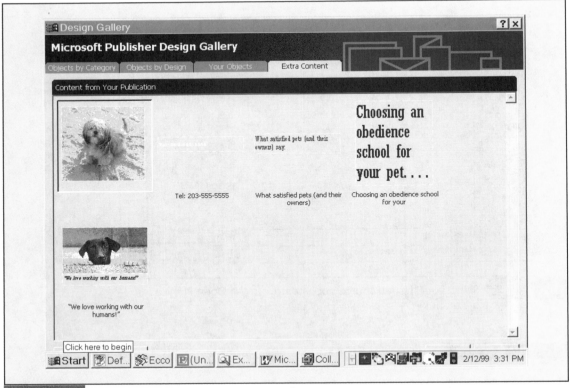

FIGURE 11-7 Publisher strips out some objects from your print publication when creating a Web site from it

Content tab to see what objects did not automatically become part of your converted Web site. You can reinsert these objects as you wish, but take some care in where you place them.

Publisher makes significant changes to your source document's organization and a few changes to your actual content. The following list contains several objects that will be changed in the print-to-Web conversion process:

- Your brochure title will be removed.
- The copy on the back of the brochure—consisting primarily of contact information—becomes part of the footer for every page.
- Any content you may have added to the back (such as the dog with hands, in this instance) will be removed.
- The copy on the inner fold of the outside of the brochure is placed on the home page (the first page of your Web site). This is not too surprising, since,

before editing, the content on this page indicates that "This is a good place to briefly, but effectively, summarize our products or services." If you used the space for this purpose, the home page text is appropriate.

- Photographs that weren't originally from Publisher's galleries may be removed, especially those scanned directly into Publisher.

- Space for a pull-quote has been added to every page except the home page. Since none of the brochure designs include pull-quotes, these will contain dummy text. You'll either have to create new pull-quotes or eliminate the placeholders.

- Fonts are replaced with new ones. Logically, the new ones should be Times New Roman and Arial, which have equivalents on almost any system your viewers are likely to use, but they may be something else.

- Even if you've replaced every image with one of your own, some of the original placeholder images will reappear.

- Publisher creates three navigation buttons, one captioned Home Page and the others captioned Story Page.

Tip: If there's an element of the Web site design you don't like, you can replace it with any number of choices from the Design Gallery, all of which will fit in with your basic design scheme.

Restoring Your Original Content and Organization

The first step is to restore your title. Although you can paste it from the Extra Objects window, it's better to select the Web site's Home Page Title. In that placeholder, enter your new Web site's correct title.

Next, you'll probably want to replace the default animated GIF. In this instance, I deleted it and moved the dog picture from the left border to the right border, to be consistent with the story pages. Finally, I moved the slogan into the left column. The result looks like Figure 11-8.

Remember, the brochure's inside pages contained a large article with one major head and two subheads. Through the conversion, Publisher doesn't exactly preserve this structure. Click on the icon for page 2. You should see the original content from the left inside fold, as shown in Figure 11-9. However, there's no indication of the sponsoring organization's name.

To place the organization's name on each page in the same position as on the home page, follow these steps:

1. Click the title of the home page.
2. Choose Arrange | Ungroup Objects.
3. Click on the text box containing the organization's name.
4. Choose Edit | Copy.
5. Draw your mouse around the title area.

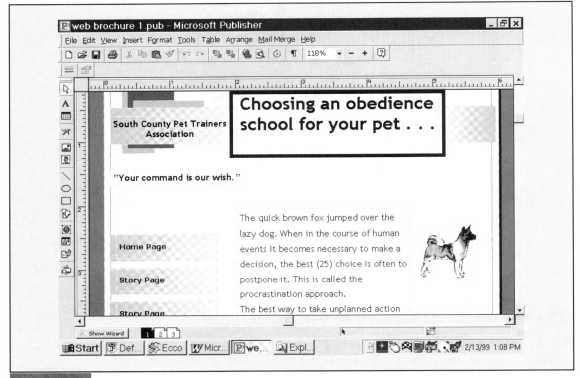

FIGURE 11-8   The brochure content rearranged in the Web version

6. Choose Arrange | Group Objects.

7. Click the icon for page 2.

8. Click the title area of the page.

9. Choose Arrange | Ungroup Objects.

10. Choose Edit | Paste to paste the text box. The title will automatically appear at the appropriate location.

11. Draw your mouse around the title area.

12. Choose Arrange | Group Objects.

Repeat Steps 8 through 12 for any additional pages.

At this point, you should change the text on the first Story Page button so that it reflects the content of the page to which it links.

Now turn to the third page. Even though this part of the brochure did not alter the design in any way, Publisher seems to have had trouble interpreting the

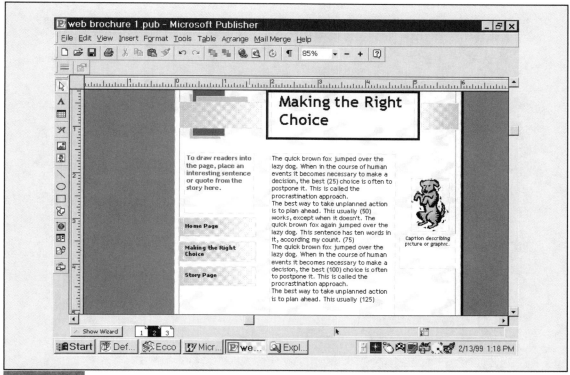

FIGURE 11-9 The first story page appears to be correct, but needs a few additions

content, as you can see in Figure 11-10. Ideally, this content should become two pages, one for each subhead.

To make your Web site's organization follow that of the brochure, follow these steps:

1. Select the first subhead.
2. Choose Edit | Copy.
3. Select the text Story Page Title.
4. Choose Edit | Paste. (In this example, I also pressed SHIFT-ENTER after the word "to" in the title, breaking the title into two lines that are better balanced.)
5. Notice that when you click outside the title box, the text on the link button at the left changes to match your title.
6. Choose Insert | Page, and make sure Add Hyperlink To Web Navigation Bar is checked.

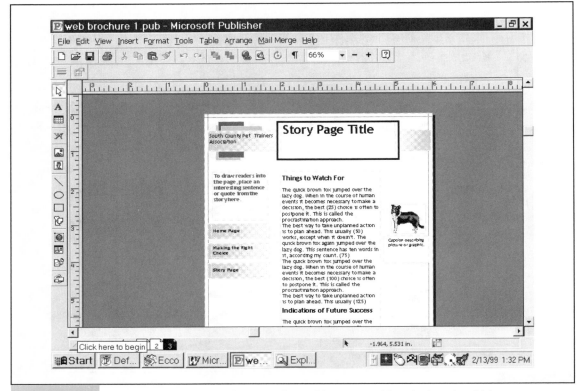

FIGURE 11-10 The second story page has no title, and has two subheads that should have become titles

7. Click the More Options button, and Publisher will display the Insert Page dialog box:

8. Specify the number of pages you want to add in the Number Of New Pages box. Click the appropriate radio button to insert the pages before or after the current page.

9. Insert any blank pages you might need (you can always delete these later). You can instruct Publisher to automatically create one text frame on each new page.

10. Decide whether you want to duplicate all the objects from any page to the newly inserted pages, and specify the page from which the content should be copied.

11. Request that Publisher automatically add hyperlinks to the navigation bar for all the new pages you insert.

If your inner front flap contained a story instead of a description of your organization or your products and services, you'll want to give it a page of its own, and edit the home page content appropriately. To make these changes, follow these steps:

1. Choose Insert | Page, and be sure to check the Add Hyperlink To Web Navigation Bar.

2. Click the More Options button, and then check Duplicate All Objects On Page 4.

3. Go to the newly inserted page 5, and delete the text from the text box.

4. Go to the home page and cut the text from the text box on that page.

5. Return to your new page 5, and paste the text into the text box on that page.

6. Enter the title of the story.

If your image from that story was placed in Extra Content, add it back in the picture space on the newly added page 5. To relocate the picture, first click on the duplicated picture, and choose Arrange | Ungroup Objects, in case the objects are grouped in the design. Then click the Extra Content button, and choose the image you want to insert. Click Insert Object.

When the selected object appears on page 5, drag the image to the space above the caption. Nudge it into place by pressing the ALT key plus the arrow keys (that is, ALT-UP moves the image up in small increments, ALT-LEFT moves it left, and so on). If a red frame flashes around the picture, you have overlapped the caption frame, and the caption will be turned into a graphic. Nudge the picture upward until the red frame disappears. Finally, if you want to group the design objects for future use, SHIFT-CLICK the caption, and choose Arrange | Group Objects. Publisher will then "lock" the picture and caption together, which simplifies any future relocation options. (If you'd rather use clip art, just double-click the picture to bring up the Clip Gallery.)

Cleaning Up the Page

Now that you've got your brochure reasonably well duplicated on your Web site, it's time to turn your attention to the design elements Publisher creates for you. First, go back to the home page. Notice that the Home Page button now shows the page title. Since the home page title is the subject of the entire site, you may want to change the button text back to Home Page. To do so, just click the button and type the new text.

Turn now to the bottom of the home page. Notice that a big box with the heading Features appears below the text box, as shown in Figure 11-11. Within the box are links to two of your pages—the original two pages. Below that is a box containing links to all the pages, so you may want to delete the Features box

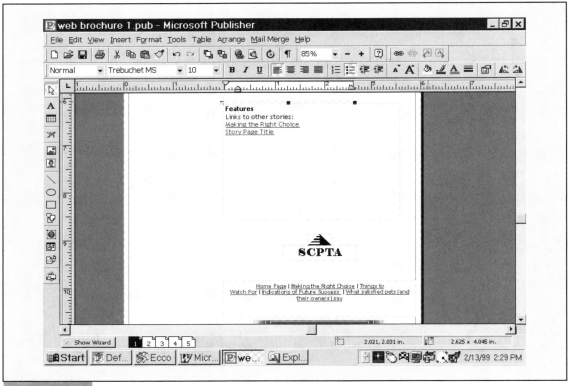

FIGURE 11-11   Publisher gives you the chance to have multiple navigation bars

as redundant. However, many of your Web site visitors may like the addition of navigation bars at more than one spot on each Web page. Leaving the multiple navigation bars as an enhancement to your site or deleting them is up to you. If you leave both link areas, make sure the names of the links are identical in each location and the links operate without any difficulty.

Remember, while white space is good, too much of it makes Web site navigation a bit more difficult. So if you have any white space at the bottom of the text box, bring up the bottom border of the box until it's just below the text, as shown in Figure 11-12.

Now scroll farther down the home page. You should see a logo, the links box, and two boxes full of contact information. There's no reason any of this content

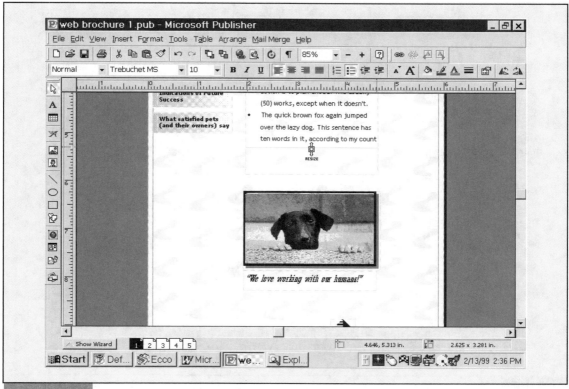

FIGURE 11-12   Resize the text box to fit the text

should be so far below the text box. Drag your mouse around the entire area to select it, and then drag upward with the Move cursor until it's just below the other
content, as shown in Figure 11-13.

Finally, note that the mailing address doesn't include the organization name,
so you may want to add it. The best way is to just type it into the text box. Press
ENTER at the beginning to make a space for it and enter the organization name.
You will probably have to lower the bottom border to display everything in the
text frame.

Now turn to the other pages. If you worked from a brochure, you'll probably
see lots of blank space on pages, where the text boxes extend too far. (In a
browser, this white space will show up as a blank screen. You don't want blank

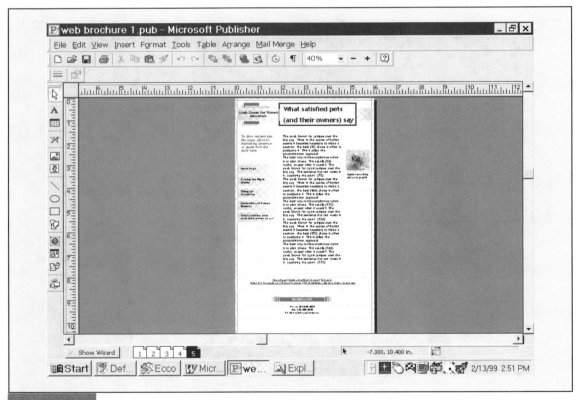

FIGURE 11-13 Move the page-end content up to just below the main content

space eating up your Web site.) Again, for each page, resize the text box to fit the text, select the page footer content, and move it up to just below the text box. (You needn't worry about the organization name being missing, because the mailing address appears only on the home page.)

All the extra white space should now be below the contact information, and when Publisher creates the actual Web pages, it eliminates the blank space, as you can see in Figure 11-14. (Notice how the right scroll bar is at the bottom of the page.) You can preview your page by clicking File | Web Page Preview.

Creating the Publishable Web Site

You may not have noticed it, but you're still working with a Publisher file. In order to use the site you created, you have to convert to HTML pages and GIF or JPG images. To do so, choose File | Save As Web Page.

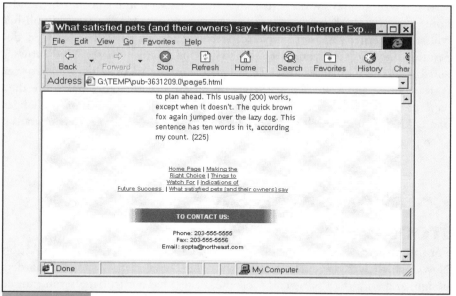

FIGURE 11-14   The extra white space at the bottom disappears when the page is viewed in a browser. The content fits in a 640 × 480 window without a horizontal scroll bar

By default, Publisher will create a folder called Publish inside the folder in which you're working. Double-click that folder. Click the New Folder icon at the top of the dialog box, and create one with a name that will help you remember what's in your Web site. Double-click the new folder, and choose OK. Publisher creates the appropriate files. Notice Publisher has preserved the JPG format of those photographs saved in that file form, while converting all other images to the GIF format.

If you want to preview the actual site, double-click on index.html, which is the home page. (In Publisher, the home page is *always* called index.html.) Publisher will start Internet Explorer or Netscape Navigator, or any other browser, depending on which one you have selected as your default browser. Your browser will display the Web pages just as they will look on the Web. While your browser is displaying your new Web site, click on all the page links to make sure they work properly. If they do, you're finished. However, if you want to make changes of any kind, you must reload the Web site into Publisher, and save it again as a Web page when you're through making modifications.

Creating a Web Site from a Newsletter

For this project, we'll use the example of the East Bridge Neighborhood Action News, which was originally created with the Newsletter Wizard, in Borders design, and with the Prairie color scheme. Page 3 has a calendar, as you can see in Figure 11-15. Also, the content required two stories on page 2, instead of

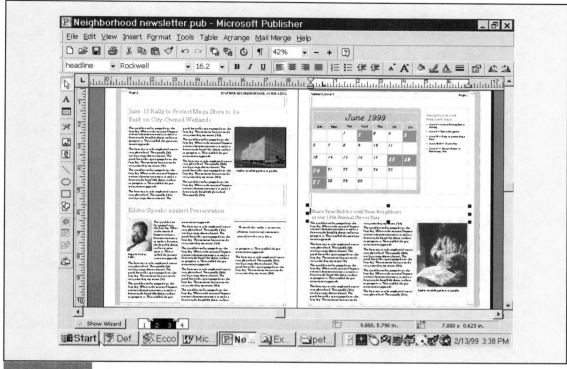

FIGURE 11-15 The right-inside page has a calendar; the left-inside page has one less story than the default

the default three stories originally planned by the Newsletter Wizard. I've replaced all the photos to make them Web-ready, as we discussed in the chapter's beginning.

Successfully converting the existing newsletter's back page will be particularly problematic. The default back page, shown in Figure 11-16, includes contact information, space for a "Who we are" paragraph, and another story. Since this newsletter was originally designed to be a self-mailer, I added a Customer Address space when I created the source document with the Newsletter Wizard.

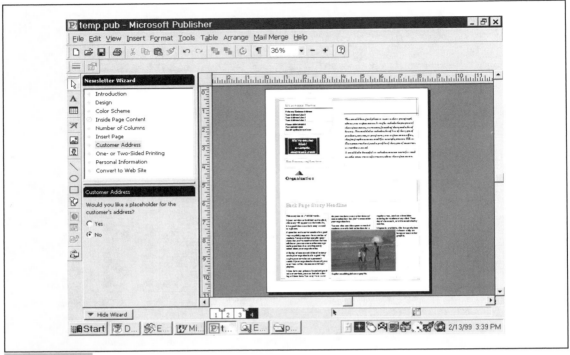

FIGURE 11-16   The default back page of a brochure is a space to describe the organization and include an additional story

Still, I wanted the "Who we are" paragraph from the back page, so I first cut it using Edit | Cut. When Publisher added the Customer Address area, I deleted the final story and pasted the previously cut paragraph. I also added a membership form to the page, so the result looked like Figure 11-17.

To begin, click Convert To Web Site and click the Create button. Choose the default method, Use the Web Site Wizard To Automatically Create A Web Design With Hyperlinks. This is the same procedure you used to create a Web site from the brochure. Next, check the Extra Content window. You'll see that you've lost the following:

- The title of the publication

- The form (you'll want a Web response form in its place, so you can collect information directly from the site)

- The "We're on the Web!" announcement; this *should* be eliminated, because it's obvious you're on the Web

- The headers for the form, the events list, and the identification story, which is now on the first page (the home page)

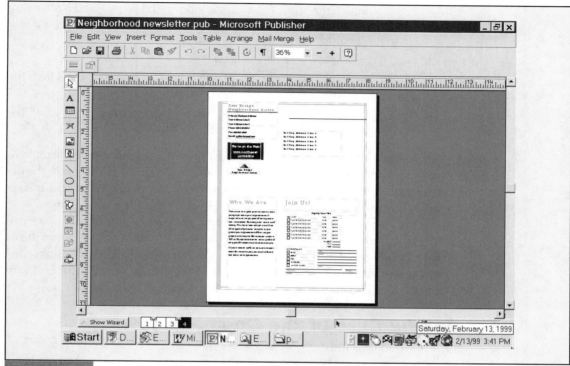

FIGURE 11-17 The edited back page has a customer address, a form, and the description in a different location

Because I grouped the form elements for convenience, the entire form was removed. If it had not been grouped, a few of the elements would have been brought over; however, most would still end up as extra content.

Now that you know what you've lost from converting your newsletter to your Web site, let's see what you've got left in the newly created Web site with which to work. The following list describes what objects successfully converted to your new Web site:

- Page 1 is a home page, which includes the "who-are-we" box, an irrelevant graphic, an animated GIF, and a Features box like the one on the brochure example's home page.

- Page 2 is the calendar, with the generic title for the event list.

- Pages 3 and 4 contain the page 1 articles from the newsletter.

- Pages 5 and 6 contain the articles from page 2 of the newsletter.

- Pages 4 and 6 contain placeholder graphics. The one on page 4 accompanies an article that had no illustration in the source document newsletter.

- Page 7 contains the photo from the second story on page 2, and is otherwise blank. The conversion process has inserted this page to replace the third article that was supposed to appear on page 2.
- Page 8 contains the article from page 3.
- Page 9 is blank, taking the place of the form, which was eliminated from the source document during the conversion process.
- Page 10 contains a text box for the story that would have appeared on the back page, along with a placeholder photo.

What does this list tell you about converting a Wizard-created newsletter to a Web site? It's pretty clear that Publisher creates one page for each item in the default design, and pours what it thinks are the appropriate articles and images from your print publication into what it thinks are the appropriate pages.

For some reason, the Web Site Wizard created only two hyperlinks. Once you load this Web site as it currently exists on the Web, the only way for your visitors to access pages other than the calendar and the home page is to use the links contained in the Features box. However, creating hyperlinks with Publisher is very easy, and you'll learn how to create them before this chapter's end.

Taking Care of the Cosmetic Issues

Before we address the more serious issues that resulted from the Web Site Wizard's process, let's start repairing the easy stuff that went awry. Use the page icons to tour each page of the newly created Web site, and when you come to a blank or irrelevant page, delete it by choosing Edit | Delete Page. Next—just as you did when you were refining the Web site you created from the brochure—go to each page and resize the text boxes to fit the text, and move the contact information to just below the text box.

In this particular publication, delete the placeholder picture from page 6, and cut the picture from page 7, which you will paste on page 6. This leaves page 7 blank, so you can delete it with Edit | Delete Page.

It would be a good idea to either eliminate the remaining placeholder pictures or replace them with appropriate ones. Similarly, since every page has a placeholder for a pull-quote, you'll want to either create pull-quotes or eliminate those placeholders.

Creating the Missing Hyperlinks

Every Web site needs hyperlinks to all of its Web pages. The horizontal hyperlink box can't be edited directly, so you'll have to work with the buttons. It's easiest if you start on the home page, because you can use the Features box for reference. The trick is that each button consists of two parts: a rectangle containing the link, and a text box containing the label. This method of construction allows you to create buttons that don't have the coloring and underlining hyperlinks normally have. See the Features box or the horizontal hyperlink box for examples.

Choose Tools | Snap To Guides and Tools | Snap To Ruler Marks to turn off these features. If you closely examine the buttons, you'll see they consist of two objects that don't entirely overlap, and neither of them falls within the guides or the ruler marks.

Drag the vertical ruler next to the buttons' edge. Hold down the SHIFT key, and right-click the mouse to set the zero point at the first button's top. You'll need to use the ruler to make sure your buttons are of uniform size and uniformly spaced. Then hold down SHIFT and point to the vertical ruler to create a vertical guide along the right side of the buttons.

Click the rectangle tool, and create a rectangle similar in size to the existing buttons, as shown in Figure 11-18. Note that the rectangles extend just beyond the vertical guide, but the text boxes don't quite reach it.

Tip: If you want to create a button that is the exact same size of an existing button, trace the existing button with your cursor. Look at the lower right corner of the document to see the proportions of the rectangle, as shown in Figure 11-18. When you create your own box, you can check in that same spot to make sure you match the measurements.

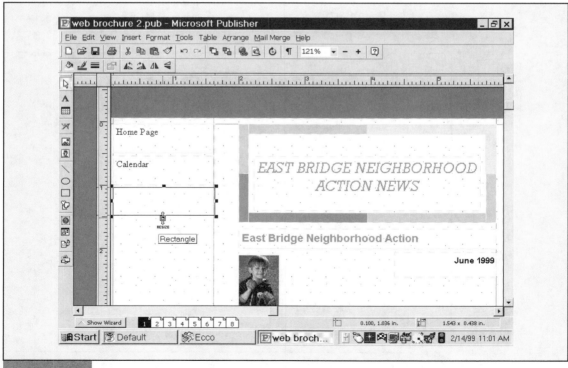

FIGURE 11-18   Create a rectangle to be used as a hyperlink

Right-click on the rectangle you created, and choose Change Rectangle | Line/Border Style | None to eliminate the visible border. Click the text tool, and create a text box on top of the rectangle.

Using the line tool, hold down SHIFT and draw a straight line across the top of the rectangle. I know you can't see any such lines, but they will show up when you preview the page in any browser.

Before you do anything else, drag your mouse around these three objects to select them, and copy them. Publisher won't take kindly to your copying and pasting a hyperlink.

Point to the rectangle. (Move in slowly from the right.) You'll know you've got it when the yellow tip says "Rectangle." When it does, click to select the rectangle.

Right-click and choose Hyperlink, or press CTRL-K. Publisher will display the Hyperlink dialog box, shown in Figure 11-19.

Choose the Another Page In Your Web Site option from the top section of the Hyperlink dialog box. In this instance, you'll specify the link to be created to page 3. Click OK when you are done with this dialog box.

When you click OK to close the Hyperlink dialog box, you will again see the full view of the Web site's home page. Now click in the text box for which you created the hyperlink to page 3, and type the title of the story on page 3.

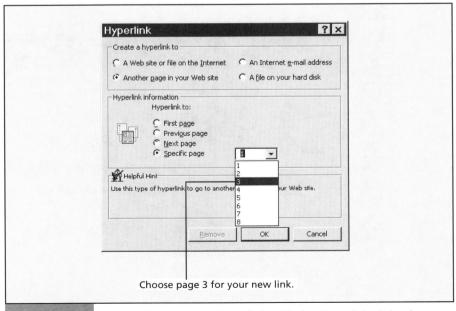

Choose page 3 for your new link.

FIGURE 11-19 Create the necessary hyperlink with the Hyperlink dialog box

Paste the pair of boxes you copied into your page, and drag them to the places you want to locate them.

Now repeat this process until you have created buttons and hyperlinks to every page, from page 4 through page 8.

Select the original two buttons, and choose Arrange | Ungroup Objects to ungroup the two objects. Remember that grouping closely related objects, such as the objects used in this example, keeps the objects grouped together so that you can easily move them as a single design unit. Using the Group Objects command makes relocating items like these hyperlink buttons a one-step process. Publisher will display all kinds of dire warnings about how it won't be able to maintain the page relationships if you do ungroup these objects, but don't worry—Publisher can't maintain these relationships very well at this point in the process anyway.

Select the entire row of buttons, and choose Arrange | Group Objects, and then copy the group. Now, with the new navigation buttons copied, go to each page in turn, delete the existing navigation buttons, and paste your new ones in their place. You can see the result in Figure 11-20.

Because Publisher forewarned you that it could not maintain the hyperlinks, you may also want to delete the horizontal link box and replace it with the Features list. You can edit the Features list so that it fits the layout better, as shown in Figure 11-21. For example, I've changed the name of that section to "Other Stories."

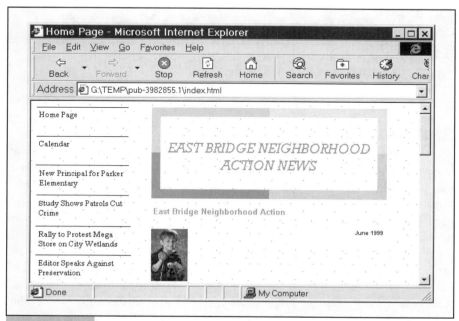

FIGURE 11-20   The new navigation buttons look and work as they should in any browser

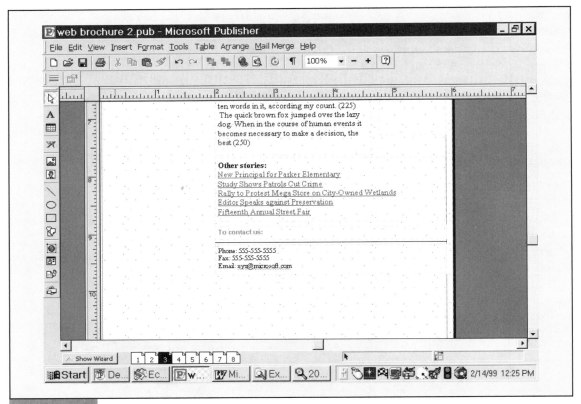

FIGURE 11-21 You can use an edited Features list in place of a horizontal navigation bar

Planning Your Future

You now know how to create a Web site from a newsletter, as well as a brochure. If you regularly publish newsletters, you will have other newsletters, or course, that you will want to add to your Web site as each new issue is published. If you want to plan your site so that it can accommodate this type of expansion, you'll need a home page for your newsletters as a group, and links to each subsequent newsletter issue. If you expand the site to include other information about your organization in addition to what appears in your newsletters, you'll want yet another level of hierarchy. Figure 11-22 shows a diagram of this structure. A real site, of course, could have many more pages. Within the diagram, the small squares inside the larger ones represent hyperlinks. If you're planning to develop a complete Web presence, keep this structure in mind. The better you plan your site, the easier it will be to enlarge and maintain.

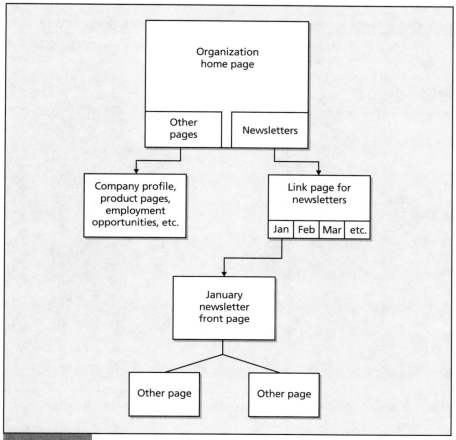

FIGURE 11-22 It's easiest to maintain a well-structured Web site

Creating Your Site and Adding Content

If you want to create a Web site from a Publisher newsletter, but want better control of the content, create the site first, and then add content from the publication. The procedure involves a lot of cutting and pasting, and is tedious, but certainly no more tedious than creating a bunch of navigation buttons by hand. This method will also give you better final results.

Start by using Publisher's Web Site Wizard to create a Web site made from the same design and color scheme as you used in your newsletter. As shown in Figure 11-23, Publisher creates a single page that's virtually identical to the home page it created when you transformed your source document newsletter into the beginning point for your new Web site.

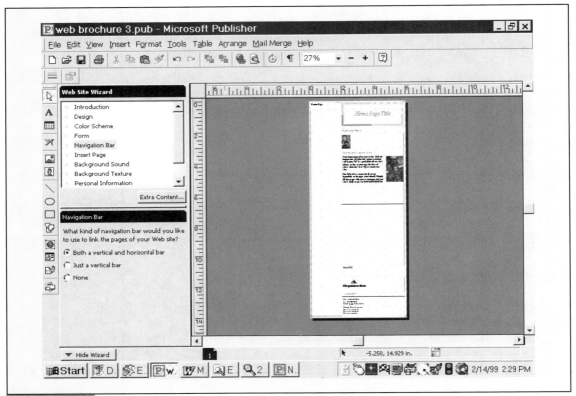

FIGURE 11-23 Publisher creates a home page based on your design and color specifications

To continue to evolve the Web site to contain most of the material you feature in your newsletter, add new pages with Insert | Page. Publisher will display the Insert Page dialog box, shown next. From the Available Page Types dropdown list, you can select the type of page you want to add. For this example, you can put a calendar on the second page, and then add six more pages (one of which is a form page) to hold the newsletter contents. (You can create the rest of your pages quickly by pressing CTRL-SHIFT-N and pressing ENTER the requisite number of times.)

Once you've added the correct title to any page, the Web Site Wizard automatically creates the appropriate hyperlinks for you, as shown in Figure 11-24. The Wizard also creates the horizontal navigation bar, shown in Figure 11-25.

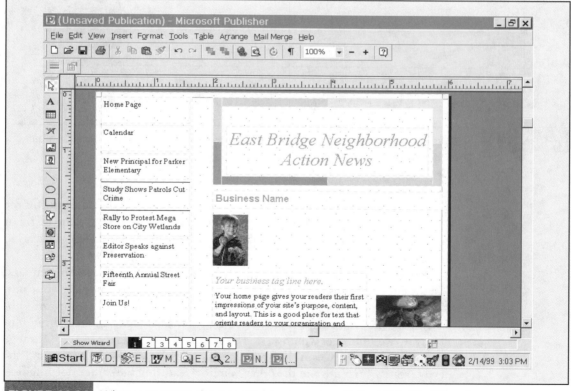

FIGURE 11-24   When you create the new Web pages yourself, the Web Site Wizard creates a proper navigation bar

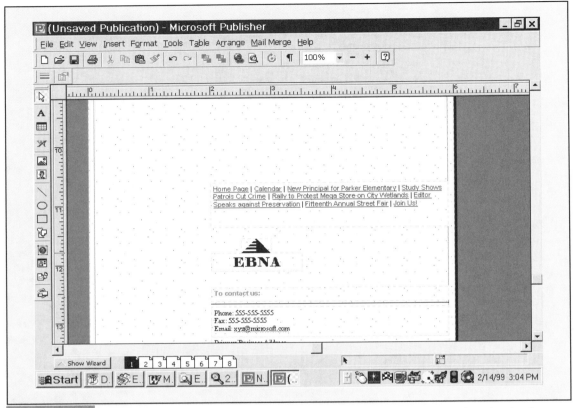

FIGURE 11-25 The Web Site Wizard maintains consistency between the horizontal navigation bar and the vertical navigation bar

If you need to edit the titles to make them fit properly on the buttons, edit the titles on the pages, not on the buttons. The two always have the same text, but Publisher may not be able to make the corrections in the horizontal navigation bar if you edit the buttons.

Now that you have your Web site structure finalized, you need only cut and paste the text, photos, and graphics to the placeholders to complete your new Web site. To make this process as easy as possible, open a second copy of Publisher from the Start menu, and load your source document publication into it. Place the two Publisher windows side by side, as shown in Figure 11-26. Arrange the corresponding pages in the two windows, with one window featuring the newly created Web site and the other Window featuring the source document—whether it is a newsletter, brochure, or another type of Wizard-created source

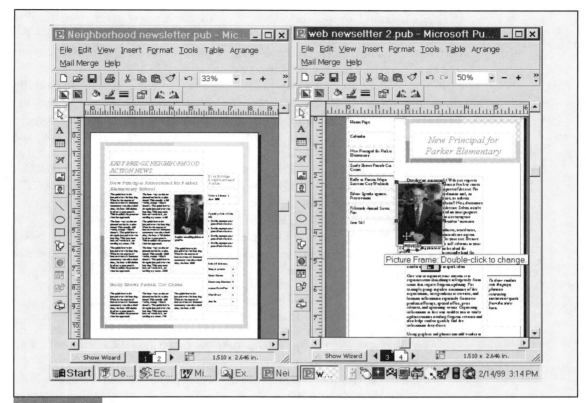

FIGURE 11-26 Lining up the Publisher windows side by side makes it easy to see where to relocate source document material in the Web site

document. Now you can easily select and copy objects from the source document window, and paste those objects into the Web site window.

Creating a Newsletter or Brochure from a Web Site

Once you've created a Web site, you can turn it back into a newsletter or brochure. However, you will experience major limitations with this conversion process, just as you did when you converted a printed document into a Web site. As with converting print to a Web site, anything that Publisher doesn't identify as the exact default design of the conversion source will not convert properly. You will have a significant amount of manual repair and redesign to do. You'll have better luck creating an empty newsletter or brochure of the appropriate design, and then manually pasting your content into it.

Publisher's steps for converting a Web site to a printed document are basically the same as those for creating a Web site from a print publication. First, open the Web site that you want to convert to a printed document. (You can only convert Web sites that were originally created in Publisher. You have to start with the Publisher file, not with the actual Web site.) When Publisher displays the existing source Web site in the right window, it will also activate and display the Web Site Wizard on the screen's left. The Web Site Wizard's last option is Convert To Print. Select this option and then choose the Newsletter or Brochure option.

When converting the Web site used for the previous demonstrations, I ended up with an eight-page publication in place of the four-page Web site with which I started. The following list shows you the types of problems you might encounter if you convert one of your Web sites to a printed document:

- The first page was perfect.

- The converted print document's page 2 and 3 both contained calendars: a blank calendar on the left page, and the calendar from the source Web site on the right. Each page had a placeholder for a story, with graphics located on each page's bottom.

- The converted print document's page 4 contained the two stories originally on the Web site's page 2.

- From the Web site, the story located under the calendar was now on the print document's page 5, along with two additional story placeholders.

- The converted print document's pages 6 through 8 contained more story placeholders, but the address area on page 8 was set up properly.

- Many elements from the Web publication that had no equivalent in the resulting brochure were placed randomly on top of stories or story placeholders.

You could make a better likeness of a print document from this Web site if you delete the dummy calendar page and the print document's pages 6 and 7. You could then move the story from the print document's page 5 to the calendar page. Regardless of any advantages using the Convert To Print option may offer, the result is a substantial amount of tedious manual cleanup to do. To avoid this, you should seriously consider using the cut-and-paste approach previously described in this chapter.

Professional Skills Summary

In this chapter, we took a look at using Publisher to convert a printed document to a Web site. We examined the features and benefits, as well as the drawbacks and problems you might encounter as you transform printed materials into Web content, including how to fix those problems and ensure that your transformed material works in the Web environment. We also discussed how to use Publisher to transform existing Web pages and material into printed documents, taking into consideration how to solve any problems you might encounter during this process. Although Publisher 2000 offers both the Convert To Web Site and Convert To Print options, you may find that you save time and stress by using the Web Site Wizard to create a Web site template, and then pasting the content from your source document into the newly created Web site, or vice versa. This approach eliminates the difficult task of manually cleaning up problems that result from either conversion process.

Now that you've taken your basic Publisher skills and fine-tuned them for maximum professional output, learn how to create logos, work with photographs, address your publications, and prepare your documents for a commercial printer in Part IV.

Part IV

Using Publisher to Project a Professional Image

chapter 12

Creating Logos with Publisher

In this chapter, you will:

- Learn how to obtain and apply clip art
- Choose the right clip art images for your projects
- Edit and personalize clip art images
- Use WordArt to create text effects
- Combine WordArt and clip art for logos and text blurbs

What a dull world we would live in if we didn't have that often-used visual enhancement called clip art to add interest to our printed and online publications. The term "clip art" became common usage long ago in printed media, because each art piece was part of a big book from which the user actually clipped the art with scissors and added it to print publications. This clip art collection was sold very inexpensively to anyone who wanted to add generic graphical elements to their otherwise text-dominated material. Often, clip art came to the user via subscription in printed books organized by topic or season, and it was also available through graphics supply stores on rub-off transfer sheets.

Welcome to the Clip Art World

With the transition of virtually all publishing activity to the PC, what is now known as clip art is a collection of graphical elements, usually distributed on CD. Anyone can purchase and use clip art in any print or online creation. The primary distinction of clip art from other forms of artwork is that it is sold with full permission for the purchaser to use it in any form without seeking additional permission. Other forms of art are considered proprietary and should not be used without the expressed written permission of the artwork's creator. With clip art, the creator has sold all the rights to the artwork to the clip art publisher, and anyone who buys the clip art on CD or off the Web can use the material freely in the public domain without any worry about rights of ownership or permission to print.

You can find clip art collections, which usually come with collections of fonts as well, sold at very affordable prices ($20–50 price range for a CD with graphics [clip art] and several new fonts) at any retail location where software is sold. Some products are available on CD and disk, and others you can download from the Web and use just as you would clip art purchased in a regular retail environment. Many word processing, Web site creation, or desktop publishing applications also come with their own smaller collections of clip art to provide the user with a modest variety of graphical objects to use in their creations.

Thousands of clip art collections are commercially available, and some individual collections come with thousands of images. Some clip art is readily identifiable by category for purchase (like religions symbols or holiday symbols). They all come in a variety of universal file types, so you can quickly place clip art into your Publisher creation without changing graphic file types, or going through some elaborate file translation process.

Here is a brief list of clip art resources you can easily find to use in your Publisher 2000 creations. Some of these sources are free:

- Publisher's Clip Gallery, which comes with the application
- Publisher's link to Microsoft's clip art library on the Web, from which you can download free graphic objects
- Most graphics software packages include some clip art, which can be imported into Publisher
- Web sites from which you can download free clip art
- Web sites from which you can download clip art for a fee per download or order on CD-ROM
- Commercially packaged, low-cost clip art collections, featuring thousands of images, which are available from any retail outlet that sells software

Later in this chapter, you'll learn how to use Publisher's Clip Gallery and Microsoft's exclusive Web site featuring its downloadable clip art collection.

Importing Clip Art

To import clip art from other packages into Publisher, open the Clip Gallery and click Import Clips. This opens the Add Clip To Clip Gallery dialog box. Browse for the folder containing the clip art you want to import.

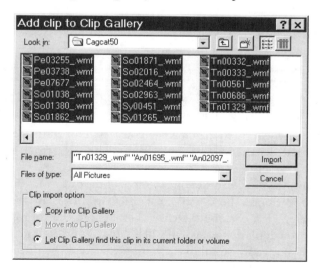

The Add Clip to Clip Gallery dialog box is a special kind of browse window, in which you can make multiple selections by clicking one item in conjunction with the CTRL or SHIFT key, as the illustration indicates, selecting more than one option. You can also choose whether to:

- **Copy into Clip Gallery**   This option makes a copy of the selected file in the Clip Gallery, while leaving the original file in its place.

- **Move into Clip Gallery**   This option moves the file from its original location into the Clip Gallery.

- **Let Clip Gallery find this clip in its current folder or volume**   This option creates a shortcut from the Clip Gallery to the file's location.

When you've made your selections, click Import. This opens the Clip Properties dialog box, once for each clip file you've selected. In the tabbed Clip Properties dialog box, you determine how the Clip Gallery will find your imported file.

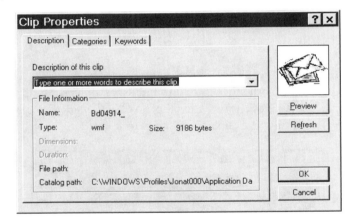

The description tab in the Clip Properties dialog box invites you to type one or more words to describe the selection. This is not just a title, but a set of search words Clip Gallery will try to match when you search for an image with particular characteristics. For the image shown, you might use cartoon-style envelope with letter, for example.

You can also add your clip art to one or more of the categories the Clip Gallery uses for quick reference. To do so, click the Categories tab and scroll down through the categories, clicking the check box next to the appropriate ones, as shown here. If you don't do this, you'll still be able to find your images through a category search, but you won't find them immediately if you open a category, as explained later in this chapter.

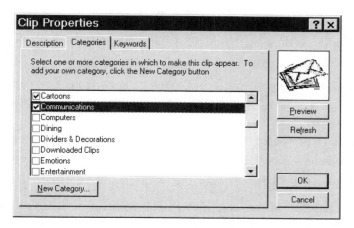

If you expect to focus on a subject area that's not included in your categories list, you can create a new category by clicking the New Category button and entering a name for the category.

Finally, you can give each image one or more keywords. Every image has its file type as a keyword, but you may want to add other categories on which to search when you import clip art into Publisher. These new categories can be more than one-word search terms or words other than those you would consider to be "categories." As you start typing a keyword, words that match what you're typing appear as a tool tip, so you can assign keywords that are already shared with other clips.

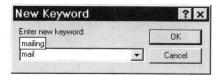

Downloading Additional Art from Microsoft's Clip Art Site

To download additional clip art from Microsoft's clip art site, click the Clip Art tabbed button on the home page. The Web site then displays the tabbed options box for selecting Microsoft clip art online. Click OK in the dialog box, and Publisher will start your default

Tip: The primary Microsoft Office CD-ROM has a collection of clip art that's as large as, but different from, the one included with Publisher. You can import this collection by placing CD 1 in your drive, and browsing for D:\Pfiles\Common\ Msshared\Clipart (assuming D is your CD-ROM drive), and then selecting each folder in turn. This does create a problem, however, in that the path to the clip art is the same as the one on the Publisher disk (CD 2). When you click on an image that's on the other CD, you see an error message asking you to insert the appropriate CD.

browser and go directly to the site. You'll be taken to the Clip Gallery Live site, a portion of which is shown in Figure 12-1. First, you choose a category of images. Then you can:

- Download a clip immediately by clicking the arrow icon below the thumbnail
- Preview a larger version of the image in the box at the left by clicking on the thumbnail
- Search for related clips by clicking the keywords next to the preview image
- Browse forward and backward
- Click the check box to add the clip to the Selection Basket

If you've checked any images, the Selection Basket icon changes to reflect the number of images you have selected. Here you can review your selections and download all the images at once.

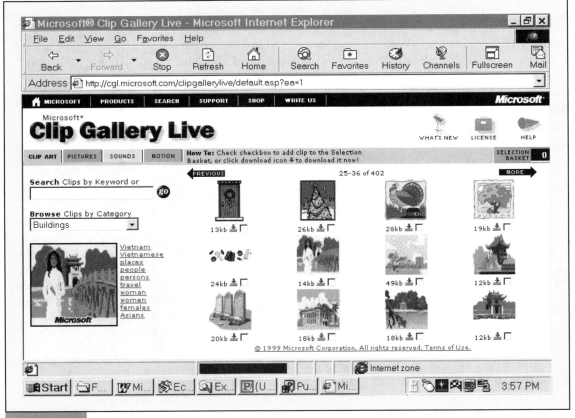

FIGURE 12-1 Microsoft's Clip Gallery Live contains a wealth of free clip art for Publisher users

If you wish, you can go directly to this site in your browser by entering the URL http://cgl.microsoft.com/clipgallerylive/.

However, there's an advantage to starting from the Clip Gallery: all your images are then placed in the category Downloaded Clips, so you can find them easily. If you want to copy or move them to other categories once they are downloaded, right-click each one and choose Clip Properties, and follow the steps just described.

A second advantage to downloading from within Clip Gallery is that each image comes with a list of keywords already attached. So even if you don't want to move the new images into more relevant categories, you'll still have at least one tool by which you can find them easily.

> **L▶ Tip:** As you're reclassifying your downloaded images, uncheck the Downloaded Clips category, so the download repository doesn't get so full it becomes useless.

Other Sources of Clip Art on the Internet

As noted, there are many sources of free clip art on the Internet. One of the best places to start is http://www.webplaces.com/html/clipart.htm, which contains links to hundreds of sites offering clip art. Most are free sites; some are commercial sites with a selection of free samples, and some are strictly commercial sites.

Among the largest sites for free clip art are:

- http://www.caboodles.com/clipart/
- http://www.clipart.com
- http://www.clipartconnection.com

Among the commercial sites offering clip art, two of the largest and best known are:

- http://www.eyewire.com
- http://www.arttoday.com.

When you download from any of these sites, you'll have to import the image into your Clip Gallery if you want it there. You can also use the Insert | Picture | From File command, and insert the image from the location to which you downloaded it.

Finding Images in Your Clip Art Collection

The Clip Gallery gives you two easy ways to find your clips: by searching and by category.

To see the categories, click the Categories icon at the top of the Clip Gallery. You'll see a layout like the one in Figure 12-2. Click on a button to open a category. In it, you'll see thumbnails of all the images and a notice the vast array of clip art categories that come with Publisher.

Special mention should be made of the New Category and Favorites buttons in the Clip Gallery shown in Figure 12-2. The New Category button lets you create a new category just as the similarly named button in the Clip Properties sheet does. The button for the new category takes on the image of the first clip you place in the category.

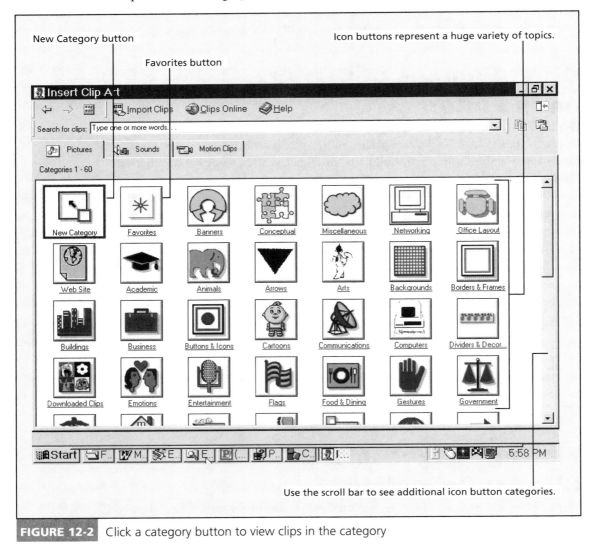

FIGURE 12-2 Click a category button to view clips in the category

You've added and changed art in most hands-on chapters in this book. To review, clicking on an image produces the visual menu in Figure 12-3, with the following four items:

- Insert clip
- Preview clip
- Add clip to Favorites or other category
- Find similar clips

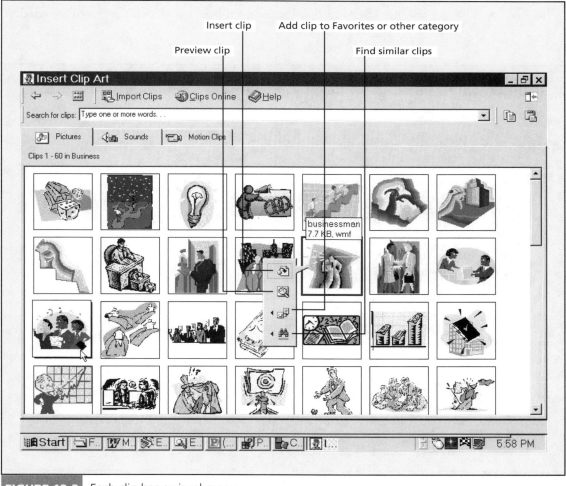

FIGURE 12-3 Each clip has a visual menu

The third button produces a drop-down list of categories, with Favorites as the default. The last button searches based on the keywords entered for the clips.

You can also rename or delete a category by right-clicking on its button and choosing the appropriate command from the context menu. The Favorites category is a good place to store images you use often. (This goes for photographs as well as drawings.) You can cross-reference any clip with the Favorites category by clicking on it, choosing the third button from the visual menu shown in Figure 12-3, and clicking Add.

If you don't see what you want in a category, most categories include a button at the end labeled Keep Looking (shown in Figure 12-4). Click it and you get another screenful of clips, selected because of some keyword association.

FIGURE 12-4   If you don't see any clip art pieces that work for you, you can expand your search with the Keep Looking button

Often, you can click several times in successive windows. However, the images are likely to be progressively less relevant as you proceed, and you can't back-track. The only way to get back to the images you've already seen is to click the Categories button and start over.

The other way to locate clips is always available in the Clip Gallery. There is an entry line at the top of the Clip Gallery labeled Search For Clips, with the words "Type one or more words…" already entered. Here you can type several search criteria, and the Clip Gallery will do its best to find what you want. For example, Figure 12-5 shows what it found when asked for "birds cartoons." Here, too, you'll usually see a Keep Looking button, with the same effects. (You have to re-enter the search criteria to start over.)

FIGURE 12-5 You can use Publisher's search tool in the Clip Gallery to find clips that meet multiple criteria

Using Clip Art in Your Publications

There are three ways to insert a clip art image into your publication. You can:

- Choose Insert | Picture | Clip Art. The image will appear in the middle of the page, slightly to the lower right, pretty much regardless of whatever other objects are there. You can freely reposition and resize your image after inserting it.

Note: When a clip art image is inserted into your document, it is always proportional, regardless of the shape you constrain it to appear in. To proportionally resize a clip art object, press CTRL while resizing.

- Create a text frame, picture frame, or other shape such as an oval or rectangle, and select it. Then choose Insert Picture | Clip Art. The clip art image will appear inside the previously created object. You can then constrain the size of the object to match the clip art, if you like.

- Use the toolbar's Clip Art Gallery tool, creating a rectangular shape approximating the desired size and position. The Clip Art Gallery will appear. After selecting your picture, the clip art will fill the shape you just created.

This command opens the Clip Gallery, where you select your image, click on it, and click on the first icon in the visual menu to insert it.

Choosing a File Format for the Clip Art You Want to Use

One criterion for acceptable clip art is the file format of the clip. Publisher's Clip Gallery includes files in the following formats:

- **BMP**   Bit-mapped images in the default Windows format. These are usually photographs, but may be drawings. Compared to other images with similar color ranges, BMP images take up a large amount of disk space.

- **TIFF**   Bit-mapped images in the Tagged Image File Format. These, too, are usually photographs. They are the preferred image format for printing bureaus, and can be read on Mac computers, as well as PCs. TIFF images have their resolution and proportion information saved with them, and thus, may appear smaller on your screen when initially inserted (they will appear at the image's true resolution, not the screen resolution). Simply resize the image in Publisher as you like. Print quality will not be affected.

- **JPEG**   Photographs that have been compressed for use on the Web. JPGs compress to a very small size, and are the image format of choice when there is a need to conserve disk space, or to keep file size down because images need to be e-mailed, or stored on floppy disks. If you repeatedly edit and save a JPG image, you may notice a loss in image quality.

- **GIF**   Drawings that have been compressed for use on the Web. GIF images are ideal for drawings with large blocks of single color, line drawings, or images with transparency information (where the background of the image is to be eliminated for online viewing). Clip art images bound for the Web should be saved as GIFs.

- **WMF**   Vector graphic drawings. WMF images are drawings and have the advantage of being resizable without image quality loss. Use a WMF clip art image, for example, when you want the same picture to appear on an envelope (very small) and in a full-size poster (much larger).

As for the various non-photographic formats (such as WMF and GIF), it's useful to think of a distinction between "drawing" and "painting." Painting—what you might do in Microsoft Paint—creates a *bit-mapped image* by changing the color of the pixels in the image. Normally, you can edit such an image only by selecting a chunk of it and copying or moving it. Drawing—the function of the Microsoft Draw module—creates *vector graphics*, images whose content is stored as a series of equations defining the various lines and curves that make up the image. Such images can be disassembled into their component parts, which is useful if you want to change the image significantly. Although Publisher includes no tools for manipulation of vector-graphic clip art, you can do so in Microsoft PowerPoint. You'll learn how later in the chapter.

Appropriate Placement and Sizing

As mentioned in Part I and as will be discussed in the following chapter, which discusses photos in more detail, the size of a picture should be proportional to the amount of information it conveys. (For this reason, "atmosphere" images—photos that create "auras" of feeling through imagery—should not be large.) It's important to establish a proper relationship between illustrations and text. Figure 12-6 shows a clip inserted into a two-column story in a newsletter. Obviously, this full-size image is too big for the space. You'll want to resize it so that it fits.

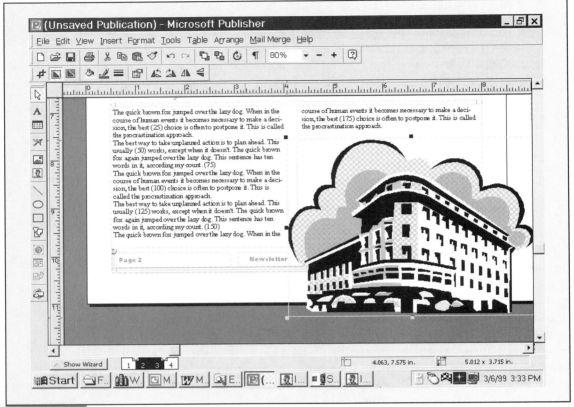

FIGURE 12-6 A full-size clip is likely to be too large for its context

Most often, you'll want to resize a picture proportionally. To do so, select the picture, then grab one of the corner handles with the pointer, click and drag in or out to make the picture smaller or larger, as shown in Figure 12-7.

Clip art can often be resized non-proportionally to good effect, as suggested in Figure 12-8. To change the proportions, use the side, top, or bottom handles. But always do the proportional resize first, so you can undo your work by pressing CTRL-Z. If you make a hopeless mess, you can get the original image back by right-clicking and choosing Change Picture | Scale Picture | Original Size.

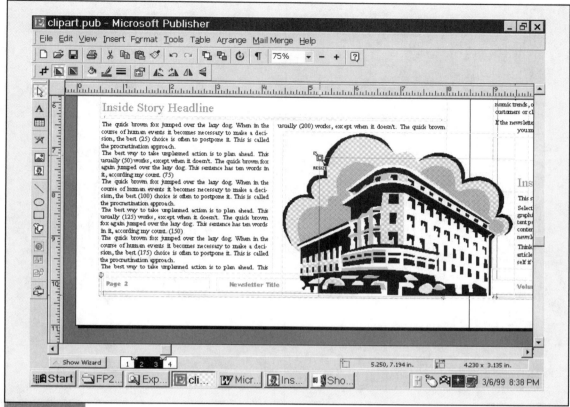

FIGURE 12-7 Drag by the corner handles to resize proportionally

The next step is to establish the proper relationship between the image and the surrounding text. You already learned in Chapter 13 how to create a border around an image to create white space where it's needed. However, with non-photographic clip art you have other options. First, you can wrap the text around the picture, rather than around the rectangle containing the picture. To do

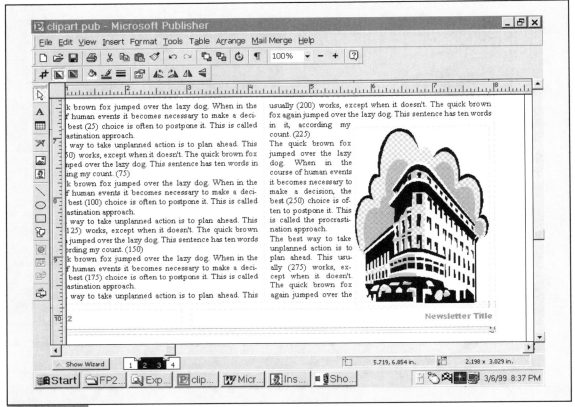

FIGURE 12-8   Sometimes resizing a clip non-proportionally creates interesting effects

so, right-click on the picture, and choose Change Frame | Picture Frame Properties | Picture Only. This produces the result you see here when you click OK.

This is not exactly the effect you want. With text pouring in on both sides of the picture, the article becomes very hard to read. Fortunately, you can change the way text wraps. To do so, click the Edit Irregular Wrap tool on the toolbar on the Picture Frame Properties dialog box. A group of handles then appears all around the picture, as seen in Figure 12-9. When you point to one, the pointer changes to a four-way Adjust arrow, as shown on the far right of the image. Use it to drag the adjustment handles away from the image to create appropriate spacing.

You may want to click outside the image, so you can see the relationship between text and graphic without the interference of all those handles. If you do, use the Edit Irregular Wrap button on the toolbar to continue adjusting. When you're finished, you should have a result similar to Figure 12-10. Notice that there's no text hanging down to the right of the image, and there's a clear white-space demarcation between the text and the graphic on the left. The wrap is indicated by a dotted line.

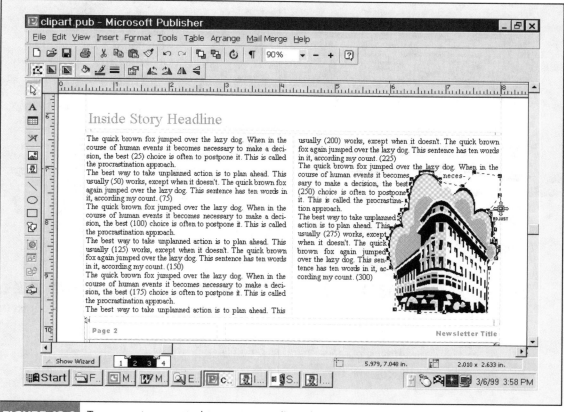

FIGURE 12-9   To prevent unwanted text wraps, adjust the irregular wrap outward

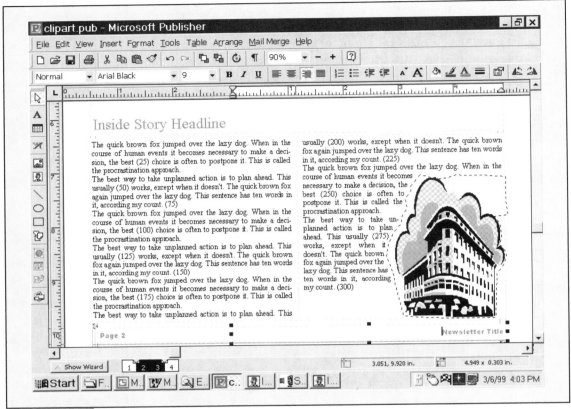

FIGURE 12-10 You should adjust the wrap to allow enough white space to clearly indicate the distinction between text and graphic. This makes the text easier to read

Creating New Images from Clip Art

Within Publisher, there are many ways you can alter clip art to suit the context or just to make it more distinctive. Among them are:

- Adding borders, shadows, and fills
- Recoloring the entire image

- Combining images to get new designs
- Taking images apart and rearranging them to get new designs

You'll learn all of these techniques in this section.

Adding Borders, Shadows, and Fills to Your Clip Art

Up to now, you've learned how to add a defining border to an image to improve legibility. Now you'll learn how to add a *visible* border. There are several other effects you can add. Although they won't necessarily improve legibility, they can add visual interest. To make a border visible, you change the line style and the line color. You can also add a drop shadow.

To change the line style, choose Change Frame | Line/Border Style. You have a choice of:

- None
- Hairline
- Three different widths

If you choose the last alternative, More Styles, a dialog box opens in which you can choose a custom width for the line, and choose a color for it at the same time. Click Apply to see whether you like the effect you've chosen, and click OK if you do.

You can see the result in Figure 12-11. I've also added a drop shadow by choosing Change Frame | Shadow. As a final effect, I've chosen Change Frame | Fill Color to fill in the background behind the image, resulting in a medallion effect.

So now you have a fancy border around your image, but it's too close to the text. You may be able to solve the problem with a custom shape. This requires 16 steps:

1. Select your image and copy it to the Clipboard.
2. Paste the copy into your publication, and drag it to the overflow area.
3. Click outside the picture to deselect it.
4. Choose Insert | Picture | New Drawing.
5. While the drawing is selected, paste your copy of the picture into it.
6. Drag the image to the left side of the drawing area.
7. Using the handles on the drawing area, not the picture, stretch the drawing area so that you have some space around the picture on all sides. If the picture is too close to the top, select it and center it vertically.

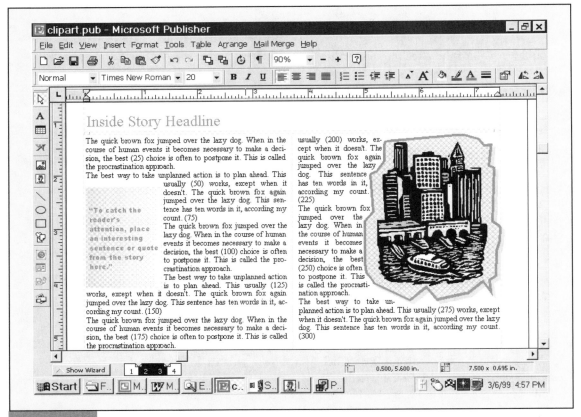

FIGURE 12-11 This picture has a 4-pt. irregular border, a drop shadow, and a filled background

8. From the AutoShapes toolbar on the lower left of the screen, choose Freeform, as shown here.

9. Draw a freeform shape around the image, being sure to fill in the corners where stray words might appear. When you've connected one end of the shape to the other, press ESC to complete the process. (You can draw true horizontal, vertical, or 45-degree-angle lines by holding down SHIFT while you draw.)

10. Using the tools on the Draw toolbar at the bottom of the screen, set the fill color to white, and the line style to none.

11. Click outside the drawing area to look at the result. You should see nothing but a white shape. Now paste the image again, and position it inside the shape, as illustrated here:

12. Select the image, then the Draw frame, and group them, as explained in Chapter 2.

13. Use CTRL-X to cut the picture, with its new, white frame, from the overflow area.

14. Delete the original.

15. Choose Edit | Paste Special | As Picture to paste the combined image back into your publication as a single object.

16. Right-click the object and choose Change Frame | Picture Frame Properties | Picture Only to create an irregular wrap.

17. Reposition the image in your publication, if necessary. The result should resemble Figure 12-12.

Recoloring Clip Art

Another effect available to you is recoloring the entire image. If your publication is in black and white, you might want to change the image to a gray scale. You can also turn any image into a half-tone by recoloring. To change the color of a clip, choose Change Picture | Recolor Picture. The Recolor Picture dialog box appears. Start by choosing a color from the Color drop-down list. (You should probably use a color from your color scheme.) When you have chosen a color, you have two options:

- Recolor whole picture
- Leave black parts black

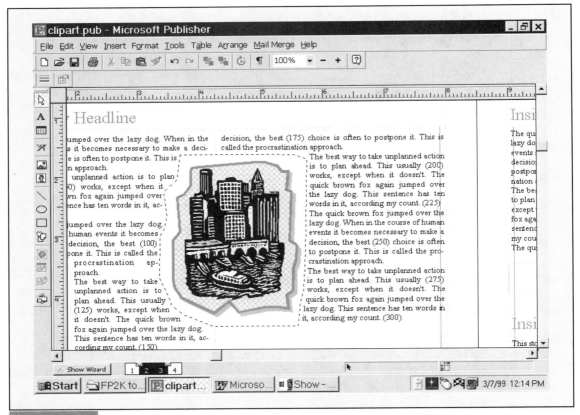

FIGURE 12-12 Your irregular shape now has white space around it, providing proper separation between the text and the graphic

Which is more effective depends on the style of your publication and the characteristics of the clip itself. If the clip has dark outlines, as this one does, leaving the black parts black can enhance the image. If it uses black only for the occasional accent, leaving the black parts black will probably look odd.

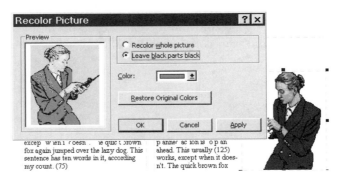

Creating Watermarks for Your Publisher Documents

Another use of recoloring is to create watermarks. The Voyage newsletter design has a compass watermark, as you can see in Figure 12-13.

To create your own watermark:

1. Press CTRL-M to display the background layer of your page.

2. Create a picture frame.

3. Find and insert an appropriate clip.

4. Choose Change Picture | Recolor Picture, and choose the palest color in your color scheme. If none of the colors is pale enough, you may prefer a very light shade of gray. Alternatively, after you've chosen the lightest shade, choose Change Picture | Recolor Picture, open the Color drop-down list, and choose Fill Effects. Choose a lighter shade of the color.

5. If you want the image at an angle, hold down the ALT key and grab a corner handle. The pointer becomes a Rotate symbol. Drag in the direction in which you want to rotate the image.

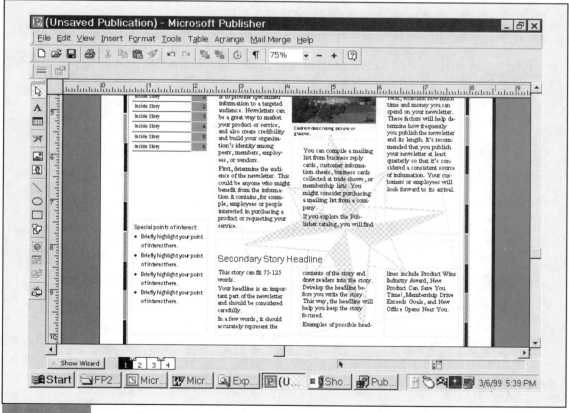

FIGURE 12-13   Some of Publisher's designs contain ready-made watermarks

6. Press CTRL-M again to bring back the foreground objects.

7. Holding down the SHIFT key as you click, select all the text boxes on the page. Press CTRL-T to toggle transparency on. The result should be something like Figure 12-14.

8. You will have to repeat Step 7 on every page in your publication.

Combining Pieces of Clip Art

You can easily combine clip art images to create new designs, to communicate more with a single picture, or to add information to a clip.

To combine two or more images for a new effect, insert each of the images into your publication. It's best to place them in the overflow space while you're working, as Figure 12-15 illustrates.

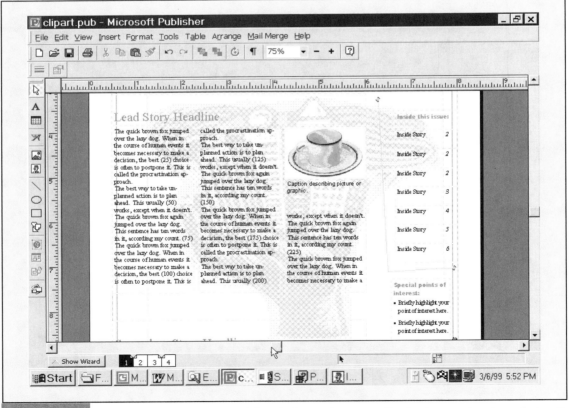

FIGURE 12-14 Create your own watermark by placing an image on the background and recoloring it so it doesn't interfere with the text

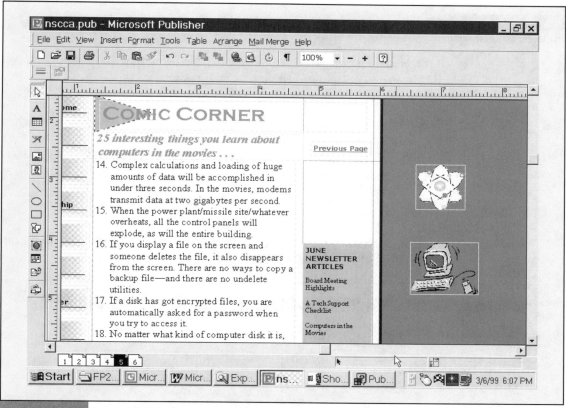

FIGURE 12-15 Place the clips you want to combine in the overflow space

Next, you get to play with them. In this publication, I'm trying to create a metaphor for an explosive computer situation, so I want the computer to be the nucleus of an atom. So the images will need to be:

- Superimposed
- Resized so they fit each other properly
- Made transparent if they aren't already
- Brought forward or backward with commands on the Arrange menu
- Grouped

The illustration to the right shows the images resized, superimposed, selected, and ready to be grouped. The easiest way to group them is to click on the group handle at the bottom. When you do, the two jigsaw pieces are shown locked together. Once they are grouped, you can move or size the entire combined image

Group Objects

Cross-Reference: For more additional information on grouping and ungrouping objects, see Chapter 2.

If there are specific items in an image to which you want to call attention, you can add arrows or callouts. To do so:

1. Place the image to be labeled in the overflow area.

2. Resize it appropriately. It will be much harder to do once you've attached callouts.

3. Deselect the clip and choose Insert | Picture | New Drawing. Publisher will place a white frame in your publication, and open the AutoShapes toolbar, as seen in Figure 12-16. As the illustration shows, it will probably place the Microsoft Draw drawing frame right on top of your clip.

4. Click outside the frame to deselect it. It will become transparent.

5. Click the frame once to reselect it without making it active. Now you can move it to an appropriate location and resize it with the handles.

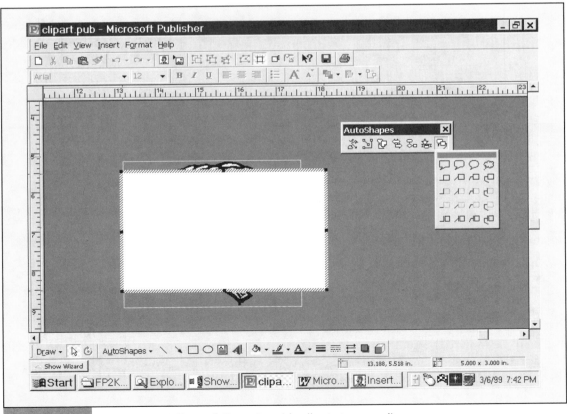

FIGURE 12-16   You can use Microsoft Draw to add callouts to your clip

6. Double-click the frame to reactivate Microsoft Draw, and click the rightmost icon to get a palette of callout shapes, which you can see in Figure 12-16. Choose your shape and draw it in the frame with your mouse. When you've drawn a box, a cursor appears inside it so you can enter a label.

7. If necessary, adjust the pointer so that it points in the right direction by grabbing the yellow handle at the end farthest from the text box.

8. Click outside the frame to deactivate Microsoft Draw, and drag the frame into its proper position. If necessary, you can reactivate Microsoft Draw and make changes.

9. If you want to change the characteristics, borders, or colors of the text box or if you want to change the orientation of text in it, double-click the text box to activate the Format AutoShape dialog box.

10. Add additional callouts, if you wish.

11. When you're finished, group the image and all the callouts, as shown in Figure 12-17.

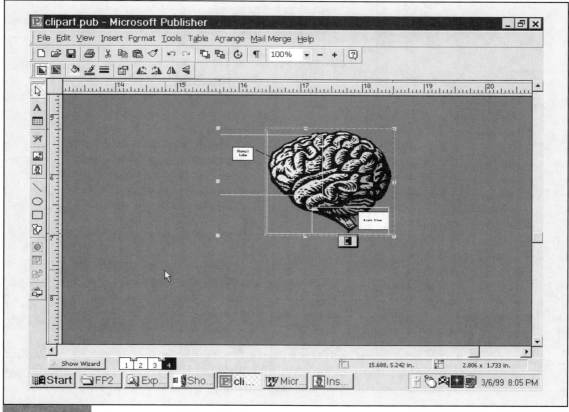

FIGURE 12-17 When you've finished labeling your clip, group the clip and the callouts so they maintain their relative positions when you drag them into place

Combining and Editing Existing Designs

Suppose you wanted a clip of a farmer standing in front of his barn. There's no such clip in the Clip Gallery. But you can create one out of existing clips using Microsoft PowerPoint as your editor.

To begin:

1. Open PowerPoint.

2. Choose Blank Presentation from the dialog box that appears.

3. Choose a blank slide form from the New Slide dialog box. This gives you your workspace.

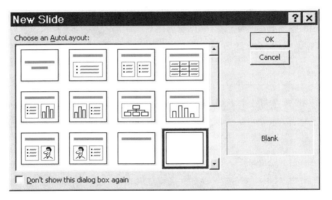

4. Choose Insert | Picture | Clip Art to open the Clip Gallery, and choose the images whose elements you wish to combine.

5. Choose the clip from which you want to extract one or more items, and enlarge it so you can see what you're doing. Right-click it and choose Edit Picture from the context menu. You will see a message saying:

   > This is an imported picture, not a drawing. Do you want to convert it to a Microsoft Office drawing group?

6. Click Yes. The picture will be broken into many elements, each with handles, as shown in Figure 12-18.

It looks daunting, but it's really not as bad as it looks. Click outside the picture to deselect all the elements, then drag your mouse around portions of the image you don't want, as Figure 12-19 shows. As a group is selected, press DELETE to delete the elements.

When all that's left is the parts you actually want, drag your mouse around the entire remaining image. Right-click and choose Grouping | Group. Now you can resize the two images so that they go together, and group them. When everything is ready, copy the grouped image and paste it into your publication, as shown in Figure 12-20. You can safely close PowerPoint without saving the presentation.

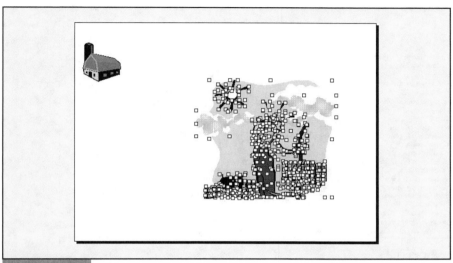

FIGURE 12-18 When you use the Edit Picture command, PowerPoint breaks the image into as many components as it can recognize

FIGURE 12-19 Delete the unwanted elements in groups

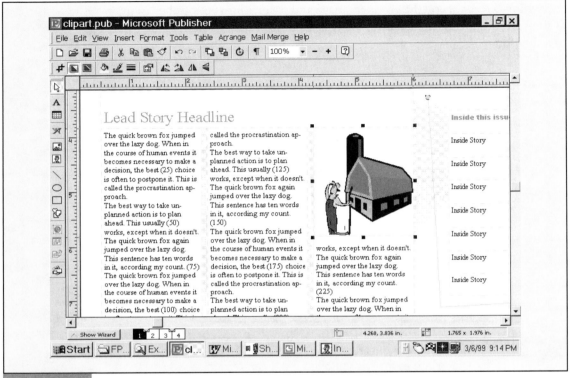

FIGURE 12-20 When you're finished, paste the edited image into your publication

Creating Text Logos and Headings with WordArt

L▶ Note: WordArt objects look especially jagged around the edges when resized. Make sure you generate your WordArt object at roughly the same size you intend to use it in.

Publisher's WordArt frame tool is the same artistic text tool you'll find in Word, Excel, and PowerPoint. With this tool, you can create decorative bitmaps from text headings, and draw your reader's eye to headlines you want to make sure get noticed. WordArt is not a professional artistic text tool. To a discerning eye, the bitmaps it generates can look jagged around the edges. You'll probably want to avoid WordArt for those million-dollar accounts and for highly professional print jobs. But WordArt can add color and pizzazz to newsletters, brochures, and flyers.

To create a WordArt object, click the WordArt tool on the toolbar (fourth icon from the top as seen in Figure 12-20; it has a W and an A), and drag in your Publisher document to create the size object you want. The menu options at the top of the screen change to WordArt options.

In addition to the new menu options, the Enter Your Text Here dialog box appears.

To add text to the WordArt frame, select the placeholder text and type over with your own.

If you want the frame in your document to reflect the new text you type, click the Update Display button.

The Insert Symbol button displays the Insert Symbol dialog box, from where you can select symbols—like scientific or Greek characters—to include in your document.

The menu has many options for creating interesting WordArt headlines. You need not close the Enter Your Text Here dialog box in order to access the WordArt menu options.

Reshape your text headings by clicking the drop-down menu on the far left (default choice is Plain Text). Click one of the shapes in the drop-down menu to see your text heading take on that shape.

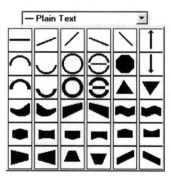

The middle drop-down menu changes your text heading's font (the default is Arial). Since WordArt generates bitmaps, you need not worry if the chosen font you use will be available for final printing at a print house or available for online viewing. Pick any font you like.

To the right of the font drop-down menu is a menu whose default choice is Best Fit. Choose a numerical font size or keep the default to allow Publisher to fit your text into your chosen shape.

To the right of the drop-down menus are bulleted menu se- 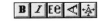 lections you can apply to your creations, such as bold text, italics, and a lowercase/uppercase toggle button.

You can also change the text orientation to be read from the side, or cause the letters to stretch to fit the entire width of the frame.

Further to the right, the buttons provide justification and text spacing options. You can choose how far apart your letters should be from each other, which is important for creating legible artistic text headings. You can also rotate and skew your text, setting it off at an angle.

To the far right are buttons for setting the Fill and Outline features of your WordArt, as well as adding a drop shadow effect.

The WordArt drop shadow effects have especially unique options, such as creating a shadow at such an offset that the entire phrase is projected clearly against the imagined surface.

L ▶ Note: WordArt menu options disappear as soon as you click outside the WordArt object. To edit your object again, double-click on it. The WordArt menu is again accessible.

Combining WordArt and Clip Art to Create Logos and Headlines

What follows are examples of combining WordArt and clip art to create logos and headlines. When applicable, the techniques for creating the effects are explained.

Using the example "Educating our Children" (Figure12-21), note that the clip art selection is a simple line drawing, and the WordArt heading was reshaped to match the upper border of the art.

I used a Deflated Bottom effect using the Comic Sans MS font. To make a text heading stretch across the entire WordArt area, use the Text Stretch button at the top of the menu.

Recycling Logos

Figure 12-22 was created with clip art from Publisher. Once you resize the image, you can place the finished product on either side of a WordArt newsletter heading.

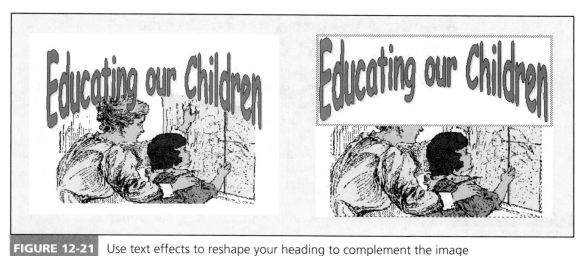

FIGURE 12-21 Use text effects to reshape your heading to complement the image

In this way, using edited versions of the same logo can give your Publisher projects a consistent appearance. The small versions of this logo were recolored. To do this, right-click, then select Change Object | Recolor Object. Choose a new color from the available color boxes. Using a uniform color helps draw attention to the heading.

FIGURE 12-22 Create your logo in Publisher and place it on your flyers, newsletters, and letterhead

Blending Text and Art to Create Interesting Text Effects

The space between the words and the image in the advertisement shown in Figure 12-23 is the key to making the message legible. It's desirable to keep the blending effect, making the kids' image appear related to the message (Youth Workers Wanted), but not so close that legibility is reduced.

To achieve this affect, after positioning your text and image, right-click on the text frame, chose Change Frame | Text Frame Properties, and increase the space of the margin the text shares with the image (in this case, the left text margin was increased to .14 inches). This sets the text off into its own tidy space.

Cross-Reference: For more information on using the Text Frame Properties dialog box with photos, see Chapter 13.

Sometimes it's best to create uniformity by placing both the text of a message and its associated image in the same text frame, as seen in Figure 12-24. The margin properties of the small drama picture are reduced to allow a snug placement inside the text frame.

FIGURE 12-23 Use the blending effect to give your ad the right tone

| **FIGURE 12-24** | Connect your text and visual messages in the same frame |

Using WordArt within Images

You can also use WordArt to create speech labels for cartoons (Figure12-25). This speech label uses the Wave 1 shape and the Kids font. The WordArt object is positioned over the clip art. The clip art is a light enough shade of gray for the WordArt to be legible. A drop shadow is applied to the WordArt, which also increases legibility.

| **FIGURE 12-25** | Use word art to create speech cartoon labels |

If your heading is clear and dramatic enough, you can get away with having portions of the text message be hidden, as in Figure 12-26. Some of the text messages, set at an angle using Publisher's text frame Rotate feature, are partially hidden. Since the heading makes it very clear what the subject matter is, no meaning is lost. The focus is still on the clip art image of the couple and the heading.

Sometimes it's possible to select a WordArt font and style that directly mimics the subject matter, such as the newsletter shown in Figure 12-27. It's important to make your clip art face your logo or heading. Notice the woman on the upper left has her head turned toward the headline, which helps draw your eye to it. Notice also the inclusion of a small, crisp photograph in the middle of the page. This draws your eye to the subheading.

FIGURE 12-26   You can use WordArt to be playful with the text when the meaning is clear

FIGURE 12-27 Use WordArt to mimic the subject matter

Professional Skills Summary

In this chapter, we covered clip art, its sources, locating and applying it to your Publisher projects, as well as the pluses and minuses of the various file types. You learned how to place clip art into your projects, reposition and resize specific pictures, and how to recolor and add borders to your clip art images. We discussed ways to combine, edit, and create logos from clip art. You also learned about WordArt, how to apply it to your projects, and how to combine it with other Publisher elements for effective logos, blurbs, and short paragraphs of text.

chapter 13

Making the Most of Photographs in Print and Online

In this chapter, you will:

- Learn how to acquire photographs for your Publisher projects

- Learn how to apply photographs creatively and efficiently

- Understand file type issues

- Store and organize your Publisher pictures for easy retrieval

- Apply creative photographic techniques to your Publisher projects

- Prepare photos for use on the Web

Photographs communicate complex ideas instantly. They can convey just about anything to the reader, or merely suggest a concept and allow the reader lots of room for interpretation. Photographs attract instant attention. Adding a picture to your Publisher document is your chance to say to your audience members, "Hey, look here!"

By selecting the correct photographs, you can set the stage and quickly frame the context by which your reader will absorb your idea, whether or not they read your words. In the world of professional photo-communication—in advertising, newsletters, magazines or other print publications, or on the Web—photographers and designers spend hours creating and selecting just the right photographs. If you've explored the photos that come with the Publisher 2000 CD and researched alternative sources of photographs, you may find yourself spending significant time selecting the right photo to reinforce your message. This time spent searching for the right photo is well spent, however, because it will draw attention to your publications or Web sites as no other object can.

How Can You Get Photos for Publisher Use?

To obtain photos for your Publisher creations, you can take your own with "old-fashioned" film or a new digital camera (if you are lucky enough to own one), or you can obtain photos on CD just like clip art, download free photos from the Web, or use images "snapped" from videos. In some cases, you will need to make sure you have legal permission to use these images.

Managing Legal Issues

If you use your own photos, you don't have to worry about permissions or rights of ownership. Using photos from any other source can cause you some legal tangles, if you don't have permission to use the photo. If you obtain permission from the photo's owner in writing, you will be able to use that photo for the purposes you described in your letter seeking permission. Sometimes, professional photographers expect a royalty or some form of payment for the use of their proprietary creations, but if your intended use for the photo is not one of commercial gain, the photo owner may grant you permission to use the photo without payment. Regardless of whether you pay for the photo's use, you always need to credit the photo's source. Required forms of photo credits vary from photographer to photographer, but be sure to credit the photo's owner and your permission to use it clearly in your Publisher creation.

One additional important point about using photos in your documents: you never should use photos from other publications, such as magazines, newspapers, books, other Web sites, music CD covers, video or DVD covers, video copies of movies, or images taken from television. To do so is a copyright violation, punishable by law. When you have any doubt about the ownership of an image or whether you need to obtain permission to use the image, the safest rule to follow is to always assume you need written permission, unless it clearly comes from a "clip-art" type source or any other source in the public domain.

Obtaining Model Releases

If you take your own photos or video captures of people for use in publications, you must obtain a *model release* to be able to use these photos for commercial use. A model release is simply a form or letter specifying exactly how the photo will be used, whether the models have agreed to grant you permission to use their likenesses for your commercial use, and whether individuals in the photos received payment for their appearance in the photo or for signing a model release. Model releases are meant to protect the privacy of individuals who are not well-known personalities—actors, musicians, singers, entertainers, political figures, or anyone else considered to be a public figure. Even if you use your own photos of public figures, you still may have to obtain written permission to use a public figure's likeness for profit. A good example of a very public figure whose likeness is closely policed for copyright infringement is Elvis Presley. If you are an average person who likes Elvis and you simply want to put photos of Elvis on a home page, chances are that no one monitoring Elvis's copyright infringement would take the time to pursue you. At worst, you might get a letter from the Elvis "copyright police," requesting that you cease using the photo on your home page unless you obtain written permission from them. If, however, you are clearly profiting from the use of Elvis's likeness, you could be found guilty of copyright infringement.

Using Your Own Photos

Even if you are just an amateur photographer, you can use your own photos in any Publisher creation. Most photographic print processors now offer not only prints and negatives, but also electronic images on floppy disk or CD. Some photo processing services on the Web will even send electronic files to your e-mail address, so you can download the files at your convenience. Note that these photos are created "traditionally," meaning that you take them with a regular film-based camera.

Scanning Your Photos

If you have still photographs, you can scan them into your PC and then fine-tune them with any one of several different software applications. Scanner quality determines the quality of the finished photo file. Scanners vary in price, with the lower-priced models geared toward home/nonprofessional use, and the more expensive models suitable for professional applications. One popular type of scanner is a flatbed scanner, which you can use to scan existing photos into a digital file form. Another common type of scanner is a film scanner. With these types of scanners, you can work directly with a 35-mm slide or negative, thus saving time by eliminating the need to transfer the image from negative to a printed photo. With film scanners, the result is a higher-quality final image.

Using Digital Still and Video Cameras

If you own a digital camera, you can transfer your digital photos directly to your PC, without the need of film processing or photo printing. Although in its infancy, the digital photography revolution is moving forward by leaps and bounds. Digital cameras range in price from a few hundred dollars to thousands. Although currently there is no dominant "standard" format—like with VHS videotape—some formats and brands are more popular than others. The digital photography topic is too large to be discussed in this chapter, but a good source for additional information is *Digital Photography Answers! Certified Tech Support,* by Dave Johnson (Osborne/McGraw-Hill, 1999).

If you shoot videotape, regardless of the video format, you can import still images into your PC with either direct video input (as offered by Sony) or through devices that "snap" still images from videotape (such as the Snap device) and then import those images into your PC.

Learning About Photographic Software

Whether you import digital photo files from a floppy disk or CD, or scan your images, you'll most likely have to fine-tune photos with software specifically designed to enhance photo images. Several different software packages in a variety of price ranges are available to make these adjustments, so that each photo you use looks as good as possible in your Publisher creations. Sometimes, versions of this type of software come free when you purchase digital cameras, scanners, and color printers. Also, some photo processing companies, such as Kodak, offer their own software to use with the digital images they provide when they develop your film. Regardless of which file format your imported photos start as, you can use these photo-enhancing software applications to change file formats to whatever file format suits your purposes. Different file formats work better in certain uses, and you'll learn more about this topic later in this chapter.

Using Clip Art and Stock Photographs

Just as with clip art, photos are available on floppy disk, CD, and via the Web for your generic, permission-free use. Some sources include photos that come with applications software—such as Publisher 2000's generic, royalty-free photo collection—and stock photo collections, which can offer thousands of images. These stock photo collections are available from a variety of sources, many of which you can preview online on the Web, or you can request catalogs of stock photo collections from which you may select the photos you want to use. Software photo collections are generally organized by subject—farming, gardening, health topics, nature, office life, and seasonal and holiday images, for example. Use stock photos to create atmosphere, evoke moods, and provide visual cues to the material they accompany. Some Web sites featuring vast photo collections are:

- http://www.eyeware.com
- http://desktoppub.miningco.com
- http://www.msubclipart.htm.com
- http://www.1stopstock.com

Some stock photography is sold on CD with very few restrictions on its use. Once you purchase the CD, you can use the photographs as often as you choose, with one exception. If you reproduce an image and sell it for profit, such as on a T-shirt or mug, you must contact the source from which the image originated. Other stock photography sources base their photo reproduction charges on the circulation of the publication in which the photograph will appear.

L▶ Note: Avoid using the images in ways that give your audience the impression that the picture is your own, for example, as part of a photo collection or included with a narrative about an experience you've had. Such use does cross legal boundaries even when using royalty-free stock photography.

Using Publisher's Photo Clip Art

Previewing and selecting photographs from Publisher's own photo collection can be an intriguing activity. If this experience with selecting photo clip art is a new one for you, be sure to set aside enough time to look through the pages and pages of photographs that come with Publisher 2000. When you are ready to begin selecting a photo for a particular need, try to stay focused on your core message and how the photo will relate to that message. Don't be sidetracked from selecting the right photo for your purpose and use a less-than-relevant photograph simply because you love it. If the photo doesn't contribute to or reinforce your message, keep looking for a photo that does fill these needs.

To locate a clip art photo, select Insert | Picture | Clip Art. Publisher will display the Clip Art dialog box. Scroll through the clip art collection and double-click on the icon called Photographs to open the Insert Clip Art dialog box, which will now have a tab called Pictures (Figure 13-1). Some PCs are slow to display photos because of their

L▶ Note: You must double-click the Photographs option icon within Publisher 2000's collection of clip art examples to access the photograph section—this extra step can make finding Publisher's photo collection more complicated than if it was accessible in another fashion.

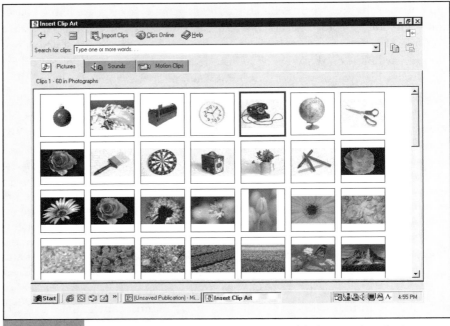

FIGURE 13-1 This unique photo collection is accessible by opening the Insert Clip Art dialog box and clicking the Pictures tab

large file sizes, so maximizing the Insert Clip Art dialog box will give you the best preview of the photos in thumbnail size.

As you move the mouse pointer over each photo thumbnail, Publisher displays a description box for each photo, revealing its keywords, size, and file type, as shown in Figure 13-2. Graphics objects—including clip art and photos—can be stored in one of several file types. Certain file types work better for certain uses, and the graphics file type topic is an enormously detailed subject—too complicated for anything but a brief discussion in this chapter. For additional information about graphics file types, see the following sections in this chapter.

Note: Thumbnails are small representations of larger pictures, organized to allow viewing of many images simultaneously.

The following list includes most of the popular graphics file types (and their extensions). These are the file types you might encounter while working with photos and graphics in your Publisher creations:

- Joint Photographic Experts Group files (.JPG)
- Windows Bitmapped files (.BMP)
- Graphics Interchange Format files (.GIF)

FIGURE 13-2   Publisher displays important file size and type information for each photo

- Windows Metafiles (.WMF)
- Computer Graphics Metafiles (.CGM)
- CorelDRAW files (.CDR)
- Tagged Image File Format (.TIF)
- Kodak Photo CD files (.CPD)
- Macintosh PICT files (.PCT)
- PC Paintbrush files (.PCX)
- WordPerfect Graphics files (.WPG)

When you click on the image you want to use, Publisher displays a toolbar along with each photo's description, as shown in Figure 13-3. You may select from four actions associated with selecting photographs to use in your Publisher documents:

- **Insert clip**   Use this button if you want to place the photograph in your document.

Note: When you are preparing documents for professional printing, the printer may ask you to provide each photo image as a separate file, not embedded in the Publisher document. In such a case, regardless of the image source type, open the image in PhotoDraw and resave it as a .TIF file.

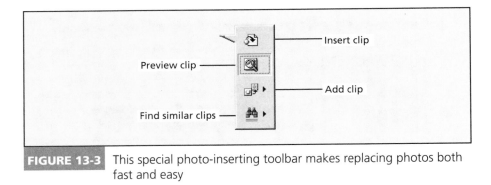

FIGURE 13-3 This special photo-inserting toolbar makes replacing photos both fast and easy

- **Preview clip** Use this button if you want to see a full-sized version of the photograph.
- **Add clip** Use this button to add a clip to Favorites (or another category) for easier retrieval at a later time.

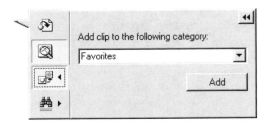

- **Find similar clips** Use this button if you want to find another image that shares the same keyword description.

Once you have inserted your selected photo in your document, you can move and resize the photograph any way you want, using the same techniques as you would use for moving and resizing text frames and clip art.

Working with Photo CDs

You may have requested that your photo developer make your pictures available on a CD, or you may have purchased a collection of images that are organized on a CD. These images usually are distributed using the Kodak PhotoCD format, which was designed for simple browsing through large collections of images. Note, however, that the PhotoCD file format, although widely recognized, is not the only file format available for putting your pictures on CD. For example, PhotoWorks (previously called Seattle FilmWorks) also has its own file format it uses to store images on CD. Figure 13-4 shows the photo index displayed

FIGURE 13-4 These digital thumbnails are organized for your easy selection

by PhotoWorks' proprietary photo-editing software displaying an index of a single CD's worth of photos.

Regardless of in which file format you first have your digital image, you can always change the image's file format to a more common file format, such as .PCX. PhotoWorks' file transfer choices don't include the Kodak file format option, and vice versa. You have to first change the Kodak PhotoCD image into any recognized format—such as .PCX or .TIF—and then transfer that file to PhotoWorks' recognized format. All the photo processing companies are in a scramble to see which format might become the dominant one as the digital photo age grows on. No one wants to be the "BetaMax" or "eight-track" of this fast-evolving industry. Figure 13-5 shows a photo scanned into a digital image processed by PhotoWorks, which is almost ready to be used in any type of Publisher creation.

Once you've decided on an image to use, you are provided with a number of image size and color depth choices.

Tip: For more information on PhotoWorks for Windows or Mac, visit http://www.photoworks.com. PhotoWorks offers free film for using their processing services, but one string is attached. The "free" film cannot be processed by any other film processor, although PhotoWorks can process any standard brand of film you might send their way, like Kodak, Fugi, and so on.

FIGURE 13-5   This larger version of the CD's stored digital image is ready for additional enhancement, if needed

To use an image from a Kodak PhotoCD, choose Insert | Picture | From File. Browse for your CD drive.

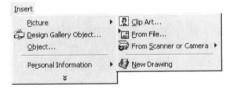

The PhotoCD should have a folder on it called Images, where the photos are stored. Click the various filenames until you see the preview of the photo you want to use. Then click Insert, and Publisher will display the figure you have selected to import into the photo placeholder waiting for it. Remember that Publisher only imports the photo as it exists as a file in whichever photo-editing software you use, and the type of file in which the file is saved will determine the photo's resolution—and therefore its appearance—in any Publisher document. If you need to make improvements or alterations to the photo, you must make those changes within your photo-editing software and then re-import the edited file image into Publisher.

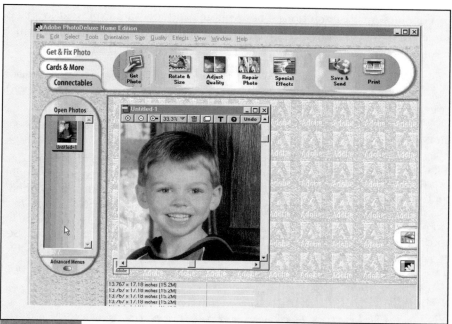

FIGURE 13-6   Adobe PhotoDeluxe is an example of photo-editing software

It doesn't matter what version or manufacturer of photo-viewing or editing software you use, as they all work in a similar fashion. Figure 13-6 shows Adobe's PhotoDeluxe Home Edition, which came with a new Sony Viao PC.

Resolution

Resolution refers to the sharpness and degree of detail in a digital image. Generally speaking, the higher the resolution, the better the image quality. On the other hand, you gain nothing from using a higher resolution than your printing technology can reproduce. And the higher the resolution of your images, the bigger the image file and the Publisher file in which the photo is embedded.

Your primary consideration in choosing the best resolution for your photos is where your selected photo is to finally appear. If you are creating a Web page, your photo and graphics file-size needs will be different than those of a print publication. If you are using a photo in a print publication, you need to consider whether you will print the final product on glossy paper by a professional print shop, on clay-coated paper by an inkjet printer, or on ordinary office paper by color xerography or photo-offset printing.

Graphics image resolutions—both photos and art—are expressed in pixels. Here are some guidelines to consider when you are trying to determine which resolution, or pixel size, will work best for the photos you select:

> **L▷ Tip:** When you place a photo into your document at a lower resolution so you can quickly print drafts, remember you will need to replace the photo with a version captured with the correct pixel measurement to ensure you get the final photo resolution you want. This step is extra, so you have to decide which is more important: quickly printing drafts or taking time to replace the photos with higher-resolution versions when you have completed your work.

- The two highest resolutions (any pixel measurement near 2 to 3 million total is the maximum resolution currently available) are for image processing: printing on glossy paper on a professional press.
- The default, 512 × 768 pixels, is fine for newsletters, flyers, and brochures.
- You might use the 256 × 384 resolution for printing drafts of your document, when all you really need to do is get the picture positions right. This resolution may also suffice for Web publications, if you don't want your visitors to be able to display more than 256 colors on their PC screens. Note, however, that selecting the correct file resolution for each application makes a big difference. For more information, see "Preparing Photos for Use on the Web," later in this chapter.
- The 198 × 192 resolution should be used only to display and print thumbnails.

Using a Scanned Photo in Your Publisher Documents

Scanning photos into Publisher is generally a two-part process. Part one is scanning the photo itself, placing it in Publisher, and resizing and repositioning it to your liking. Part two is making any adjustments in color, contrast, focus, and so on to make the photo look as good as it can for your desired use. Rarely can you simply import a photo into Publisher without making some fine-tuned adjustments to the photo once you are satisfied with your selection. Some Publisher users place and size their photos and then worry about enhancements and solving artistic issues. Other users prefer to ensure that each photo is artistically suitable before they place it in their Publisher creations. Sometimes the alterations you make in sizing and placement affect the photo's appearance in terms of color and clarity, so you may prefer to make adjustments first and then see how the result looks in your creation. Regardless of which step you do first, sometimes it comes down to a back-and-forth process to get each photo to look absolutely perfect in every instance.

To prepare your scanned photo for Publisher, you can use PhotoDraw (which comes with the Deluxe version of Publisher 2000 or Office 2000), Paint Shop Pro (which is available as *trialware*—a type of shareware where you try the software and then pay the author after you try it—on the Web, downloadable for free at http://www.jasc.com), or any of several other commercially available photo-enhancing software applications. Before bringing the picture into Publisher, use these tools to restore lost color saturation to your picture, remove red-eye from photograph subjects, or even erase creases and damages to the picture.

Scanning an Image into Publisher

First, we'll assume your image is just fine as it is, and scan directly into Publisher. To scan an image into Publisher, choose Insert | Picture | From Scanner Or Camera. If you have both devices, then choose Select Device and select your scanner from the devices listed. Then repeat the procedure and choose Acquire Image. If you have only a scanner, you can skip selecting the device.

This series of steps should launch your scanner software and begin a scan of the image you have placed on the bed of your scanner. The actual steps to take and the options available will vary with your scanner software. A preview should appear in the view pane of your scanner software. If your software retains the image of the previous scan, click the Preview button to show the current image.

Depending on your software, you may be able to do a great deal of preprocessing before you save the image. Most software packages have controls for sizing, scaling, cropping, contrast, brightness, and horizontal flip, among other facilities. You can also choose image type (black and white or color, photo or drawing) and control resolution to some extent. Since Publisher has *no* preprocessing capabilities, you may want to make use of such controls if you have them.

One factor that must be determined before you scan is image resolution. Images used in documents bound for high-end printing should be scanned at 300 dots per inch (commonly abbreviated as dpi). That's because those images will have to be made available as separate files to the printer and need to be of high quality. Images embedded into the Publisher document, ultimately printed, for example, on a commercial desktop printer for distribution throughout an office or organization, can be scanned at 150 dpi. Images scanned for Web-bound documents, such as Web pages or online catalogs need only be scanned at 72 dpi, which is the highest resolution a computer monitor can display.

Note: Regarding using your scanner's preprocessing tools, it is often impossible to predict what sort of treatment your image will require once it is scanned. It is usually a better idea to do preprocessing (brightness/contrast, increasing saturation, and such) with photo-editing software after you scan, rather than before.

Once you've applied any pre-scan image adjustments and selected your resolution settings, click Scan, and the image should show up in your publication. Be patient. A large, full-color image scanned at a high resolution can take up to five minutes to scan.

Once you've scanned your image, you'll want to test it. Since your computer monitor can be quite flattering to even a poor scan, go ahead and print your document on a desktop printer, to give you an idea how it really looks. If you're scanning an image for the Web, place the image in your document and test the Web page in a browser, making note not only of image quality, but also of page loading time.

Scanning into an Image-Editing Program

Scanning your image into Publisher makes it available to a Publisher document, but does not save the image as a standalone file. You first need to scan your image into PhotoDraw, Paint Shop Pro, or some other photo-editing software with specific photo-editing tools. Use these programs to edit your image's file directly, not simply as an embedded Publisher 2000 object.

In addition to the changes you make using the scanner's software, you can use image-editing software to alter your photo's color balance, which subtly alters your image's hues in the shadows, highlights, and image midtones. Figure 13-7

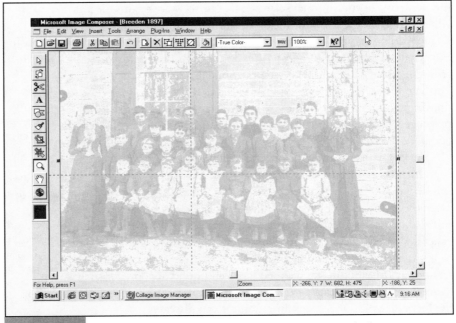

FIGURE 13-7 The old photo is badly in need of enhancement before you can use it with Publisher

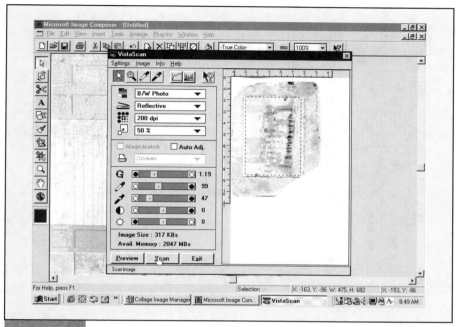

FIGURE 13-8   Image-editing software adds enhancements to improve the image quality

shows an unenhanced image, an antique photo of students from 1894 taken in Lancaster, Indiana. Figure 13-8 shows the photo undergoing enhancements to improve the contrast. The result, shown in Figure 13-9, shows some improvement to the aged image.

If you've scanned into PhotoDraw or another graphic editing program, save your image before editing its color components (brightness/contrast, color balance, hue/saturation/lightness, and such). That way, if you make unadvisable color correction choices, you can always revert back to your untreated, original image.

When using photo-editing tools (whether those from PhotoDraw, Paint Shop Pro, or some other editing program such as Adobe PhotoDeluxe—or perhaps you got one of those Limited Edition versions of Photoshop tossed in with your scanner), here are some factors to keep in mind:

- **Aim for clarity**   Use tools such as Color Balance and Hue/Saturation/Lightness to assist the viewer in understanding the image subject matter instantly. After treating the image, are the objects in the image clearer, more distinct?

- **Aim for depth**   Have you ever seen a photo so rich in color, it seems you can reach your hand in and touch the objects inside? The mountains in the background look like they have real dimension, the people in the foreground look like they could almost pop out of the photograph? Tools like Color

FIGURE 13-9   The same photograph, enhanced with image-editing software

Range and Color Balance add depth to images. Experiment with your color tools, keeping your eye on what happens to the image depth.

- **Go easy on special effects**   Although image-editing software comes with fascinating special effects such as paintbrush tools, starburst, and various framing effects, such treatment may not be right for your message. What is your document trying to say?

- **Keep output size and medium in mind**   If your newsletter or brochure is going to be printed in black and white, don't spend time on color adjustment. Use Brightness/Contrast and Saturation to bring out the shades of gray in your image. If your image is going to occupy a small corner of the page, go for simple clarity, making the objects pronounced and obvious. Don't spend much time on subtleties that no one will appreciate.

Using Images from Digital Cameras

To use an image from a digital camera, choose Insert | Picture | From Scanner Or Camera. If you have both devices, choose Select Device and select your camera from the devices listed. Then repeat the procedure and choose Acquire. If you have only a digital camera, you can skip selecting the device.

Of course, the same principles apply as with scanning. For example, you should create and size a picture frame to place the image into. If you can do pre-processing in your digital camera conversion software, you should make use of its capabilities; if you can't, you should acquire the image with software that can.

Placing Photographs in Your Publisher Document

Many design factors are involved in the proper placement of photographs in your publication. The most important are:

- Size
- Placement relative to other photographs
- Placement relative to text

Size and placement are intimately linked. Where you place a photo has an effect on the appropriate size.

There are two ways to place a photograph in a publication: *embedding* and *linking*. Embedding places a *copy* of the photo—in other words, the entire file—into your publication. Linking just places a link to the file on disk. There are three significant advantages to linking a photo:

- You can make changes to the original image without having to reinsert the image after each change.
- You don't have to resize (and possibly recrop) the photo in Publisher every time you reinsert it since the photo will be inserted from the file location you specify.
- The file size for Publisher documents with linked images will be much smaller than those that use embedded pictures.
- When you're preparing a publication for commercial printing, the printer can do color separations on the original photo, if necessary (this cannot be done with an embedded file).

The advantage of embedding a photo is that it always stays with its intended use, but it makes the overall file size a huge storage and movement problem, should you ever need to print copies from a home PC, for example. We'll look at how to specify either process.

Embedding Photos into Your Publisher Document

When you embed a photo file, the procedure is essentially the same whether the file is from your scanner or digital camera, from a clip art package, or from a photo CD. If you want to preselect the photo's location, click the Picture icon and draw a picture frame where you want the picture inserted (this step is optional). Next, choose Insert | Picture | From File, and you'll see the Insert Picture dialog box. Notice that at the left there are four preset areas to look for pictures. If you know your photo is in one of the indicated locations, click it. Otherwise, browse for the file. When you click a filename, a preview appears in the right pane of the dialog box to help you locate the correct photo. When you've found the photo you want, click Insert.

If you're working with one of Publisher's preset designs, double-click the filename of the Publisher-provided photo to preview it in the browse area. (If the item you select is clip art, right-click and choose Insert | Picture | From File instead.) The new image will appear in place of the photo. The size will be similar, although the proportions will be adjusted appropriately. If—for some reason—you did not add a photo placeholder for this photo in your layout, Publisher places the image right in the middle of the current page (see Figure 13-10), which is probably not where you want it. Point to it, and you should see the pointer change to a Move icon. You can then click and drag the picture to your preferred location.

Figure 13-11 shows the resizing of the image by pointing to one of the *corner* handles of the frame to resize the picture proportionally. Resizing with either the top, bottom, or side handles changes the image's dimensions. You may use the corner handles to resize the dimensions as well (make the image taller without making it wider, for example). To do this, press the SHIFT key while dragging a corner handle.

> **Tip:** If you've inserted multiple photos and want to align them, use Publisher's Align Tool (from the Arrange menu, choose Align). You can align images along an imagined vertical or horizontal axis, or align them to the margin or center of a page. This tool is also helpful for aligning a single image to the exact center of a document.

> **Note:** The Crop tool does not change the image file. You can restore the image to its previous appearance simply by using the Crop tool, but dragging outward. The cropped image segment will appear. You can do this even after saving the Publisher file with the cropped image.

Cropping a Photo to Match the Available Space

Maybe you have a photo you want to use in your document, but you only want to use a portion of the image. Publisher's Crop tool allows you to "zero in" on an image segment and delete the parts of the image you don't want.

To crop your image, click the Crop tool. When you point the mouse at one of the picture's handles, it turns into a special Crop pointer. You can't mark an area—you can only crop from the edges inward. Using a

FIGURE 13-10   In the absence of a picture frame, Publisher inserts the image as shown. Use the mouse to drag the picture to its desired location

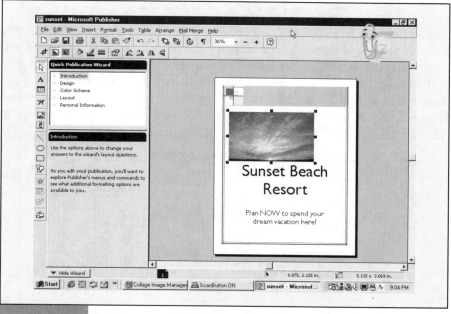

FIGURE 13-11   Drag a corner handle to resize a picture proportionally

corner handle allows you to crop from both a side edge and a top or bottom edge at once. Click on the corner handle and drag it until you have eliminated the unwanted area. If you want to crop from both sides, or from the top and bottom, you have to do each of these edges individually. If you make a mistake, undo it with CTRL-Z. When you're finished, turn off the Crop tool by clicking on it again.

Linking Photos to Your Publisher Document

There are times when you may want to link an image to a Publisher document, rather than embedding. To link a photo, choose Insert | Object. The Insert Object dialog box will appear, shown in Figure 13-12. The options determine how the linked file will function in your document:

- **Create New**   Click this radio button to create a new file.
- **Create From File**   Click this radio button to create a link to an existing photo file.
- **Link**   Check this box to link a photo file to your Publisher photo's placeholder within your document. The text box shows the current folder, along with any associated subdirectories.
- **Browse**   Click to see Publisher's standard Browse dialog box, used to specify files.
- **Display As Icon**   Check this box if you want Publisher to display an icon in your document rather than a large, slow-to-access photo file.

If you work in a collaborative environment in which several individuals may be working on and editing the document's image files, using linked images will ensure that the final Publisher document reflects everyone's most recent input.

To link an image, choose Create From File, then click the Browse button. Publisher will display the standard Browse window, shown in Figure 13-13. There is no Preview feature available for this step, so you'll soon appreciate the use of descriptive

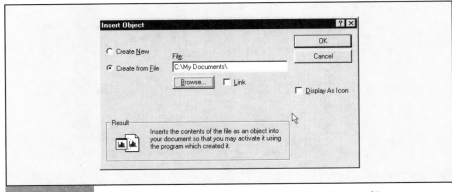

FIGURE 13-12   Use the Insert Object dialog box to link an image file

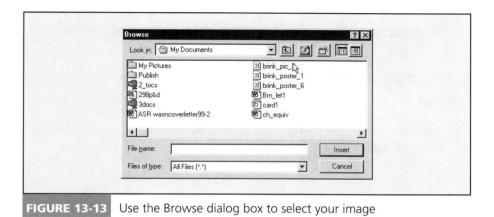

FIGURE 13-13   Use the Browse dialog box to select your image

filenames to help you quickly locate an image. When you've found the file you want, click Insert to close the window, and then click OK.

Rather than have Publisher display and load—and reload—large, slow photo files in your publication as you work, you can choose to have Publisher assign an icon to each photo, and place just the icon in each photo's placeholder for editing and fine-tuning activities. In the Insert Object dialog box, check the Display As Icon check box, and Publisher will make the substitution in your document, as shown in Figure 13-14.

How Large Should Photos Be in Your Documents?

Real estate on your Publisher page is at a premium. You want to utilize it well. How much text, and how to arrange that text? Columns or paragraph style? How big should your headlines be? And then there are photography considerations. Should you use one large descriptive picture that takes up perhaps one-third of your page? Or two or three strategically located images? Here are some guidelines for using photos in Publisher documents:

- Make sure you get all your text in first. If you splurge on photo space, what does that decision do to text flow? By inserting that Himala-yan-sized photo, have you unwittingly added a page to your final output?

- Don't sacrifice legibility. If your photo idea seems to demand that you shrink your text below an easily read font size, it's a bad photo idea. Shrink the picture instead.

L▶ Note Publisher can display erratic behavior when working with more than two or three linked files. For example, it may refuse to display linked images, show messages about low memory situations, or otherwise behave unpredictably. Publisher documents using linked images should be saved often, and saved sequentially—after a number of linked images are added, use a new filename to save the new additions. To save yourself hours of work, please take these precautions.

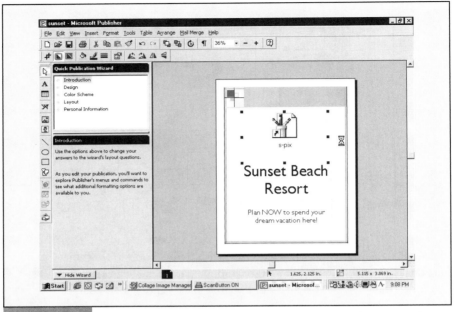

FIGURE 13-14   Publisher can insert a temporary icon into your document that acts as a placeholder for your selected photo

- If you are picking a photo that has lots of colors in it, make sure your output can display all those lovely colors. Additionally, appreciating lush color detail requires a larger image. Before choosing a detailed photo with nuances that will be lost at a smaller size, make sure you can afford the space on your page.

- If an image simply has to be large, consider straddling the image across two columns. This technique is used often to great effect in professional publishing.

- If an image seems flat and lifeless, consider using a drop shadow effect (available with most image-editing software) to give the picture a bit more dimension.

Cross-Reference: For information on using WordArt's drop shadow effect in combination with text and photos, see Chapter 12.

- Consider the role of the caption in your image. How much of the image's significance needs to be explained with a text caption, and how much can you leave to the reader's visual impression alone?

- If only one segment of a photo really adds content to the project, then crop to that segment. No need to display an entire photo just because it came off the shelf that way.

Use Low-Resolution Images to Speed Screen Redraws

If you place a high-resolution image in your publication, you'll notice a paint-brush appearing at the mouse pointer each time you resize your page or return to a page containing such an image. When you see the paintbrush pointer, Pub-lisher is redrawing the screen. If you plan to use high-resolution images, you might want to use lower-resolution versions while you're designing the publica-tion, and replace them with the high-resolution versions only when everything else is done. (This is called placement *for position only*, or *FPO*.) You might even use a clip-art line drawing, which is much less detailed, and therefore ap-pears more quickly (and takes less space on your hard drive). Alternatively, you could just use a picture frame, possibly with a background color added for the vi-sual weight:

1. Place the image you plan to use; get it right in every detail.

2. Use CTRL-C to copy your image and CTRL-V to paste it into another application, such as PhotoDraw, where you can save it.

3. In your Publisher document, draw a picture frame around your image so you get the size right.

4. Choose Arrange | Send Backward to place the new frame behind the finished picture.

5. Delete the picture from the publication, and reinsert it when your document is complete.

> **Tip:** If you just use an empty frame, you'll save a great deal of time printing your early proofs, the stage at which you'll want to be primarily checking out how your headlines, text, and overall layout appear.

Adding Borders and Captions to Your Photos

You can avoid a lot of placement problems by adding borders to your pictures. In some instances, you can get the same results with captions.

Adding Borders to Your Photos

Borders can help you avoid placing photographs too close to text or to each other. The image in Figure 13-15 has a wide border at the top and not much space on the left. To make sure the photo stays near the center, you can use Change Frame | Picture Frame Properties, which brings up the Picture Frame Properties dialog box shown in Figure 13-16. Here you can add a border to any or all sides of your photo. If you don't want to use increments of a tenth of an inch, you can type the values into the boxes instead of using the up and down arrows.

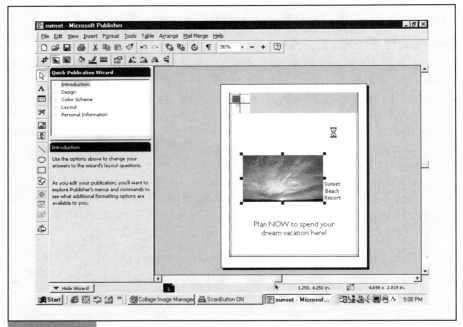

FIGURE 13-15 A badly placed photo can be repositioned using borders

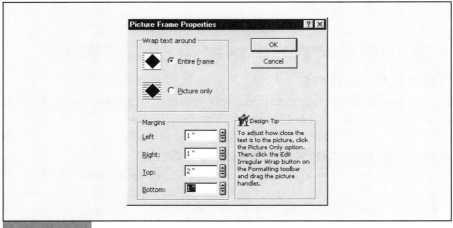

FIGURE 13-16 Use the Picture Frame Properties dialog box to ensure that your photo isn't too close to surrounding text

Inserting Captions for Your Photos

A caption can serve several purposes. Obviously, it identifies what's in the picture, but it can also act as a design element and set off the photo to which it's attached.

You can insert captions in two ways: add a simple text box, or use a Caption Design Object.

When using a text box, keep the following points in mind:

- Allow enough space to set the caption off from regular text.
- Use a font that contrasts with regular text. If your normal text is Times New Roman, use a sans serif font. If your text is a sans serif font, use a font with serifs for your captions. Consider using italic or possibly bold.
- Keep the font size small—generally smaller than your normal text.
- Avoid hyphenating in captions. If Publisher breaks the line in the middle of a word, press ENTER to move the entire word to the next line.
- Don't center your captions. Place them flush left or flush right.
- Don't use justification for captions.

When you have added a caption to a figure, select both by holding down SHIFT as you click in each box, and select Arrange | Group Objects. You will see an icon at the bottom of the image and caption that shows that they are grouped, as shown in Figure 13-17. This allows you to move or resize the image with its caption, without losing the relationship between the two.

This figure also shows how a deep text box can be used to provide white space around the image. Since the picture had a border, Change Frame | Text Frame Properties was used to display the properties sheet and give the frame a left border equivalent to the one on the picture frame.

Publisher's Design Gallery has a variety of formatted picture captions, as you can see in Figure 13-18. Using them is something of a two-edged sword, however. On the one hand, these are "smart objects," which come with a Wizard to manage their construction, and you can also pick a different caption design so that you can modify the colors to fit your color scheme.

> **Tip:** Use Format | Text Style to create a text style just for your figure captions, and apply it to all your captions. Then if you decide to change the style, you can do it through the Format menu, and all captions will take on the change.

On the other hand, because it's a smart object, if you ungroup its elements you can't use the Wizard anymore, and there's no way to insert a different picture into the picture frame in the caption without ungrouping the objects.

The Design Gallery captions all consist of three objects: an image placeholder, a text frame, and a caption graphic, such as a frame or a background. To insert your own picture, first use Arrange | Ungroup Objects to ungroup the parts. Then select the frame and insert the picture in the usual manner. At that point, you'll still have some work to do to tailor the caption to your use and regroup the individual objects as a single design element.

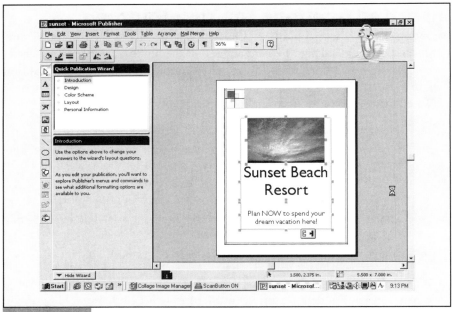

FIGURE 13-17 Use plenty of white space in a caption box, and group it with the illustration it accompanies

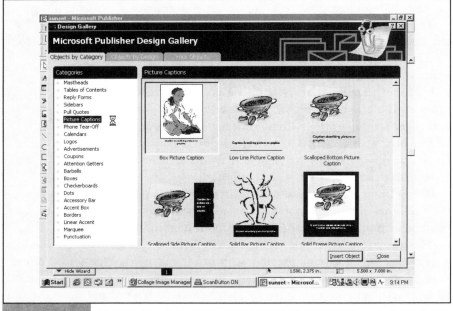

FIGURE 13-18 The Design Gallery has a variety of picture caption designs. For a consistent look, use only one style in a publication

Publisher Photo Design Concepts

The capability to directly edit photographs within Publisher is limited, since Publisher is a publishing application, not a program designed for photo editing. If you need to edit your photo before you use it in a document, it's best to work with a dedicated photo-editing application, such as Microsoft Image Composer. If you have imported a photograph into Publisher and have manipulated it, moved it around, and tried to do something interesting with it, and have run out of ideas, here are a few suggestions to get the creative juices flowing again.

Rotating, Overlapping, and Framing

One way to avoid the blocky, repetitive appearance of simply placing a photo inside some text is to rotate the photo perhaps 20 degrees to the left to provide a little variety. Or you could overlap the corners of two photos, creating a "stacked" appearance. Figure 13-19 shows an example of photos overlayed on a map and accented with a drop shadow effect, then pasted into Publisher. Figure 13-20 shows an image treated with a paintbrush effect and framing.

The Tyranny of the Rectangle

One problem with positioning photographs in Publisher is that the images are so, well, square. It's hard to get away from the linearity that makes readers say to themselves "Ho-hum, another newsletter." Here are some tips to avoid rectangle-itis.

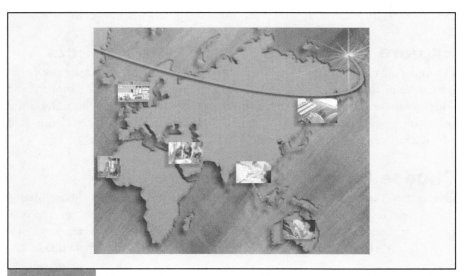

FIGURE 13-19 These small photos were positioned over a map, then pasted as a single image into Publisher

FIGURE 13-20 Here is a photograph treated with a paintbrush effect and framing, techniques both available in PhotoDraw

Use PhotoDraw's Designer Edges tool on your pictures. With this tool, you can blend the edges of the photos into the background using a variety of interesting shapes. To try another program that does something similar, but to an even more amazing degree (see Figure 13-21), download the plug-in Photo/Graphic Edges 10,000, by Auto FX. You can try it out free at http://www.autofx.com.

Explore PhotoDraw's Paintbrush Effects

Figure 13-22 displays a photo treated with a paintbrush effect. Notice the circular nature of the brush strokes emphasizes the subject's focus, the mother and daughter in movement. These techniques are easy to learn using PhotoDraw and other image-editing programs such as RightHemisphere's Deep Paint and MetaCreation's Painter.

Choose Images with Movement

One important concept in bringing a flat document to life is to choose images that appear to be going somewhere. Think travel, running, flying, blurred motion, sports, and expressions of affection. Figure 13-23 displays an image of a highway and clouds. Yet because of the intense rectangularity of the image, the

FIGURE 13-21 An interesting effect you can achieve with a photograph treated by the Auto FX Photo/Graphic Edges 10,000 tool

road seems to move upward. The word "upward" appearing on the image emphasizes the perspective already implied by the image itself.

FIGURE 13-22 A photograph treated with a heavily stroked paintbrush effect adds the impression of movement

FIGURE 13-23   An image with intense perspective, emphasized by the words overlaid on the picture, also adds the impression of movement

Keeping Track of Your Photos

When you insert a picture from a file, the Browse window contains a bar at the left with four icons, representing shortcuts to specific locations:

- **History**   A list of recently opened documents.
- **My Documents**   A system folder created by Microsoft Office, used as the default location for storing all your documents created with Office applications, unless you direct them otherwise. If you use PhotoDraw, this contains a folder called My Pictures, which is PhotoDraw's default storage location.
- **Favorites**   A tree of folders containing the locations of all your Internet favorites established in Internet Explorer.
- **The Desktop**   A convenient location for files in transit, such as those recently downloaded from the Web.

You can make use of all of these locations to help you keep track of your photo images. You might find My Pictures a convenient location for your .MIX files—those PhotoDraw files you're still working on. However, as you're putting publications together, and setting up space to store the images you're going to put in the FPO picture frames, you'll find it more convenient to group your images with the publications in which they will appear.

To do this, create a folder on your hard drive called Publications. Within it, create other folders, one for each publication or type of publication. Once you've done that, choose Tools | Options. Select the General tab, go into the File Locations box, click on Pictures, then click Modify. Browse for the location you've set up as the default for your pictures for publication, click Insert, then click Close to save this as the default location for pictures.

The Favorites folder is a good location for photos you use frequently. There's no point in copying them to each publication folder, as this folder is always available with a single click in the dialog box. To add an image to the Favorites list, locate the image in Explorer, click it, and select Favorite from the Explorer menu. Choose Add To Favorites. A dialog box appears, prompting you to name the file, or you may accept the name provided. Use the Create In button to create a new folder (a fly-out folder that appears when you select Favorites) for these images. After saving your images to Favorites, they'll be available from the Start menu (Start | Favorites), from the My Computer or Explorer menus, or by clicking the Look in Favorites button that appears in the Open dialog box of almost every Windows program.

Preparing Photos for Use on the Web

Preparing photos for the Web involves two main issues: acceptable file formats and download time.

If you're using photographs in your Publisher document, and you're going to place that document on the Web, they should be in a compressed format to reduce download time. There are three compressed formats in use on the Web: .JPG, .GIF, and .PNG. Because .PNG does not yet have widespread acceptance, and many browsers can't see images in this format, your best option is to limit yourself to the first two formats. The .JPG format is generally preferred for photographs, because it compresses them significantly without losing too much quality.

Because Web photos are displayed at 72 dpi, there's absolutely no reason to use any higher resolution than that if you have a choice (as you do when scanning or using photo CD images). This, too, reduces file size and therefore download time.

A third way to reduce download time is to reduce the size of your images. Remember, many Web surfers are using a 640 × 480 screen resolution; big photos will hardly fit in a browser window at that resolution.

Finally, pay attention to the filenames you use on the Web. Many Web servers use the UNIX operating system, which is sensitive to the use of upper- and lower-case type. Since most people probably enter filenames in all lowercase letters, it's a good idea to use lowercase when naming your files, including file extensions (.jpg, .gif, and so on). You may also want to limit filenames to eight characters, for those people who are still using Windows 3.1. This becomes an issue, however, only when you're building links to the location of the files in your Publisher documents. If you choose to simply place your photos in a Publisher Web publication, Publisher saves the files with names such as img0.gif, img1.gif, img2.jpg, and so on.

Professional Skills Summary

In this chapter, you learned how to obtain photos for your Publisher projects, and how to insert, reposition, and resize them. We discussed how to determine the best file type and file size for various output configurations, such as brochures printed from a desktop printer, professionally printed output, or Web viewing, and gave you details on how to choose the best images for your particular use. You learned about different sources of photographs, how to scan in your own, and how to quickly locate images for your various requirements in a Publisher document. Finally, you learned how to enhance your photos and add special effects with the use of image-editing software.

chapter 14

Addressing Postcards, Newsletters, and Brochures

In this chapter, you will:

- Create and edit address lists
- Import address data from other databases
- Merge address data with your Publisher projects
- Print address data
- Sort data and eliminate entries from specific projects
- Understand direct addressing versus creating address labels
- Print envelopes

Many of Publisher's designs are for items to be mailed: postcards, newsletters, catalogs, and sometimes brochures and flyers. To mail these items, you need to address them. Publisher will print addresses on many of these items as you print them, provided you can give it a list of addresses. So where do you get the list? Publisher allows you to use a variety of sources:

- An internal list called the Publisher Address List
- A single file from a Microsoft Access database
- Address lists from Microsoft Outlook
- A page from a Microsoft Excel worksheet notebook
- Other types of database files

If you already have address lists in any of these forms, you can use the addresses from them when you're ready to add addresses. Excel and Access files require some special handling, which will be discussed in the section "Addressing Your Publications."

Using Publisher's Address List

You can create one or more address lists from within Publisher itself. If you do a regular mailing to a select group that you don't do anything else with—say, an organization for which you provide publication services on contract—this is probably the best tool for the job. (If you already have address lists in other Office applications, you can use those lists just as easily. That's the topic of the next section.)

The Publisher Address List is a Microsoft Access database, and it is one-way compatible with the complete Access application. This means you can exchange data between the Publisher Address List and other Access tables, and you can also edit the Publisher Address List in Access. However, you can't view or edit an address list created by Access in Publisher, although you can use the data. If you don't already use Access, and don't want to take the time to learn how, you can easily use Publisher's scaled-down portion of it.

It's particularly easy to import address data and contact information created in an Excel spreadsheet. An Excel spreadsheet can be opened and linked to a Publisher project just as if it were a Publisher database.

Creating Address Lists by Entering Data

To create a Publisher Address List, choose Mail Merge | Create Publisher Address List. This produces the New Address List dialog box, shown in Figure 14-1. You can use just the fields you need or you can customize the list of fields.

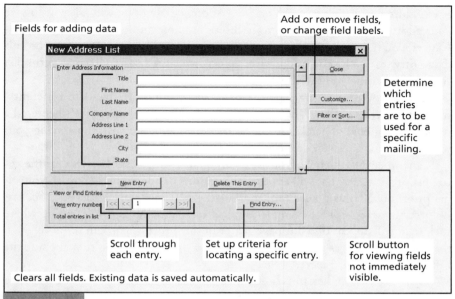

Fields for adding data

Add or remove fields, or change field labels.

Determine which entries are to be used for a specific mailing.

Scroll through each entry.

Set up criteria for locating a specific entry.

Scroll button for viewing fields not immediately visible.

Clears all fields. Existing data is saved automatically.

FIGURE 14-1 The Publisher Address List is an empty database to which you can add your own information

Begin entering data by typing in the Title field—for example, Mr., Mrs.—or you may simply leave this field blank. Press TAB to move to the next field, entering data as you go. You'll do no harm by leaving any fields blank, because Publisher will eliminate the empty lines when it addresses your document during printing.

Please note that an address entry is saved to this list as soon as you complete the new entry. The form has no Save button, and you should only click the Close button when you have finished all your entries. Clicking the New Entry button clears all fields so you can begin again. Use the Delete This Entry button to delete the entry currently visible. You can scroll through existing entries and use the Delete This Entry button to erase entries you no longer need.

The View Entry Number control box offers VCR-like controls for scrolling through all entries. Use this feature to determine if you've forgotten any entries, or use the Find Entry button on the right to set up criteria for searching for a specific entry (for example, finding everyone in your Address List who lives in California).

To save the entries you make during each data-entry session (if you need to break up your address entry time) click on the New Address List Close button, and Publisher will display the

Tip: You can press SHIFT-TAB to move backward through the fields of your data.

Save Address List dialog box. The Save Address dialog box will ask you to give your address list a name. Enter your choice of name and click OK. If you press Cancel, you'll lose all your changes and discard everything you've added on this data-entry session for this address list. Cancel will also discard all work on this list since the last time you saved data to it.

Because you're working in a database, some things are handled differently from other types of files. There's no Undo function, and once you've entered a record, it's entered. There's no way to quit the application without saving your work. You can, however, delete a record once you've entered it.

Remember that the fields you are creating here are placeholder text for the entire list of addresses that will appear, one address per document copy, in your final print job. You won't see those addresses now, only placeholder text, such as <<First Name>>, <<Last Name>>, and so on. Your job is to determine where each field will appear on your page. Later in this process, you can scroll through the actual addresses as they really will appear in your document, to make sure the results are what you expect.

L▶ Note: It's easy to figure out where you've stored your address lists, since when you reopen an Address List, Publisher will always return to the last Address List used. If other lists also appear in the same Browse window, it will be easy to locate them.

Click the Close button to access the Save Address List dialog box. Browse for the folder in which you want to save your file, enter a filename (the default extension is .mdb, which signifies an Access database), and click OK. Your list is not saved until you've completed this step. In fact, the only way to bring up the option to save your list (or save your current edits) is to click the Close button.

Where should you save your file? It depends on how many address lists you expect to create, which in turn may depend on whether you customize the Address List. If you expect to have many Publisher Address Lists, create a separate folder for them so they're easy to find and don't get lost among your other Publisher files.

Customizing Your Address List

To customize your Address List, select Mail Merge | Edit Address List, and then select the Address List you want to customize. Publisher will open the selected Address List. Click the Customize button on the Address List's dialog box, which displays the Customize Address List dialog box, shown here. With this dialog box, you can change the order of the fields, rename fields, delete fields, or add new fields. Use the Add button to add new fields. To change the order in which fields in the Address List are arranged, select the field you want to move, and click the Move Up or Move Down button.

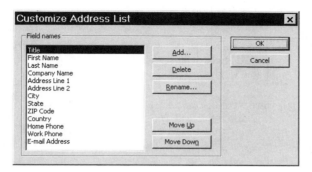

Which fields you need to use in your address database will depend on the purpose of your Address List. If your mailing list is a business list, for example, you may not need the home phone number. In fact, unless you export the list to Access, you can't really use this list for dialing phones, so you may want to delete both phone number fields. If it's a personal list, you may not need the business information. If it's a roster of everyone who applied to join a Little League team, you'll probably want additional fields for parents' names and team names.

> **L▶ Note:** It's fine to add a second Address line even if some of your addressees only have a single line to their address. When you print any document with that person's address, Publisher automatically removes the second blank line.

Most importantly, if you expect to send some publications to only some of the people in the Address List, you must have some way of distinguishing those who should receive the publication from those who shouldn't.

To be able to select who should receive certain, but not all, publications, you need to add *criterion fields*—fields to hold some kind of indicator by which you can select records. You might, for example, add a Type field, and enter either Business or Personal as the value in that field. Or you might distinguish between Major Clients, Ordinary Clients, Hot Prospects, and everybody else.

You'll have to remember what types of data the fields you create are supposed to contain. Unlike a full-strength database, the Address List doesn't let you distinguish between types of data (alphanumeric, numeric, date, logical, and so on). It also doesn't give you any controls, such as a list of values from which to choose, or a default value for some fields. Every field you create is a text field. But you can go far enough with that for many purposes. Table 14-1 shows the actions you can take to alter the structure of any Address List.

Editing an Existing Address List

You may want to edit an existing Address List so you can remove inactive entries or make changes to addresses when people move.

Action	Description
Add a new field	Choose a field in the list that is adjacent to where the new field should appear, then click the Add button. A dialog box asks for a name for the new field, and whether you want it to appear before or after the selected field.
Delete a field	Select the field and click Delete. A message box will warn you that if you delete the field, you also delete any data in it, and ask you to confirm. Click Yes to continue or No to cancel.
Rename a field	Select the field and click Rename. Enter the new name in the dialog box and click OK.
Move a field	Select the field and click Move Up or Move Down.

TABLE 14-1   Actions That Alter the Structure of an Address List File

If a contact's address data has changed, or you want to add or eliminate entries to an existing list, use the Edit Address List function.

To edit an existing Address List, choose Mail Merge | Edit Publisher Address List. To create a new record, click New Entry. This creates an empty record for you to fill. You can click this button any time, but the record is always added to the end of the list.

To update the information in an existing field, you can use the browse buttons at the bottom of the window, enter the record number if you know it, or search for some item in the record to be altered. To search, click Find Entry. This displays the Find Entry dialog box. Enter the text to search for. The default is to search all fields, but you can click This Field and choose the field in which to search from a drop-down list. When you've entered the information, click Find Next. If the record isn't the one you're looking for, keep clicking Find Next until you find it.

Once you've found the record to change, you can edit the text in a field the same way you would any other text. Highlight the entire field to delete the contents and enter something new, or just edit the text in place. When you are finished with the Address List, click Close, and the window closes without further ado.

Addressing Your Publications

Addressing your publications takes two or three steps:

1. Inserting fields in your publication to hold the address information
2. Optionally *filtering* your address list to select only some of the addresses
3. Performing a mail merge

Using Address Panels in Publications

For three types of publication—brochures, newsletters, and catalogs—there is a Publisher Wizard that includes a Customer Address item. Click this item and you're offered the choice of adding a customer address to your publication.

If you add a customer address to a brochure, the center pane on the outside is set up like an envelope, with your Personal Information (your own address and contact info) in the upper-left corner and an address placeholder in the usual location. In a newsletter, adding a customer address reorganizes the top half of the last page. It's assumed you'll fold your newsletter in half before mailing, and the address information is laid out accordingly, as shown in Figure 14-2.

If you want to get more copy onto the back page of your Publisher document, and you are willing to fold your newsletters twice, you can rearrange the elements once they are placed, so that they take only a third of a page, as Figure 14-3 shows.

When you've created a catalog in Publisher, and you want to add an address to it, you'll see that the entire back cover is replaced by a mailing page that includes your Personal Information and a customer address placeholder.

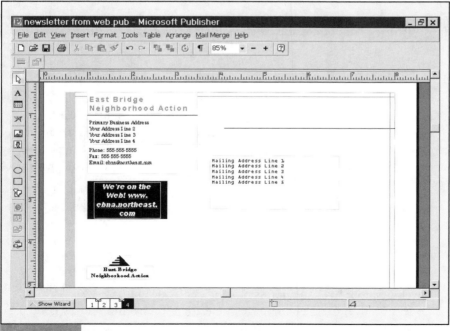

FIGURE 14-2 Publisher reserves half of a newsletter page for an address area

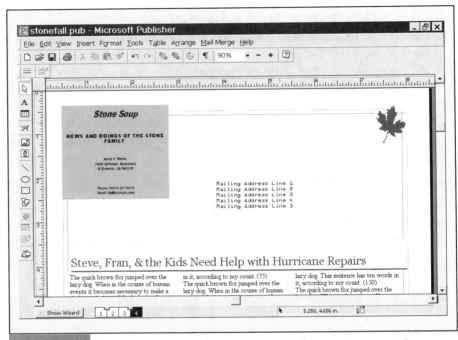

FIGURE 14-3 You can rearrange the address area of a newsletter to take less space

Of course, if you create a postcard or an envelope, the address placeholder is added automatically. Figure 14-4 shows the address side of a postcard. The return address information is, as usual, added from the Personal Information file. However, for postcards, you have the option of adding several other types of copy as well. Click Address Side in the Postcard Wizard, and you can add any one of the following:

- A map with directions
- Speaker names
- A promotional message
- Details regarding an appointment and cancellation information

Envelopes, too, have an address placeholder by default.

To set up a flyer or other one-page publication for mailing, add a second page with a return address from the Personal Information file and a text frame containing the mail merge fields for a mailing address, as shown in Figure 14-5. This

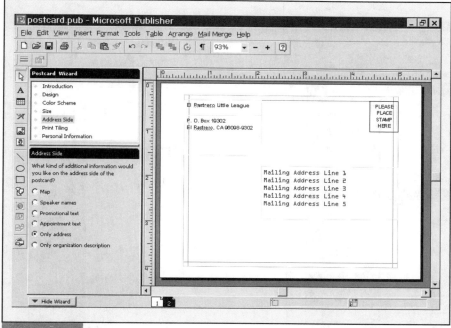

Postcards automatically contain an address placeholder. You can add several types of additional information to the address side

allows the publication to be folded over and mailed as a flyer, saving the cost of envelopes.

Choosing a Data Source

Before you can insert the merge fields, you must choose a data source. To insert address fields in your publication, first select and delete the placeholder text. Then choose Mail Merge | Open Data Source to open the file containing the addresses you want to use. You'll see the following dialog box:

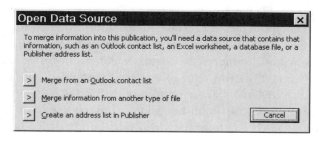

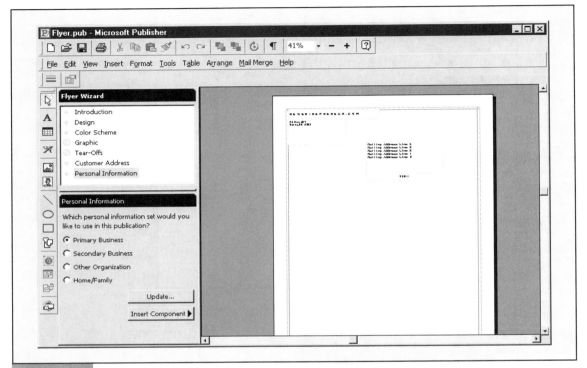

FIGURE 14-5   The same merge fields can be repeated for easy mailing

You can choose from these options:

- An Outlook contact list
- Another type of file
- A new address list you'll create in Publisher

To use an Outlook contact list, choose Merge From An Outlook Contact List. You'll be taken to Outlook's Choose Profile window, where you choose the list to use. Choose the profile you want to use and click OK.

To use another type of database, choose Merge Information From Another Type Of File. In the Open Data Source browse window, you have a choice of Access Database, Excel files, and many other types of database files, as you can see in Figure 14-6.

Choose the type of file you want to use, or choose All Database Files or All Files, choices that are hidden at the bottom of the list.

If you're using an existing Publisher Address List, choose Merge Information From Another Type Of File from the Open Data Source dialog box to locate it.

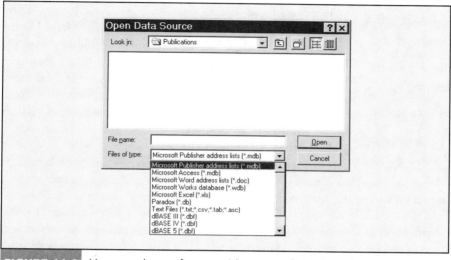

FIGURE 14-6 You can choose from a wide range of database file types as a source of addresses for a mail merge

(Publisher Address Lists are the default type of file.) Open the data source from which you will use the addresses.

Merging Data from an Excel Worksheet

If you would like to create your address database with Excel (in the worksheet "column-row" arrangement), or if you already have an existing Excel address worksheet, you can use Publisher's Mail Merge features to merge the Excel address data fields into your Publisher document. If you are creating a new Excel worksheet to use with your Publisher Mail Merge operations, be sure to use the worksheet's first row to provide descriptive names to each column. (With Excel, the columns represent fields and can be handled like any database's fields; Excel calls them column headers.)

Don't, however, use an Excel worksheet without descriptive names for each column header. Because Publisher is designed to use your Excel column headers to identify each mail-merge field, using Excel column headers is extremely important to the simplicity of mail merging Excel worksheets with Publisher documents. If the Excel worksheet you want to use does not have column headers, take time to add the descriptive header field names in the Excel worksheet's first row. Once you have added the descriptive column headers to your Excel worksheet, return to Publisher and add the Excel column headers as descriptive fields to your mail-merge document.

Tip: Putting extra effort into adding header field names will ensure that you'll easily be able to identify the fields if you can't recall them when you enter your mail-merge fields into your Publisher document, or if you simply don't recall the significance of your Excel worksheet's organization.

Once you have correctly created or altered your Excel worksheet to include column headers, choose Mail Merge | Open Data Source | Merge Information From Another Type Of File. Change the file type to Microsoft Excel (*.xls), as shown in Figure 14-7. Look through the folders to find the file. Make sure the Excel file you want to merge is not already open in Excel. (Publisher cannot use an open Excel worksheet as a data source—you must save the file and close the worksheet before you begin the mail merge.) Use the Look In subdirectory folder drop-down list to display a list of existing Excel worksheet files. Select the file you want, and Publisher will display a prompt asking you if you want to use your Excel worksheet's column headers as mail-merge field names. If you have taken the time to make sure your Excel worksheet has descriptive column headers, answer Yes. If you know that the Excel worksheet you want to use as a data source has no column headers, but begins its first row with actual data, you can answer No to the column headers prompt. What works best, however, is to return to Excel and add the descriptive column headers, as described earlier in this chapter section.

If your Excel worksheet has more than one page, Publisher will prompt you to enter the name of the page that has the data you want to use, as shown here. If you haven't named your sheet, then type **Sheet1** into this field. (There is no space between Sheet and 1.) If you don't remember the name, you'll have to open the worksheet in Excel and check on it. Be sure to close it before you proceed, or Publisher won't be able to open it.

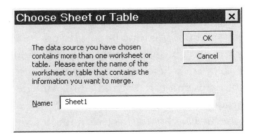

The data you use from an Excel file is updateable. If you make a change in the Excel spreadsheet you've merged with, the change will be reflected in Publisher. However, the data is not "live updateable." After making the change in Excel, you have to save the file, then open Publisher and open the document. You can't make a change to the Excel file, and expect Publisher to automatically see the new or revised address info. The good news is you don't have to remerge the data in order to see the new information.

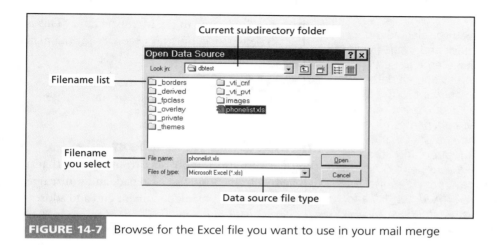

FIGURE 14-7 Browse for the Excel file you want to use in your mail merge

Merging Data from an Existing Microsoft Access Database

You can use any Microsoft Access database with appropriate records in a Publisher mail merge. To use an Access database as the data source, choose Mail Merge | Open Data Source | Merge Information From Another Type Of File, as was shown in Figure 14-6. Browse for the file. (You can, but need not, change the file type to .mdb.) If the database has multiple tables, you'll be asked to choose a single table because Publisher only lets you merge using one table.

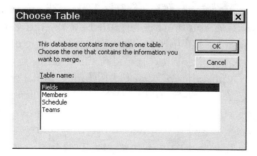

Therefore, if some of your information is in linked tables, you'll have to create a single table containing the information in both tables that you need for your merge. In the figures shown in this chapter—a Little League member welcoming letter merged with a league management database—the coaches' names were in the Teams table. Since the welcoming letter to new players had to include the name of the coach of the member's team, the fields containing the coaches'

L ▶ Note: Once you've selected a data source, you can go back and insert fields later by choosing Mail Merge | Insert Field. There's no need to open a data source again unless you want to use a different one. If you switch to another source, however, the field names may not be the same, and Publisher will remove any from your publication that don't match names in your new source. Even though they may contain equivalent information, "Addr1," "Address_1," and "Address Line 1" are regarded as different entities. Publisher notes the fields that must be erased, so you can easily delete them.

names were duplicated in the Members table. This is bad database practice, but was necessary for the mail merge.

Cross-Reference: To learn more about entering and using Personal Information, see Chapter 4.

Merging Data from a Text File

Publisher can also import data from an ASCII text file, such as from Windows Notepad, and utilize it as a database. Create a blank document and add address data to it, separating each "field" by pressing the TAB key. Publisher can import this data as a legitimate database just as easily as data from a database program or spreadsheet. Just type the salutations or title, then press the TAB key, type the first name, then press the TAB key, type the last name, press the TAB key, the address lines, each separated by a tab entry, and so forth. The first row of entries you type should be the field names (Title, First Name, Last Name, Address 1, and so on), since Publisher will offer to use the first row of entries as the names it uses as placeholder text in your address text frame.

You can use Word, Notepad, WordPad, or any other text program for this purpose, as long as you save the file as plain text (.txt).

Inserting Fields into Your Imported Database

After creating a database, you must determine how the individual entries should appear on your document. Publisher needs to be told where each field will appear on your projects. Create a blank text frame or table, and use the Insert Field feature to sequence the appearance of your fields (for example, the Title comes first, such as Mr. or Mrs., followed by the First Name, if applicable, followed by the Last Name). This text frame or table can be moved or repositioned after you initially create it. It will not lose its connection to the database by being moved.

When you've selected your data source, you'll see the Insert Fields dialog box, which is shown in Figure 14-8. With either a text frame or table selected, double-click a field name to insert the placeholder for it. As you move down the list of fields in the Insert Fields dialog box, selecting as you go, Publisher places fields right next to each other with no spaces in between. You'll have to manually organize the information in the target text frame to look like an address. To do so, click inside the frame, and use the SPACEBAR and ENTER keys to appropriately

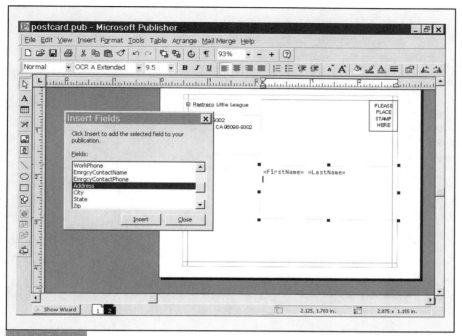

FIGURE 14-8   Enter field placeholders from the Insert Fields list. Arrange them appropriately in the text box as you go

space the fields apart. To enter the inside address, you'd choose First Name, press the SPACEBAR, choose Last Name, press ENTER, and choose Address. For the City/State/Zip line, enter a comma and a space between City and State, and a space between State and Zip, as shown in Figure 14-9. The field names take their formatting from the document defaults, the text frame defaults, or Excel column headers.

When you're finished inserting fields, click Close.

> **Note:** You can also change font type, color, size, and other text formatting in the target frame. The placeholder data names (Name, Address, City, State) will change to reflect your text choices.

If you want to add personalized content to the publication appropriate to each addressee, you simply insert the appropriate field placeholders in the publication, wherever they should be. There's no reason you can't also create an inside address if you want.

If you want to add more fields later, place your cursor where you want to insert the field and choose Mail Merge | Insert Field. If, perhaps, you forgot to add a needed name or other address option, you can use this feature to add fields to an existing address list. In our example, the letter needs to include the name of the

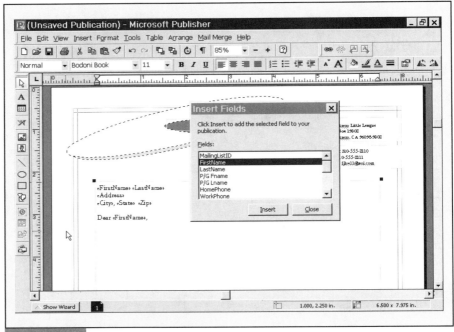

FIGURE 14-9 Insert field names in the order in which you want them to appear in your publication

player's team and coach, so they are inserted, as shown in Figure 14-10. When you add fields in this way, Publisher automatically matches the new fields to any Publisher document.

Filtering and Sorting

If you want to send your publication to only a portion of your address list, you can filter the list. You can also sort your list. In fact, if you're doing a bulk mailing in the United States, you *must* sort your list by zip code if you plan to take advantage of bulk mailing rates. The postal service requires it.

If your data source is a Publisher Address List, there are built-in filtering and sorting tools. Use this feature to narrow down the number of people from your database who will be included in the Publisher print job. To sort or filter a Publisher Address List, choose Mail Merge | Edit Publisher Address List, and open the list you want to work with. When the dialog box appears, click Filter or Sort. You'll see the Filtering and Sorting dialog box, shown in Figure 14-11. Use this dialog box to select from a larger address list only those addressees who live in

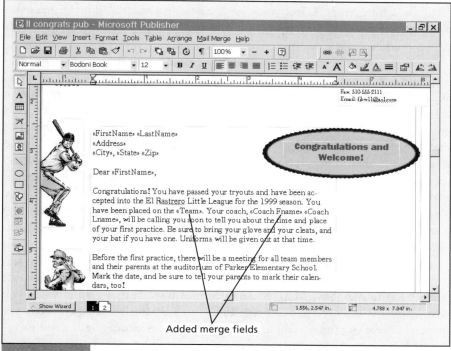

Added merge fields

FIGURE 14-10 Merge fields can be entered at any time

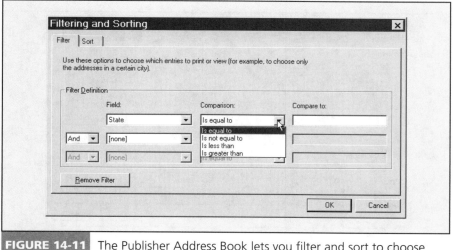

FIGURE 14-11 The Publisher Address Book lets you filter and sort to choose which records to include in a mail merge

California, for example. Here you choose a field from a drop-down list, a comparison from another drop-down list, and then enter something to which the data should be compared.

To filter by just one item—say, only personal addresses—you could use a Type field and use the values "Type," "Is equal to," "Personal," or perhaps, "Company Name," "Is equal to," " " (a blank field). Once you've created the first filter criterion, the drop-down lists to the left of the field lists become available, and you can create multiple criteria using And and Or. Figure 14-12 shows an example of multiple criteria. (You do not need to use multiple criteria. It's fine to leave the bottom drop-down menus in their default position so they do not affect your filtering.) Here, the Type field is used twice, once to select hot prospects, and the second time to select those who are neither hot prospects nor clients. These are joined with an Or, so either type will be included. Finally, the mailing is restricted by state, so the only people who will receive this mailing are non-clients in the state of Washington.

To sort your list, click the Sort tab to access the available options. Use this feature to determine which addressees will be printed first, and will appear first when you use the Show Merge Results control box. This is helpful when you have a long list and need to make sure all intended addressees are included in the print job. Here you can sort on up to three fields, in ascending or descending order. When you use more than one criterion, values in the first field listed are sorted first, then each group of matching items is sorted by values in the second field, and so on. Figure 14-13 shows a typical three-field sort for a mailing list.

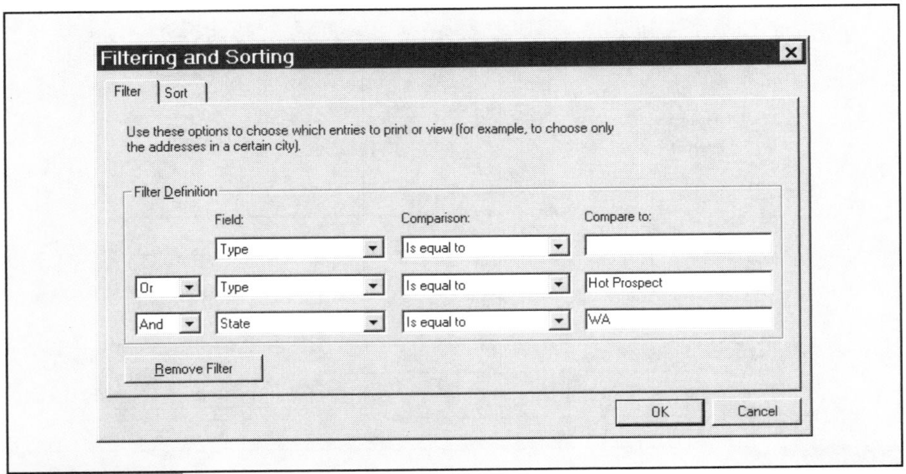

FIGURE 14-12   You can filter your list by up to three criteria

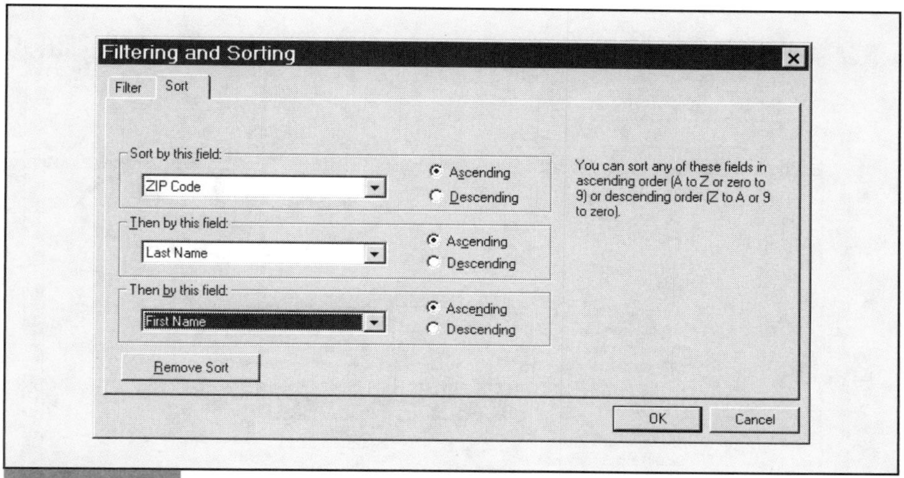

FIGURE 14-13 You can sort on up to three fields, in ascending or descending order

If you're using another type of data source, you can still filter and sort your data after you've completed a merge, as described in the next section (you'll have to save your file as a Publisher .mdb file first, before filtering). Once you've completed the merge, the command Filter Or Sort appears on the Mail Merge menu. This opens the Filtering and Sorting dialog box you saw in Figures 14-11 through 14-13. You use it as described, but the field drop-down lists display the fields from your chosen source.

Completing the Merge

Once you've got everything set up as you want it, choose Mail Merge | Merge to complete the job. This creates a set of hidden copies of your publication, each based on a different record in your data source. As it proceeds, you can preview the data with the Preview Data window that automatically opens (see Figure 14-14). Be sure to enlarge your publication so you can see what's being placed in each merge data field. As you click through the list, you can verify that each is set up correctly. If it isn't, you can skip it during the printing process. Please note that once you've merged, you can no longer add fields.

When you're ready to print your merged publications, choose File | Print Merge, which replaces the normal Print command after you've done a merge. Your options are different in this type of print operation, as you can see in Figure 14-15. The print range includes the option to print a range of entries by number, so you

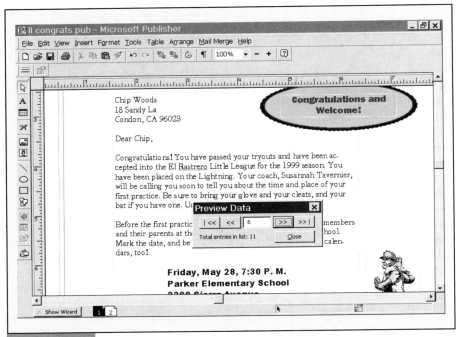

FIGURE 14-14 You can preview your merge, one record at a time

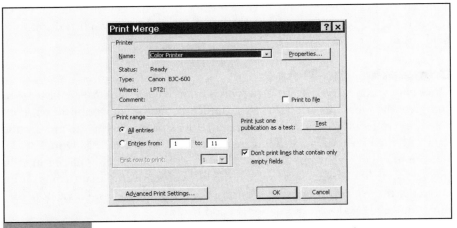

FIGURE 14-15 Printing a merge affords you different options from normal printing

can do two passes with different ranges to skip a copy for which the merge didn't come out correctly in the preview. You also have the options to print a single copy as a test and to skip blank lines. The latter is selected by default. You might use it if you include two address lines and some of your addressees have only one address line. This makes the result look more finished and professional than including an empty line.

Direct Addressing Versus Address Labels

When should you address your publication directly as part of printing it, and when should you prepare address labels or envelopes? As a general rule, it's easiest to address your publication directly if you're printing it yourself, and to use labels if you're having it printed professionally.

On the other hand, if there's some reason to print your publication well in advance of mailing, you may not know exactly who will be on the recipients list. And sometimes, you need to mail only one or a few copies after the regular mailing. For these circumstances, it makes sense to use a label.

Addressing Professionally Printed Flyers and Brochures

It would be extremely difficult to squeeze a newsletter or catalog that's already been commercially printed through your printer, since the paper stock will likely be thicker than what your printer can accommodate. But a three-fold brochure or a flyer is another matter. You proceed by creating a one-page publication from a blank document of the same size as your brochure or flyer. Think of this blank document as a template for where the address will appear on your printed job. Test the placement of the address, repositioning the address and printing again on blank paper, until you are happy with the results. For a brochure, you'll want the address information in the middle of the page; for a flyer, at the top or bottom.

1. Choose File | New | Blank Publications | Full Page | Create.

2. From the Wizard, choose Personal Information. Choose the proper organization for your publication and click Insert Component. Insert as many Personal Address components as you think appropriate, and arrange those elements along the left side of the page in the return address area, as shown in Figure 14-16.

3. Create a text frame in the proper location for the recipient's address.

4. If you have a bulk rate permit, you can create the bulk rate tag at the same time, using a text frame with a border.

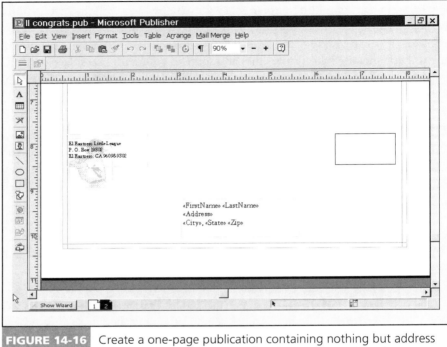

FIGURE 14-16 Create a one-page publication containing nothing but address information to address preprinted one-page publications

Figure 14-16 shows a mailing page to be used with a flyer, with the information at the bottom, including a text box for a bulk rate permit.

At this point, you're ready to perform the merge. Don't forget to run a test print on some scrap paper that's already been printed on one side, to ensure that you'll be printing on the blank side of your publication.

Printing Labels

As mentioned earlier, sometimes you will have a need to create mailing labels instead of directly addressing your publication, and Publisher 2000 provides you with a simple way to do this.

To create mailing labels, choose File | New, then choose Mailing Labels from the list at the left. Choose the type of label on which you will print. As you can see in Figure 14-17 they are all coded to Avery stock numbers, which are industry standard. Select and delete the placeholder text, and insert the merge fields as

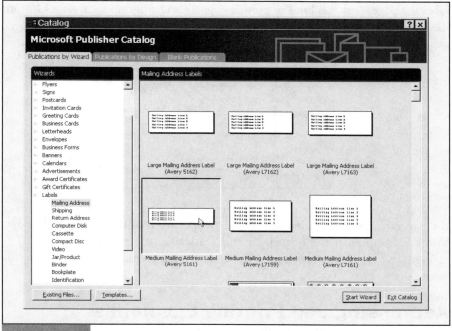

FIGURE 14-17   Choose a preset label type by stock number

described earlier. Be sure to select and delete the box containing the "This label is ready to print" message, or it will be printed too. Room on the label for large amounts of address data can be tight. Expect to spend a few minutes editing the spacing, removing blank lines, space, and extra carriage returns that can force some of your address data off the page.

Remember that when you are determining spacing for an entire sheet of labels, a small alignment discrepancy in the first label will multiply, and each subsequent label will be that much more out of alignment when your sheet is actually printed. Take the time to make sure the labels are well centered before printing. To avoid unintentional offsetting, make sure your printer paper feed mechanism is snugly aligned to the label sheets.

The Print Merge dialog box for labels has somewhat different options from the standard Print Merge dialog box. A Page Options button lets you print one label per page, which is kind of pointless, and also brings up a Custom Options dialog box. This lets you control fine details of spacing on and between the labels.

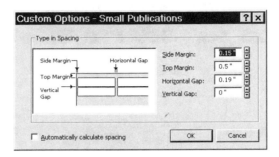

As you can see, you can choose the precise size of the side and top margins of the page, to align your print with the actual positions of the labels on the page. You can also adjust the horizontal and vertical gaps between the labels. The changes you make are immediately illustrated in the graphic pane on the left side of the dialog box.

Addressing and Printing Envelopes

The Publisher 2000 Envelope Wizard provides more than a dozen custom envelope styles. These include graphics and labeling options. These Wizards create fields on the envelope for merging address data from a database. The Wizard also lets you specify standard, extra-large, or a number of custom envelope sizes.

After specifying the envelope design, you can determine where the address information should be printed on your envelope and what data should appear. After the Wizard has finished providing basic content for your envelope, click Print Merge from the Merge menu. The Merge control box appears, allowing you to click through the list of addressees who will receive this mail from you.

The nuts and bolts of printing your envelope depends on your printer. Some printers provide a special attachment or other mechanism for aligning envelopes for accurate printing. Some printers are just not too good about preventing envelope slippage, meaning that with each subsequent envelope being printed, the printer offset increases, eventually to unacceptable levels. In such cases, print a handful of envelopes at a time. Then stop or pause the print job, and reposition the envelopes for more accurate printing.

Publisher 2000 does provide a control for printing a test page. For envelopes, printing a test page to see exactly where the print truly appears is a must.

Professional Skills Summary

In this chapter, you learned to use the Publisher Address List to create data for your mailings, as well as importing data from Excel, Access, or even a text file. We discussed how to edit a database and save it to apply to all your Publisher projects. You also learned how to merge databases with your projects, determining where on your page fields should appear, sorting fields, or eliminating certain data from existing mailing projects. You learned about the pros and cons of direct addressing versus creating address labels, and how to print address information on envelopes. In Chapter 15, we'll take a look at choosing between your desktop printer or a commercial printer, depending on the quality you want in the final product.

Choosing Between Desktop and Commercial Printing

In this chapter, you will:

- Evaluate your project's needs to pick the best output option

- Manage your part of the printing process if you choose commercial printing

- Use Publisher's Pack and Go Wizard

- Learn to use Publisher's new Commercial Printing Tools

- Manage graphics and font files

Until Microsoft released Publisher 2000, you had primarily two ways to print the brochures, newsletters, and letterheads you created with Microsoft Publisher: your ink-jet or laser printer for lesser quantities, or a duplicating center or commercial printer for larger quantity duplication. Neither option, of course, was ideal. Although desktop ink-jet or color printers are capable of excellent results, they are inefficient and uneconomical for printing large numbers of finished publications. If you need to print more than 50 to 100 final copies, printing time can become unreasonably long, and ink cartridges or toner refills can cost more than having your final copies professionally duplicated.

In the past, if you used a commercial service to make quantity copies of your final document, you had to prepare high-quality master paper copies, requiring the commercial printer to work from hard-copy originals that might not have been true in terms of color reproduction or reliability for quality duplication. This drawback might have caused some desktop publishers to refrain from using color in their publications or using color to the extent they might like. For commercial printers, color selection and duplication has always been considered an art, so dealing with less-than-precise methods of color processing is not something printers take lightly.

To specify color placement the old way, you had to explain where you wanted color by creating a printed tissue overlay that matched black-and-white originals. These overlays indicated where you wanted color. To specify color selection, you had to select your color(s) with an elaborate color-selecting method, standardized as the Pantone Matching System (PMS). This system, however, is reminiscent of selecting paint colors from hundreds of paint chip samples: what you select might work, but maybe when you paint the whole room, you'll wish you'd selected another tint, which is, of course, now impossible. With the old-style of color selecting, you could forget about having the capability to see beforehand how colors and color combinations interrelate. Experimentation with color was reserved for the rich, the brave, or the extremely well-experienced desktop publisher. Adding color to a publication drastically increased the chances for errors—not only in accurate color duplication, but in correct color registry and color placement.

Those days are over. Publisher 2000 now offers you total control over color, giving you an easy and dependable way to create colorful publications. New to Publisher 2000 are several key feature enhancements that give you the capability to easily and efficiently prepare and submit four-color documents for quantity duplication with predictable results.

New in 2000:   The Pack and Go Wizard makes preparing your files for commercial printing a quick and painless process.

Pros and Cons of Home and Office Desktop Printing

Desktop printing in color or black and white, depending on your ink-jet or laser printer, is suitable for small quantities of brochures, business cards, flyers, newsletters, and postcards. It's perfect for situations where consistency is more important than quantity—for example, when you just want to print a dozen or so flyers every day or every week.

Desktop printing is also appropriate if you want to prepare an event's worth of brochures or flyers at a time. Use desktop printing when you just want to prepare enough business cards or marketing materials for a meeting or convention, or when you want to prepare proposals, event signage, and seminar materials in color.

As quantities increase, however, you'll probably quickly reach the upper boundaries of efficient desktop printing. When you need to print more than 25 two-sided brochures or 50 flyers, you'll probably get frustrated by the time it takes to print them. Hold to this limit especially if you have an ink-jet printer that slows down or ties up your computer while printing, preventing you from doing any other work until the printer is done.

If you decide to print black-and-white paper masters on your desktop printer, your finished publication will be constrained by the quality of that printer. For most practical purposes, this restricts you to including black-and-white photographs in your publication. Worse, preparing paper masters decreases the quality of any photographs you have included in your publication. Quality is lost at each generation of printing.

Creating a Final Electronic Output File

The alternative to preparing black-and-white masters for duplication is to submit electronic files to your duplication center or commercial printer. Submitting electronic files for commercial duplication offers the following major advantages:

- **Color accuracy**   You enjoy total control over color, permitting you to specify the exact colors and tints you desire, relying on printed color-matching reference books and resources used by commercial printers.

- **Quality and creativity**   Electronic files deliver sharper text and visuals. They also permit you to include special effects such as edge-to-edge printing—known as bleeds—which desktop printers are not able to prepare.

- **Photographic quality**   Black-and-white photographs will be sharper and include more shades of gray. In addition, the capability of using four-color process printing means you can include color photographs. The quality of both black-and-white and color photographs will be significantly higher.

- **Printing quality** Color quality will be higher because commercial printers can "trap" colors, making sure there are no gaps between adjacent colors.
- **Paper options** Commercial printers have access to far more paper colors, textures, and weights than are available at office supply stores or duplication centers.

Dealing with Commercial Printers

Successful publications are the result of a close working partnership between publisher and commercial printer. The sooner you begin communicating your publication goals to the printer, the smoother the project will flow, the better results you'll get, and the less you'll have to pay.

Disappointment is certain if you go ahead and design, produce, and submit your project without consulting with your printer and working with them at every stage. Once you move beyond photocopier-quality levels into two-, three- and four-color printing, you'll find far more things to go wrong and far more opportunities for increased costs.

By closely working with your printer, you can identify and avoid potential problem areas and also investigate—with the printer's guidance—ways of reducing printing costs.

Choosing the Right Commercial Printer

The starting point is to visit several commercial printers in your area and find out which ones are most interested in printing your project. All printers are not alike. Commercial printers vary in the types of projects they handle, the size (physical dimension and number of pages) of the publications they print, as well as the size of the print run (quantity printed) and quality level they're comfortable working with. Printers also differ in their turnaround times and in their familiarity with working with Publisher 2000 files.

Some printers, for example, specialize in fast turnaround of business forms, letterheads, and envelopes. Others specialize in newsletters and brochures for ad agencies and other quality-conscious clients. Still others specialize in long documents such as instruction books and catalogs. Your first job is to match the printer to the project. If you work for a busy firm or organization, you may end up working with several different printers, sending different projects to each one.

Most of your pre-qualification can be done on the telephone, although you'll probably want to meet face-to-face with the printer as early as possible. Try to visit their premises and ask for a tour of their facilities. Pay particular attention to the firm's overall cleanliness and organization.

When visiting printers, bring along samples of the type of publication you want. For example, bring along copies of printed newsletters or brochures similar to the one you want to print, so the printer can evaluate the quality level and the paper stock it's printed on. It doesn't do much good to visit a printer and say: "I want a newsletter." It's a lot better to say: "I want a newsletter like this, but printed in blue."

When making preliminary contact with printers, it helps to find out if they are comfortable working with Windows files in general and Publisher 2000 files in particular. Many printers are most comfortable working with files prepared for the Apple Macintosh and actually convert Windows files to Macintosh files before printing—which increases the opportunities for problems.

Obtaining Printing Quotes

Always get at least three different printing quotes for each print job. Even if you typically work with the same printer, getting more than one printing quote will guarantee that you don't overpay. Printing quotes simplify your job by making it easy to compare apples to apples, oranges to oranges.

Your printing quote should specify the following information:

- **Type of project**   Brochure, letterhead, or newsletter, for example.
- **Final printed piece size**   8.5 by 11-inch pages or "standard trim" book-size pages, for example.
- **Pages and folds**   Three-panel brochure with two folds, for example.
- **Type and number of colors**   Black-and-white, black plus one spot color, or four-color process.
- **Quantity**   You usually get a better price if each printer bids on three different quantities—for example, at breaks of 2,000, 5,000, and 10,000, plus a price per additional 1,000 copies at each level.
- **Paper**   Brand, color, texture, and weight.
- **Proofs**   When you want to see proofs in the process, how many proof copies, and at what final printed quality levels.
- **Special printing requirements**   Heavier than normal ink coverage, bleeds, or special die-cuts, for example.
- **File submission**   Via the Internet, disks, or zip drives, for example. Any special file compression protocols to observe.
- **Final printed product delivery and/or pick-up**   How the printed pieces will get from the printer to your place of business. Any special packing or storage requirements.

- **Late charges and alterations**   How much extra it will cost if you are late providing the files, and how much alterations (not corrections due to the printer's error, which should be free) will cost you once your project is on the printing press.

- **Flexibility in delivery**   Often, if you can be a bit flexible, your printer will charge less if your job can be done during a "down" period when the presses would otherwise be idle.

- **Rush charges**   How much extra it will cost for fast turnaround if you are facing a deadline situation. Rush jobs *always* cost more.

Most importantly, find out in which file format they'll want you to submit your Publisher file. Ask whether they want you to use the Microsoft MS Publisher Color Printer or MS Publisher driver to create the final files for them—or if they want you to install a printer driver specifically designed for their particular printing hardware and software. (If so, they will provide the driver for you and detailed instructions.) Or perhaps they want you to prepare PostScript files ready for printing. At the same time, find out if there are any specific settings they want you to use or if they can take care of "tweaking" your files as they prepare your publication for printing.

Check with your printer to see if they will fill out a standard printer's quote form. With this form, you can easily make sure that each printer quotes on exactly the same printing job, so you can compare prices and make the best-informed decision.

Be flexible when it comes to paper. Find out if the printer has a similar paper in stock or knows of a similar paper that can save you money. Find out if the printer regularly works with the specific paper stock you have chosen, or if they can recommend something similar and save you money. Sometimes, a printer will submit a low bid if they have the paper in stock and want to use it up.

Working with Distant Printers

Although you may have an ongoing relationship with a local printer, it's also possible that you may choose to work with a distant printer, especially if you are printing large quantities of a standardized format, such as a newsletter or three-panel brochure.

Some printers specialize in high-volume/long-distance printing, permitting you to take advantage of economies of scale. Your project may be matched with other, similar projects that use the same colors, permitting drastic price savings.

You can upload your files to their Web site, and the printer can send proofs to you via overnight courier. In some cases, you can check your proofs on their Web site.

The downside of working with distant printers is that their prices are based on standard formats and paper stocks. Be sure that their low prices do not force you to compromise the quality you hope to achieve.

Preparing and Submitting Files

Publisher 2000 makes it easy to prepare and submit a publication designed for high-quality commercial printing.

Microsoft has worked closely with commercial printers, optimizing Publisher 2000 to the needs of commercial printers. As a result, the entire process from start to finish is likely to be simpler than you anticipated—even if you have never prepared a four-color publication before.

Setting Up Your Publication

The starting point for creating a publication ready for a commercial printer is to choose the printer driver your commercial printer requires. Remember that the printer's output device is an expensive piece of hardware with which you are probably unfamiliar. The printer has to process your electronic files through some type of output mechanism to be able to render hard-copy finals of your publication. This part of the process is critical—it's the foundation of your reason for deciding to use a professional printer, because different output devices print final products of varying quality. Choose your final output device based on the level of quality you want your final product to have.

Before beginning work on your publication, select File | Print Setup. When Publisher displays the Change Printer Settings dialog box, as shown in Figure 15-1, select either Microsoft Publisher Imagesetter (for spot-color or black- and-white publications) or the Microsoft Publisher Color Printer driver. Choose whatever printer driver option your commercial printer has asked you to use.

The choice is based on their specific hardware and the number of colors used in your publication. For example, if your printer is using an Agfa ProSet 9500 or Linotronics 330 or 530, and you are printing spot-color or black-and-white publications, they will probably recommend you use the Microsoft Publisher driver.

In some cases, the printer may request that you download and install a special printer driver from the Internet, or they may provide you with a copy of the driver on disk.

Tip: Remember that your commercial printer may have an output device that is completely new to you. If the printer intends to use that output device, they will also be able to provide you with the driver you'll need to create the output files in the proper format. Your printer should also be able to give you specific instructions for how to install the driver. If you need to download a driver from the printer off the Internet, or if you aren't sure how to download a file or install a new driver, don't be afraid to ask your printer for help.

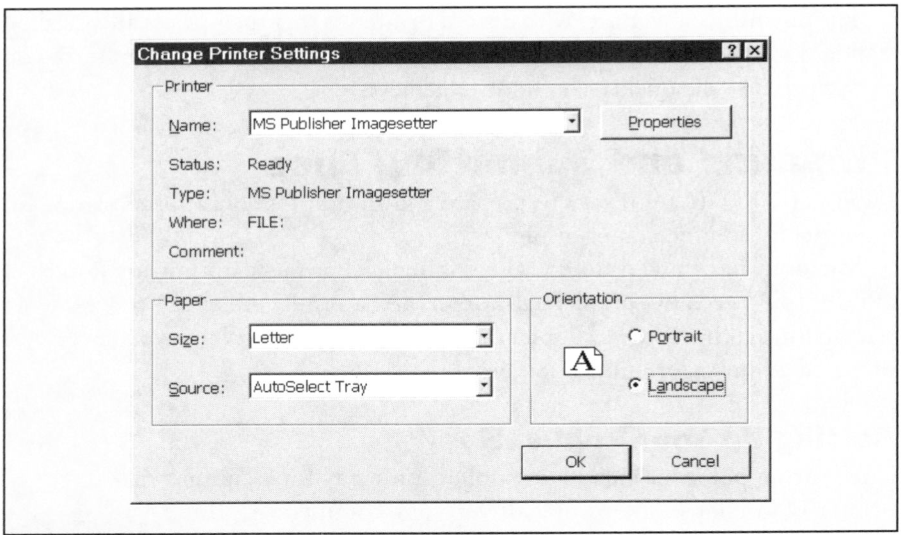

FIGURE 15-1 Select the printer driver your commercial printer recommends in the Change Printer Settings dialog box

Proofing Your Work

Although you are preparing your publication for commercial printing, at any time you can return to the Print Setup dialog box and reselect your desktop printer so you can proof your publication.

After you have printed your proof, select File | Print Setup to reselect the printer driver your commercial printer requires.

Making Things Easy with Publisher's Pack and Go Wizard

You have two ways to deliver your files to the commercial printer. The simplest approach is to use Publisher's Pack and Go Wizard to copy your Publisher files to a disk or to several disks. The second alternative is to prepare a PostScript file on your computer's hard drive and send it to your printer by one of three methods: upload the file to your commercial publisher's Web site, send it via e-mail as an attached file, or copy it to a zip drive and deliver the zip drive to your commercial printer.

Publisher's Pack and Go Wizard offers several advantages in preparing color files for commercial printers. One benefit is that the Wizard spares you from making any of the advanced decisions involved in preparing your files for commercial printing—important decisions that adapt your files to your printer's specific software and hardware needs. The Pack and Go Wizard also makes it easier for your printer to make any changes to your file that may be necessary to ensure the best possible final printing.

To submit files to your printer, select File | Pack and Go | Take To A Commercial Printing Service, as shown in Figure 15-2. Publisher will then activate the Pack and Go Wizard, which will guide you through the steps and decisions you need to make Publisher 2000 files, complete with fonts and graphics, for your commercial printer.

Note that Publisher offers the special option called Take to Another Computer. Use this option if you want to copy your publication to disks, so you can share it with a coworker not connected to your computer network, or if you want to continue working on your project on your home computer.

The first Pack and Go Wizard dialog box, shown in Figure 15-3, describes the steps involved in gathering together the various files you'll need to take to your commercial printer. Click the Next button.

When Publisher displays the second Pack and Go Wizard dialog box, enter a name for your publication. The default is the A drive, or 3.5-inch disk drive. If you select the lower radio button, you can click the Browse button to select a different folder on your network or a removable drive such as a zip drive. If you

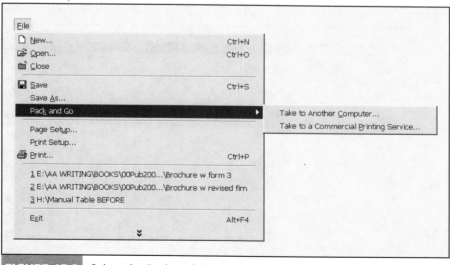

FIGURE 15-2 Select the Pack and Go Wizard to prepare your files for commercial printing

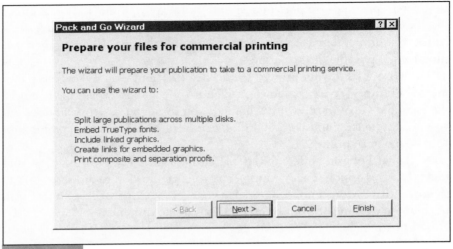

FIGURE 15-3 The first Pack and Go Wizard dialog box begins the process of preparing your files

accept the default—the A drive—the Pack and Go Wizard will divide large publications and their associated files among two or more disks.

The third Pack and Go Wizard dialog box, shown in Figure 15-4, is the most important of the dialog boxes in this operation. Use it to fine-tune the associated font and graphic files you'll need to send along with the Publisher files.

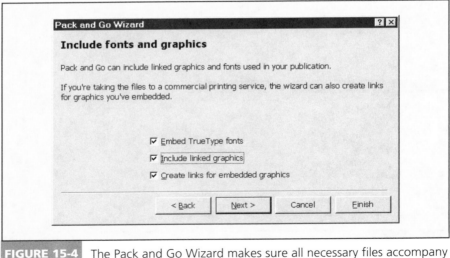

FIGURE 15-4 The Pack and Go Wizard makes sure all necessary files accompany your Publisher files to the commercial printer

The Wizard's default settings include copies of all necessary font and graphics files, should anyone at the commercial printer need to adjust your publication as they prepare it for printing. The Pack and Go Wizard ensures you have all you need for commercial printing by providing important default choices in the following three areas:

- By default, the Pack and Go Wizard embeds TrueType fonts in the Publisher file. This font storage method increases the Publisher's file size, but eliminates a major cause of printing headaches: when fonts you use in your publication are not fonts the printer owns or uses. By embedding TrueType fonts into your publication, you'll eliminate this potential problem.

- Unless you deselect the option that copies all linked graphics, by default the Pack and Go Wizard will copy all your publication's linked graphics to the disks you take to the printer. This feature ensures that all your graphics will print properly.

- Unless you deselect the option that copies all embedded graphics, by default the Pack and Go Wizard creates links for all your publication's embedded graphics. This feature ensures that your commercial printer can access any of your graphical objects, such as photographs. This allows for minor changes the printer may have to make to ensure quality reproduction.

Click the Finish button when you're ready to continue. Publisher displays the Pack and Go Wizard's Progress Bar, accompanied by any prompts that let you know what the Wizard is doing and how much work remains.

When your disk is filled, Publisher displays a warning prompting you to remove the current disk and insert a blank one.

When Publisher packs the last file, the Wizard names it Unpack.exe, which your printer will use to unpack (decompress) the individual files so the printing staff can access them.

Preparing Optional PostScript Files

Experienced Publisher users in high-volume environments, such as corporate departments preparing similar documents over and over again for in-house printing departments, may find it more efficient to prepare PostScript files.

The advantage of PostScript files is that they can reduce printing costs by saving the printer some time. The Publisher user can now make many of the decisions that commercial printers would otherwise make. The files arrive at the printer ready to use. The disadvantage of PostScript files is that the printer cannot easily modify them—for example, optimize graphics for best reproduction, and so on.

To prepare a PostScript file, after selecting either the Microsoft Publisher or the Microsoft Publisher Color Printer driver, select File | Print. Rather than the familiar Print dialog box, Publisher's Pack and Go Wizard displays a different Print dialog box, shown in Figure 15-5.

The dialog box offers several options. For example, click the Properties button to reveal the Microsoft Publisher Imagesetter Properties dialog box, shown in Figure 15-6. This allows you to choose the size of paper your publication will be printed on. By clicking one of the Custom icons, followed by the Custom

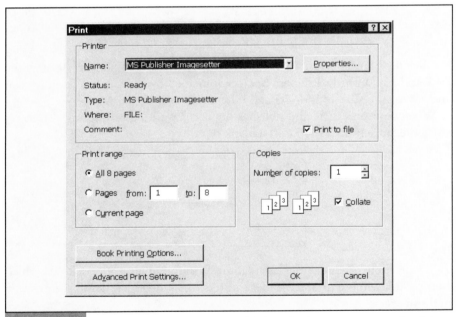

FIGURE 15-5 If you select Imagesetter, Publisher displays a more complex Print dialog box

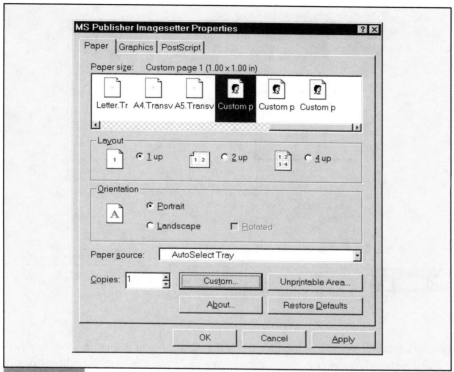

FIGURE 15-6 Use the Microsoft Imagesetter Properties dialog box to set a custom paper size and how many pages will appear on each sheet

button, you can create a custom paper size and determine whether one, two, or four copies will be printed on each sheet.

Depending on your publication's size, Publisher may display the Book Printing Options button. If Publisher displays the Book Printing Options dialog box, select Print As Book. This option prints multiple pages of your publication on 11 by 17-inch sheets, as shown in Figure 15-7.

If you click the Advanced Print Settings button, Publisher will display the tabbed Print Settings dialog box. Click on the Publication Options tab to determine if you want to print your publication's linked graphics, including information such as

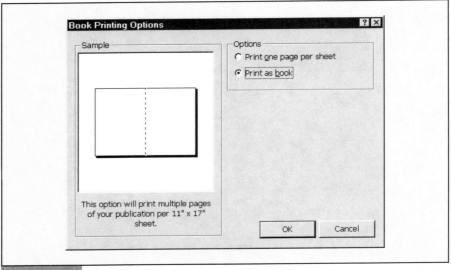

FIGURE 15-7   With the Book Printing Option, you can print two 8.5 by 11-inch pages on 11 by 17-inch sheets of paper

crop marks and bleeds. Use the Device Options tab, shown in Figure 15-8, to determine whether the printer will create a printing press plate face up, face down, or as a negative.

Click OK, and Publisher will display the Print To File dialog box. Name the file and specify the location where Publisher will save it.

Working with Publisher's Commercial Printing Tools

With Publisher 2000's new commercial printing tools—or with Publisher's Pack and Go Wizard—your printer can prepare color separations and fine-tune the subtlest aspects of color printing. To access these valuable tools, which bring Publisher 2000 to a new level of functionality, select Tools | Commercial Printing Tools, and choose from the four options: Color Printing, Trapping, Graphics Manager, or Fonts, as shown in Figure 15-9. Use these tools when you are printing proofs of your publication on your desktop printer, as well as when you are preparing PostScript files at your office or at the commercial printer.

New in 2000:   In addition to the new Pack and Go Wizard, Publisher also has a new set of Commercial Color Printing Tools.

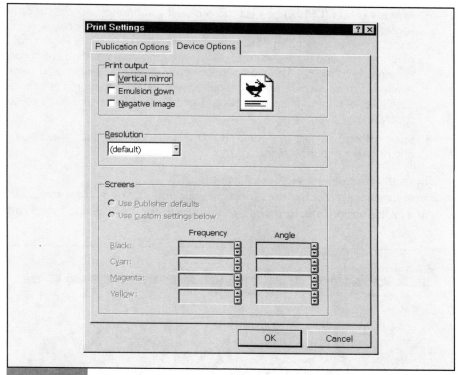

FIGURE 15-8 Use the options offered by the Advanced Print Settings button to adjust the PostScript file to your commercial printer's needs

Printing Color Separations To print color separations, first make sure that your document will print properly as a proof in black ink before you tackle the task of printing color separations. When you have checked your proof and made sure that your creation looks just as you want when printed only in black, then you can see how the color separations will print. To check color separations, select Tools | Commercial Printing Tools | Color Printing. When Publisher displays the Color Printing dialog box you can select from the following three options:

- **Composite RGB** Select this option if you want each page of your publication to print as it looks on your screen, with each page on a single sheet of paper, regardless of the number of colors on it.

- **Process colors (CMYK)** Select this option if you have included color photographs in your publication. This option converts Publisher's color scheme colors to colors created by mixing the four basic printing colors—cyan, magenta, yellow, and black—in precise amounts. Individual sheets of paper corresponding to the necessary amounts of cyan, magenta, yellow, and black needed to reproduce the colors of your publication will be printed as individual sheets of paper (or as individual printing plates). These sheets are called separations.

- **Spot color(s)** Select this option if you want to print in black plus tints of one or two additional colors.

Click OK, after you make your selection(s).

If you have selected either the process or spot option, you will see two additional printing options the next time you return to the Print dialog box: Print

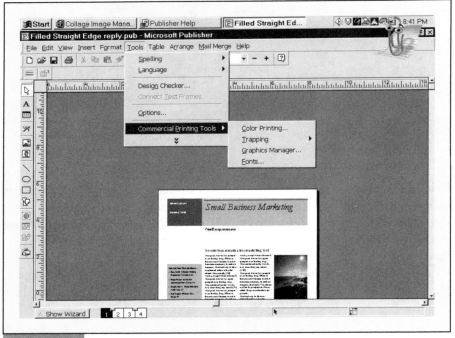

FIGURE 15-9 Publisher's commercial printing tools bring a new level of control to advanced users and commercial printers

Composite and Print Separations. If you select the Print Separations option, you can choose to print all four color separations for each page, or you can select just the separation—or layer—that corresponds to a single color, as shown in Figure 15-10.

If you have chosen spot colors, you can print the Black, Spot Color 1, and/or Spot Color 2 (if available) separations, or just a single color separation, as shown in Figure 15-11.

For more control over the separations that print, click the Advanced Print Settings button. When the Print Settings dialog box appears, you can determine whether or not to print linked graphics. You can also decide if you want to include printer's aids such as crop marks (which indicate the trim area of a page), registration marks (which help printers accurately place each separation on top of each other) and job information (file and date information), as shown in Figure 15-12.

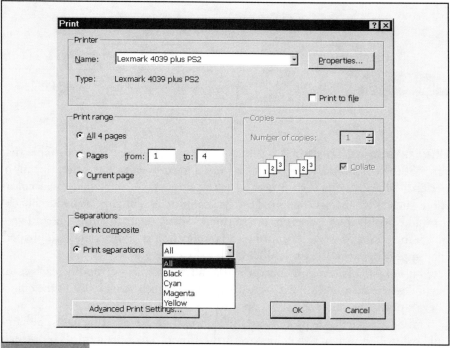

FIGURE 15-10   When choosing process printing, you can print the separation associated with just one of the four process colors

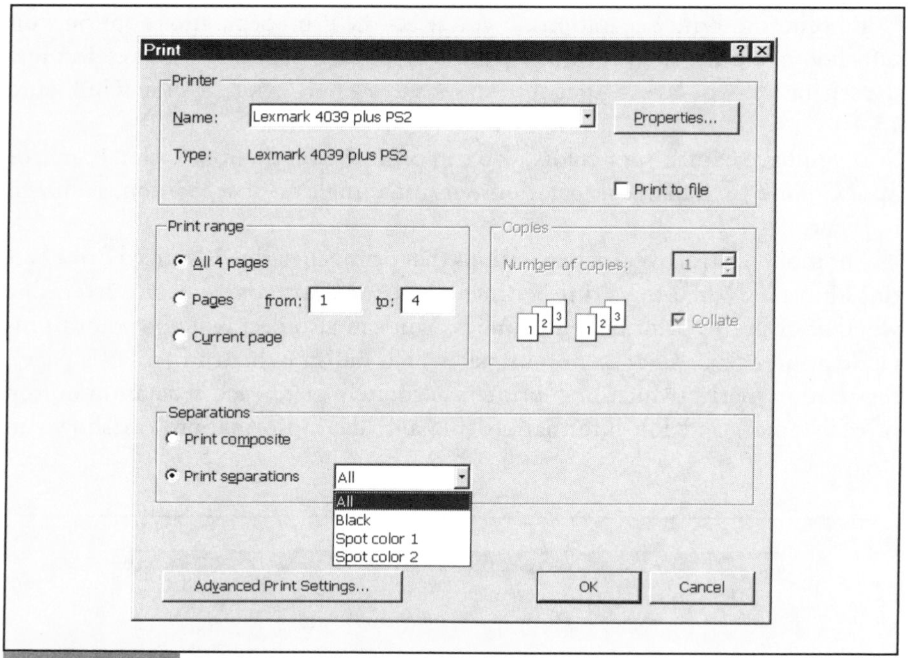

FIGURE 15-11 When you are printing spot color separations, you can print black or the other spot colors

Understanding Trapping   When printing separations, it is inevitable that some of the color separation layers may not appear in exactly the right location, perfectly aligned with each other. This can cause problems where two colors meet, such as when a large colored text or graphic element appears inside a background color. If the separations are not perfectly aligned, an annoying and very noticeable sliver of white (assuming the publication is printed on white paper) may appear between the two colors.

Trapping involves slightly overprinting the two colors—extending each color beyond where it should appear—creating a buffer zone so that if one of the colors doesn't print, the other color will appear.

Trapping is a delicate process, and the amount of overprinting has to be carefully controlled. When two colors overprint, they often create a third color (such as blue ink on top of yellow ink might create a thin green outline).

You, or your commercial printer, can control the amount of printing overlap by selecting Tools | Commercial Printing Tools | Trapping, Preferences.

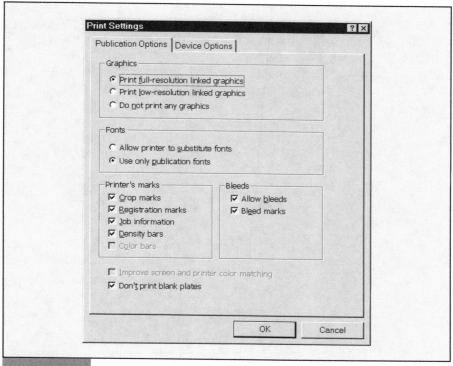

FIGURE 15-12 Use the Advanced Print Settings button to control both the publication options and device options

Publisher will display the trapping Preferences dialog box, shown in Figure 15-13, which allows you to control trapping settings throughout your document when you have selected either process or spot color printing.

You can increase or decrease the amount of overprinting, or the width of solid colored objects, such as text and objects, by increasing or decreasing the Width specification. You can increase or decrease the amount of trapping for WordArt object frames containing gradient fills by increasing or decreasing the Intermediate figure.

By default, Publisher 2000 will overprint black lines, fills, and black-and-white photographs on top of background colors. If, instead, you prefer that these objects be trapped, deselect the objects in the Black Overprinting section of the Preferences dialog box. You can also decide at exactly what location in your design to use overprint rather than trapping.

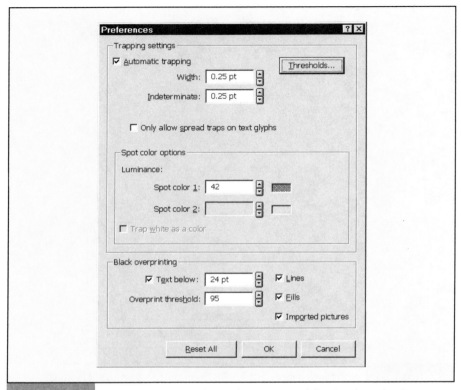

FIGURE 15-13 Activate trapping throughout your publication by selecting the automatic trapping option from the trapping Preferences dialog box

If you are an experienced press technician, click the Thresholds button. When Publisher displays the Trapping Thresholds dialog box, shown in Figure 15-14, you can select the exact point that trapping occurs, thereby preventing separation trappings of approximately the same density. Without this option, your final publication would show distracting outlines.

In addition to making global trapping adjustments that will affect every page of your document, you can also modify the way individual text and graphic elements placed against colored backgrounds will print. You can fine-tune the way a headline placed against a colored fill will print, for example.

To adjust trapping of individual text and graphic elements, select a headline placed against a colored fill or a headline placed against a photograph. Select Tools | Commercial Printing Tools | Trapping | Per Object Trapping. When Publisher displays the Per Object Trapping dialog box, shown here, choose from several alternatives, including overprinting the text color on top of the

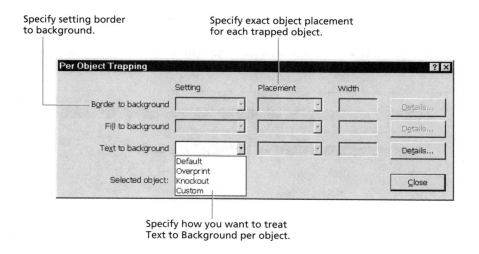

FIGURE 15-14 If you are a commercial printer, you can modify the trapping thresholds on the basis of your experience with your printing hardware

background fill, or knocking out the fill color behind the text, thus permitting the text to appear more readable.

Handling Graphics Publisher 2000's Graphics Manager lets your printer access and modify your publication's original source files, making whatever changes might be necessary to improve printing quality. By accessing the original PhotoDraw files for scanned images in your publication, for example, your printer may be able to improve photo reproduction by lighting certain portions of the image or adjusting the image's color balance.

Source files cannot be accessed, of course, if they are embedded within a Publisher document. To allow access to the original files, Publisher 2000 makes it easy to replace embedded files with linked files. Select Tools | Commercial Printing Tools | Graphics Manager. The Graphics Manager dialog box opens, shown in Figure 15-15.

To create a link to the file, select the filename of the desired graphic, and click the Create Link button. When Publisher displays the Create Link dialog box, shown here, you can either browse to locate the original file and link to it (the best choice) or create a new file from the full-resolution graphic stored in Publisher and link to the new file. (Choose this option if the original graphic file is no longer available.)

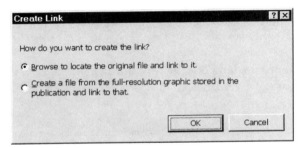

When you next select Publisher's Pack and Go Wizard, Publisher will follow the links to all linked graphics and include them as separate files.

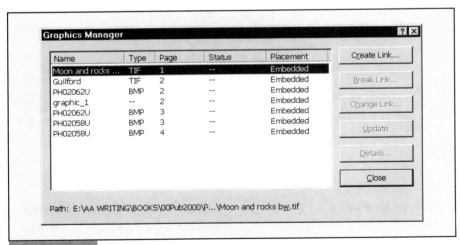

FIGURE 15-15 The Graphics Manager lets you replace embedded graphics with linked graphics, so printers can make any last-minute adjustments

After you have selected a graphic file and created a link to the original file, new options appear in the Graphics Manager dialog box. Click the Break Link button to unlink individual graphics objects you may have previously embedded. Click on the Link button to re-embed the graphic objects, and click the Change Link button to link to a different file. Click the Details button to preview the file and examine its properties, such as file type, the file's last date of change, the file's folder, and—most importantly—the file size, as shown in Figure 15-16.

Working With Fonts   Select Tools | Commercial Printing Tools | Fonts, and Publisher will display the Fonts dialog box, shown in Figure 15-17. With this dialog box, you can determine the number of fonts used in your publication and decide whether to embed the entire font file or just the characters used in your publication.

The Fonts dialog box displays the fonts used in your publication, regardless of whether you have embedded them in your publication. Select Embed TrueType fonts when you save the publication if you want Publisher to save the font files as part of the publication file. (Although the Fonts dialog box reveals the presence of Type1 fonts, you cannot embed these fonts.)

Select the Embed TrueType Fonts When Saving Publication option. Including the fonts will increase your Publisher's file sizes. Select the Subset Fonts When Embedding option when you want to embed the fonts. When you choose this option, Publisher saves only those characters that you used in your

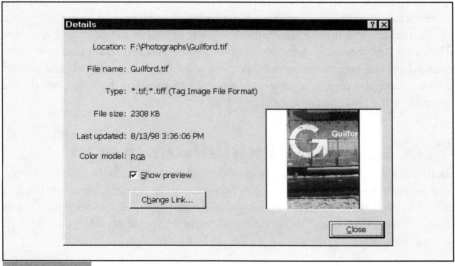

FIGURE 15-16   Use the Details dialog box to examine file size, file type, and the folder where you have saved the file

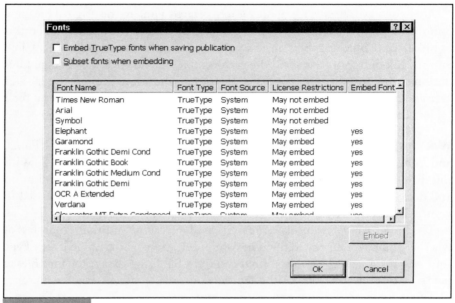

FIGURE 15-17   Use the Fonts dialog box to decide whether you want to embed the entire character set or just the characters used in your publication

publication. This option reduces file size, but if you need to make revisions, your printer may not be able to make them (unless you have already used the characters).

To prevent Publisher from embedding a font, select the font, and click the Don't Embed button. If you use this option, you must be certain that your commercial printer has access to the font on the printer's hardware. If the printer doesn't have the font you have used or want to use, you have to provide the printer with a separate file containing the font.

Professional Skills Summary

In this chapter, we discussed the important decision of whether to use your desktop printer or a commercial printer when generating your final printed project. We discussed the criteria for making this decision, which includes number of final copies, use of color, final document purpose, frequency of update or revisions, and costs.

We also examined how to manage your part of the printing process if you decide to use a commercial printer. This discussion included getting competitive quotes, understanding your role when coordinating with the printer, managing cost issues, and understanding the steps involved in working with most commercial printers.

Later in the chapter, we prepared a publication for commercial printing with Publisher 2000's new Pack and Go Wizard. We also took a look at each one of Publisher 2000's new commercial printing tools, including color selection, color matching, and trapping.

Index

Note: Page numbers for illustrations and tables are in italics.

Looking for more ideas about using Publisher 2000 as a profit-builder for your business?

Visit Roger C. Parker's www.NewEntrepreneur.com Web site. Discover:

- Descriptions and schedule of upcoming seminars and workshops
- Customized Publisher 2000 staff training
- Additional Publisher 2000 articles, tips and suggestions
- Customized "Web Mentor" project advice and consultation
- Lists of additional marketing, design and web resources
- Discounted design and marketing books

Visit www.NewEntrepreneur.com today!

Over a million and a half readers in more than 37 countries rely on books by Roger C. Parker. Roger's clients have included Apple Computer, ArsDigita, Bose, Hewlett-Packard, Lexmark, Microsoft and Yamaha. In 1996, Roger was appointed to the Microsoft Small Business Council.